TOURISM IN THE TWENTY-FIRST CENTURY

Also available from Continuum:

Tourism in the Twenty-first Century

Reflections on Experience

Edited by
Bill Faulkner, Gianna Moscardo
and Eric Laws

CONTINUUM
London and New York

Continuum

The Tower Building
11 York Road
London SE1 7NX

370 Lexington Avenue
New York
NY 10017–6503

First published in 2001

British Library Cataloguing-in-Publication Data
A catalogue record for this book is available from the British Library.

ISBN 0-8264-4827-5 (Hb)
ISBN 0-8264-4828-3 (Pb)

Designed and typeset by Ben Cracknell Studios
Printed and bound in Great Britain by the Cromwell Press, Trowbridge, Wilts

Contents

List of Tables
and Figures

TABLES

FIGURES

The Contributors

Nell Arnold

Professor in Marketing and International Business at Queensland University of Technology, received her Bachelor of Music in opera performance, and her research masters and doctorate with dual majors in opera production and in arts administration. Her university career, melded with leadership and council positions in government and industry, concentrated on research in the development and marketing of new technologies. From 1972 to 1982, she served as Professor and Director of the USA Centre for Transnational Studies at San Jose State University and chaired the International Business Council of the Silicon Valley of Northern California. A second area of specialization concentrated on arts development. Her festival tourism and community transformation research began in 1967 and extended to 52 countries. Highlights include service as director of special events, marketing and development of the arts, heritage sites and cultural festivals for the State of California Department of Parks and the California Arts Council in the four years leading into the 1984 Olympics of Los Angeles; director of the Cabrillo Opera Festival, 1986–92, and director of the Soil of Flame Festival, a rural festival tourism training series of projects in Queensland, 1995–99.

Pierre Benckendorff

PhD student at James Cook University, having graduated with 1st Class Honours and a University Medal from JCU. He holds a Commonwealth Postgraduate Scholarship and is interested in future technology and tourism and strategic management issues in tourist attractions. His previous work has focused on best practices in Internet marketing for regional tourist bodies.

Dimitrios Buhalis

Senior Lecturer in Tourism at the University of Westminster, London, and Adjunct Professor at the Institut de Management Hotelier International (Cornell University–Ecole Superieure des Sciences Economiques et Commerciales ESSEC) in Paris. He earned his BBA from the University of the Aegean in Greece, and his MSc and PhD from the University of Surrey, where he contributed to the teaching, research and international consultancy undertaken by the tourism team. He is Chair of the

Association of Tourism Teachers and Trainers and committee member of the International Federation of Information Technology and Tourism. He has chaired the ENTER 1998, 1999 and 2000 conferences and is a consultant to the World Tourism Organization. He is also Reviews Editor of the *International Journal of Tourism Research*; Books Editor of the *IT and Tourism: Applications-Methodologies and Techniques Journal*; and Associate Editor for the *Encyclopaedia of Tourism*.

Richard Butler

Taught at the University of Western Ontario, Canada, from 1967 to 1997, leaving as Professor having served two terms as Chairman of the Department of Geography. Joined the School of Management Studies at the University of Surrey in 1997 as Professor of Tourism, and is currently also Deputy Head of School (Research). Past President of the International Academy for the Study of Tourism (1993–97), former President of the Canadian Association of Leisure Studies, former executive member of the Canadian Association of Geographers, and currently a Fellow of the Royal Geographical Society and the Royal Society of Arts (UK). Editor of the *International Journal of Tourism and Hospitality Research*, and a member of the editorial committees of several referred academic tourism journals (UK, USA, Australia, New Zealand). External Assessor for the University of the South Pacific, the University of North London and Strathclyde University (tourism programmes). Author/editor of several academic books on tourism, including *Tourism and Indigenous Peoples*, *Tourism and Recreation in Rural Areas* and *Contemporary Issues in Tourism Development*. Current research includes tourism development models, seasonality in tourism, indicators of sustainable tourism and capacity of tourism areas.

Graham Dann

Professor of Tourism at the University of Luton, UK. Founder member of the International Academy for the Study of Tourism and of the research committee on international tourism of the International Sociological Association, he is on the editorial board of several leading tourism journals. His research interests focus on tourist motivation and the sociolinguistics of tourism promotion, and he has published extensively in both areas.

Ross Dowling

Associate Professor of Tourism at Edith Cowan University, Western Australia. He is an international speaker, researcher and consultant on ecotourism and has particular interests in environmental education, the greening of tourism, tourism planning, the cruise ship industry and wine tourism. In 1998 he convened the First Australian Wine Tourism Conference at Leeuwin Estate, Margaret River, and co-edited the proceedings *Wine Tourism – Perfect Partners* (1999). He prepared the *Draft Western Australian Wine Tourism Strategy* (1999) and is an adviser for the

First New Zealand Wine Tourism Conference to be held in Marlborough in November 2000. Dr Dowling is the Program Convener of the First Global Wine Tourism Conference & Expo to be held in Australia, 24–28 March 2001.

David Edgar

Senior Lecturer in the Caledonian Business School at Glasgow Caledonian University, Scotland, UK. His research interests focus upon the nature of value creation of organizations and the strategic dynamics of resources that lead to a sustainable competitive advantage. His interest in short break markets stems from his PhD work and has proven to be an interesting research context, when exploring the strategic dynamics of organizations.

Bill Faulkner

Director of the Centre for Tourism and Hotel Management Research, Griffith University, Australia. He is also Deputy CEO of Australia's CRC for Sustainable Tourism. Prior to taking up this position, he was the founding director of Australia's Bureau of Tourism Research (BTR). His earlier career included senior tourism policy positions in the Australian Federal administration and he entered the tourism field after an earlier career in urban/transport planning research.

Daniel Fesenmaier

Professor and Director of the National Laboratory for Tourism and e-Commerce at the University of Illinois. His research focuses on the use of information technology in tourism from the local to the international level.

Donald Getz

Professor of Tourism and Hospitality Management, Faculty of Management, at the University of Calgary, Canada. Professor Getz has particular interests in destination management and marketing, entrepreneurship and family business, rural tourism, impact assessment, event tourism and event management. He is the author of two books: *Festivals, Special Events, and Tourism* (1991) and *Event Management and Event Tourism* (1997). He has also co-edited and contributed to a third book, entitled *The Business of Rural Tourism* (1997) and has worked with several colleagues to produce a workbook entitled *Planning For Sustainable Tourism Development at the Local Level* (1997). His next book, entitled *Wine Tourism Management*, has been completed and will be available in 2000.

Suzanne Johnstone

Holds a degree in tourism from the University of Canberra and has worked as an executive assistant in Canberra tourism and in the Cooperative Research Centre for Sustainable Tourism. She also works for the Cooperative Research Centre for the Great Barrier Reef World Heritage Area as a research officer managing survey data collections.

Eric Laws

Author of four books on aspects of tourism management and has edited three others. His research interests include the management of destination systems, and the modelling of service quality in tourism. He is a visiting researcher at the University of Queensland, Australia, and Visiting Professor at the University of Limerick, Ireland.

Laura Lawton

PhD student and research assistant in the School of Tourism and Hotel Management, Griffith University, where she has been based since 1996. For eight years prior to that, she was a senior Research Officer in Saskatchewan Environment and Resource Management. Ms Lawton is the author of many government reports and refereed journal articles, and conducts research in the areas of sustainable tourism, time-sharing, protected areas and ecotourism. She is actively involved in various research projects sponsored by the CRC for Sustainable Tourism.

Gianna Moscardo

Principal Research Fellow in the Tourism Program at James Cook University, Townsville, Australia. She leads a team of researchers concerned with supporting the development and management of sustainable tourism in the Great Barrier Reef and Wet Tropics World Heritage Areas. The writing of her chapter was supported by funding from the Rainforest Cooperative Research Centre.

Trevor Mules

Professor of Tourism at the University of Canberra. He has published widely in tourism economics, the economic impacts of tourism and the economic impact of special event tourism. He has carried out numerous economic impact studies, including forecasting work on the 2000 Sydney Olympics, and he has written on other economic aspects of tourism, including a cost–benefit analysis of Gold Coast beach erosion.

Joseph O'Leary

Professor of Outdoor Recreation and Tourism at Purdue University. He has published more than 200 articles on travel and recreation behaviour. His research focuses on secondary analysis of large-scale, domestic and international travel and recreation behaviour survey data.

Nick Parfitt

Principal of 2003 Pty. Ltd., Brisbane.

Philip Pearce

Foundation Professor of Tourism at James Cook University. He holds a DPhil (Oxon) in psychology and has maintained a long-standing interest in tourist behaviour. He is the author of four books on tourism and numerous scholarly articles. He is the editor of the *Journal of Tourism Studies* and is a Program Leader in the Rainforest CRC. He is an active representative in the World Tourism Organization's network for elite education and training centres in tourism.

Joan Phillips

Postgraduate student at the University of Luton, UK. Specializing in sex tourism, she conducted a study of bar girls in Bangkok which resulted in the successful completion of her MPhil dissertation at the University of the West Indies. Currently she is writing up her fieldwork on beachboys in Barbados which she intends submitting for her doctoral thesis.

Bruce Prideaux

Lectures in tourism at the University of Queensland. His teaching centres on tourism transport, tourism economics and Asian tourism. His major research interests are tourism transport, Asian tourism, tourism and crime and destination development. Prior to accepting the lecturing position, Bruce worked for the Queensland Department of Transport.

Roslyn Russell

Lecturer in the Tourism Department of La Trobe University, Melbourne, Victoria. Prior to taking up this position she was a PhD student at Griffith University (Gold Coast). Her current research includes applications of chaos theory to the analysis of the evaluation of tourism, using the Gold Coast as a case study. In this context she is specifically interested in the role of entrepreneurs as 'chaos-makers'.

Chris Ryan

Professor for Tourism at the University of Waikato, Hamilton, New Zealand. He is also editor of *Tourism Management*. His publications include six books, the latest being *Sex Tourism: Liminalities and Marginal People*, co-authored with Professor Michael Hall and published by Routledge, and *Tourism Management: Towards the New Millennium*, co-edited with Professor Stephen Page and published by Elsevier. He says he has now lost count of the number of other articles, reports, conference papers, etc. he has written. While his output appears eclectic, it has constant themes based in psychology and economics. Chris is on the Advisory Committee of Tourism Waikato and currently is undertaking research for New Zealand's Department of Conservation, Tourism Coromandel, Hamilton International Airport, the Maori Arts and Crafts Institute and Australia's CRC for Sustainable Tourism. Internationally he is Visiting Professor at the Australian International Hotel School, Canberra, and the University of Northumbria, UK.

Noel Scott

Noel Scott has 20 years of experience in research and development in the Petrochemical, Finance, Electricity and Tourism industries. He has spent over ten years in research management roles, most recently at Tourism Queensland as Research and Strategic Services Manager. He has been a state representative on National Tourism Research Committees, is a past State Chairman of the Market Research Society of Australia (Queensland Division) and holds an Honours Degree in Chemistry, a Masters of Business Administration and a Masters in Marketing. For further information contact Tourism Queensland on (07) 3406 5382 or noelscott@ug.net.au.

Renata Tomljenovic

PhD student at the School of Tourism and Hotel Management, Griffith University. Her research interests include contact between travellers and their hosts, social impacts of tourism and cultural tourism.

Stephen Wanhill

Travelbag Professor of Tourism, School of Service Industries, Bournemouth University and Director of the Unit for Tourism Research, Bornholms Forsknings-center, Nexø, Denmark. His principal research interests are in the field of tourism destination development and policy. He has undertaken a wide range of tourism development strategies, tourism impact assessments, project studies and lecture programmes, both in the UK and worldwide, covering some 45 countries. He has acted as tourism policy advisor to the Select Committee on Welsh Affairs, House of Commons, and has been a Board Member of the Wales Tourist Board with responsibilities for the development and research divisions. He is the editor of the journal *Tourism Economics*.

David Weaver

Associate Professor in the School of Tourism and Hotel Management, Griffith University, where he has been based since 1996. He obtained his PhD in geography at the University of Western Ontario in 1986. His research interests are in the areas of sustainable tourism, ecotourism and destination development. He is the author of two books and over 40 refereed journal articles and book chapters. Several of his current projects are funded by the CRC for Sustainable Tourism.

Xinran You

PhD student in the outdoor recreation and tourism programme at Purdue University, USA. She has had seven years of professional experience in destination marketing and travel product planning with the China National Tourism Administration and private travel firms in Singapore. With a special interest in international travel marketing, she has been actively engaged in several destination marketing research projects and has published three journal articles and several other proceedings articles while at university.

Preface

If, in the minds of most people, the turn of the century is a momentous occasion, then the birth of the new millennium is even more so. The fact that such benchmarks in our history should stimulate a heightened degree of debate on past events and the future is perhaps symbolic of humankind's interest in both who they are and where they are going. By reflecting on past events, we can gain a better understanding of the sequence of events that define our heritage and identity. Knowing our place in the world and understanding how we have become what we are has potentially positive effects to the extent that this may reinforce the cohesion of social, economic and political systems, and/or highlight anomalies that require remedial action. Also, by reviewing how events have unfolded in the past, and the factors and relationships that have influenced these, we can provide a better foundation for planning in the future. Conversely, a preoccupation with the past can undermine our preparation for the future. An unduly nostalgic or uncritical interpretation of history, or a less than informed and balanced analysis of it, can produce distortions that result in inequities and inefficient practices becoming entrenched. The individual, organization or society that allows itself to become bound by history will become less adaptable to the changes that confront it in the future. Equally, however, if it disregards its past entirely, it denies the benefits a common history provides with regard to cementing mutually beneficial relationships and risks repeating the mistakes of the past.

The theme and purpose of this book springs from the above interpretation of the value and pitfalls of the reflective processes we are inclined to engage in at significant points in history. Such activity is demonstrably productive if it helps us to learn from past experiences and, therefore, prepares us to face the future through a heightened understanding of our predicament. It is counter-productive if it draws us into a fixation on the past that does not illuminate any warning signs for navigating the future. Specifically, the purpose of this book is to provide a series of reflections on aspects of tourism development in the twentieth century in order to produce a foundation for considering key issues and challenges in the twenty-first century.

As an area of human activity, tourism has a history that extends back as far as some of the earliest forms of trade. However, it was not until the second half of the twentieth century that it became prominent in terms of both the geographical extent of tourism flows and the scale of these movements. The contributions to this book therefore tend to concentrate on developments in the later part of the twentieth century, although this is not at the expense of ignoring relevant trends that were evident in much earlier times.

In organizing the content of the book, we have endeavoured to cover a broad spectrum of issues without being comprehensive. In doing so, we have sacrificed breadth in order to provide some depth in the areas that are examined. We therefore begin with an introductory chapter that puts the remainder of the book into perspective by elaborating the 'reflecting on experience' theme introduced above. In Part 1, the impacts of recent socio-economic and tourism supply-side trends on tourist activities and experiences are explored in selected settings. Part 2 focuses on the changes in the operational environment of tourism organizations and responses to these changes. Both private and public sector organizations are examined, and the relationships between such organizations and other organizations, their customers and destination communities are considered. Finally, in Part 3 some methodological challenges and innovations that may have a significant influence on the tourism research agenda in the twenty-first century are discussed.

The Editors wish to thank Lana Vikulov for the role she played in consolidating and formatting manuscripts for this book.

INTRODUCTION

Moving Ahead
and Looking Back

Gianna Moscardo, Bill Faulkner and Eric Laws

The beginning of a new year is seen in many cultures as a time for individuals to reflect on the past year. It is a time when many reflect on the highlights and low points of the past year, and look forward to, and make plans for, the year ahead. The beginning of a century generates widespread reflection, contemplation and prediction not only at the level of individual lives but for whole societies. The beginning of a millennium, not surprisingly, is associated with even more contemplation about the future and analysis of the past. The years 1999 and 2000 offer an almost irresistible opportunity for academics to research and write about the history and future of their area of interest. The editors and contributors to this book aim to ensure that tourism, both as a human activity and field of academic interest, will be recognized as an important part of this dialogue.

The actual change of the century, and for some the millennium, is expected to be a boom time for tourism. There appears to be an overwhelming urge amongst people from all over the world to be somewhere significant for key dates in the year 2000. Reports in the media and on the World Wide Web list many specialist tours, hot spots for accommodation, major events and initiatives by cities all over the world to attract visitors (see *www.everything2000.com/news/events/eveceremonies.asp* for details). Major parties have been planned in virtually every major city, with many spending large amounts of public money on major attractions in the hope of attracting additional tourism income. Britain's Millennium Dome at Greenwich (on the 0-longitude line) is one of the largest of these efforts. With a circumference of 1000 feet this will be the largest cable-supported arena in the world covering sufficient area to house two football fields (Johnson, 1998).

Two opposing views are readily distinguished as the new century gets under way. While one perspective celebrates the future with festivities, the other view is much more sanguine. There has been an enormous growth in literature, especially web pages, devoted to those who predict that the world is coming to an end. Certainly during the last change of millennia much of medieval Europe was gripped by predictions about the end of the world (Ancer, 1999). One of the most popular sets of doomsday scenarios is that associated with the Y2K computer bug. The latter problem could have a profound impact on tourism if some of the more pessimistic scenarios foreshadowing disastrous disruptions to transport systems, for instance, actually eventuate.

SOME THOUGHTS ON THE NATURE OF THINKING ABOUT THE FUTURE

The existence of two such opposing viewpoints at the outset of the new century, catastrophe versus celebration, highlights one of the interesting features of predictions or prophecies – there are multiple futures. Given the focus of this book on contemplating both the future and the past in tourism, it is worth considering the nature of predicting the future in some more detail. A literal interpretation of the Oxford dictionary implies that there is little distinction between 'forecasting' and 'futurology', with the former being defined as a 'conjectural estimate of something in the future' and the latter as 'systematic forecasting of the future'. Both involve a systematic analysis of information relating to past events and relationships in order to produce predictions about the future. Among practitioners broadly concerned with predicting the future these two terms have not been used interchangeably. There has been a tendency for forecasting to involve an emphasis on quantitative analysis of the past trends and relationships as a basis for producing projections about the future, although qualitative methods have also been utilized as a supplementary tool. This is certainly the case in tourism demand forecasting, at least (Calantone *et al.*, 1987; Faulkner and Valerio, 1995; Uysal and Crompton, 1985). Futurologists, on the other hand, tend to rely more heavily upon qualitative methods, mainly because they are more concerned with producing predictions about the longer-term future, in relation to which quantitative methods become less effective. Also, once we become involved in the production of longer-term predictions, many broader societal, economic, technological and environmental factors have to be taken into account, and it is often difficult to quantify these factors (and their interactions) precisely.

The work of forecasters and futurologists is not an end in itself. They provide an essential foundation for planning and policy formulation in various domains and in such circumstances they should be required to present evidence and some set of logical arguments to justify their predictions. For decision-makers in modern businesses and government agencies, it is advisable to be circumspect in their attitude towards forecasting and only to accept a set of forecasts as a basis for decisions after their credibility has been thoroughly tested. Historically, this approach has not been particularly prevalent in business and government. In ancient Rome, the basis of the prophets' forecasts was shrouded in the mystique of reading the entrails of a slaughtered beast and the credibility of the prophet hinged on his position in the religious hierarchy, rather than the underlying logic or accuracy of his past predictions. Even where the latter considerations may have become an issue, as Stephen Hawking (1993) has observed with regard to the great oracle at Delphi, this was deftly sidestepped by ambiguities which enabled any eventuality to be interpreted as being consistent with the prognosis.

Unfortunately, the above reference to ancient oracles, and the blind faith of political leaders who relied on their predictions, has many parallels in modern-day practice in the tourism planning and development context. Too frequently, naivety on the part of tourism entrepreneurs and planners results in the uncritical acceptance of forecasts produced by 'experts', and a lack of appreciation of the nature and role of forecasting distorts the planning process (Faulkner and Valerio, 1995). In the process of anticipating and addressing the challenges that will confront the tourism sector in the twenty-first century, we need to bear in mind the following observations regarding the limitations of past trends in the industry's approach to forecasting (Faulkner, 1994).

The alienation of the forecasting process

As alluded to in the above reference to the naivety of some decision-makers, the complexity and sophistication of forecasting techniques has resulted in this particular activity becoming alienated from the remainder of the strategic planning process. Schaffer (1993, p. 54) has observed this phenomenon in a broader context:

> Experts need their own private world where ignorant outsiders cannot penetrate. The very obscurity of the sums in which cost benefit analyses of astrologers engage helps give them impressive authority. But the expert predictors also need outsiders' trust: they need to show that the terms they use are, in some way, connected to what matters to the customers.

Forecasting is too frequently seen as an end in itself by the specialist forecaster, rather than as an integral part of the strategic planning process. Meanwhile, many users of the forecasts become mesmerized by the 'science' of forecasting and are too intimidated by the experts to question underlying assumptions in the manner that is so necessary for all potential scenarios to be adequately explored. In this respect, many present-day decision-makers are not unlike their counterparts in ancient Rome or Greece.

The myth of accuracy

Partly as a consequence of the naivety referred to above, forecasts that predict events and trends with some degree of precision are generally praised as being accurate. There are two rejoinders to this position. First, many forecasts might be right for the wrong reasons. That is, while the forecast might appear to have provided a reliable prediction, this has happened as a consequence of an unexpected and fortuitous combination of events that were not anticipated. In such situations the forecasts can play a counter-productive role in the planning process because they reinforce a limited, and possibly distorted, understanding of the underlying dynamics of the environment in which the organization is operating. Second, the corollary of assuming that only 'accurate' forecasts are good forecasts is that the converse is also true – that is, inaccurate forecasts are necessarily deficient or useless. The following two points clearly refute this proposition.

The good forecast might be the one that never eventuates

This is particularly so where the forecast foreshadows an unsavoury future, which can be avoided through remedial action. Thus, the prospect of large-scale famine and endemic poverty identified by the Club of Rome in the 1960s (Meadows *et al.*, 1972) was instrumental in triggering a range of public health and agricultural development initiatives, which eventually averted the projected population pressures. A parallel to this in the tourism context is, perhaps, the way the generalized prognosis encapsulated in Butler's (1980) Destination Life Cycle model has activated planning strategies aimed at rejuvenating maturing destinations. Similarly, the momentum of the growing acceptance of sustainability as a guiding principle for tourism development has been fuelled by predictions of what will happen in the absence of such measures (Inskeep, 1991).

Forecasts can be self-fulfilling prophecies

Many forecasters are vindicated not so much because their assessment of emerging trends was particularly astute, but rather because their forecasts stimulated an awareness of opportunities and concerted action to realize these opportunities. Thus, optimistic forecasts for growth at a particular destination can create impetus for public and private investment in infrastructure, product development and innovation and increased marketing efforts. However, optimistic forecasts based on a less than astute assessment of market trends and opportunities can be equally instrumental in stimulating overinvestment in the expansion of infrastructure, resulting in underutilized capacity and profitless volume problems. Conversely, unduly conservative forecasts can also be self-fulfilling prophecies if they result in underinvestment in infrastructure development and associated capacity constraints which limit growth to the forecast level.

The certainty of the unexpected

One of the features of the twentieth century observed by social commentators such as Alvin Toffler (1970) has been the accelerating pace of change in modern society, which has been propelled in particular by technological innovations. Within this more volatile environment, there are increasing levels of uncertainty, greater pressure on the adaptive capabilities at government, institutional and individual levels, and forecasters have been increasingly haunted by the reality that the only certainty is that the unexpected will happen. The need for policy-makers and entrepreneurs to deal with uncertainty and ambiguity is stressful. 'The ability to think futures is believed to be a uniquely human characteristic . . . the part of the brain that deals with futures thinking (is) also where worry is located' (Paskins, 1997, pp. 259–60).

The final point is particularly poignant when we consider the challenges confronting forecasters in the twenty-first century because it appears that, if anything, the pace of change will continue to accelerate in the future. In the twentieth century, forecasting generally, and tourism forecasting in particular, has both implicitly and explicitly assumed the relationships that have prevailed in the past will continue in the future and, accordingly, the path of change can be mapped in terms of linear or quasi-linear trends. As will be argued in Chapter 18, where the potential relevance of chaos theory to our understanding of tourism phenomena is discussed, the 'certainty of the unexpected' predicament highlights the failure of the prevailing paradigm to keep up with the changes of the twentieth century. We live in an increasingly turbulent rather than linear world, where single events can precipitate large-scale displacements of systems from previously linear paths. If this is the case already in the twentieth century, then fundamental changes in our approach to tourism management and research will be necessary if we are to cope with the problems of the new millennium.

In summary then, this book recognizes that good predictions about the future rely heavily on good understandings of the past and thorough analyses of the present. The mission of the book is to analyse the key factors or trends that have influenced the nature of tourism in this century, to describe current trends in tourism and to look ahead to what tourism might be like in the next century.

A BRIEF HISTORY OF TOURISM

Tourism is often considered to be a twentieth-century phenomenon, yet literature exists which describes travel for purposes other than trade, warfare and exploration, as an activity of ancient times. Both ancient Greek and Roman citizens travelled to sporting events, festivals and sites of archaeological interest such as the Egyptian pyramids (Anthony, 1973). The Romans also participated in spa tourism and developed coastal and mountain resorts to escape the summer heat (Wolfe, 1967).

Casson (1994) has pointed out that tourism has been a feature of society since the earliest recorded times, and it appears from his study that many of the contemporary industry structures and the problems experienced by tourists were also features of classical tourism. Early tourism to remote places was motivated, as it is largely today, by pleasure (the pleasure periphery), and by curiosity about other societies or earlier eras. By the Roman era, destination areas were well established, exemplified by the Bay of Naples, a natural vacation land because of its beauty and climate, which is ringed with hot springs. The whole shore, as a consequence, 'sprouted a line of watering places which became the most fashionable in the roman world' (pp. 133–4). Casson (1974) adds that these travellers were wealthy, able to use the extensive road system developed for trade and administration and encouraged by political stability. Pearce, Morrison and Rutledge (1998) also provide evidence that Chinese and Japanese citizens have travelled for curiosity and recreation for at least 2000 years.

In the European context, about which the most is written, the political instability and decay of the road system which accompanied the decline of the Roman Empire was associated with a major decline in travel that persisted for several hundred years. When wealth and political stability again began to rise in the Middle Ages in Europe, so too did travel. In this era the most common form of travel was the religious pilgrimage. Shrines and destinations such as Jerusalem and Rome grew in popularity. Both Murphy (1985) and Rowling (1971) note that, while the primary focus of travel at this time was religious, social and recreational activities and opportunities quickly developed along and around the pilgrimage routes and destinations.

The seventeenth century saw the advent of the Grand Tour in Europe (Hibbert, 1969). The Grand Tourist was typically a young son of a wealthy and aristocratic family sent to travel throughout Europe for two to three years. The purpose of this exercise was to gain an education in the arts, culture, politics and languages of Europe. The Napoleonic Wars brought this form of tourism to an end.

In the eighteenth century European tourism again began to increase encouraged by widespread political stability, a growing middle class with wealth generated by the Industrial Revolution and a new technology, the steam engine. This engine in turn encouraged the development of extensive rail systems and faster, more reliable ships (Swinglehurst, 1974; 1982). For the middle class recreational travel began to be seen as a necessary feature of their lives, an escape from their work responsibilities and a way to restore their health. This changing attitude towards travel as a form of health activity and the new faster transport systems led to the development of day tours for the working class. These tours were designed to provide factory workers with a chance to escape temporarily the unhealthy atmosphere of industrial towns and to spend time at seaside resorts (Pearce, 1982). In parts of the United States a similar pattern emerged, adding mountain resorts as another destination (Murphy, 1985). The existence of new markets (travellers with time, independent means and motivation) and new infrastructure (railroads and steamers) provided the ideal circumstances for a new type of entrepreneur, the tour organizer. Thomas Cook was the first to seize this opportunity in a major way, beginning day tours in 1841. In the next three decades he developed larger and more extensive packages, creating both international and domestic options for a variety of travellers (Burkart and Medlik, 1974; Brendon, 1990).

Tourism continued to grow throughout the early twentieth century particularly after the First World War. In this era tourism was fuelled by the advent of regular paid holidays, the building of large ocean-going liners and the increasing popularity of the automobile (Pearce, 1982). After the Second World War another technological advance, the development of jet aircraft, supported a further rapid growth, both in numbers travelling and destinations visited. Murphy (1985) plots the change in travel time and cost across the century. In 1929 travel from New York to Sydney took two weeks by ship, by 1969 it took one day by air, and in 1999 it can take as little as 18 hours. This new technology opened up the world to many tourists from the wealthier, more developed countries and created what could be referred to as mass tourism. In this era the travellers were predominantly from the developed West travelling in North America and Europe, and by the 1980s, to destinations in the developing East.

In more recent times there has been much discussion and analysis of major changes in the nature of tourism, particularly international tourism. According to the World Tourism Organization (1996) there has been a substantial shift in the nature of international travellers with the greatest growth in terms of both the origin of international travellers and destinations being in the Asia Pacific region rather than Europe. In this decade international travellers are much more likely to be Asian and/or to be visiting an Asian destination than in any other period. This reflects the rising standards of living in many Asian countries and accompanying changes in work practices and government regulations that have allowed residents from Asian countries the means and the opportunities for international travel, as well as encouragement of their inbound and domestic sectors by these governments (Pearce *et al.*, 1998; Oppermann and Chon, 1997).

In addition to these changes in the origins and destinations of international travellers, there has been much discussion of changes in the nature of travel more generally. Poon (1992) and Urry (1990), for example, provide detailed analyses suggesting a fundamental shift in the nature of tourism away from a mass production industry providing standardized holiday packages towards greater individuality, independence, more flexible itineraries and greater variety in the experiences desired and sought. One consequence of these new tourists has been the proliferation of a greater variety of types of tourism products and many more specialized and niche options.

THE BIG TRENDS

In this brief history several factors were repeatedly noted as factors supporting the growth of travel and tourism. More specifically, tourism seems to thrive in times of political stability and responds rapidly to the development of infrastructure, such as airports, roads and resorts. The development of new transport technologies in particular seems to create opportunities for tourism entrepreneurs to expand and grow. Tourism is linked to growing wealth, to changing work practices which allow for paid recreational leave and to shifts in sociocultural values and attitudes towards seeing travel as a human necessity or right rather than a luxury (WTO, 1990). In addition there has been an increasing attention paid to the impacts of broad scale changes on the nature of travel and tourism. It is therefore worth considering what some of these broader changes are and how they might affect tourism in the future.

THE WORLD WIDE WEB

There is substantial agreement amongst many commentators and authors that changing computer technology, especially changing and increasing use of the Internet and World Wide Web, represents a fundamental shift in the way we organize our social, cultural, political and economic lives. Toffler (1990) has referred to this as a 'Powershift', arguing that the basis of power has become knowledge and that access to the Internet will allow a fundamental redistribution of power and wealth around the world. According to Naisbett (1994), this new technology will result in a more global society with the creation of new 'tribes' as people use this system to find and connect to others around the world who share their interests. The Internet also allows for greater dissemination of knowledge and greater participation in politics (Johnson, 1999). As a result of greater freedom of information and connections across national boundaries there has been a decline in the relevance and importance of national boundaries. According to Naisbett these trends create a number of paradoxes. First, as the world becomes more global, the importance of regional and group cultural identity increases. Here, it seems as if there is a greater need to define groups by culture and language as economic and business traditions become more uniform. Second, as the potential markets for businesses become greater, smaller companies have greater opportunity to become successful. Smaller companies are no longer restricted by limited access to markets, are more flexible and can respond more quickly to changing conditions. The solution to this paradox has been the development of strategic alliances. Naisbett (1994) uses the analogy of shifting from a mainframe to personal computers to personal computers connected through a network. Another paradox is that the more we rely upon computer technology for conducting our business and everyday lives, the more we value and seek human contact. Many authors have noted that few workers have taken up the opportunities now possible to work entirely from a home office (Naisbett, 1994; Matathia and Salzman, 1998)

In addition to these more general trends and predictions there has been much discussion of the possibilities the Web offers for electronic commerce. Matathia and Salzman (1998) offer a variety of statistics on the number of people on-line and the volume of business based on this growing system. In South-East Asian countries more than US$125 million was spent on Internet purchases in 1997, with more than US$1 billion spent in Western Europe in the same time period. There are estimated to be more than 36 million Internet users in Asia (excluding Japan) and the number of Internet users worldwide is on track to have tripled by the end of the year 2001 (Matathia and Salzman, 1998). Not only is the volume of e-commerce and Internet-based consumption increasing, the nature of purchase decisions and approaches to marketing are also changing dramatically. The Internet allows customers to connect directly to companies, opening the way for much more individualized service responses and product design. One of the paradoxes with this development is that the explosion of options threatens to overwhelm many Internet users. There is a rising demand for, and use of, services which filter the information and select products to create personally tailored and limited options for Internet users (Naisbett, 1994; Matathia and Salzman, 1998).

At the same time, the growing numbers of more confident Web users have easy and rapid access to up-to-date information about destinations, attractions, hotels and travel arrangements. Increasingly, destination web sites are illustrated with good quality photographs or video clips of the area and provide current information on temperatures, exchange rates and the latest activities. There are webcam sites, which provide real time video of street scenes, seascapes or mountain scenery and the effect of this on future travel behaviour is a matter of debate. Technology associated with the NASA Mars lander mission gives us the potential to take this trend a step farther by providing a video and audio web site capable of allowing everyone the opportunity to 'visit and experience' neighbouring planets.

The first manned lunar landing, by Neil Armstrong and Buzz Aldrin, took place on 20 July 1969. Aldrin now lobbies for ShareSpace, a non-profit company he founded to promote mass market space travel. He forecasts Earth-orbiting ships carrying 100 people, and clusters of modules as orbiting hotels. Space tourism could be said to have already begun with the flight of a Japanese TV reporter in 1990. Two firms now offer tourists basic cosmonaut training at Star City and ten minutes of weightlessness in an Ilushin 76 for US$ 5000 or a flight in a MiG 25 to an altitude of 28 kilometres (*The Economist*, 1999). Richard Branson has already registered Virgin Galactic Airways as a trading name (Ajello, 1999). Hilton International has drawn up preliminary plans for a moon-based hotel. Interestingly, a textbook on organizational behaviour in hotels and restaurants concludes by speculating how the career experiences of students in the early decades of the twenty-first century may encompass a spell as Manager, Hotel On The Moon (Guerrier, 1999).

CHANGING SOCIAL STRUCTURES AND VALUES

It is difficult to disentangle the effects of new technology from other factors when discussing changes in social life. Clearly the trends described in the previous section have major implications for social and cultural life. We have already noted that the Internet allows people to be connected to like-minded others all over the world. It is also changing the nature of business and commerce such that more flexible working hours and arrangements are not only possible but often necessary. If a major strategic partner is based in a time zone twelve hours different from yours it makes greater sense to have at least someone in your team who works at a matching time. In addition to these effects, however, there are also some changing socio-demographic factors that are important to note.

Much attention has been given to the consequences of an ageing population. Concerns over the health and welfare bills that such a population might generate are common. Equally common are discussions of the possibilities that might exist from a group of people with greater wealth, health and freedom than any previous generation (Henderson, 1998; Molitor, 1998). Changes in socio-demographics have also been extensively discussed. The ageing of many populations has been a topic of major interest, and with earlier retirement there is a trend amongst this group to longer holidays. Two examples are the popularity of month or longer Mediterranean stays during the Northern European winter utilizing discounted charter flights and hotel rates, while the appeal of long tourism holidays is still growing in North America where many retired people use their own RVs and the extensive network of well-equipped camper sites. In contrast, another trend in many countries has been a move away from a single long annual vacation to multiple shorter holidays to fit around greater work pressures and the difficulties of matching holiday time to two working schedules. (Pearce *et al.*, 1998).

Frequently claimed changes in the attitudinal and emotional disposition of modern society are summarized in Table A.1. The changing role of women is another common theme. Increasing power, wealth and opportunities for women have corresponded to changes in workplace practices, such as the provision of childcare and more flexible hours, changes in marketing practices, with more of a focus on products and services for women, and changes in child-rearing and domestic activities, such as the rise in childcare and outsourcing of domestic tasks (Matathia and Salzman, 1998).

Such changes in demographic, consumption and work practices are relatively easy to measure and to demonstrate. What is harder to quantify are the changes in values, attitudes and emotional responses that have been suggested as resulting from all the changing circumstances we have already listed. Matathia and Salzman (1998) and Eckersley (1999) suggest a number of such changes, which are summarized in Table A.1.

IMPLICATIONS FOR TRAVEL AND TOURISM

One thing that many authors agree upon is that demand for travel and tourism will continue to grow (Naisbett, 1994; Toffler, 1990; Matathia and Salzman, 1998). The World Tourism Organization (1997) predicts that in the year 2020 there will be 1.6 billion international tourist arrivals, compared to 564 million in 1995. This figure is based on projected annual growth rates of 4.3 per cent each year. The highest levels of growth are expected to be in Asia, particularly in China, which is predicted to be the world's most popular destination in the year 2020. The Russian Federation is also expected to enter the list of ten most visited destinations. Both the Russian Federation and China are also forecast to enter the top ten tourism-generating countries. Overall, however, Asia will be the region with the greatest growth in outbound tourism. Other forecasts from the WTO include greater growth in long-haul travel, greater intraregional travel in the Asia Pacific region and growth in domestic tourism in Asia, Latin America, the Middle East and Africa.

In addition to these more general forecasts about the growth in tourism there are a number of more specific predictions, which are summarized in Table A.2. Some of these are extensions of existing trends, especially those related to the use of the Internet. Matathia and Salzman (1998) provide some figures to demonstrate the recent growth in e-commerce related to travel. One web-based company, Preview Travel, made a total of US$80.4 million worth of bookings in 1997, as compared to US$20.3 million in the previous year. Microsoft's Expedia travel service sold more than US$100 million worth of travel in 1997 and gets more than 1 million visits each month. Many analysts have suggested that this will reduce the role of travel agents (Tarlow and Muehsam, 1992). Matathia and Salzman (1998) disagree, arguing that the explosion of information available on the Internet overwhelms many users who will turn to professional services to help them make sense of what is available. In this scenario, on-line travel agents will continue to have a role in assisting time pressured and information-overloaded travellers to choose the options that best suit their needs.

Table A.1 Changes in attitudinal and emotional disposition in modern society. *Source*: Based on Matathia and Salzman (1998)

- resistance to change and stress, resulting from the pace of change (also noted by Toffler, 1990, and Bertman, 1998);
- increasing concerns over security and personal safety;
- increasing interest in environmentally friendly products and practices (also noted by Monitor, 1998, and Eckersley, 1999);
- a change in consumption patterns from products to services and experiences (also in Poon, 1992);
- increasing spirituality (see also Minerd, 1998); and
- a change towards taking greater personal responsibility for health and welfare (see also Minerd, 1998).

Table A.2 Some tourism predictions. *Source*: Based on WTO (1997); Naisbett (1994); Matathia and Salzman (1998); Schley (1997); Kistler (1999); Tarlow and Muehsam (1992)

Contributing Factors	Tourism Prediction
Greater availability, flexibility and use of the Internet for business and leisure.	Increased use of the Internet for travel information, planning and purchasing. Need for sophisticated communication access to allow tourists to stay connected while travelling. Increasing competition from computer-based entertainment will create pressure to create even higher levels of service in tourism products. Increasing demand for more flexible, individualized options. Growth in shopping as a travel experience.
Changes and advances in transport technology.	Faster, larger aircraft will decrease travel time and costs, opening some new destinations and offering opportunities for the development of some forms of tourism, such as cruising, to develop in a wider range of locations. Faster, more accessible rail systems will provide an alternative to automobile and aircraft travel. Some form of space travel is likely to be available in the near future for the very wealthy
Changes in working hours, job conditions and the rise of working mothers.	A continuation of the trend towards more shorter trips in a year. Increased combinations of business and recreation. Greater clustering of attractions and experiences to allow for maximum options in a limited time.
Increased concern over health and well-being.	Growth in travel to health spas and resorts.
Increased concern about the environment.	Continued growth in nature-based tourism. Increasing use of information about environmental practices to choose between tourism products.

CHALLENGES FOR TRAVEL AND TOURISM

All these changes, trends and predictions present both opportunities and challenges for the tourism industry. Five key issues or challenges can be identified from the literature.

1. *The need to get more accurate and uniform statistics on the size and economic contributions of tourism* (WTO, 1997; Hawkins, 1993; Naisbett, 1994). Currently tourism is often given a low priority by governments and little attention in terms of the development of policy or support. One reason often cited for this lack of recognition is that, compared to other economic activities, tourism has a poor level of data collection and presentation.

2. *Pressure to compete more effectively with other recreational and entertainment options* (Naisbett, 1994; WTO, 1997; Buhalis and Cooper, 1998). This is particularly a challenge for the many small and medium enterprises that make up a substantial part of the tourism industry in many destinations. Buhalis and Cooper (1998) have noted the problems that many of these businesses have in recognizing who they are competing with. In tourism there is a tendency to focus attention on other operators in the same destination, or on neighbouring destinations, and to ignore the very real competition from other destinations further afield and other forms of entertainment or leisure. Buhalis and Cooper then describe a system for developing strategic alliances between operators to assist them to deal with these other competitors.

3. *The need to deal with increasing diversity amongst tourists* (WTO, 1997; Hawkins, 1993). The markets for tourism will become increasingly diverse in terms of cultural backgrounds, age, family structures and experience, creating challenges for the development of products and the management of the interaction between tourists and hosts and tourists and other tourists.

4. *The need to ensure that infrastructure development and maintenance keep pace with growing demand* (WTO, 1997; Hawkins, 1993). In this case, infrastructure refers not just to the transport systems and built facilities, but also to the training and education of the human resources of tourism.

5. *The need to ensure sustainable tourism development* (WTO, 1997; Hawkins, 1993; WTTC, WTO and the Earth Council, n.d.). The potential for tourism development to produce adverse environmental and social impacts that undermine the longer-term attractiveness of destination has been recognized on the basis of the experience of many maturing destinations. The sustainable tourism development agenda, therefore, becomes a dominant philosophy, with the preservation of social and environmental assets and the well-being of the host community becoming primary objectives.

CONCLUSION

Tourism is a rapidly developing sphere of human activity, reflecting the changing economic and social conditions which underlie modern views of individual freedom of expression through consumer choice, and the new technologies of transport and data communications which make it possible for large numbers of people to spend their leisure in distant places. Just as the emergence of tourism as a significant domain of human activity is attributable to changing social, economic and technological conditions, therefore, the evolution and dynamics of this sector is affected by ongoing changes in these conditions. Within the context of the array of changes alluded to in this chapter, however, the above attempt to distil the challenges confronting the industry in the twenty-first century into just five areas clearly misrepresents the complexity of the task. The one certainty of the future is that change will continue and those tourism operators and destinations who are both aware of these changes, and develop effective responses to them, will achieve longer-term viability. At the same time, however, it needs to be appreciated that tourism is itself an agent of change. The exploitation (and creation) of new opportunities by entrepreneurs and destination planners can be instrumental in initiating change through the influence they have on consumers and other operators, both within and beyond the tourism sector.

REFERENCES

Ajello, R. P. (1999) 'How far will the vacation take us?' *Asiaweek*, 20–27 August, 74–5.

Ancer, J. (1999) 'Prophets of da doom'. *Sunday Times Lifestyle*, 24 January, 1–2.

Anthony, I. (1973) *Verualamium*. Hanley, UK: Wood Mitchell and Co.

Bertman, S. (1998) 'Hyperculture'. *The Futurist*, **32**(9), 18–24.

Brendon, P. (1990) *Thomas Cook: 150 Years of Popular Tourism*. London: Secker.

Buhalis, D and Cooper, C. (1998) 'Competition or cooperation?'. In E. Laws, B. Faulkner and G. Moscardo (eds) *Embracing and Managing Change in Tourism*. London: Routledge, pp. 324–46.

Burkart, A. J. and Medlik, S. (1974) *Tourism*. London: Heinemann.

Butler, R. W. (1980) 'The concept of a tourist area cycle of evolution: implications for management of resources'. *Canadian Geographer*, **24**(1), 5–12.

Calantone, R. J., Benedito, A. and Bojanic, D. (1987) 'A comprehensive review of tourism forecasting literature'. *Journal of Travel Research* (Fall), 28–39.

Casson, L. (1974) *Travel in the Ancient World*. London: Allen and Unwin.

Eckersley, R. (1999) 'Is life really getting better?' *The Futurist*, **33**(1), 23–7.

Economist, The (1999) 3–9 July, 70.

Faulkner, B. (1994) 'The future ain't what it used to be: reflections on the nature and role of tourism forecasting in Australia'. In *Tourism Forecasting*. Proceedings of the 1993 Australian Tourism research Workshop, Canberra: Bureau of Tourism Research, pp. 5–11.

Faulkner, B. and Valerio, P. (1995) 'An integrative approach to tourism demand forecasting'. *Tourism Management*, **16**(1), 29–37.

Guerrier, Y. (1999) *Organizational Behaviour in Hotels and Restaurants: An International Perspective*. New York: Wiley.

Hawking, S. (1993) 'The future of the universe'. In L. Howe and A. Wain (eds) *Predicting the Future.*
Cambridge: Cambridge University Press, pp. 8–23.

Hawkins, D. E. (1993) 'Global assessment of tourism policy: a process model'. In D. G. Pearce and
R. W. Butler (eds) *Tourism Research: Critiques and Challenges.* London: Routledge,
pp. 175–200.

Henderson, C. (1998) 'Today's affluent oldsters'. *The Futurist,* **32**(8), 19–24.

Hibbert, C. (1969) *The Grand Tour.* London: Weidenfeld Nicolson.

Inskeep, E. (1991) *Tourism Planning: An Integrated and Sustainable Development Approach.*
New York: Van Nostrand Reinhold.

Johnson, D. (1998) 'Millennium: the biggest party ever – and you are invited'. *The Futurist,* **32**(7), 41–6.

Johnson, D. (1999) 'Politics in cyberspace'. *The Futurist,* **31**(1), 14.

Kistler, W. P. (1999) 'Humanity's future in space'. *The Futurist,* **33**(1), 43–7.

Laws, E. (1995) *Tourist Destination Management: Issues, Analysis and Policies.* London:
Routledge.

Matathia, I. and Salzman, M. (1998) *Next: Trends for the Future.* Sydney: MacMillan.

Meadows, D. H., Meadows, D. L., Randers, J. and Behrens, W. W. (1972) *The Limits of Growth.* New
York: Universe Books.

Minerd, J. (1998) 'The new individualism'. *The Futurist,* **32**(9), 12–14.

Molitor, G. T. T. (1998) 'Trends and forecasts for the new millennium'. *The Futurist,* **32**(6), 53–60.

Murphy, P. E. (1985) *Tourism: A Community Approach.* New York: Methuen.

Naisbett, J. (1994) *Global Paradox.* New York: Avon Books.

Naisbett, J. (1997) *Megatrends Asia.* London: Nicholas Brealey.

Opperman, M. and Chon, K. (1997) *Tourism in Developing Countries.* London: Thompson Business
Press.

Paskins, D. (1997) 'Thinking futures. How to survive and thrive in a fast changing (business) world'.
Futures, **29**(3), 257–66.

Pearce, P. L. (1982) *The Social Psychology of Tourist Behaviour.* Oxford: Pergamon.

Pearce, P. L., Morrison, A. M. and Rutledge, J. L. (1998) *Tourism: Bridges Across Continents.*
Sydney: McGraw Hill.

Poon, A. (1992) *Tourism, Technology and Competitive Strategies.* Wallingford, UK: CAB
International.

Rowling, M. (1971) *Everyday Life of Medieval Travellers.* London: B.T. Batsford.

Schaffer, S. (1993) 'Comets and the world's end'. In L. Howe and A. Wain (eds) *Predicting the
Future.* Cambridge: Cambridge University Press.

Schley, R. (1997) 'Travel planning online: virtual visits give travellers a head start'. *The Futurist,*
31(6), 12.

Swinglehurst, E. (1974) *The Romantic Journey.* London: Pica.

Swinglehurst, E. (1982) *Cook's Tours: The Story of Popular Travel.* London: Blandford Press.

Tarlow, P. E. and Muehsam, M. J. (1992) 'Wide horizons: travel and tourism in the coming decades'.
The Futurist, **26**(5), 28–33.

Toffler, A. (1970) *Future Shock.* London: Bodley Head.

Toffler, A. (1990). *Powershift.* New York: Bantam Books.

Urry, J. (1990) *The Tourist Gaze.* London: Sage.

Uysal, M. and Crompton, J. L. (1985) 'An overview of approaches used to forecast tourism demand'.
Journal of Travel Research (Spring), 7–15.

Wolfe, R. I. (1967) 'Recreational Travel: The New Migration'. *Geographical Bulletin,* **2**, 159–67.

World Tourism Organization (1990) *Tourism to the Year 2000.* Madrid: WTO.

World Tourism Organization (1996) *The WTO's 1995 International Tourism Overview.* Madrid: WTO.

World Tourism Organization (1997) *Tourism: 2020 Vision.* Madrid: WTO.

World Travel and Tourism Council, World Tourism Organization and the Earth Council (n.d.).
Agenda 21 for the Travel and Tourism Industry.

PART 1

Forms of Tourist Activity

Edited by Gianna Moscardo

In the first chapter we identified both the changing nature of tourism and described and contemplated the various forces that are associated with these changes. In this part the focus of attention is narrowed to tourists and what they do. A number of major trends relevant to understanding the changing nature of tourists and their activities can be identified. First, there appear to be changes in the motivations and expectations of tourists related to greater opportunities to travel, greater travel experience and higher levels of education. The most obvious consequence of these changing patterns of tourist motivation are a move from mass packaged relatively inflexible options for travel to an exponential increase in the range of travel options available and sought and a major shift to more independent, flexible and personalized itineraries. This theme of increasing variety in forms of tourist activity is one that runs through all the chapters in this part, but especially through the chapters on 'Cultural and Heritage Tourism', 'Nature-based Tourism and Ecotourism' and 'Wine Tourism'.

A second major theme that can be identified with regard to the changing nature of tourist activity is the increasing focus on the sustainability of tourist activities. Again this is discussed in all chapters in this part but is central to the arguments in Gianna Moscardo's chapter on 'Cultural and Heritage Tourism: The Great Debates', and Laura Lawton and David Weaver's chapter on 'Nature-based Tourism and Ecotourism'.

A third theme is the changing nature of tourists and their social and work worlds. One major new pattern of tourism has been that of the increasing diversity of travellers with many more countries becoming major sources of international tourists. Increasing cross-cultural contacts can bring issues of cultural sustainability to the fore and these are central to the discussion of Renata Tomljenovic and Bill Faulkner in their chapter on 'Tourism and World Peace: A Conundrum for the Twenty-first Century'.

A final theme of relevance to this part has been the changing nature of travel activity, which results from changes in the patterns of work and social life. One consequence of increasing social and economic complexity has been a move away from single annual long holidays to multiple shorter breaks. David Edgar in his chapter on 'Short Break Markets – from Product Positioning to a Value-Based Approach' provides a detailed review and analysis of this form of tourist activity.

In addition to these themes, two core concepts run throughout the chapters in this part. One is a focus by all the authors on taking what Jafari (1990) has referred to as a knowledge-based approach to the particular tourist activities reviewed. Thus Moscardo balances a review of the major negative impacts of cultural and heritage tourism with a discussion of some of the potential benefits, especially for less powerful groups, from changing forms of cultural and heritage tourism. Lawton and Weaver also take up a knowledge-based approach in assessing the potential for ecotourism to deliver on its early promises for a truly sustainable and viable alternative form of tourism. A further example can be found in Tomljenovic and Faulkner's critical analysis of the conditions under which cross-cultural contact in a tourism setting can contribute to improved relationships and cultural understanding. The other important and major concept that runs through the chapters in Part 1 is that of learning from the experiences of the past to suggest guidelines for the future. Ross Dowling and Don Getz's chapter on 'Wine Tourism Futures' and David Edgar's chapter on 'Short Break Markets' are clear examples of this approach, with each chapter providing a set of guidelines for the future development of these two forms of tourism.

REFERENCE

Jafari, J. (1990) 'Research and scholarship: the basis of tourism education'. *Journal of Tourism Studies*, **1**(1), 33–41.

CHAPTER 1

Cultural and Heritage Tourism: The Great Debates

Gianna Moscardo

INTRODUCTION

Recent decades have seen an explosion of interest in the past embracing everything from fossils and furniture to folklore and faiths: . . .

No longer are only aristocrats obsessed with ancestry, only the super-rich collectors of antiques, only academics antiquarians, only a cultured minority museum-goers; millions of ordinary folk now search out their roots, mobilize to protect beloved scenes, cherish their own and other people's mementoes, and dote on media versions of history. (Lowenthal, 1993, p. 3)

In these eloquent statements Lowenthal describes two simple but critical features of heritage – growth and change. Arguably growth and change are characteristics of virtually all aspects of late twentieth-century life. Throughout this book many authors attempt to describe succinctly and analyse critically growth and change in many aspects of society and particularly tourism. The challenge for this chapter is to do the same for cultural and heritage tourism. This author's response to this challenge will be to chart the debates, describe the rival social representations of heritage and cultural tourism and identify the gaps in existing academic discussions of this particular form of tourism.

Definitions

This chapter is concerned with two interrelated forms of tourism, that which is focused on the past (heritage) and that which is focused on the present (cultural) way of life of a visited community. Many authors have used more explicit behavioural definitions following on from Smith (1978). Smith defined these two

Table 1.1 Some site and activity definitions of cultural and heritage tourism

Ashworth (1993)	Historic architecture Places associated with historical events and personalities Artistic achievements Accumulations of cultural artefacts
Richards (1996)	Archaeological sites and museums Architecture (ruins, famous buildings, whole towns) Art, sculpture, crafts, galleries, festivals, events Music and dance Drama Language and literature study, tours, events Religious festivals, pilgrimages Complete (folk or primitive) cultures and subcultures*
Prentice (1997)	Palaces, cathedrals, temples and galleries Study of or focus of history, archaeology and literature
Richter (1999)	Museums, historic districts Re-enactments of events Statues, monuments and shrines

Note: * This component is often seen as a separate form of tourism referred to as Ethnic or Indigenous tourism.

forms of tourism by listing the sites and activities that characterize them. In her typology, historical tourism includes 'the Museum–Cathedral circuit' and 'guided tours of monuments and ruins' (Smith, 1978, p. 3). Cultural tourism includes meals, performances and festivals. Table 1.1 lists some of the sites and activities included in more recent definitions.

In addition, and sometimes in opposition, to these descriptive resource and behavioural definitions are those which focus on the experiential components of these forms of tourism. In these definitions attention is paid to what tourists seek and get out of cultural and heritage experiences. In summary, cultural and heritage tourism is a form of tourism in which participants seek to learn about and experience the past and present cultures of themselves and of others (Ashworth, 1993; Jansen-Verbeke, 1997; Nuryanti, 1996; Prentice, 1997; Richards, 1996).

An important component of many of these experiential definitions is the recognition that cultural and heritage experiences are produced from the interactions of visitors and the objects and/or ideas presented at the sites. Figure 1.1 is a simple model of this production process derived from models presented by

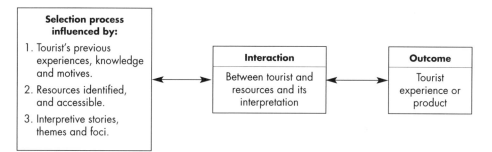

Figure 1.1 A simple model of cultural and heritage tourism production.

Source: Developed from Jansen-Verbeke, 1997; Prentice, 1997; and Ashworth, 1993

Prentice (1997), Ashworth (1993) and Jansen-Verbeke (1997). Each of these authors includes a component related to the interpretation of the place, history, idea or people. The importance of interpretation is recognized by many authors and this is a theme that will be taken up later in this chapter. Table 1.2 lists some of the common characteristics of definitions of interpretation. Interpretation is sometimes referred to by European authors as animation (Bauer, 1996; Krippendorf, 1987).

In summary, this chapter is concerned with describing and analysing growth and change in the nature of visitor experiences at places associated with the past and/or present culture of some groups of people. By explicitly arguing that cultural and heritage tourism is best understood as an experience which is produced by the interaction of the visitor with the resource, this definition focuses attention on the selection and interpretation of past and present culture. It is these three processes of selection, interpretation and experience production that have been at the centre of the major debates over cultural and heritage tourism.

Table 1.2 Components of definitions of interpretation

Component	Definitions
Education	Tilden (1977)
Significance	Shepherd (1993); SIBH; Knudson *et al.* (1995)
Explanation	SIBH (Society for Interpreting Britain's Heritage)
Understanding	SIBH; Shepherd (1993); Knudson *et al.* (1995)
Access	Knudson *et al.* (1995)
Awareness	Shepherd (1993)
Enjoyment	SIBH; Shepherd (1993)
Discovery	Shepherd (1993)
Creating a conservation ethic	SIBH; Shepherd (1993)
Inspiration	Shepherd (1993)

This chapter will describe the long-running and ongoing debates over the authenticity or inauthenticity of tourism experiences and over historical accuracy or inaccuracy. The chapter will then examine other issues related to the sustainability of cultural and heritage tourism. The next section of the chapter will concentrate on interpretation. In particular, this section will explore the role of interpretation in sustainability. Finally, the chapter will briefly look towards the future and the challenges and opportunities of new technologies for cultural and heritage tourism.

THE AUTHENTICITY DEBATE

The case against tourism

The earliest criticism of tourism that is most commonly cited is that of Boorstin (1964). Boorstin's argument was a simple one – modern tourists are shallow individuals seeking only entertainment, who are easily satisfied by the inauthentic 'pseudo-events' presented to them by the tourism industry. MacCannell (1976) then provided both a more complex analysis of the concept of inauthenticity and a boost for its status in academic discussions of tourism. While MacCannell agreed with Boorstin's analysis of tourism, he disagreed with Boorstin's descriptions of the modern tourist. According to MacCannell all modern tourists were seeking real or authentic experiences. In this analysis, the tourist is an individual on a secular pilgrimage trying to create meaning in his/her own life by seeking out and learning from authentic experiences in other places. Although MacCannell gives tourists more worthy motives, he does not appear to afford them any greater intelligence than Boorstin. Like Boorstin, MacCannell argues that the tourism industry inevitably creates inauthentic or staged experiences and the tourist is happy with these because he/she is incapable of recognizing these 'pseudo-events' as fake. MacCannell goes on to describe in detail how these inauthentic experiences are created and this process is summarized in Table 1.3.

An offshoot of MacCannell's argument is that led by Hewison (1987). Hewison is more specifically concerned with cultural and heritage tourism than MacCannell and argues that pressure from the tourism industry to create entertainment inevitably leads to a superficial and often inaccurate presentation of history. In a similar vein Fowler (1989) states that:

> We can do what our ancestors did and learn something of what they might have experienced physically. But even here we tend to be somewhat selective, going mainly for the fun things like jousts and fayres and banquets. I doubt if all this activity has contributed one iota to a deeper popular understanding of history. Indeed, the cynic could see evidence in

Table 1.3 MacCannell's steps in the creation of a tourist attraction or site sacrilization

1. Naming	A site is identified as significant and markers are used to identify the site.
2. Framing and elevation	The site is made available for visitation and/or displays are created. Framing refers to creation of an official boundary to protect and enhance the site.
3. Enshrinement	The boundary areas or displays become sites in their own right.
4. Mechanical reproduction	Prints and models of the site are produced.
5. Social reproduction	Groups, cities and regions take the name of the site.

the heritage product to argue that, far from being educative, it has had the effect of buttressing already deeply embedded perceptions. Nevertheless it is easier, more fun, and more revenue earning that the perpetuities for so many, the cold and damp and hunger, the weariness and illness . . . Would the public let us display death, disease and dismay rather than the pap which panders to their expectation? I doubt it. (Fowler, 1989, p. 63)

Like Boorstin (1964) and MacCannell (1976), this argument is based upon the assumptions that tourism inevitably creates inauthentic experiences and that tourists uncritically accept these.

Horne (1984) makes a slightly different suggestion. He again assumes that tourists are gullible and that many of their cultural and heritage experiences are shallow and inauthentic. His particular focus is, however, on the nature of this inauthenticity. His argument is that the presentation or interpretation of culture and history in tourism settings is biased towards that of the dominant groups. In this version of the debate, women, ethnic and minority groups, the powerless and the poor are left out and ignored. This selectivity means that cultural and heritage tourism serves to bolster the power of those who dominate. This is a criticism that continues to create concern amongst those who write about the presentation of the past (see Fladmark, 1993; Richter, 1999; and Rickard and Spearritt, 1991, for further discussions of these issues).

The reply

Not surprisingly these arguments about the inauthenticity of tourism have been criticized. The most vocal critics have been Cohen (1979a, 1979b, 1988) and Urry (1990, 1995). Cohen and Urry have suggested that MacCannell's and Hewison's arguments are based upon two incorrect assumptions about tourists. First, it is suggested that tourists exclusively seek either authenticity or entertainment and that they cannot tell the difference between authentic and inauthentic or staged experiences. Urry (1990, 1995) has argued in some detail that, not only are tourists capable of perceiving the staged nature of tourism, but that postmodern tourists will sometimes actively seek staged experiences as part of their desire for play and the value they place on eclecticism.

Several authors (Cohen, 1988; Salamone, 1997; and Waller and Lea, 1999) have taken this analysis further, claiming that MacCannell also assumes the existence of some objective measure of authenticity. Pearce and Moscardo (1986), Cohen (1988), Salamone (1997) and Waller and Lea (1999) all dispute this, proposing instead that authenticity is a quality that emerges from an individual's experience and is a perceived rather than an objective feature of tourist attractions. While Pearce and Moscardo (1986) claimed that authenticity was primarily a feature of the visitor or tourist's perception, Salamone (1997) adds the perspective of the other participants in cultural tourism, the hosts. Salamone (1997) provides an interesting analysis of the experience provided by the San Angel restaurants in Disneyworld and Mexico. This analysis suggests that authenticity is a multidimensional concept, an idea taken on by Waller and Lea (1999). Waller and Lea go on to make a connection between Moscovici's (1984) concept of social representations and perceptions of authenticity.

Moscovici has argued that much social behaviour and interaction is guided by, or based upon, social representations. Social representations are the theories and stereotypes that people develop and use to understand the world around them. People often adopt the dominant social representations of the social groups they belong to. In this sense social representations are both outcomes and mechanisms of socialization and components of group identity.

Crick (1989) and Pearce, Moscardo and Ross (1996) have used this concept of social representation to explore some of the prevailing academic literature about tourists. They argue that many of those who are concerned with the inauthenticity of tourism appear to be using a social representation which sees tourists as passive, powerless, ignorant and easily duped. According to Crick (1989), these assumptions in turn serve to support social distinctions between the academics and the tourists they study.

In addition to these conceptual analyses, there is a growing body of evidence that tourists differ widely in their interests and motivations and in their perceptions of the cultural and heritage experiences on offer. Table 1.4 lists some of the motivation-based market segments identified in three recent studies of cultural and heritage tourism. This table is not meant to represent a comprehensive review but rather provides some recent examples which demonstrate the range of different types of motives and benefits sought and experienced. Some further examples can be found in Herbert (1996), Beeho and Prentice (1997) and Jansen-Verbeke and van Rehman (1996).

Table 1.4 Some cultural and heritage tourism market segments

Authors	Sample Details	Segments
Alzua, O'Leary and Morrison (1998)	1200 UK international travellers who participated in a cultural or heritage experience on their most recent holiday	*Backpackers* – visit cultural and heritage sites because they are icons of the destination. *Family group* – cultural and heritage activities are often associated with visiting families and as opportunities for the family to spend time together. *Urban Heritage group* – older, better-educated couples seeking more intense cultural experiences. *Family Resort group* – seek relaxation and recreation.
Formica and Uysal (1998)	278 visitors attending the Spoleto Festival in Italy.	*Enthusiasts* – specifically attracted to the festival to experience a range of cultural activities and to share cultural interests with like-minded others. *Moderates* – less interested in culture experiences and not at all interested in interacting with others.
Prentice, Witt and Hamer (1998)	403 visitors to the Rhondda Heritage Park in South Wales.	*Visitors with a strong personal interest* in local history. Feel sense of identity with industrial Wales and nostalgia. *Visitors with little sympathy* for present trade unions but who believe they have had an educational experience. *Visitors with children* who visit to spend time together as a family.

In addition to those who argue that a singular view of tourists is not accurate, there are those who have responded to Hewson's critique of heritage by suggesting that there is no single version of history (Craig, 1989; Schofield, 1996; Uzzell, 1996). Ashworth (1993), for example, proposed that much of the debate over historical authenticity is better described as a clash of conflicting versions of the past. According to Crang (1996) 'careless critiques of the heritage industry can end up advocating a single means of enjoying the past' (p. 417). He goes on to suggest that many academics have taken on the role of 'legislator' (p. 419), or those in charge of determining what is significant in history. In this scenario 'much of the drive of heritage and contemporary society consists in previously silenced groups striving to overturn this hierarchy' (Crang, 1996, p. 419).

Nuryanti (1996) takes up this theme, portraying the authenticity and accuracy debates as resulting from the tension between traditional forms of cultural and historical consumption and modern forms, and between power and continuity and change. Bourdieu (1984) coined the phrase 'cultural capital' as a consequence of his studies of French museum and gallery visitors. Cultural capital was gathered through education and socialization and allowed for the appreciation of what have been called 'high' cultural forms such as art, opera and architecture. This cultural capital was thus a form of social class distinction. If changing patterns of consumption and tourism allow for greater access and appreciation across a wider range of people (which is Urry's 1990 and 1995 argument), then these new forms of cultural and heritage tourism threaten existing power and class hierarchies. It is not surprising then that these new forms are criticized by those who previously controlled this cultural capital.

A number of studies have identified the increasing participation in cultural and heritage tourism of generalists rather than specialists (Alzua *et al.*, 1998; Edwards and Llurdes i Coit, 1996; Formica and Uysal, 1998; Herbert, 1996; Prentice *et al.*, 1998; Richter, 1999). In a parallel fashion there is also clear evidence of the increasing democratization of those whose heritage and culture is presented (Lowenthal, 1993; Richter, 1999). Numerous newly vocal and previously marginalized groups are now using tourism to present and reaffirm their history and experience (Edwards and Llurdes i Coit, 1996; Jansen-Verbeke, 1997; Jones, 1993; Urry, 1995).

Another change in the nature of cultural and heritage tourism is the increasing development of, and interest in, sites of conflict and tragedy (Dann, 1994; Richter, 1999). Examples include Dachau concentration camp, the Holocaust Museum in Washington, DC, and the Beit Itashoah Museum of Tolerance in Los Angeles. While Dann (1994) portrays this trend as a macabre form of entertainment, Richter (1994) suggests it is possible that such sites can create powerful experiences for visitors. This is an argument also made by Uzzell (1989), who proposed that greater attention needed to be given to these 'hot' or emotional topics and that effective interpretation in these settings could be a powerful force for peace and tolerance.

THE IMPACTS OF CULTURAL AND HERITAGE TOURISM

Another area of debate in regard to cultural and heritage tourism is that of the balance between negative and positive impacts. Using Jafari's (1990) terminology there is a strong advocacy platform in the literature describing these types of tourism. The advocates typically focus on the economic benefits of developing cultural and heritage tourism. Many authors present case studies where urban regeneration projects have been supported based on the belief that the resulting tourism boost will outweigh the investment costs. See Lavery (1993) for an example of the European Union support for restoration projects in Venice and Athens; Tuppen (1996) for an example of restoration in French cities; Bull and Church (1996) for examples in London; Blank (1996) for examples in the United States; Richards (1996) for examples in Scotland; McGregor (1993) for an example in New Zealand; and Crookston (1998) for examples in Arab countries. These advocates often also suggest that such regeneration and restoration projects provide social benefits for residents and are examples of tourism supporting conservation.

Ashworth (1993) and Richards (1996) offer a different view. Ashworth (1993) particularly concentrates on the economic aspect of developing resources for cultural and heritage tourism and describes the difficulties of accurately measuring both benefits and costs. Both Ashworth and Richards note that many centres for cultural and heritage tourism suffer from congestion and overcrowding, pollution and overuse of resources. One of the common consequences of these problems is the displacement of locals who move away from these pressures. Ashworth (1993) describes some of the mechanisms and strategies that have been used in attempts to alleviate these problems including directly limiting visitor numbers to sites, limiting facilities such as car parks and increasing prices to deter or discourage visitation. To date there is only limited evidence that these strategies have had any significant successes.

Several authors have argued that greater control, regulation and organization from more powerful management agencies may be necessary to alleviate the negative impacts of tourists to cultural and heritage sites (Jansen-Verbeke, 1997; Jansen-Verbeke and Lievois, 1999; Jones, 1993; Van der Borg *et al.*, 1996). Richter (1999) in turn points out that such actions can disenfranchise local communities. The recognition of a site's significance and possible or actual tourism damage often results in a takeover of the site by a management agency which takes control of the site out of the hands of locals. This loss of power can undermine the goals of the agency. In an Australian study of World Heritage listing it was found that substantial proportions of those surveyed held negative views of this process, believing that listing was imposed upon local communities and that management control was taken over by the United Nations (Moscardo *et al.*, 1998).

11

THE ROLE OF INTERPRETATION IN SUSTAINABLE CULTURAL AND HERITAGE TOURISM

One management tool given little attention in the previous discussions is that of interpretation. Effective interpretation can contribute to the sustainability of tourism in a number of ways. One way is through relieving congestion at high pressure sites. Visitors often concentrate at particular sites because they are unaware of alternatives. Roggenbuck (1992) reports on a study demonstrating that the provision of information on alternatives was successful in encouraging visitors to visit alternative sites thus alleviating pressure on high profile sites. A more extreme version of providing information on alternatives is to provide a substitution experience. Moscardo (1999) provides the example of the Tyrrell Museum of Palaeontology in Canada. In this case the museum presents the fossils of the Dinosaur Provincial Park. The park is a very fragile setting with little capacity for visitation. The museum is located quite a distance from the site but provides a variety of interactive audio-visual and diorama displays. Many of those who already decry the creation of staged experience are likely to see such substitution experiences as the ultimate degradation of the cultural or heritage experience. Such a view denies visitors the opportunity to recognize that their own presence can have negative impacts and that the best action they can take to conserve the site is to accept a substitute.

Krippendorf (1987) has noted that, while many managers, hosts and academics discuss the negative impacts of tourism, few include the tourists themselves in the discussion. An analysis of interpretive messages provided on signs to visitors to the Wet Tropics World Heritage Area of north-eastern Australia found that fewer than 5 per cent of the signs provided information on minimal impact behaviours. This was in contrast to the views of visitors, the majority of whom were seeking advice on how to minimize their impacts (Moscardo *et al.*, 1998). Another way in which interpretation can contribute to sustainability is through informing visitors about their impacts and educating them with regard to minimal impact behaviours.

Interpretation – 'the Emperor's new clothes'

Despite widespread support in the literature for the use of interpretation to enhance the sustainability of cultural and heritage tourism, there continues to be criticism of the entire concept. The most common concern is that interpretation interferes with, or acts as a barrier to, the visitor's own experience of a place or object. According to O'Toole (1992), 'the whole notion of the interpretative centre can be seen as the product of an overactive mind, a mind that must always substitute meaning for experience' (p. 14). He goes on to quote Susan Sontag as stating that 'To interpret is to impoverish, to deplete the world – in order to set up a shadow world of "meanings"' (p. 14). At core, the argument here is that places we often believe need interpretation can speak for themselves and once a visitor experiences someone else's interpretation they will never be able to have their own direct experience.

This argument is based on two questionable assumptions. First, that visitors have sufficient background and understanding to appreciate the significance of a place on their own. Second, that visitors come without their own pre-existing interpretations. Despite these weaknesses, the possibility does remain that interpretation can overwhelm visitors and interfere with their experience. It is not an uncommon experience for an overly enthusiastic interpreter to move from presentation to propaganda.

These problems often arise because of the tendency to conceptualize interpretation as a one-way flow of information from the interpreter who knows the 'truth' or the 'facts' to the visitor (Crang, 1996). Faggetter (1996) refers to such approaches as the straight arrow model of communication. The prevailing belief amongst those who adhere to such models is that, if the right arrow can reach the right target, then the interpretation will be successful. Such assumptions are consistent with the focus of much evaluation research on quiz or multiple choice tests to measure knowledge gains.

The straight arrow communication model and its passive visitor is inconsistent with much of existing evidence available from psychological and educational research. People actively construct their understandings of the world by seeking patterns and adding to, or adjusting, what they already know (Moscardo, 1999). Pines and West (1986) suggested that there are several possible combinations in communication situations. One common situation is that visitors and interpreters have very different or conflicting understandings or beliefs. There is evidence that in many of these instances visitors extract the information that makes sense to them (Miles, 1989). Another common combination occurs when interpreters over-estimate the knowledge that visitors bring with them. In these cases visitors simply cannot understand the information presented (Borun, 1991; Tilden, 1977).

Moscardo (1996, 1999) has proposed an alternative model based on the work of psychologist Ellen Langer on mindfulness (1989a). According to Langer, in any situation we can be either mindless or mindful. When mindless, people follow familiar routines, accept existing definitions and perspectives, and fail to pay attention to and use new information. Mindlessness is not a lack of thought, but rather a lack of attention and processing of new information. People are capable of conducting much complex behaviour mindlessly. What they are not capable of is changing their perspective or learning new information.

The opposite state is that of mindfulness. Mindful people actively process new information, create new categories for this information, change their perspectives and create new routines for their actions. Moscardo (1996, 1999) proposes that the most appropriate goal of interpretation is to encourage visitors to be mindful. Mindful visitors can then play an active role in the interpretation, process new information, contemplate other perspectives and change their behaviour.

Mindful visitors have the power to create their own personal experiences and take what makes sense to them from what is presented by the interpreters. Mindfulness can itself be encouraged by giving visitors greater power or control over the interpretation they experience. Control encourages mindfulness as it requires choices or decisions and these in turn require active information processing. An example of giving visitors greater control would be a tour guide directly asking them what they would like to do or hear about and then organizing the tour to match the responses. Another example can be found in the South Australian Maritime Museum where visitors are asked to write a short story about their experiences of a local sea voyage. The result is a constantly changing and popular exhibit created entirely by the visitors themselves. The increasing availability and use of technology offers many new options for visitors to have some control over their interpretive experiences. Computers and their networks can provide flexible and interactive options.

Not only can new technologies be used to offer visitors greater control, they can also act as a pressure to do so. As visitors arrive with increasing experience of interacting with information through media such as the World Wide Web, they may expect greater sophistication and flexibility in their experiences. This new technology is another force which seems likely to support the trend, described earlier, towards greater access to 'cultural capital'. Giving greater control to visitors is a further example of the shift in traditional power structures within cultural and heritage tourism.

Langer (1989b, 1993) has also suggested that one way to encourage mindfulness in formal educational settings is explicitly to recognize that a complete and agreed-upon body of knowledge rarely exists. Most fields are characterized by debate, by gaps in knowledge and explanation, and by alternative and often competing theories. Langer argues that often in formal education these gaps, debates and alternatives are downplayed or even ignored. The consequence of presenting knowledge as a complete and unambiguous whole is to deny the learner any opportunity to be critical or to make choices and this encourages mindlessness. This description seems to fit much cultural and heritage interpretation.

According to Langer, teachers (and interpreters) should recognize and focus on the gaps and debates and encourage students (and visitors) to make choices and to speculate. One suggestion is to use the question 'what if?' as a recurrent theme. The increasing recognition of alternative histories, of debate and conflict, and of gaps in our historical records, has been noted by Richter (1999) as another force for encouraging mindfulness.

A single theme can be identified that runs through all the discussions of cultural and heritage tourism: the increasing democratization and participation by a broader range of people. These trends apply both to the visitors who seek to experience the heritage and cultures of others, and to the communities and groups who are those others. For some authors this change is a negative one, for others it represents opportunities for improving the sustainability of this type of tourism. What is clear is that these trends are likely to continue, supported by computer technologies with the potential for all the participants in cultural and heritage tourism to create, present and enjoy a wider range of experiences.

REFERENCES

Alzua, A., O'Leary, J. T. and Morrison, A. M. (1998) 'Cultural and heritage tourism: identifying niches for international travellers'. *Journal of Tourism Studies*, **9**(2), 2–13.

Ashworth, G. (1993) Culture and tourism: conflict or symbiosis in Europe. In W. Pompl and P. Lavery (eds) *Tourism in Europe*. Wallingford, UK: CAB International, pp. 13–35.

Bauer, M. (1996) 'Cultural tourism in France'. In G. Richards (ed.) *Cultural Tourism in Europe*. Wallingford, UK: CAB International, pp. 147–64.

Beeho, A. J. and Prentice, R. C. (1997) 'Conceptualizing the experiences of heritage tourists'. *Tourism Management*, **18**(2), 75–87.

Blank, U. (1996) 'Tourism in United States cities'. In C. M. Law (ed.) *Tourism in Major Cities*. London: International Thomson Business Press, pp. 206–32.

Boorstin, D. (1964) *The Image: A Guide to Pseudo-events in America*. New York: Harper.

Borun, M. (1991) 'Confronting naïve notions through interactive exhibits'. In *Doing Time, Museums, Education and Accountability*. Proceedings of the 1991 Museum Education Association of Australia Conference, Sydney.

Bourdieu, P. (1984) *Distinction: A Social Critique of the Judgement of Taste*. London: Routledge and Kegan Paul.

Bull, P. and Church, A. (1996) 'The London tourism complex'. In C. M. Law (ed.) *Tourism in Major Cities*. London: International Thomson Business Press, pp. 155–78.

Chang, T. C., Milne, S., Fallon, D. and Pohlmann, C. (1996) 'Urban heritage tourism: the global–local nexus'. *Annals of Tourism Research*, **23**(2), 284–305.

Cohen, E. (1979a) 'A phenomenology of tourist experiences'. *Sociology*, **13**, 179–201.

Cohen, E. (1979b) 'Rethinking the sociology of tourism'. *Annals of Tourism Research*, **6**(10), 18–35.

Cohen, E. (1988) 'Authenticity and commodization in tourism'. *Annals of Tourism Research*, **15**(3), 371–86.

Craig, B. (1989) 'Interpreting the historic scene'. In D. L. Uzzell (ed.) *Heritage Interpretation Volume 1: The Natural and Built Environment*. London: Belhaven Press, pp. 107–12.

Crang, M. (1996) 'Magic kingdom or quixotic quest for authenticity'. *Annals of Tourism Research*, **23**(2), 415–31.

Crick, M. (1989) 'Representations of international tourism in the social sciences'. *Annual Reviews in Anthropology*, **18**, 307–44.

Crookston, M. (1998) 'Conservation and regeneration: two case studies in the Arab world'. In E. Laws, B. Faulkner and G. Moscardo (eds) *Embracing and Managing Change in Tourism*. London: Routledge, pp. 264–78.

Dann, M. S. (1994) 'Tourism: the nostalgia industry of the future'. In W. F. Theobald (ed.) *Global Tourism*. London: Butterworth-Heinemann.

Edwards, J. A. and Llurdes i Coit, J. C. (1996) 'Mines and quarries: industrial heritage tourism'. *Annals of Tourism Research*, **23**(2), 341–63.

Evans, M. (1991) 'Historical interpretation at Sovereign Hill'. In J. Rickard and P. Spearritt (eds) *Packaging the Past*. Melbourne: Melbourne University Press, pp. 142–52.

Faggetter, R. (1996) 'The interpretive environment creating place and space for rich experiences'. In *Interpretation in Action,* Proceedings of the Fifth Annual Interpretation Australia Association Conference, Bendigo, pp. 19–24.

Fladmark, J. M. (ed.) (1993) *Heritage: Conservation, Interpretation and Enterprise.* London: Donhead Publishing.

Formica, S. and Uysal, M. (1998) 'Market segmentation of an international cultural-historical event in Italy'. *Journal of Travel Research,* **36**(4) 16–24.

Fowler, P. (1989) 'Heritage: a post modernist perspective'. In D. L. Uzzell (ed.) *Heritage Interpretation Volume 1: The Natural and Built Environment.* London: Belhaven Press, pp. 57–63.

Herbert, D. T. (1996) 'Artistic and literary places in France as tourist attractions'. *Tourism Management,* **17**(2), 77–86.

Hewison, R. (1987) *The Heritage Industry.* London: Methuen.

Horne, D. (1984) *The Great Museum.* London: Pluto Press.

Jafari, J. (1990) 'Research and scholarship'. *Journal of Tourism Studies,* **1**(1), 33–41.

Jansen-Verbeke, M. (1997) 'Urban tourism: managing resources and visitors'. In S. Wahab and J. J. Pigram (eds) *Tourism Development and Growth.* London: Routledge, pp. 237–56.

Jansen-Verbeke, M. and Lievois, E. (1999) 'Analysing heritage resources for urban tourism in European cities'. In D. G. Pearce and R. W. Butler (eds) *Contemporary Issues in Tourism Development.* London, Routledge, pp. 81–107.

Jansen-Verbeke, M. and van Rekom, J. (1996) 'Scanning museum visitors: urban tourism marketing'. *Annals of Tourism Research,* **23**(2), 364–75.

Jones, M. (1993) 'The elusive reality of landscape'. In J. M. Fladmark (ed.) *Heritage: Conservation, Interpretation and Enterprise.* London: Donhead Publishing, pp. 17–41.

Kimmel, J. R. (1995) 'Art and tourism in Santa Fe, New Mexico'. *Journal of Travel Research,* **33**(3), 28–30.

Knudson, D. M., Cable, T. T. and Beck, L. (1995) *Interpretation of Cultural and Natural Resources.* State College, Pennsylvania: Venture.

Krippendorf, J. (1987) *The Holidaymakers.* London: William Heinemann.

Langer, E. (1989a) *Mindfulness.* Reading, Massachusetts: Addison-Wesley.

Langer, E. (1989b) 'Conditional teaching and mindful learning: the role of uncertainty in education'. *Creativity Research Journal,* **2**, 139–50.

Langer, E. (1993) 'A mindful education'. *Educational Psychologist,* **28**(1), 43–50.

Lavery. P. (1993) 'A single European market for the tourist industry'. In W. Pompl and P. Lavery (eds) *Tourism in Europe.* Wallingford, UK: CAB International, pp. 80–98.

Lowenthal, L. (1993) 'Landscape as heritage'. In J. M. Fladmark (ed.) *Heritage: Conservation, Interpretation and Enterprise.* London: Donhead Publishing, pp. 3–15.

MacCannell, D. (1976) *The Tourist.* New York: Schocken.

McGregor, R. (1993) 'Napier, the Art Deco city'. In C. M. Hall and S. McArthur (eds) *Heritage Management in New Zealand and Australia.* Auckland: Oxford University Press, pp. 209–17.

Miles, R. (1989) *Evaluation in its Communication Context.* Technical report No. 89–30. Jacksonville, Alabama: Center for Social Design.

Moscardo, G. (1996) 'Mindful visitors'. *Annals of Tourism Research,* **23**(2), 376–97.

Moscardo, G. (1999) *Making Visitors Mindful.* Champaign, Illinois: Sagamore Publishing.

Moscardo, G., Greenwood, T., Clark, A. and Green, D. (1997) *Public Perceptions of World Heritage Areas and Responses to Proposed Interpretive Text.* Report prepared for the Queensland Department of the Environment.

Moscardo, G., Verbeek, M. and Woods, B. (1998) 'Effective interpretation and sustainable tourism'. In *The Fourth Asia Pacific Tourism Association Conference Proceedings – The Role of Tourism: National and Regional Perspectives Series B.* Pusan, Korea: Asia Pacific Tourism Association, pp. 148–55.

Moscardo, G. and Woods, B. (1998) 'Managing tourism in the Wet Tropics World Heritage Area: interpretation and the experience of visitors on Skyrail'. In E. Laws, B. Faulkner and G. Moscardo (eds) *Embracing and Managing Change in Tourism: International Case Studies*. London: Routledge, pp. 285–306.

Moscovici, S. (1984) 'The phenomenon of social representations'. In R. M. Farr and S. Moscovici (eds) *Social Representations*. Cambridge: Cambridge University Press, pp. 3–69.

Nuryanti, W. (1996) 'Heritage and postmodern tourism'. *Annals of Tourism Research*, **23**(2), 249–60.

O'Toole, F. (1992) 'The emperor's map makes us tourists in our own land'. *Interpretation Journal*, **51**, 13–14.

Pearce, P. L. and Moscardo, G. M. (1986) 'The concept of authenticity in tourists' experiences'. *Australian and New Zealand Journal of Sociology*, **22**(1), 121–32.

Pearce, P. L., Moscardo, G. M. and Ross, G. (1996) *Understanding and Managing the Tourism Community Relationship*. London: Elsevier.

Pines, A. L. and West, L. H. T. (1986) 'Conceptual understanding and science learning'. *Science Education*, **70**, 583–604.

Prentice, R. (1997) 'Cultural and landscape tourism'. In S. Wahab and J. J. Pigram (eds) *Tourism Development and Growth*. London: Routledge, pp. 209–36.

Prentice, R., Witt, S. F. and Hamer, C. (1998) 'Tourism as experience: the case of heritage parks'. *Annals of Tourism Research*, **25**(1), 1–24.

Richards, G. (1996) 'The scope and significance of cultural tourism'. In G. Richards (ed.) *Cultural Tourism in Europe*. Wallingford, UK: CAB International, pp. 19–46.

Richter, L. K. (1999) 'The politics of heritage tourism development'. In D. G. Pearce and R. W. Butler (eds) *Contemporary Issues in Tourism Development*. London: Routledge, pp. 108–26.

Rickard, J. and Spearritt, P. (eds) (1991) *Packaging the Past*. Melbourne: Melbourne University Press.

Roggenbuck, J. W. (1992) 'Use of persuasion to reduce impacts and visitor conflicts'. In M. J. Manfredo (ed.) *Influencing Human Behavior*. Champaign, Illinois: Sagamore Publishing, pp. 149—208.

Salamone, F. A. (1997) 'Authenticity in tourism: the San Angel inns'. *Annals of Tourism Research*, **24**(2), 305–21.

Schofield, P. (1996) 'Cinematographic images of a city: alternative heritage tourism in Manchester'. *Tourism Management*, **17**(5), 333–40.

Shepherd, I. (1993) 'Explaining the local heritage'. In J. M. Fladmark (ed.) *Heritage: Conservation, Interpretation and Enterprise*. London: Donhead Publishing, pp. 175–84.

Smith, V. L. (1978) 'Introduction'. In V. L. Smith (ed.) *Hosts and Guests*. Oxford: Basil Blackwell, pp. 1–14.

Tilden, F. (1977) *Interpreting our Heritage* (3rd edn). Chapel Hill, North Carolina: University of North Carolina Press.

Tuppen, J. (1996) 'Tourism in French cities'. In C. M. Law (ed.) *Tourism in Major Cities*. London: International Thomson Business Press, pp. 52–88.

Urry, J. (1990) *The Tourist Gaze*. London: Sage.

Urry, J. (1995) *Consuming Places*. London: Routledge.

Uzzell, D. (1989) 'The hot interpretation of war and conflict'. In D. L. Uzzell (ed.) *Heritage Interpretation Volume One*. London: Belhaven Press, pp. 33–47.

Uzzell, D. (1996) 'Heritage interpretation in Britain four decades after Tilden'. In R. Harrison (ed.) *Manual of Heritage Management*. Oxford: Butterworth Heinemann, pp. 293–302.

Van der Borg, J., Costa, P. and Gotti, G. (1996) 'Tourism in European heritage cities'. *Annals of Tourism Research*, **23**(2), 306–21.

Waller, J. and Lea, S. E. G. (1999) 'Seeking the real Spain? Authenticity in motivation'. *Annals of Tourism Research*, **26**(1), 110–29.

CHAPTER 2

Tourism and World Peace: A Conundrum for the Twenty-first Century

Renata Tomljenovic and Bill Faulkner

INTRODUCTION

One of the sadder realities of humankind is that national, racial, religious, ethnic and cultural differences have been the root cause of conflicts of one kind or another throughout the history of our civilization. It is equally sad that the intensity of such conflicts have not abated, despite the growth in knowledge and technological capabilities in the twenty-first century. With the spread of education and the increased capacity for objective and critical thinking this should bring, along with developments in communications technology that have resulted in the 'global village' prediction of McLuhan and Powers (1989) becoming a reality, one might have hoped that the world of today would be a more harmonious, conflict-free community than it has in fact become. Looking back on the last century of the second millennium, however, it would appear that many of the technological advances of this period have been channelled into increasingly large-scale forms of destruction, rather than towards more constructive ends. Thus, as this millennium draws to an end, deep-seated ethnic hatreds are unleashed with such a force that ethnic cleansing has become a term as often present in the human consciousness as the global village which symbolizes world peace, harmony and mutual interdependence.

Ironically, the same technological and communication developments that have contributed to the escalating scale of tensions and conflict have also facilitated an unprecedented growth in international tourism which has been lauded as an instrument for world peace. This belief is fuelled by the rapid growth of international tourism in the second half of the twentieth century and the fact that this growth has brought an unprecedented number of people of different national, racial, ethnic, religious and cultural persuasions into contact with each other. It is believed that, through such contact, people will get to know and understand each other better and, as a consequence, they will become not only more tolerant of their differences but also embrace the diversity of humankind as a stimulus for personal growth. Thus, in the 1960s tourism was proclaimed the 'noblest instrument of this century for achieving international understanding, harmony and world peace' (Hunziker in Krippendorf, 1987, p. 57). In the 1980s it was heralded as having the potential to become the 'world's great peace industry' (D'Amore, 1988a, p. 23), while one of the World Tourism Organization's uppermost objectives is to 'accelerate and enlarge the contribution of tourism to peace, understanding, health and prosperity throughout the world' (in McIntosh *et al.*, 1995, p. 72).

While the prospect of tourism becoming an instrument for world peace is appealing, there are sceptics who question some of the assumptions that underpin this interpretation of the industry's role. First, the extent to which tourism experience could influence improvements in attitudes towards others has been questioned. It has been suggested, for instance, that an increased frequency and/or intensity of contact between tourists and hosts may perpetuate, rather than ameliorate, misconceptions travellers have about people in foreign countries (Cohen, 1972). Crick (1989, p. 328) considers the rhetoric of 'peace and understanding' to be a 'mystifying image that is a part of the industry itself', while Bruner (1991) goes a step further by arguing that travel's supposed contribution to international understanding and personal growth is a construct of popular Western discourse, rather than a reflection of the actual travel experience. Second, for the tourism experience to have a bearing on the attainment of world peace one has to believe that mutual respect and understanding at the individual level have the capacity to overcome conflicts of interest and the quest for security and power at the national level. According to Kelman (1962), this proposition is naïve, although favourable attitudes may decrease the amount of mutual hostility and actual contact may make it easier to establish negotiation mechanisms for co-operation and peaceful resolution of conflicts (Kelman, 1962).

These opposing views of tourism's role in world peace present a challenging conundrum for tourism development in the third millennium. If the optimists, who see tourism as a catalyst for peace and harmony, are correct, then the task that lies ahead is a relatively uncomplicated one of simply continuing to promote international travel and facilitating visits to foreign countries. On the other hand, if the pessimists are correct and tourism is potentially counter-productive in terms of its contribution to international understanding, the tourism industry needs to consider changes in the way it conducts its business in order to remedy this negative effect. This chapter examines the problem by, first, reviewing the arguments presented by these two opposing schools of thought. These arguments are then evaluated in the context of empirical evidence derived from two case studies of tourists' reactions to their experience in foreign countries. Finally, some conclusions are drawn about the implications of this issue for tourism development in the third millennium.

TWO OPPOSING SCHOOLS OF THOUGHT

The basis of the claim of tourism's contribution to improved intercultural understanding arises from the contact theory of social psychology (Allport, 1954; Cook, 1962; Amir, 1969, 1976; Pettigrew, 1986), which simply states that contact between different ethnic groups will improve intercultural attitudes and reduce intergroup tension. This hypothesis was 'elevated to a cultural truism and a plan for action' in the USA after the Second World War (Pettigrew, 1986, p. 173), where urban social planners linked rising levels of racial conflict with ghetto formation in major cities. It was believed that, by separating racial groups physically, ghettoes inhibited contact and therefore reinforced the prejudices that fuelled conflict. Many of the urban social programmes of the era therefore involved strategies aimed at reducing ghetto formation (Pettigrew, 1986).

While political, civic and church leaders embraced the contact hypothesis on the domestic front, its relevance to foreign policy was not lost. For example, the first US ambassador to China founded a scientific exchange programme on the basis of the argument that 'the perceptions of two nations with different opinions, goals and activities change when one experiences a USA exchange trip and learns through one-on-one contact that others' dreams are also our own' (Wei *et al.*, 1989, p. 323). In another context, following the improvement in relationship between the USSR and the USA, a joint statement from General-Secretary Gorbachev and President Reagan declared: 'There should be greater understanding among our peoples and to this end we will encourage greater travel' as this people-to-people contact will enable them to 'share, enjoy, help, listen and learn from each other' (in D'Amore, 1988, p. 25).

However, this unqualified faith in the contact hypothesis was almost immediately tested by empirical research. Such research began to reveal that it was not contact, per se, that reduced prejudice and enhanced mutual understanding, but only certain types of contact that achieved this. In general, it was found that improved attitudes are associated with intimate and voluntary contact among participants of equal status, who share common goals within a supportive social atmosphere. Where these conditions are lacking contact either fails to produce any attitude change, or reinforces initially held attitudes (Allport, 1954; Cook, 1962; Amir, 1969, 1976).

The opponents of the tourism-intercultural understanding platform argue that contact in tourism settings seldom involves the conditions necessary to produce positive changes. It is argued that foreign tourists have fewer and less intensive encounters with hosts than is often assumed or claimed by the tourism industry (Nettekoven, 1979). Also, it is believed that tourism promotional material, for example, predisposes travellers to a narrow view of the host country (deKadt, 1979), while the tourism infrastructure at the destination often creates an isolated enclave (Cohen, 1972; Evans, 1976). Frequently, poorly qualified tour guides contribute to the confirmation of preconceived ideas by anticipating the sentiments of the travel party (Anastasopoulous, 1992; deKadt, 1979; Pearce, 1982), while members of the travel party often focus their attention on building relationships among themselves rather than with members of the host community (Anastasopoulos, 1992; Scott, 1965). Furthermore, intimate contact is often hampered by the language barriers and cultural differences (Pool, 1965; Hewstone and Brown, 1986), and communication difficulties are likely to cause stress which can reinforce cultural differences (Taft, 1977; Steinkalk and Taft, 1979). Moreover, status disparity is often noticed when tourists visit less developed countries, where they feel superior, and this affects the dynamics of the contact situation, as Guldin (1989) reported to be the case of the American tourists visiting China. Status disparity is also evident in encounters with service personnel, where tourists may display a tendency to project the inferiority of this relationship onto the host population as a whole. Finally, if the tourists are focused on enjoying themselves, while members of the host population are seen as being primarily there to serve them, there is little possibility of the two parties having common goals and communicating with each other on an equal footing (Sutton, 1967).

Although these general features of tourism all point to a role which is counterproductive in terms of improving intercultural understanding between visitors and hosts, it is nevertheless plausible that tourism may have the desired effect in situations where meaningful contact is facilitated. Thus, D'Amore (1988) advocates 'properly designed tourism', where people come in contact through students or cultural exchanges, twinning of cities, international sporting events and other forms of travel that bring people into a mutually rewarding dialogue. Similarly, McIntosh *et al.* (1995) stress that observing the world from the hotel's balcony contributes very little to improving intercultural understanding, but this would be achieved if visitors and hosts mingle socially and become better acquainted with each other. Notably, those who question the tourism-intercultural understanding–world peace nexus focus their attention on the organized mass-traveller end of the spectrum in developing countries.

Both schools of thought apparently have a tendency to emphasize the particular form of travel that suits their argument, and make generalizations to the overall travel phenomenon on the basis of this narrow focus. It therefore seems likely that both points of view are correct for different types of tourism experience. Accordingly, where the tourist is involved in a fully organized coach tour, where his or her exposure to locals and their culture is filtered by the interpretation of the tour guide (who is often not a local), contact would be minimal and the entire experience would have a minimal impact in terms of changing the attitudes of visitors. On the other hand, where the travel arrangements are both flexible and amenable to the frequent high-quality contact with the host, we would expect travel experience to enhance the travellers' understanding of the people visited. However, those who are inclined to choose the latter option are often highly motivated to learn about different cultures and are therefore predisposed to developing intercultural exchange in any case. While there has been a sufficient body of research to test these propositions to some degree, the results of such research have been inconclusive. This issue is explored further in the next section.

THE EVIDENCE SO FAR

The few studies that have been carried out so far have tended to concentrate on conventional tourists and generally appear to confirm those aspects of the above interpretation concerning this form of tourism. Anastasopoulos (1992) surveyed Greeks visiting Turkey and Milman, Reichel and Pizam (1990) investigated the attitude change of Israelis visiting Egypt. Both Turkey and Egypt were regarded less favourably by their Greek and Israeli visitors as a consequence of their visit. In other words, the traditional hostilities associated with the nationalities in each of these studies were reinforced by the visit. Pearce (1982) surveyed British tourists on organized holidays to Greece and Morocco and in both instances their attitudes moved in the negative direction. This was more so for those visiting Morocco than Greece. Here, the actual travel experience was, in fact, detrimental to the process of enhancing mutual understanding and, given that the self-esteem of visitors returning home was improved as the result of this experience, Cohen's (1972) speculation that travel perpetuates misconceptions about foreign people and places appears to be supported.

On the other hand, will this be so in situations such as student cultural exchange programmes, where the travel experience is specifically structured to facilitate meaningful contact between hosts and visitors? While the evidence here is somewhat mixed, aspects of the research focusing on this type of tourism provide some encouragement to those advocating tourism's role as an instrument for peace and understanding. Australian students on an education tour to Israel, in spite of the many contact situations designed in their itinerary, returned home less favourably disposed towards Israelis. On the other hand, while they acknowledged that this experience has broadened their horizons, only a third thought that their experience has resulted in them developing greater tolerance towards others (Steinkalk and Taft, 1979). In an early study, Smith (1955) investigated the influence of spending a summer in Europe among a sample of US college students. Regardless of their travel arrangement, students did not change in some of the more deeply rooted social attitudes such as ethnocentrism, authoritarianism or political and economic conservatism. However, their attitudes towards the country visited changed. A decrease in favourable attitudes occurred for those visiting Germany and France, while those spending a summer in England evaluated their British hosts more favourably. Elsewhere, US students on an education tour to the USSR returned home with mixed attitudes. After the trip, many thought the USSR was less clean but more reliable, while the Soviet government was thought to be less concerned with the welfare of its people than its socialist roots implied (Pizam *et al.*, 1991). Furthermore, participants in the Semester at Sea programme (where students from all over the world board a ship equipped with classrooms and a library for a 100-day around the world journey with a dozen ports of call) were reported to have developed a more sophisticated perspective by becoming less reliant on their first impression of people and places, and becoming less judgemental (Welds and Dukes, 1985).

While these studies have generally employed sound quasi-experimental designs to measure change in attitudes, they have used the contact hypothesis as an ad hoc explanatory device, rather than actually measuring the contact. For example, as a possible explanation of the patterns they observed in their studies, Anastasopoulos (1992) and Milman *et al.* (1990) simply suggested that the contact was limited to service personnel, and it was assumed that such contacts did not feature situational factors thought necessary for attitude shifts to occur. Furthermore, neither satisfaction with the contact and the overall trip nor the travellers' motivation was measured, despite there being evidence that the more satisfying contacts lead to improved attitudes toward the ethnic group evaluated (Amir and Garti, 1977) and motivation is an important predictor of the post-trip attitudes (Fisher and Price, 1991).

Since these studies do not explicitly test the contact hypothesis in the tourism setting, their explanatory power in terms of the role of the contact is limited. The two exploratory studies described below were conducted in an effort to test the contact hypothesis more explicitly. The first study evaluated shift in attitudes among Croatian students visiting Spain, Greece and the Czech Republic in a travel arrangement resembling the organized mass tour model, and where neither meaningful contact nor significant shifts in attitudes were expected to occur. The other study focused on Australian students enrolled in an undergraduate Japanese studies programme on a four-week cultural immersion tour of Japan. As the latter example is more aligned with the 'quality tourism' approach advocated by D'Amore, it was expected that this would be more conducive to producing enhanced intercultural understanding and favourable attitude shifts among the Australian students involved.

THE CROATIAN STUDY

Every September, Croatian students who are about to enter their final year of high school undertake a seven-day organized coach tour to a destination of their choice. While these tours are incorporated into the educational programme with the explicit purpose of creating a better understanding of other cultures, the travel arrangements involved resemble a form of organized mass tourism, rather than a cultural immersion experience. Students are escorted by their teacher and their activities are structured by a tightly packed itinerary designed by a commercial tour organizer with no particular experience or expertise in organizing educational or special interest tours. However, some free time is normally available in the late afternoons and evenings.

Of the 73 respondents who were surveyed, 40 visited Spain, 15 Greece and 18 went to the Czech Republic. Students responded to a pre-trip questionnaire in the coach before departure, while the post-trip survey was administered during the class time just after their return from the trip. The survey instrument combined closed and open-ended questions, with contact being measured in terms of the number of people students had conversations with, the duration of the encounters and the overall pleasantness of these contacts on a 7-point scale (extremely unpleasant to extremely pleasant). While this approach had the advantage of being easy to administer, the imposition of an arbitrary five-minute cut-off for measuring the duration factor was clearly a limited indicator of the depth of the dialogue. This measure was therefore complemented by a question, which asked students to describe one of these contacts in an open-ended format.

Attitudes towards the host and the country in general were measured by Likert type statements which were factor analysed and yielded a reliable alpha reading (0.85) for the attitudes towards the people, and a somewhat lower but acceptable alpha of 0.74 for attitudes towards the country. While the national stereotypes of the hosts may be different according to the country visited, it should be stressed that the purpose of the study was to ascertain shifts in these, rather than the actual content of these stereotypes. Given that such attitude measures have been criticized as superficial indicators of the contact outcome by several authors (Kelman, 1965; Pool, 1965; Bochner, 1982), they were complemented by measures of perceived group variability and ethnocentrism. The former refers to the extent to which members of the host population are seen to be similar or different from each other. It was expected that, as the travellers became more familiar with their hosts, they would be able to differentiate better between members of the host society, rather than perceiving them as a homogeneous group (Islam and Hewston, 1993; Stangor *et al.*, 1996). A univariate measure of the perceived group variability was therefore included, where respondents were asked to indicate, on a 7-point scale, the extent to which they perceived host nationals to be completely similar or different from each other. The ethnocentrism scale used was developed specifically for the Croatian circumstances and, considering the small sample size, the six-item scale used achieved an acceptable alpha of 0.75.

The survey revealed that, despite the educational goals of the tour, students' primary motivation was to have fun in the company of their schoolmates and to see the destination's landmarks. Increasing their knowledge about the host country or developing friendly relationships with some of the locals were the least important motivational factors. Students' initial attitudes towards the country visited were either positive, as in the case of Spain, or neutral in the case of Greece and the Czech Republic. The host nationals were perceived as being mostly similar to each other and their ethnocentrism was relatively high with a mean of 5 on a 7-point scale. Post-trip attitudes towards both the host population and the country in general improved for those students visiting Spain and the Czech Republic, but they did not change significantly for those visiting Greece. If anything, a slight negative shift was noticeable in the latter.

This pattern of results was reinforced by students' responses to an open-ended question asking them how, if at all, their perceptions about the country visited changed. Almost half of those going to Spain said that they had previously thought this country would be an excellent place to visit and their travel experience confirmed their expectations. This sentiment was captured well in the following comment: 'Even before the trip I have formed good impression about Spain and Spanish people and during my stay there they have remained the same if not better.' Similarly, half of the students visiting the Czech Republic thought they had returned with better opinions about that country, while the others believed that their perceptions had not changed. However, while the attitude statements did not indicate a statistically significant shift in attitudes among the students visiting Greece, more than half said that they did not expect much and that their opinion had changed for the worse. Students visiting Spain were extremely satisfied with their trip. While those returning from the Czech Republic also indicated satisfaction, they were irritated by the unprofessional attitudes of drivers provided by their Croatian tour operator. Nevertheless, this appears to have had little bearing on the formation of their attitudes towards Czechs and the Czech Republic. The students visiting Greece experienced not only problems with the substandard transport facilities provided by the tour operator, but also with accommodation on the ferry and in hotels. At the same time, the Greek tourism operators were not perceived as being professional in rectifying these problems. These incidents might have had some impact on the way that the entire country was perceived. While highly speculative at the moment, it may be that the students distinguished between the services provided by tour operators of the same nationality and those provided by the hosts. It appears that service failure in the former situation might not influence attitudes towards the host country, but this may not be so when local providers are responsible. In the latter case, students may not differentiate between the hospitality personnel directly responsible for the services provided and the host population in general, leading to the negative impression of those in the hospitality industry contaminating the overall assessment of host nationals as a whole.

A surprising aspect of the survey results was the fact that, despite the homogeneity of this group and the fact that they were in a situation where this homogeneity was reinforced by peer group pressure and a tightly packed itinerary under the watchful eyes of their teachers, students displayed a marked variability in their propensity to explore the destination and interact with locals, with some of them not reporting any contact at all and others engaging in conversation with up to ten people. More importantly, an examination of responses to open-ended questions revealed a strong relationship between the quantity and the quality of contacts. Those not having any contact with locals for longer than five minutes reported mostly mundane exchanges with the hospitality and sales people, such as: 'How much is this T-shirt? Ooo, it can't be tried on! OK, I'll take it anyway.' The longer conversations appear to be where students responded to questions initiated by sales people and were mostly limited to talk about Croatia, their accommodation and places visited. However, a small proportion reported longer conversations with local youths encountered on streets or on the ferry in Greece, while one student reported that spending a day with a Spanish guy, who showed her all the interesting sites, was a highlight of her trip.

The main departure of both the studies reported here from previous research is that details of contact situations and satisfaction levels were collected. After variations associated with pre-trip attitudes, destination influences and the overall trip satisfaction had been controlled in a regression analysis, the quantity and quality of contact emerged as statistically significant predictors of the post-trip attitude change. Thus, the more contacts students have had with the host nationals, the more their post-trip attitude, to both host nationals and the country overall, changed in a favourable direction. However, with regard to perceived group variability, the more contact students had the more likely it was that host nationals were perceived in a stereotypical fashion. Theoretically, quantity of contact should be related to the greater perceived variability among host nationals. However, in instances where there are some strong situational biases, such as contact occurring within a restricted range of situations, a tendency to perceive higher levels of homogeneity is probably to be expected (Islam and Hewstone, 1993). Finally, ethnocentrism was also not affected by the students' travel experience. While it is possible this could be an artefact of the scale used for the study, it is equally plausible that the relatively short travel experience is not sufficient to affect deeply rooted attitudes such as ethnocentrism (Smith, 1955).

THE AUSTRALIAN STUDY

The Australian students included in the study were involved in a four-week education tour to Japan. They all had a keen interest in Japanese language and culture, and most of them spoke Japanese sufficiently well to feel comfortable in situations where they were required to interact with Japanese residents. Most members of the group had previous extensive contacts with Japanese people, either through work or through hosting Japanese visitors. However, while all students had developed a sound understanding of the historical, cultural and religious background of modern-day Japan through their involvement in the Japanese studies programme, for most of them this trip represented the first opportunity actually to visit that country and interact with Japanese people. Compared with the Croatian students' travel arrangements, the Australian students' itinerary was relatively unstructured. A tour of the country was included, but this involved the use of public transport systems. While standard tourist accommodation was used for part of the trip, this was complemented by home-stays, both in rural and urban settings. Finally, ample free time was available in the itinerary so that students would have the opportunity to interact with locals. The students were keen to practise their Japanese language skills and were therefore open, proactive and receptive to contact with Japanese.

Given that there were only seventeen students involved in the December, 1997 trip, statistical tests similar to those employed in the Croatian study could not be applied and a directly comparable approach was not feasible. A case study approach involving a combination of questionnaires, trip diaries, a focus group session after the trip and an in-depth interview with the lecturer organizing the trip was used. While this approach might be considered more comprehensive than in the Croatian study, the research was endorsed by their teachers and the students themselves have had a keen interests in the outcome of the survey. This has made the diary technique and a subsequent focus group session possible. The Croatian students, being younger and embarking on a journey of fun and excitement, would have been less receptive to the more intrusive techniques such as the diary, but the richness of their experiences was, nevertheless, captured through the open-ended questions incorporated in the survey.

The questionnaire measured students' attitudes towards the Japanese on a semantic-differential scale (Anastasopoulous, 1992; Milman *et al.*, 1990; Pizam *et al.*, 1991), while their general level of prejudice was measured using a scale based on Altemeyer's (1988) Manitoba Prejudice Scale. An anxiety scale was included following the suggestion that high intercultural anxiety hampers effective communication (Stephen and Stephen, 1992). Since students were aware of the highly structured nature of Japanese social relationships and the associated rules of conduct, there was a possibility that this awareness may have heightened their anxieties, especially in the home-stay situations. While it was not considered necessary to measure contact given the home-stay arrangements, in the diaries students documented the type and nature of the contact, the most pleasant and unpleasant experiences of the day and any specific thoughts about Japan or Japanese people and their customs. The subsequent focus group session was used to obtain further insights into the nature of their impressions of Japan and their trip. Of the seventeen participants in the tour, twelve have responded to a questionnaire while seven returned their diaries. Of those five not completing the post-trip questionnaire, one student returned to her native Sweden, while another spent the entire summer in Japan.

On average, the students perceived Japanese favourably, although somewhat stereotypically. They perceived their hosts as peace-loving, reliable, friendly, intelligent, hard-working, moral, educated, honest, clean, kind, warm-hearted, modest, good and nice. At the same time they saw Japanese as being tense, sexist, rigid and old-fashioned, although the strength of agreement with these negative traits was lower than in the case of positive traits. Examination of the post-trip responses revealed that very little shift in attitudes had taken place. Given the students' favourable predisposition towards Japan and Japanese at the outset, the attitudes could not move much in a favourable direction owing to the ceiling effect. Stangor et al. (1996) have suggested that, when the attitudes are extremely favourable, it is to be expected that these would be modified as a result of the actual experience of the country visited and, under such circumstances, the variability of responses might be a more meaningful measure of attitude shift. However, judging by the variability of the scores, students' tendency to perceive Japanese in a stereotypical fashion was not reduced following the trip.

As might be expected in such a group, the prejudice of these students was low. On the 8-point scale, where a higher score indicates more prejudice, they averaged 3.79 in the pre-trip questionnaire. The score increased slightly to 4.05 in the post-trip questionnaire, but this was not statistically significant and may have been affected by the higher non-response factor at this stage. Similarly, statements dealing with Asian migration and the status of Asian migrants in Australia received slightly lower endorsement after the trip, although again this shift was not statistically significant. However, these should be taken tentatively as these slight shifts may be due to chance. Anxiety of the students was 6.63 on a 10-point scale prior to the trip and this was reduced to 5.84 following the trip, a statistically significant reduction.

While no effort was made to quantify the extent of contact with locals in the manner attempted in the Croatian study, the diaries provided evidence of student engagement in intensive contacts with host families, especially where they were taken to schools or universities to mix and mingle with people of their own age. Many impromptu contacts also occurred during the touring part of their trip, with conversations taking place with the people they encountered on the trains, in shops and at attractions visited. Despite the richness of these encounters, examination of the diaries revealed mostly superficial observations about Japan. Students frequently noticed that Japanese in general, and especially their host families, are nice and friendly, they are shy and poor in expressing themselves and they have a tendency to stare at foreigners, and even become unexpectedly assertive when they want their photographs taken with a blonde Western girl. The diaries did not reveal any unpleasant situations, apart from a female participant noticing tense relationships among some of the girls in the group. In the focus group session, students were briefed in detail about the purpose of the study and asked to help interpret the pattern of these results. They suggested that the quantitative data was consistent with their general impressions about the trip and that their opinions about Japan did not change much as a consequence of the trip. They reported being surprised by the mutual independence between members of their host families, by the contrast between rural and urban Japan and by the beauty of the scenery. However, in general they felt that the insight into the Japanese culture and customs they obtained from the trip represented more of a confirmation of their original views, rather than involving any substantial shift in their position.

CONCLUSION

The two studies described in this chapter provide a somewhat paradoxical perspective on the outcomes of cultural interaction in the tourism context. On one hand, in the Australian students' case, the experience designed to maximize cultural learning has done very little in terms of shifting students' attitudes, even though this represented the form of 'quality tourism' D'Amore advocated as being a potential contributor to world peace. Their pre-trip preparation through the courses they had attended meant that they were already relatively open-minded and well informed about, and receptive to, Japanese culture. On the other hand, Croatian students' travel arrangements epitomized the form of tourism critics of the world peace – tourism nexus proposition considered as being either irrelevant or even detrimental to the process. Croatian students received no formal instruction on the cultural background of their hosts and had, at best, fuzzy preconceptions about the nature of the people they would encounter. Yet, when compared with their Australian counterparts, there were changes in perceptions of their hosts, albeit limited.

It seems likely then that those who are motivated by a strong desire to gain cultural insights into the country they visit have both a predisposition to cultural understanding and well-developed normative stereotypes of the destination country prior to their departure. Normative stereotypes, as argued by Triandis and Vassiliou (1972), are formed in response to historical events, mass media or education. Once learned, they are only modified by the actual experience to the extent that they become more realistic. Thus, the Australian students based their responses to the pre-trip questionnaire on relatively informed judgements, and actual experience has resulted in these being confirmed with only slight adjustments. The Croatian students, on the other hand, had very poorly formed preconceived notions about their hosts and the host country in general and, as a consequence, there was more scope for their attitudes to be affected by the actual experience of the country visited. Moreover, the contact in itself, though limited and superficial, along with the level of satisfaction with the contact, emerged as significant predictors of the post-trip evaluation.

The small sample size and the unrepresentative nature of the sample in both studies mean that any conclusions that may be drawn will be unavoidably speculative. However, the results nevertheless challenge the conventional wisdom about the nexus between tourism and intercultural understanding. It has been assumed that those travellers who are highly motivated by cultural learning and open to contact with hosts would benefit from the travel experience in terms of gaining improved understanding of other cultures and increased intercultural tolerance. It appears, however, that these individuals may have those qualities at the outset and the actual travel experience simply contributes by reinforcing their established beliefs. There is, therefore, a self-selection process that introduces a tautological element to the problem. That is, those who are predisposed to cultural understanding and tolerance are more inclined to enter educational programmes, read literature and view media that reinforces this predisposition.

At the other end of the scale, those who are not particularly motivated to engage in intercultural experiences, and therefore have had little prior exposure to the host country's culture, stand to benefit most from the actual travel experience, that is, provided that the content and structure of their travel itinerary involves ample free time with opportunities for relatively meaningful contacts with locals. Under these circumstances, visitors may even be aware of the constraints imposed on the nature of the contact with their hosts and may even prefer relatively superficial contacts (Selltiz and Cook, 1962). Particularly in situations where the visitor knows very little about the host country at the outset, it is not inconceivable that by simply observing locals and through relatively superficial encounters in shopping excursions, one might arrive at a better appreciation of the host country and its people. However, this observation is subject to an important caveat regarding the quality of the experience. It is important to bear in mind that neutral or even positive attitudes can be quickly eroded if there are service quality failures or negative events that impinge upon the enjoyment of the trip. This was illustrated in the case of Croatian students visiting Greece, where the dissatisfaction with the trip spilled over into the attitudes towards both Greece and Greek people.

Bearing in mind the caveat regarding service quality considerations, it appears that contact, however superficial or limited, can be beneficial to the overall trip experience. It follows that tourism operators and destination managers should recognize this in their approach to itinerary development and broader planning activities. However, before tour operators and planners start thinking about incorporating the contact into the overall travel experience, it is important to remember that the crucial ingredient of contact situations, in terms of their potential role in bringing about favourable shifts in attitudes, is that the engagement is voluntary from both the hosts' and the visitors' points of view. In the case of the Australian students, they were prepared and open to the contact with Japanese. They also spoke Japanese and were familiar enough with the Japanese culture and customs to be reasonably comfortable communicating with their hosts and staying in their homes. In the case of the Croatian students, while their itinerary did not feature any structured contact experiences, those so inclined could engage in a dialogue with the locals during their free time. Forcing contact on all students, regardless of individual differences in their preparedness to do so, might have been counter-productive in terms of both the enjoyment of the trip and intercultural understanding outcomes. The earlier study of Australian students visiting Israel by Steinkalk and Taft (1977) indicated how a situation where students are forced into contact beyond their comfort zone can produce a negative reaction. Indeed, Steinkalk and Taft (1977) conceded that stress during the contact situation might have been the critical factor that moved students attitudes in a negative direction and reinforced ethnocentric tendencies.

The implications for the tourism industry arising from the observations contained in this chapter can be summarized in terms of three simple propositions. First, while tourism has the potential to promote intercultural understanding and tolerance, it has an equally strong potential to have the opposite effect. Second, one of the core conditions for ensuring positive outcomes is the quality of services provided at the destination. A low standard of services generally, or major failures, will create an inverse halo effect that will result in the visitors' disappointments spilling over into negative impressions of the country visited and its people. Third, in planning itineraries and in destination product development, consideration needs to be given to the possibility of highly contrived contact situations resulting in both guests and hosts being pushed beyond their respective comfort zones. This will result in stress on both sides of the encounter, which will in turn result in a deterioration in intercultural understanding and reduced enjoyment in the trip. It would appear that better results would be obtained if tour schedules allowed some flexibility, with scope for free time in situations where visitors may have the option to mix with locals in a manner that suits their preferences. With the emergence of tightly scheduled packaged tours as the normal expression of mass tourism in the twentieth century, the flexibility required for meaningful contacts has been largely lost. Finally, the likely nexus between meaningful intercultural contact and enjoyment of the travel experience may mean that, by becoming more attuned to the above requirements, tourism operators and destination planners might simultaneously enhance the viability of their product and make tourism's role as the peace industry a reality.

REFERENCES

Allport, G. W. (1954) *The Nature of Prejudice*. Cambridge: Addison-Wesley.

Altemeyer, B. (1988) *Enemies of Freedom*. San Francisco: Jossey-Bass Publishers.

Amir, Y. (1969) 'Contact hypothesis in ethnic relations'. *Psychological Bulletin*, **71**, 319–42.

Amir, Y. (1976) 'The role of intergroup contact in change of prejudice and ethnic relations'. In P. A. Katz (ed.) *Towards Elimination of Racism*. New York: Pergamon Press, pp. 245–308.

Amir, Y. and Garti, C. (1977) 'Situational and personal influence on attitude change following ethnic contact'. *International Journal of Inter-Cultural Relations*, **1**, 58–75.

Anastasopoulos, P. G. (1992) 'Tourism and attitude change'. *Annals of Tourism Research*, **19**, 629–42.

Bochner, S. (1982) 'The social psychology of cross-cultural relations'. In S. Bochner (ed.) *Cultures in Contact: Studies in Cross-cultural Interaction*. New York: Pergamon Press, pp. 5–44.

Bruner, E. M. (1991) 'Transformation of self in tourism'. *Annals of Tourism Research*, **18**(2), 238–50.

Cohen, E (1972) 'Toward a sociology of international tourism'. *Social Research*, **39**(1), 164–82.

Cook, S. W. (1962) 'The systematic analysis of socially significant events: a strategy for social research'. *Journal of Social Issues*, **18**(2), 66–84.

Crick, M. (1989) 'Representations of international tourism in social sciences: sun, sex, sights, savings and servility'. *Annual Review of Anthropology*. **18**, 307–44.

D'Amore, L. J. (1988) 'Tourism: a vital force for peace'. *Tourism Management*, **9**(2), 151–4.

deKadt, E. (1979) 'The encounter: changing values and attitudes'. In E. deKadt (ed.) *Tourism: Passport to Development?* Oxford: Oxford University Press, pp. 50–67.

Evans, N. (1976) 'Tourism and cross-cultural communication'. *Annals of Tourism Research*, **3**, 189–98.

Fisher, R. J. and Price, L. L. (1991) 'International pleasure travel motivation and post-vacation cultural attitudes'. *Journal of Leisure Research*, **23**(31), 193–208.

Guldin, G. E. (1989) 'The anthropological study tour in China: a call for cultural guides'. *Human Organisation*, **48**(2), 126–34.

Hewstone, M. and Brown, R. (1986) 'Contact is not enough: an intergroup perspective on the '"contact hypothesis"'. In M. Hewstone and R. Brown (eds) *Contact and Conflict in Intergroup Encounters*. New York: Basil Blackwell, pp. 1–45.

Islam, M. R. and Hewstone, M. (1993) 'Dimensions of contact as predictors of intergroup anxiety, perceived out-group variability, and out-group attitude: an integrative model'. *Personality and Social Psychology Bulletin*, **19**, 700–10.

Kelman, H. C. (1962) 'Changing attitudes through international activities'. *Journal of Social Issues*, **18**, 68–87.

Kelman, H. C. (1965) 'Social-psychological approaches to the study of international relations: the question of relevance'. In H. C. Kelman (ed.) *International Behaviour: A Social-Psychological Perspective*. New York: Holt, Rinehart and Winston.

Krippendorf, J. (1987) *The Holiday Makers: Understanding the Impact of Leisure and Travel.* Oxford: Butterworth & Heinemann.

McIntosh, R. W., Goeldner, C. R. and Ritchie, J. R. B. (1995) *Tourism: Principles, Practices and Philosophies.* New York: John Wiley and Sons.

McLuhan, M. and Powers, B. R. (1989) *The Global Village: Transformation in World Life and Media in the Twenty-first Century.* New York: Oxford University Press.

Milman, A., Reichel, A. and Pizam, A. (1990) 'The impact of tourism on ethnic attitudes: the Israeli-Egyptian case'. *Journal of Travel Research,* **29**(2), 45–9.

Nettekoven, L. (1979) 'Mechanism of intercultural interaction'. In E. deKadt (ed.) *Tourism: Passport to Development.* Oxford: Oxford University Press, pp. 135–45.

Pearce, P. L. (1982) 'Tourists and their hosts: some social and psychological effects of inter-cultural contact'. In S. Bochner (ed.) *Cultures in Contact: Studies in Cross-cultural Interaction.* Oxford: Pergamon Press, pp. 199–221.

Pettigrew, T. F. (1986) 'The intergroup contact hypothesis reconsidered'. In M. Hewston and R. Brown (eds) *Contact and Conflict in Intergroup Encounters.* Oxford: Basil Blackwell.

Pizam, A., Jafari, J. and Milman, E. (1991) 'Influence of tourism on attitudes: US students visiting USSR'. *Tourism Management,* **12**(1), 47–54.

Pool, I. de S. (1965) 'Effects of cross-national and international images'. In H. C. Kelman (ed.) *International Behaviour: A Social-Psychological Perspective.* New York: Holt, Rinehart and Winston, pp. 106–28.

Scott, W. A. (1965) 'Psychological and social correlates of international images'. In H. C. Kelman (ed.) *International Behaviour: A Social-Psychological Perspective.* New York: Holt, Rinehart and Winston, pp. 71–103.

Selltiz, C. and Cook, S. (1962) 'Factors influencing attitudes of foreign students toward the host country'. *Journal of Social Issues,* **18**, 7–23.

Smith, H. P. (1955) 'Do intercultural experiences affect attitudes?' *Journal of Abnormal and Social Psychology,* **51**, 469–77.

Stangor, C., Jonas, K., Stroebe, W. and Hewstone, M. (1996) 'Influence of students exchange on national stereotypes, attitudes and perceived group variability'. *European Journal of Social Psychology,* **26**(4), 663–75.

Steinkalk, E. and Taft, R. (1979) 'The effect of a planned intercultural experience on the attitude and behaviour of the participants'. *International Journal of Inter-cultural Relations,* **3**, 187–98.

Stephen, C. W. and Stephen, W. G. (1992) 'Reducing intercultural anxiety through intercultural contact'. *International Journal of Inter-cultural Relations,* **16**, 89-106,

Sutton, W. A. (1967) 'Travel and understanding: notes on the social structure of touring'. *International Journal of Comparative Sociology,* **8**(2), 218–23.

Taft, R. (1977) 'Coping with unfamiliar cultures'. In N. Warren (ed.) *Studies in Cross-cultural Psychology, Volume 1.* London: Academic Press, pp. 121–53.

Triandis H. C. and Vassiliou, V. (1972) 'A comparative analysis of subjective culture'. In H. C. Triandis, V. Vassiliou, G. Vassiliou and Y. Tanaka (eds) *The Analysis of Subjective Culture.* New York: John Wiley and Sons, pp. 299–335.

Wei, L., Crompton, L. J. and Reid, L. M. (1989) 'Cultural conflicts: experiences of US visitors to China'. *Tourism Management,* **10**(4), 322–32.

Welds, K. and Dukes, R. (1985) 'Dimensions of personal change, coping styles and self-actualisation in a Shipboard University'. *Annals of Tourism Research,* **12**, 113–19.

CHAPTER 3

Nature-based Tourism and Ecotourism

Laura Lawton and David Weaver

The purpose of this chapter is to discuss the phenomenon of 'nature-based tourism' as a discrete subdivision of the broader tourism sector, and to address issues that are relevant to this area at the cusp of the new century. Of particular concern is the plethora of often incompatible meanings that are assigned to the term, which leads to much confusion and misunderstanding. Some stakeholders, for example, confine its definition to hard-core ecotourism-type activities, while others take a much broader perspective and include such contrasting activities as beach resort tourism. Following an overall review of the meaning of nature-based tourism, attention will be focused on its specific components. An emphasis is placed on the area of ecotourism, given the contention associated with that particular term. The final section of this chapter considers the magnitude of nature-based tourism, its spatial patterns and the relationships that exist among its components.

REALM OF NATURE-BASED TOURISM

Many publications point out, with varying degrees of conviction and authority, that 'nature-based tourism' is one of the fastest growing sectors within the tourism industry. Yet, there is considerable ambiguity, confusion and dispute regarding the definition of this tourism sub-sector (Nature Based Tourism Advisory Committee, 1997). At one extreme, some sources consider the term to be synonymous with such relatively specialized tourism components as ecotourism or, less commonly, adventure tourism (e.g. Boo, 1990; Sherman and Dixon, 1991; Whelan, 1991; WTTERC, 1993). This perspective is largely predicated on the equation of 'nature-based' settings with relatively undisturbed natural environments. The other extreme, that all tourism is nature based because of the ultimate dependency of

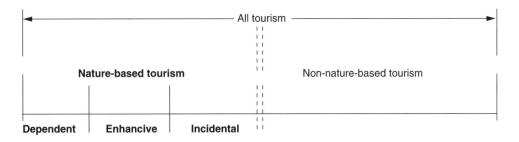

Figure 3.1 The tourism continuum and the nature-based component

all activity on the natural environment, is seldom expressed, since this trivializes the term, and eliminates its usefulness as a means of identifying a distinct subdivision of the broader tourism sector. More prevalent than either of these extremes is the tendency to see nature-based tourism as essentially those tourist activities that involve the direct use of a destination's natural resources as either a setting or an attraction (e.g. Ceballos-Lascurain, 1997; Fennell, 1999; Goodwin, 1996; Ingram and Durst, 1987). Valentine (1992) refines this perception by suggesting that the interaction between the activity and the natural environment can occur in three ways:

- Some activities are dependent upon nature for the attraction and/or setting
- Some activities are enhanced by nature
- The natural environment or nature is incidental to the activity

Hence, nature-based tourism can be defined as incorporating

> forms of tourism that maintain a dependent, enhancive or incidental relationship with the natural environment, or some aspect thereof, in terms of their utilised attractions and/or settings.

The entire tourism continuum, and the place of nature-based tourism and its sub-types within this continuum, is depicted in Figure 3.1. Activities that normally situate in the non-nature-based segment include casino gambling, stadium-based sporting events, cultural festivals, historical attractions, shopping, VFR (visiting friends and relatives) and business tourism. Activities that qualify under the nature-based rubric include 3S tourism (i.e. sea, sand, sun), adventure tourism, ecotourism, consumptive tourism, captive tourism and health tourism. Each of these is described below.

3S TOURISM

3S tourism is the largest, most conventional and in some quarters perceived as the most controversial manifestation of nature-based tourism. Largely a phenomenon of the latter half of the twentieth century, 3S tourism is closely associated with the emergence of a leisure-dominated 'pleasure periphery' occupying a significant portion of the Mediterranean and Caribbean basins, along with parts of the South Pacific, south-eastern Asia and the Indian Ocean basin (Weaver, 1998). The element of controversy is the extent to which this form of tourism has become symbolic of the negative economic, environmental and sociocultural impacts that can ensue from tourism. Furthermore, 3S tourism is equated with mass tourism, and with hedonistic impulses and motivations that are commonly seen to be less meritorious than those that underlie ecotourism or adventure tourism (see below).

At the end of the twentieth century, 3S tourism is facing a paradox. On the one hand, it continues to be subjected to a sustained barrage of criticism, accompanied by accusations that it constitutes a 'sunset' sector more in harmony with an older, unsustainable paradigm than with the contemporary dynamics of sustainability (e.g. Poon, 1993). Moreover, the wisdom of participating in 3S tourism activities has been called into serious question by evidence linking prolonged sun exposure with skin cancer, due to the continued erosion of the so-called ozone layer. On the other hand, 3S tourism remains an extremely popular vacation option, and the pleasure periphery continues to expand relentlessly through the world's subtropical and warm temperate coastal regions. Certain facets of 3S tourism, such as golf and scuba-diving, are among the fastest growing forms of tourism-related activity. The paradox is partly accounted for by the interest expressed by the industry in regenerating itself through the adoption of 'sustainable tourism' practices, and in forming a closer relationship with alternative tourism practices such as ecotourism (e.g. Ayala, 1996; Weaver, 1998). The establishment of the Green Globe accreditation scheme is but one sector-wide indication of this philosophical shift, as is the emphasis on beach/safari packages in destinations such as Kenya.

CONSUMPTIVE AND CAPTIVE TOURISM

Also controversial are the areas of consumptive and captive tourism, which are generally dependent upon natural settings or specified elements of the natural environment. Although all tourism activities incorporate elements of consumption, consumptive nature-based activities per se are generally perceived as those that intend to offer not just experiences to the participant, but also tangible products (Applegate and Clark, 1987). Hunting and fishing (except perhaps for 'catch and release' fishing), the commonest forms of consumptive tourism, are controversial in many quarters because of their emphasis on the deliberate attempt to seek out, kill and remove an organism from its environment. This ethical argument is often accompanied by accusations that wildlife consumption is environmentally unsustainable, even though there is considerable evidence to suggest that hunting and fishing can be an effective means of wildlife conservation under some circumstances. Nevertheless, like 3S tourism, consumptive tourism is associated with older, unsustainable forms of tourism. However, unlike 3S tourism, the popularity of consumptive nature-based tourism, and hunting in particular, has actually declined within the past two decades. In a comprehensive survey of American adult participation in outdoor recreational activities, the number of active participants in hunting declined by more than 11 per cent between 1982 and 1994, a rate of erosion that was exceeded only by tennis (Cordell *et al.*, 1995).

Captive nature-based tourism incorporates settings such as zoological parks, aquariums, aviaries and botanical gardens where elements of the natural environment are presented under variably confined and controlled conditions. Like 3S tourism and hunting, the traditional concept of a 'zoo' has been subject to increased criticism on ethical grounds, prompting their reconfiguration as 'wildlife parks' that attempt to replicate, as far as reasonably possible, the natural habitats of their resident wildlife. Concurrently, conservation goals are also more apparent, as in the pursuit of captive breeding and reintroduction programmes. Wildlife parks, zoos and the like tend to be located within or near urban areas, and hence often attract very large visitor numbers.

HEALTH TOURISM

Nature-based health tourism, as a discrete sub-sector, is most closely associated with spas and other facilities that rely on a supply of purportedly therapeutic water or mud. Such forms of health tourism enjoyed a prominent status in global tourism prior to the Second World War, but declined in importance with the emergence of relatively inexpensive 3S alternatives. Ironically, 3S tourism itself originated as a salt-water oriented variation of the spa phenomenon.

ADVENTURE TOURISM

Three elements distinguish adventure tourism from other types of nature-based tourism. First, adventure tourism, as implied by the name, contains an element of risk (Hall, 1992; Fennell, 1999). Second, a certain amount of skill is generally required to carry out the activity in a way that does not endanger the participant. Third, adventure tourism often involves higher levels of physical exertion (Ewart, 1989). Adventure tourism is usually, although not exclusively, associated with natural environments. Related activities include white-water rafting, skydiving, wilderness hiking, sea-kayaking, mountain climbing, diving, caving and orienteering (Sung *et al.*, 1996/97). In all of these pursuits, the natural environment offers a venue that provides a suitable level of challenge to the participants, thus allowing them to achieve the desired level of thrill or excitement. Thus, in terms of Valentine's categories, the relationship with the natural environment can range from incidental to dependent, depending on the type of activity pursued. One common way of classifying adventure tourism, aside from the specific activities pursued, is along a continuum from 'soft' to 'hard' adventure, wherein the levels of risk, skill and exertion increase from minimum to maximum levels.

ECOTOURISM

In the literature of the 1980s and early 1990s, there was a tendency to equate ecotourism with 'nature-based tourism' and even 'adventure tourism'. While there is still no consensus on the precise definition of ecotourism, a review of the relevant literature reveals three core characteristics that are usually associated with this type of tourism (Blamey, 1997). These are relation to the natural environment, educational/appreciative motives and sustainability.

Relation to the natural environment

The primary attraction base in ecotourism is focused on the natural environment, or some constituent element thereof – hence the strong affiliation with nature-based tourism, and with the nature-dependent component in particular. Some definitions of ecotourism, such as the original definition put forward by Ceballos-Lascurain in 1983, cite associated cultural attributes as a secondary basis of attraction (cited in Boo, 1990), and this is a logical addition given that most so-called 'natural' landscapes have been impacted to a greater or lesser extent by human activity. A corollary to the nature-based link is that ecotourism is commonly associated in the literature with protected areas and other relatively undisturbed 'natural environments'. These, without doubt, offer a high-quality venue for accessing wildlife and other natural attractions. However, the inclusion of constituent elements of the natural environment in the definition of ecotourism, as above, offers considerably more latitude for extending the types of venues that can accommodate this activity. For example, if the ecotourist is especially interested in peregrine falcons, then the central business districts of some large North American cities are an ideal viewing environment, though far removed from the pristine landscape of a National Park. Similarly, some waste disposal sites, such as the Leslie Street Spit in Toronto, provide outstanding opportunities for bird observation.

The implications of this observation are not merely academic, since the ability to extend the range of ecotourism into significantly modified environments could help to ease the pressure that this rapidly growing sector is placing upon the declining pool of relatively undisturbed space. Being modified already, the environmental carrying capacity for ecotourism is presumably greater in such areas, which are also more accessible to the tourist market. Aside from specific types of wildlife that frequent particular modified environments, the product base of this extended ecotourism could in some areas emphasize landscape restoration efforts.

Educational/appreciative motive

The relationship between the ecotourism participant and the natural environment is focused around an element of education and appreciation that can be situated on a continuum from casual interest to deep commitment, depending on the type of ecotourism practised (see below). This contrasts with 3S and adventure tourism, where the natural environment offers a convenient setting for the realization of extrinsic motivations such as relaxation or thrill-seeking, respectively. One potential ambiguity occurs where the product incorporates an educational or interpretive element, but the tourist accessing that product is not particularly interested in this learning component. Conversely, the participant might desire to learn about the resource, but the associated product provides no interpretation. Whether these scenarios of market/product nonconformity meet this criterion of education/appreciation is open to debate.

Sustainability

The third core characteristic of ecotourism is sustainability, a concept that is discussed in detail elsewhere in this book (see Chapter 16). As that chapter demonstrates, there is widespread support for the principle of sustainable tourism, but many serious problems that are encountered when the actual implementation process is engaged. Hence, this raises the question as to whether any instance of ecotourism can be definitely assessed as being sustainable. If not, then the criterion that ecotourism must be sustainable is too harsh, with little or nothing remaining in this category. The solution to this dilemma is to emphasize the intent and apparent substance of sustainability. Thus, an operation would fall under the category of ecotourism if every reasonable attempt is made to operate in a sustainable matter, and if remedial measures are undertaken in a situation where environmental stresses are inadvertently induced.

Another relevant matter is the scope of sustainability. Many definitions only refer to ecological or environmental sustainability, but it is difficult to see how this context can be divorced from the cultural, social and economic dimensions of a destination. This is partly because of the significant role played by indigenous people in particular in shaping the character of the so-called 'natural' environment. In addition, local communities that are disadvantaged and alienated by tourism and protected area managers, in the supposed interests of an area's ecological integrity, are likely to do what they can to sabotage this resource base. This was demonstrated by the anti-wildlife actions of certain Masai tribesmen in Kenya during the 1980s and 1990s (Sindiga, 1995).

Hard and soft ecotourism

It is argued here that tourism activities that meet the above criteria, as with adventure tourism, can be positioned on a continuum that ranges from the more 'hard' pursuits to those of a 'soft' variety. Figure 3.2 presents these two ends of the continuum as 'ideal types' that provide an undistorted standard against which real-life situations can be assessed. Thus, the hard ecotourism ideal type involves specialized trips undertaken over a relatively long period of time by small groups of dedicated environmentalists who expect few if any services, and prefer to immerse themselves in a wilderness or other relatively undisturbed environment. At the other end of the spectrum, soft ecotourism involves larger groups of less committed tourists whose encounter with nature is diversionary and temporary, usually one incidental component of a multi-purpose trip. These tourists tend to concentrate in more modified areas, often on the edge of a protected area or within its interpretive centre, where a high level of services is available. Of course, in reality, most trips fall somewhere in between these two extremes, although the difference in scale dictates that activity will be concentrated on the right-hand side of the spectrum.

The hard-soft continuum has been recognized in many of the theoretical and operational definitions of ecotourism that have been proposed to date. For example, Lindberg (1991) distinguishes between 'hard-core' or 'dedicated' ecotourists on one side, and 'casual' or 'mainstream' ecotourists on the other. The Queensland ecotourism plan recognizes 'self-reliant' and 'popular' ecotourism, but acknowledges the middle ground by adding an intermediary 'small group ecotourism' category (Queensland, 1995). Not all definitions, however, accommodate the possibility of a soft ecotourism component, this omission usually being based on the assumption that a relatively large-scale and modestly committed level of activity cannot be

HARD	SOFT
Small group	Large group
Specialized trip	Diversionary experience
Prolonged encounter with nature	Temporary encounter with nature
Immersive	Incidental
High level of interest/commitment	Moderate level of interest/commitment
Wilderness/undisturbed setting	Modified setting
Few or no services	Ample services

Figure 3.2 Hard and soft ecotourism: ideal types

compatible with the sustainability of the resource base in a relatively undisturbed natural environment. This reluctance raises the issue of the association between ecotourism and mass tourism, which is discussed further in the following subsection.

RELATIONSHIP BETWEEN ECOTOURISM AND MASS TOURISM

When originally conceived during the 1980s, ecotourism was almost invariably described as a form of Alternative Tourism, that is, a small-scale form of tourism that was deliberately managed to avoid the characteristics that were associated with mass tourism. This conception of ecotourism is strongly associated with the dominance at that time of the 'cautionary' and 'adaptancy' platforms (Jafari, 1989), which tended to see mass tourism as an inherently negative and unsustainable form of tourism, and Alternative Tourism as the preferred option. Hence, ecotourism was seen as being inherently incompatible with mass tourism – a position that accounts for the tendency of some definitions to emphasize only the hard component of ecotourism, or at least to emphasize preference for the latter.

While often justified as a position that occupies the high moral ground and resonates with the ideal of what ecotourism should be, this focus on only the hard component is questionable on several grounds. First, the association with Alternative and mass tourism respectively as 'good' and 'bad' tourism is giving way under the 'knowledge-based' platform of the 1990s to a disassociation between scale and value. Thus, depending on how they are managed and the idiosyncratic circumstances that pertain to each destination, small and large-scale tourism can both be either a positive or negative force. As discussed in Chapter 16, there is growing evidence that the mainstream mass tourism industry is becoming more sustainable in its practices, and an argument can be made that associated economies of scale better facilitate the implementation of sustainability in comparison to smaller enterprises. Under the knowledge-based platform, there is therefore no a priori basis for suggesting that ecotourism cannot have a large-scale dimension, and it is no longer an oxymoron to consider the possibility of 'mass ecotourism' as being applicable to some types of soft ecotourism.

Secondly, the potential problems of adhering to a highly restrictive definition of ecotourism must be raised. When such a view is promulgated, just one of two scenarios is possible:

*   Ecotourism is effectively restricted to the small handful of individuals who have the money, time, fitness, motivation and skills to engage in immersive hard ecotourism. This marks ecotourism as an elitist activity, and one that does

not generate sufficient income to warrant any further consideration of ecotourism as a serious generator of revenue that can justify its claim on natural environments continuously under threat from other stakeholder groups; or

- Hard ecotourism is promoted as the preferable mode of activity that should be followed by the tens of millions of travellers who otherwise fall under the soft ecotourism umbrella. Assuming that this market can somehow find the money, time and fitness to engage in such pursuits, one can only imagine the ecological consequences of this invasion on the unserviced, relatively undisturbed venues that would be affected.

If, on the other hand, the concepts of soft and mass ecotourism are acknowledged, then it is possible to rationalize local site hardening measures that will confine visitors to service intensive portions of protected areas in a sustainable way. Concurrently, enough revenues are generated to justify maintaining the remainder of the park in a pristine condition, and to manage this resource base to ensure that it remains so.

Finally, even where ecotourism itself does not become mass tourism, there is an argument to be made for the possibility of synergy between mass tourism and (soft) ecotourism. The inclusion of an incidental ecotourism experience appears to make a conventional mass tourism holiday more diverse, and hence more attractive. Destinations that offer soft ecotourism opportunities are therefore more desirable than those that provide only the basic 3S product. For example, the great majority of inbound tourists in Kenya would qualify as mass tourists, but 70 per cent of this total market selected Kenya for their vacation because of the opportunity to see African wildlife as part of the package (Akama, 1996). Based on an analysis of activity and preference patterns, a similar situation pertains to Costa Rica and many other high profile ecotourism destinations (Weaver, 1998). In the other direction, there is the aforementioned clout given to ecotourism by the revenues generated through mass tourism. In addition, it may be that the exposure of conventional tourists to ecotourism will contribute to the 'greening' of consumer values, and accelerate the implementation of sustainable tourism measures within the mainstream industry. The argument for mass tourism to become more engaged with ecotourism is also based on the growing popularity of the latter. Although claims of annual growth in the vicinity of 20–25 per cent are almost certainly exaggerated, strong anecdotal evidence does point to robust growth in related activities. The US survey cited earlier identified birdwatching as by far the fastest growing form of outdoor recreational activity among American adults, with 155 per cent growth recorded between 1982 and 1994. In the number two and three positions, respectively, were hiking (93 per cent) and backpacking (73 per cent) (Cordell *et al.*, 1995).

RELATIONSHIPS AMONG THE VARIOUS FORMS OF NATURE-BASED TOURISM

The relationships and relative magnitudes of the nature tourism sub-sectors described above are depicted in Figure 3.3. 3S tourism is undoubtedly the largest component, and is largely discrete except for some overlap with ecotourism, adventure tourism and health tourism. The best illustration of an overlap with ecotourism is scuba-diving, snorkelling, reef visits and related pursuits, where the latter are undertaken in a sustainable way. The overlap with soft adventure tourism occurs in such areas as jet skiing, windsurfing and water-skiing. The non-nature-based component of 3S tourism is also differentiated, as is the cultural component in ecotourism, adventure tourism (e.g. visits to war zones) and health tourism (e.g. medical treatment). Ecotourism, even with the inclusion of its soft component, is smaller than 3S tourism, and overlaps with adventure tourism to a

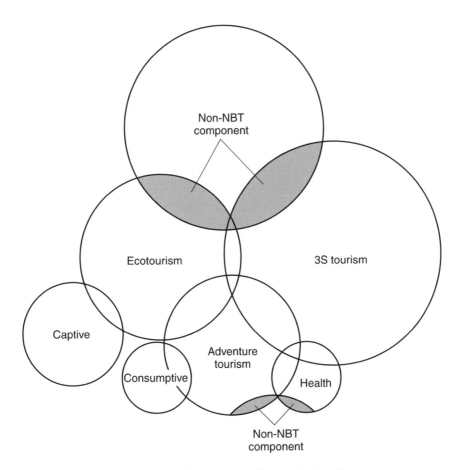

Figure 3.3 Nature-based tourism sub-sectors and interrelationships

fairly large extent (as with trekking, canoeing, safaris, bushwalking, etc.). Among the smaller sub-sectors, captive tourism has some overlap with ecotourism where the site succeeds in replicating a natural habitat. Consumptive tourism and ecotourism, however, are mutually exclusive, although the former does link with adventure tourism in such areas as big game hunting and deep-sea fishing.

Thus, after identifying the components of nature-based tourism, and recognizing that each of these sub-sectors has a discrete core and an element of overlap, it is now possible to estimate the magnitude of nature-based tourism both in terms of participation and spatial extent. The presence of overlap will of course make this task more difficult, as will the increasing popularity of multi-purpose travel. For example, a trip undertaken primarily for social or business purposes may incorporate a strong secondary nature-based component, but is excluded from the nature-based ledger because the participant proclaims only 'business' or 'family visit' as the purpose of trip. Similarly, a trip undertaken mainly for purposes of 'ecotourism' may incorporate a visit to an urban historical attraction. Notwithstanding these qualifiers, it is contended here that nature-based tourism constitutes one-half or more of all international tourism activity. The proportion for domestic tourism is probably smaller due to the higher prevalence of VFR (visiting friends and relatives) and business tourism at that scale.

This contention is predicated on several observations. First, nature-based 3S tourism accounts for perhaps 20–25 per cent of all international tourism activity, and a much higher proportion in pleasure periphery regions such as the Caribbean and Mediterranean basins, the South Pacific, and parts of south-east Asia and the Indian Ocean rim. The share that one attributes to ecotourism depends on the willingness to incorporate its soft elements. If this is granted, then ecotourism accounts for between 20 and 40 per cent of all leisure travel by some estimates (e.g. Ecotourism Society, 1998; Hawkins (cited in Giannecchini, 1993)). Nature-based adventure tourism has a similar discrepancy between its hard and soft elements, but in total is not as large as ecotourism. Captive nature-based tourism is a considerable element in its own right by merit of the fact that most large cities possess zoological parks and botanical gardens that attract very large numbers of visitors. Once consumptive and health-related tourism is added, it is apparent that nature-based tourism accounts for over one-half of all international tourism.

Any attempt to quantify nature-based tourism more precisely at the global level is impeded by the lack of reliable cumulative activity/frequency statistics. However, some indication of frequency can be obtained by focusing on countries where such data are available. One such example is Australia, where the activity and visitation patterns of inbound tourists are monitored continually on a sample basis by the International Visitor Survey. As depicted in Table 3.1, this survey in 1996 found that nature-based sites were among the most popular generic attractions to be visited by international tourists. Especially remarkable, because of their concentration in

Table 3.1 Places visited by inbound tourists to Australia in 1996. *Source*: Bureau of Tourism Research, 1997

Type of Place	Percentage of all International Tourists Visiting*	Relation with Nature-Based Tourism
Restaurants	91	Ubiquitous; may be associated with n-b attractions
Zoos, animal parks, aquariums	48	100% captive n-b tourism, with ecotourism overlap
Botanical or other public gardens	45	100% captive n-b tourism, with ecotourism overlap
National Parks	42	Strong association with ecotourism
Historic/heritage buildings, sites, monuments	33	No direct association
Museums, art galleries	28	No direct association
Casinos	25	No direct association
Amusement/theme parks	20	No direct association
Aboriginal sites and cultural displays	15	Some association with n-b tourism
Art/craft workshops/studios	12	No direct association
Performing arts/concerts	12	No direct association
Mines, mills, wool centres, farms	11	No direct association
Wineries	10	No direct association
Festivals/fairs	8	No direct association

Note: * Proportion of tourists visiting this type of attraction at least once during their visit.

highly modified urban areas, are captive settings such as wildlife parks and botanical gardens. The popularity of national parks is also apparent in Table 3.1.

In terms of spatial patterns, an interesting relationship can be discerned between the magnitude of an activity's participation, and the amount of space that is used for that activity. At one end of the continuum is a cluster of nature-based activities that involve large numbers of participants within restricted spatial environments (Figure 3.4). While such a relationship can be easily imagined for a zoological park or 3S resort, a similar pattern applies to ecotourism. Evidence from Costa Rica, Kenya and many other ecotourism destinations indicates a strong concentration of soft ecotourism activity within just a handful of protected areas, and a similarly strong concentration of visitor activity within those few parks

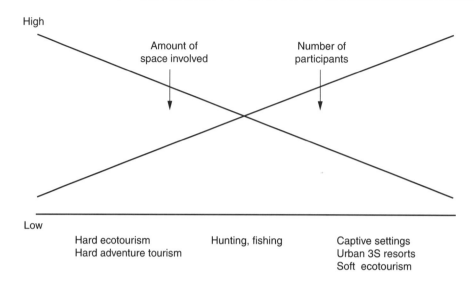

Figure 3.4 Spatial concentration and magnitude of nature-based tourism sub-sectors

(Weaver, 1998). At the other end of the continuum, activities such as hard ecotourism and hard adventure tourism involve very small numbers of participants who undertake these pursuits within a very large spatial venue, such as a wilderness area or the open seas. In between these two extremes are activities such as hunting and fishing that involve intermediate levels of spatial and participation intensity.

CONCLUSION

Nature-based tourism, globally, is a diverse and large-scale phenomenon, involving such pursuits as 3S tourism, ecotourism, adventure tourism, captive tourism, consumptive tourism and health tourism. Each of these activities, to a greater or lesser extent, entails a relationship with the natural environment, or some element thereof, that is either dependent, enhancive or incidental. Among the issues that are pertinent to the managers of nature-based tourism is the need to disengage from the view that ecotourism and mass tourism, two of the biggest components, are mutually exclusive and non-complementary. Instead, effort should be put into identifying the opportunities for synergy and mutual reinforcement, given that mass tourists and soft ecotourists are to a large extent the same people and, moreover, people that are seeking a diversified and rewarding holiday experience. Another major observation is the recognition that for the vast majority of participants, nature-based tourism is something that involves a very small amount of space. This is paradoxical for several reasons. First, the intuitive notion of a high-quality nature-based experience is associated with uncrowded, wide open spaces, not small and intensively utilized areas. Second, the spatially intensive/high participation model presents both opportunities and threats to both the physical environment and the quality of the tourism experience. The threat is that large magnitudes are more likely to result in a breaching of site-carrying capacities, while the opportunity is that the revenue derived from large visitation levels can be used to implement site hardening techniques which will better ensure that those capacities will not be exceeded. While sustainability is increasingly recognized as a core prerequisite for ecotourism, it is clear that all other types of nature-based tourism as well must adhere to this principle if they are to prosper in the twenty-first century.

REFERENCES

Akama, J. (1996) 'Western environmental values and nature-based tourism in Kenya'. *Tourism Management*, **17**(8), 567–74.

Applegate, J. and Clark, K. (1987) 'Satisfaction levels of birdwatchers: an observation on the consumptive-nonconsumptive continuum'. *Leisure Sciences*, **9**, 129–34.

Ayala, H. (1996) 'Resort ecotourism: a paradigm for the twenty-first century'. *Cornell Hotel and Restaurant Administration Quarterly*, **37**(5), 46–53.

Blamey, R. (1997) 'Ecotourism: the search for an operational definition'. *Journal of Sustainable Tourism*, **5**(2), 109–30.

Boo, E. (1990) *Ecotourism: The Potentials and Pitfalls. Volume 1*. Washington, DC: World Wildlife Fund.

Bureau of Tourism Research (1997) *International Visitor Survey 1996*. Canberra: Bureau of Tourism Research.

Ceballos-Lascurain, H. (1997) 'Introduction'. In K. Lindberg, M. Epler Wood, and D. Engeldrum (eds) *Ecotourism: A Guide for Planners and Managers. Volume 2*. North Bennington, VT, USA: Ecotourism Society, pp. 7–10.

Cordell, H. K., Lewis, B. and McDonald, B. L. (1995) 'Long-term outdoor recreation participation trends'. In J. L. Thompson, D. W. Lime, B. Gartner, and W. M. Sames (eds) *Proceedings of the Fourth International Outdoor Recreation and Tourism Trends Symposium and the 1995 National Recreation Resource Planning Conference*. St Paul, MN, USA: University of Minnesota, pp. 35–8.

Ecotourism Society (1998) *Ecotourism Statistical Fact Sheet*. North Bennington, VT, USA: Ecotourism Society.

Ewart, A. (1989) *Outdoor Adventure Pursuits: Foundations, Models, and Theories*. USA: Publishing Horizons.

Fennell, D. (1999) *Ecotourism: An Introduction*. London: Routledge.

Giannecchini, J. (1993) 'Ecotourism: new partners, new relationships'. *Conservation Biology*, **7**, 429–32.

Goodwin, H. (1996) 'In pursuit of ecotourism'. *Biodiversity and Conservation*, **5**, 277–91.

Hall, C. M. (1992) 'Adventure, sport and health tourism'. In B. Weiler and C. M. Hall (eds) *Special Interest Tourism*. London: Belhaven Press, pp. 141–58.

Ingram, D. and Durst, P. (1987) *Nature Oriented Travel to Developing Countries*. Research Triangle Park, NC, USA: Southeastern Center for Forest Economics Research, FPEI Working Paper No. 28.

Jafari, J. (1989) 'An English language literature review'. In J. Bystrzanowski (ed.) *Tourism as a Factor of Change: A Sociocultural Study*. Vienna: Centre for Research and Documentation in Social Sciences, pp. 17–60.

Lindberg, K. (1991) *Policies for Maximizing Nature Tourism's Ecological and Economic Benefits.* Washington, DC: World Resources Institute.

Nature Based Tourism Advisory Committee (1997) *Nature Based Tourism Strategy for Western Australia.* Perth: Western Australian Tourism Commission, Department of Conservation and Land Management.

Poon, A. (1993) *Tourism, Technology and Competitive Strategies.* Wallingford, UK: CAB International.

Queensland (1995) *Draft Queensland Ecotourism Plan.* Brisbane: Department of Tourism, Sport and Youth.

Sherman, P. and Dixon, J. (1991) 'The economics of nature tourism: determining if it pays'. In T. Whelan (ed.) *Nature Tourism: Managing for the Environment.* Washington, DC: Island Press, pp. 89–131.

Sindiga, I. (1995) 'Wildlife-based tourism in Kenya: land use conflicts and government compensation policies over protected areas'. *Journal of Tourism Studies,* **6**(2), 45–55.

Sung, H., Morrison, A. and O'Leary, J. (1996/97) 'Definition of adventure travel: conceptual framework for empirical application from the providers' perspective'. *Asia Pacific Journal of Tourism Research,* **1**(2), 47–67.

Valentine, P. (1992) 'Nature-based tourism'. In B. Weiler and C. M. Hall (eds) *Special Interest Tourism.* London: Belhaven Press, pp. 105–27.

Weaver, D. (1998) *Ecotourism in the Less Developed World.* Wallingford, UK: CAB International.

Whelan, T. (ed.) (1991) *Nature Tourism: Managing for the Environment.* Washington, DC: Island Press.

WTTERC (1993) *World Travel and Tourism Environment Review 1993.* Oxford: World Travel and Tourism Environment Research Centre.

CHAPTER 4

Wine Tourism Futures

Ross Dowling and Donald Getz

INTRODUCTION

A recent surge of interest in the formal planning, development and marketing of wine tourism reflects a major, late twentieth-century mega-force, the intensification of global competition for tourism, leading destinations and the industry to seek competitive advantage through niche marketing. Also stemming from this force is the increasing linkage of tourism to other industries, in this case agriculture and wine, for mutual benefit. This has resulted in many new partnerships and a growing emphasis on joint marketing efforts. A subset of this 'partnership' trend is the linkage of various niche markets, such as wine, industrial, cultural or agritourism into more comprehensive, lifestyle packages.

In this chapter we examine specific trends in wine tourism within this context. Key issues and challenges are identified, especially research needs. Wine tourism is such a recent innovation, at least in terms of formalized study, that considerable gaps exist in our knowledge of the wine tourism system.

By way of examining future developments in this field, a planning scenario is developed and its implications evaluated. This scenario is based on work conducted in Western Australia as part of a wine tourism planning process for the state. The scenario rests on a realistic but hypothetical vision statement and major goals, followed by speculation on how actions based on the vision and goals are likely to influence the future.

WHAT IS WINE TOURISM?

Most existing definitions of wine tourism relate to the traveller's motivation and experiences. For example, Hall and Macionis (1998) defined it as visitation to vineyards, wineries, wine festivals and wine shows for which grape wine tasting and/or experiencing the attributes of a grape wine region are the prime motivating factors for visitors. The South Australian Tourism Commission (1997) focused on activities suggesting that wine tourism is any experience related to wineries or wine production in which visitors participate when on a day trip or longer visit. It added that wine tourism can range from a visit to a single cellar door outlet while en route to a main holiday destination, to intensive, week-long experiences focused on the wine process.

The *Draft Australian National Wine Tourism Strategy* (Global Tourism and Leisure, 1998) also concentrated on the experience, but deliberately broadened the definition to include visitations to wineries and wine regions to experience the unique qualities of contemporary Australian lifestyle associated with the enjoyment of wine at its source – including wine and food, landscape and cultural activities. The *Draft Western Australian Wine Tourism Strategy* defines wine tourism as travel for the experience of wineries and wine regions and their links to the local lifestyle, and encompasses service provision and destination marketing (Dowling *et al.*, 1999). It comprises a number of characteristics which inform the definition as well as a range of features which provide the wine tourism experience (Table 4.1).

These are consumer-focused definitions, which makes a lot of sense because ultimately it is the consumer who defines the wine tourism 'product', but it should be remembered that there are at least three major perspectives on the subject – that of wine producers, tourism agencies (representing the destinations) and consumers. Thus, wine tourism is, simultaneously:

- a form of consumer behaviour;
- a strategy by which destinations develop and market wine-related attractions and imagery; and
- a marketing opportunity for wineries to educate, and to sell their products, directly to consumers.

MAJOR TRENDS IN WINE TOURISM

There are a number of trends emerging in wine tourism. They include its rapid growth, the unfolding of wineries as tourist attractions and complete destinations, the importance of cellar door sales, the proliferation of wine festivals and events, the synergy between food and wine and the recognition of the need for the formalized planning of wine regions or precincts.

Cambourne (1999) asserts that wine tourism has replaced ecotourism as 'the hot new buzz word' and as an important new niche market with significant growth

Table 4.1 Characteristics and features of wine tourism. *Source*: Dowling *et al.*, 1999

Wine tourism is travel for the experience of wineries and wine regions and their links to the local lifestyle and encompasses service provision and destination marketing.

Characteristics – various characteristics inform this definition including:
- It is a lifestyle experience.
- Wine tourism should take account of both supply (the wineries and tourism operators) and demand (consumer behaviour) factors.
- It can be part of a broader tourism experience.
- It has an educational component.
- Wine may be one of many attractions of a region.
- There are linkages to food, accommodation, arts and crafts and the environment.
- It is a marketing opportunity.
- It enhances the economic, social and cultural values of the wine region.
- It should form part of the national and international tourism image of the region.

Features – the wine tourism experience can be provided for in a number of ways including:
- Events, festivals and vintage celebrations.
- Restaurants and fine dining.
- Education and interpretation.
- Hospitality and accommodation.
- Wine touring.
- Travelling around a region – including wine trails.
- Information centres.
- The provision of information about wine – including verbal detail and written documentation.
- Tasting and cellar door sales.
- Retail outlets – selling locally produced art, craft and speciality foods.
- Architecture and heritage features.
- Specialist accommodation in or close to wineries.
- Winery tours – including wine production processes and viticulture.
- Wine villages – including wineries, events and themed accommodation.

potential. In the 1990s both the wine and tourism industries achieved high levels of growth and, combined, they have the potential to create significant benefits to all involved in the wine and tourism industries. In New Zealand it is estimated that wine-related tourism is undertaken by 17 per cent of domestic tourists and 13 per cent of international visitors (Hall and Johnson, 1999).

According to the Australian International Visitor Survey conducted by the Bureau of Tourism Research (BTR), 390,400 international visitors visited wineries during their stay in Australia in 1996. This represents about 10 per cent of total visitors to Australia and an increase of 68 per cent on winery visits in 1993 (Robins, 1999). The Winemakers' Federation of Australia estimates total Australian wine tourism figures to be in the order of 5.3 million visits per annum, worth $428 million in 1995 and which is expected to grow substantially to around $1100 million by 2025 (Australian Wine Foundation, 1996). As stated by Kennedy (1998), the industry, already worth $400 million plus, is young but surprisingly full-bodied. Australia also had a record 72,707 hectares of vines in 1995 and exported 113.6 million litres valued at a record $385.3 million (Australian Bureau of Statistics, 1996). These figures provide an indication of the size and value of the wine tourism industry to Australia's economy.

The Napa Valley (USA), probably the busiest wine destination in the world, receives approximately 5 million visitors annually (Shapiro, 1998). Mondavi receives about 300,000 at his winery alone, and that is at capacity (personal communication, 1998). Denbies winery in England, built specifically as a tourist attraction, receives about 200,000 visitors annually (Howley and van Westering 1999).

Another indicator of the growth of the industry is the number of conferences being planned on the subject. The First Australian Wine Tourism Conference was held at Leeuwin Estate, Margaret River, Western Australia in May 1998. The conference had 260 participants from five continents and ten countries, illustrating the recognition of wine tourism as an emerging growth industry, and has now become an annual event. Some key elements which arose from the conference were the need for:

- branding and imagery and the differentiation of wine regions;
- the co-ordination of marketing efforts;
- wine tourism to benefit the wineries;
- staff training and education;
- co-operation at a range of planning levels; and
- national development planning and co-ordination.

At the time of writing a number of other wine tourism conferences are being planned, including national Australian conferences in Victoria (August 1999) and Adelaide (November 2000) as well as in New Zealand (Marlborough, November 2000). In addition, two international conferences to be held include the first

European Wine Tourism Conference at the University of Surrey, England, in September 1999 and the First International Wine Tourism Conference and Expo (Western Australia, March 2001).

As stated by Shelmerdine (1999, p. 160) 'clearly the growth in tourism to wine regions is directly linked to the growth of wine consumption, both domestic and international.' Public awareness of wine has increased, resulting in growth in regards to all aspects of the wine industry. Care must be taken, however, to make sure that any development which occurs is of a sustainable nature. Lessons can be learned from more developed wine tourism regions overseas such as the Napa Valley where congestion has become a big problem. Here the quality of the wine experience has decreased and visitors are actually discouraged from visiting the region (Dodd and Bigotte, 1997, p. 47).

Wineries are emerging as tourist attractions and even as complete destinations in themselves. By adding quality restaurants, gift shops, special events, meeting rooms and accommodation, wineries have the ability to capture longer visits and enhance their revenue all year round. As self-contained destinations they can offer the cultural or rural tourist a unique wine country experience. Small wineries can get into this market through bed and breakfast accommodations or providing meals to groups. Larger wineries have many more options. A risk, however, is that restaurants and other product expansions might not be profitable in the context of growing competition among wineries or with other service providers in the area.

Cellar door sales account for a significant percentage of the total revenue from wine sales (Table 4.2). A comprehensive study carried out in 1996 of over 600 visitors to wineries in the Margaret River wine region of Western Australia indicated that three in every four visitors purchased wine at the cellar door (King and Morris, 1999). However, a tracking study of 56 of these visitors carried out two years later found that only one-third had purchased further wines produced by the region and only twelve respondents (21 per cent) were able to recall brand names purchased.

Wine festivals, related food festivals and wine trade shows, have all been proliferating. Numerous wine villages in Europe produce annual, community wine events, but in newer wine regions the impetus has often come from individual wineries or tourism agencies. These festivals and events can attract new and repeat visitors, especially outside the main tourist seasons and tourist traffic areas, help develop a positive destination image themed on wine and mobilize new partnerships between wine, tourism, event sponsors and the community.

In Australia, the Victorian Wineries Tourism Council (VWTC) has given a great deal of assistance to the creation and marketing of wine events in all of its wine regions. One of the state's major successes has been the establishment of 32 wine festivals, up from an original 12 in the days before the Council. The VWTC has an annual events grant scheme which draws on AUS$100,000 in funding to match event

Table 4.2 Percentage of wine sold at cellar door sales in selected regions

Source	Country	Wine Region	Sales (%)	Notes
Howley and van Westering (1999)	England	–	65	–
Dodd (1995)	USA	Texas	60	7 of 19 wineries
King and Morris (1997)	Australia	Margaret River	34	76% of visitors purchase wine
Reilly (1996)	Australia	Barossa	30	–
		Clare Valley	25	A high of 60%
Choisy (1996)	France	Alsace	23	–
		Burgundy	19	–
Hall and Johnson (1999)	New Zealand	–	20	–

budgets and it has produced quality guidelines for events receiving their assistance. The scheme has concentrated on generating new wine events, rather than on the provision of operating funds. Growth in attendance at wine events is reported to have increased by 19 per cent since 1993. The Yarra Valley Grape Grazing Festival alone attracts over 30,000 visitors annually. So successful has this programme been, drawing on enthusiasm in the regions, that it is now a real question as to how many wine events the state can successfully support.

The synergy between food and wine is an integral part of a wine region's lifestyle experience. Food is a key component of wine tourism and underpins the visitors' experience. Thus the establishment of food outlets on the wineries can highlight the quality of regional produce adding further economic value to the individual winery and the region. Finally there is the recognition of the need for the formalized planning of wine regions. Such regions or precincts provide a coherent all-inclusive destination for the tourist encompassing attractions, transport and accommodation. Fundamental to the whole experience is the centrality of the winery visit.

MAJOR ISSUES AND CHALLENGES

Notwithstanding the rapid rise of interest in, and development of, wine tourism, a range of issues and challenges face the future growth of the industry. They include generational, health, environmental, co-operation, demonstration of benefits, competition and planning.

The generational challenge

Baby boomers will dominate wine consumption and wine tourism for the next two decades, but what then? These are the boom years for wine and wine tourism, especially in North America, and the industries must capitalize on these now. But they cannot take for granted that growth will continue indefinitely. Somehow the younger generations have to be brought into the culture of food and wine. Price is a major related issue, as younger consumers are possibly being left behind as the costs of wine production continue to rise.

The health challenge

Although the health benefits of moderate alcohol consumption are now widely recognized, with wine in particular being associated with a healthy lifestyle, enough questions and challenges remain to ensure that health will remain a major issue. The wine industry must be proactive in stressing responsible drinking, and encouraging the food and wine synergy.

The environmental challenge

Organic viticulture and winemaking are spreading rapidly, but many environmental issues remain for the wine and tourism industries to tackle. The basic challenge is to preserve and enhance the resources upon which sustainable wine tourism rests, including soils, land for grapes, water for irrigation, community support and cultural authenticity. If wine tourism leads to mass tourism, many small towns and rural areas will suffer from congestion and too many visitors to accommodate without problems. Wine tourism should always remain a niche market stressing high-yield, high-quality visitors who come for the special attractiveness of the wine region's unique attributes.

Where wine tourism has reached mass tourism levels, as in the Napa Valley of California, the policy is to continue to move upmarket and attract mainly overnight, price-indifferent consumers. Other regions can avoid the congestion and commercialization experienced by Napa through early planning.

The challenge of co-operation

Destinations are policy 'domains' in which stakeholders agree to co-operate for mutual gain because independent actions do not work. The wine industry must form effective partnerships with food, tourism and hospitality, secure strong community and political support, and demonstrate the benefits of wine tourism. A regional wine tourism planning process can be the tool for attaining these goals.

The challenge of demonstrating benefits

To ensure community and political support, wine tourism must demonstrate its benefits and deal with its impacts. So far, little research has been undertaken on impacts and related management strategies.

The competitive challenge

Wine tourism is a highly competitive specialty market and competition is growing rapidly. This unprecedented growth has led to an increase in wineries, a rise in aggressive destinations and more sophisticated marketing. Thus individual wine regions must find their own distinctive appeal within the broader national and state strategies. Some can compete on their unique environmental attributes, others on festivals and events. Those close to major urban centres or tourist gateways have an advantage in terms of accessibility, but more remote wine regions can stress cultural authenticity, peace and quiet. A few will be able to brand their identity internationally, based on quality and exports.

THE NEED FOR LOCAL PLANNING

The success of a vibrant wine tourism industry depends on the availability and quality of land suitable for viticulture. Thus a key strategy is to initiate local planning policies which minimize the potential for conflict between viticulture and other land uses and ensure the preservation of prime quality viticultural land and adequacy of water resources. This security of resource protection underpins the successful development of the wine tourism industry in the state because the long-term viability of the wine tourism industry ultimately depends on maintaining the integrity of wine regions. This in turn provides the basis for quality visitor experiences and hence the potential regional benefits generated through wine tourism.

CRITICAL SUCCESS FACTORS

A number of critical success factors have been identified by research involving the industry in both Washington State, USA, and in Australia (Getz *et al.*, forthcoming). They include a range of generic factors which will influence wine tourism development in the future. The factors considered to be the most important in regard to the future success of wine tourism include the quality of the product, the nature of the experience, winery appeal, effective marketing and co-ordinated development. In addition there is a need for more research to be undertaken on all aspects of the industry.

The quality of the product

The foundation of wine tourism was judged to be quality – of the wine, of the wine region experience, the regional cuisine and of service provided to visitors. Poor wine, and unknown wine, will not attract very many tourists. The image and reputation of wines and wine regions must be earned, then effectively communicated. Visitors must receive high-quality service and enjoy their experience in order to ensure good reputation and repeat visits.

The nature of the experience

Understanding the motives and benefits sought by wine tourists is a critical success factor. While a great deal more consumer research on this key issue is needed, the industry professionals are undoubtedly well placed to know a lot about what is attracting their clientele.

In addition to the essential ingredient of good wine, wine country experiences require quality dining opportunities and other attributes to create a unique experience and ambience, especially for short breaks. These can include a variety of cultural opportunities, especially festivals and events. The Australians also highly valued preservation of architecture and heritage as part of the wine country product.

Winery appeal

Respondents believed that visitors come primarily for the wine – to taste before buying, to find unique offers and to learn about the process and the region (Table 4.3). Meeting owners and winemakers is part of the appeal, but friendly and knowledgeable staff are thought to be absolutely essential to satisfy the customer. Attractive, well-designed wineries are important, but with regard to its features, the Australians were much more certain that having a café was necessary. Good sign posting was important to both samples, but special events/functions appealed more to the Washington group.

Research by Dodd (1995) confirms the importance of friendly staff and good service, particularly with regard to influencing wine purchases at wineries. He emphasizes the role of wineries in educating wine consumers and influencing word of mouth communications that could lead to future decisions to visit.

Effective marketing

Strong tourism marketing is essential to fostering wine tourism. Critical marketing efforts will include joint marketing efforts involving wine and tourism industries, focused target marketing and communications, branding and image-enhancement, and packaging. Much of the necessary marketing effort can be thought of as positioning, that is, shaping the mental image of potential wine tourists regarding the attractions and benefits of visits to wine regions.

Table 4.3 The appeal of wineries in Australia and the USA.[1] *Source*: Getz *et al.*, forthcoming

The attractions of wineries	Australia (%)	USA (%)
Quality wine/taste before purchase/special offers	30.9	31.3
Ambience/mystique	19.1	2.5
The winery/setting	19.1	–
Talking with (or meeting) owners or winemakers	16.2	6.3
Total winery experience	10.3	8.8
Knowledgeable cellar door staff	4.4	3.8
Education/to learn	–	16.3
Staff/friendly reception	–	7.6
Tours	–	3.8
Reputation/brand	–	3.8

Note: 1. The samples consisted of participants at the First Australian Wine Tourism Conference, held in Margaret River in 1998, and participants in a wine tourism seminar (the first of its kind) held in the Tri-Cities of Washington State's Columbia Valley appellation in 1998.

Co-ordinated development

Co-operation between the tourism and wine industry bodies is needed as effective co-ordination is a prerequisite to wine tourism progress. Key developmental factors include staff training for wine knowledge and service quality; achieving a critical mass of wineries, attractions and services; effective sign posting and interesting wine tourism trails; wine country tours; and a programme of special events. Leadership is also an important issue and may come from wineries, industry associations or government agencies. Americans and Australians have different perspectives on the roles of government. Americans are primarily concerned with reforming government regulations which they believe hinder their business and wine tourism in general whereas Australians look to government more for planning, funding and taxation reform.

The need for research

Wine tourism can create many benefits, however, on both national and regional scales, and has the potential to give a strong competitive advantage to regions with a grape and wine industry, and to generate profitable business for wineries, other wine-related products and for visitor services (Getz, 1999). As stated by Carlsen and Dowling (1999, p. 12) 'wine tourism is a field that is ripe for research and it is hoped that a bunch of researchers can network via the grapevine to harvest a vintage crop of information, thereby acquiring a taste for wine tourism research and enjoy the fruits of their labour.'

Finally, Getz *et al.* (forthcoming) argue that ultimately the consumer decides what is important. Knowing what the industry thinks is useful, but future research must determine what correlation, if any, exists between consumer and industry opinions. They suggest that success stories of regions, tour companies and wineries should be evaluated as to critical factors influencing wine tourism. Suppliers, organizers and consumers all shape the wine tourism system, but their interactions are only beginning to be probed.

CASE STUDY – WINE TOURISM IN WESTERN AUSTRALIA

In 1998 Western Australia attracted 579,000 international visitors, approximately 13 per cent of Australia's total, and they came mainly from Asia and Europe (WA Tourism Commission, 1999). The international visitors came mainly to visit Perth and the south-western part of the state and their preferred activities were shopping, dining out and visiting friends and relatives. WA also had about the same number of interstate visitors (from other parts of Australia) and over 6 million intrastate visitors (from within the state). In 1997 tourism contributed 3.9 per cent to WA's Gross State Product, generated approximately $2 billion of tourism expenditure and employed approximately 75,000 people or 8.5 per cent of the state's workforce. The state's key products are its nature-based tourism and the two emerging sectors of cultural (Aboriginal) tourism and wine tourism

Western Australia is recognized as possessing world-class wines and wine tourism regions. It attracts dedicated, high-yield wine tourists who travel to the state specifically because of the quality wines, as well as other cultural tourists who seek the unique blend of wine, food, lifestyle and natural attractions. Wine tourism has an important place in establishing the desired image and branding of WA, and is given prominence in promotion of the main wine regions.

The Western Australian Tourism Commission (WATC) and the Wine Industry Association of Western Australia (WIA) have developed the strategy in order to maximize the tourism potential of the Western Australian wine industry. The strategy complements, supports and is integrated with the overall directions of several other industry strategies (Table 4.4). Key goals of the strategy are to raise the awareness and understanding of the value-added benefit of tourism to the wine industry; establish an industry standard for wine tourism outlets and facilities; increase the skill level of employees in the wine tourism industry; foster the links between wine, food and the Australian lifestyle; and identify the impediments to the development of wine tourism in Western Australia and devise strategies to overcome them.

The vision for the development of wine tourism in the state is that, by 2005, Western Australia will be universally recognized as a world premier wine tourism

Table 4.4 Wine and tourism strategies in Australia and Western Australia. *Source*: Dowling *et al.*, 1999

Level	Wine	Tourism	Wine Tourism
National	Strategy 2025 – the Australian Wine Industry (1996)	Tourism – Australia's Passport to Growth	National Wine Tourism Strategy (1999)
State	Western Australian Wine Industry Strategic Plan (1997)	Western Australian Tourism Development Strategy (1997)	Draft Western Australian Wine Tourism Strategy (1999)

destination, based on the reputation of its wine-producing regions, the quality of its wines and their synergy with lifestyle, cuisine, environment and climate.

For the Western Australian wine tourism industry to grow and mature into an internationally recognized premier wine tourism destination, the government and industry should foster a symbiotic partnership to capitalize on, and further develop, a number of competitive advantages. According to the Western Australian Wine Industry Association these include the state's climate, land available for expansion and premium wines. In addition they encompass the state's growing reputation as an exciting tourism destination which is of extremely high quality and diversity. Together the two industries have a unique opportunity to deliver considerable benefits to the state through the increased development of the wine and tourism industries, especially in wine regions.

This can be achieved through building awareness and understanding through the development of a wine tourism culture; establishing industry standards; establishing training and development as well as education; establishing food, hospitality and lifestyle links; fostering integrated regional planning; infrastructure development; creative marketing and promotion; implementing research; the co-ordination of government, tourism and the wine industry; and by establishing wine and tourism links.

Key developmental strategies

There is an opportunity to capitalize on WA's 'unique selling propositions' of the imagery of Margaret River as the state's best-known wine region; the quality of Western Australian wines; and the idyll of WA lifestyle. One of the key strategies is effective co-ordination of the development process through the establishment of a Wine Tourism Council which can represent all interested parties. The state has many different wine regions, each of a diverse nature and level of maturity in wine tourism. For these proposals to succeed it is essential that the strategy creates a structure for the development of promotion of the state as a whole, and the development of further, local 'Tourism Action Plans' for the wine-producing regions. These 'Action Plans' should address the specific local needs of the regions and produce strategies to address them, and develop an active local wine tourism industry. Amongst other issues they could consider are regional branding, regional promotion and access issues.

Individually the wine and tourism industries are well established in the state. There is an opportunity for them to combine their immense resources, skills and knowledge to develop a framework for developing wine tourism in the state. Education of both the wine and tourism industries is necessary to realize the potential of each industry, the value-adding they can have and to understand the constraints they are working under. Winemakers can use tourism as a means of selling their product and tour operators and accommodation providers need to be more knowledgeable about what wineries are trying to achieve.

There should be promotion and selling of regional wine tourism as a total experience, not just the promotion of wine. Recent studies indicate that the major attractions of wine regions are the quality wine, regional cuisine and the unique experience (Table 4.5). Furthermore, the development and expansion of tourism supply in less established wine regions is essential. Consistent wine and tourism experiences should be developed throughout the state through the establishment of a hallmark Wine Tourism Event, tour routes, signage and information and a centralized wine tourism information centre.

Table 4.5 The appeal of wine regions in Australia and the USA.[1] *Source*: Getz *et al.*, forthcoming

The attractions of a wine region	Australia (%)	USA (%)
Quality wine/regional cuisine/food/unavailable wine	32.4	18.8
Total experience/lifestyle/socializing/unique experience	41.2	10.1
Unique setting/environment/scenery/climate	13.2	10.1
Interaction with owners or winemakers	8.8	5.8
Reputation/ image of the area	4.4	1.5
Getaway/excuse for trip	–	7.2
Culture/cultural tourism	–	11.6
Learning/education/seeing the process/ talking about wine/see where it is made	–	18.8

Note: 1. The samples consisted of participants at the First Australian Wine Tourism Conference, held in Margaret River in 1998, and participants in a wine tourism seminar (the first of its kind) held in the Tri-Cities of Washington State's Columbia Valley appellation in 1998.

There is an opportunity to develop Western Australian food and wine as an integral part of the region's lifestyle experience. Food is a key component of wine tourism and the synergy and quality of the regional food and premium wine experience provide a competitive marketing advantage for the state. The food and wine industry should work with local tour operators to develop a food and wine touring package of the wine regions. This package should be promoted at domestic and international food and wine trade shows. Additionally, there should be exploration of the ways that the wine product can be sold and promoted through local restaurants. Emphasis could be placed on regional foods to complement regional wines.

There should be repositioning of the wine regions as lifestyle areas with natural food and wine produce being catalysts for increased wine tourism activity and visitation. Co-operative marketing amongst the food, wine and tourism industries to promote and develop the identity of the wine regions centring on lifestyle issues is crucial. This can be achieved by the development of a regional food and wine event in the regions to draw in domestic and international visitation.

There is a need to build on the existing skills base in wine tourism and provide educational and training opportunities throughout the state to raise the profile of the industry and improve the quality of knowledge, service levels and managerial ability within the industry. Research should be conducted into existing skills levels in the industry and skill demands for the future.

An extensive training needs analysis and a skills profiling exercise to be completed within the industry. Opportunities for career pathing and multi-skilling of employees across all parts of the wine tourism industry should be developed. A directory and database of wine tourism courses in the state should be developed and disseminated to industry. Courses need to be aimed at a wide range of operators including cellar door staff, accommodation providers and tourism organizations.

Accreditation of aspects of wine tourism provision would increase standards of service delivery, and improve customer confidence. Accreditation would provide industry and consumers with an assurance that an accredited product or service is backed by a commitment to best practice management and the provision of quality wine tourism experiences. The programme would provide benefits to wine tourism businesses, clients, regional tourism managers and local communities. The major benefit of this is that tourists have a recognized means of identifying bona fide wine tourism operators.

There is a need to establish consistent and effective signage, and a common statewide policy would facilitate visitation. A key development would be the publication of a comprehensive wine and touring guide (possibly in book format, or maybe a series of pamphlets including both a state overview with a number of regional guides). This would give a basic introduction to the wines, wine regions and touring options within Western Australia.

Developing and promoting a number of wine tourism packages should be a priority as it is a very cost-effective means to promote regions and generate new business. The key types of packages include those incorporating wine and food events, short breaks, pre- and post conventions, fly-drive, and other special interests such as nature tours and golf. Events can be focused on either a single winery or an entire region, but both bring wider benefits to the community. These events do not have to be solely wine-focused and linkages to food as the environment and the arts will produce positive outcomes.

The major goals are to be internationally recognized as a significant producer of quality wines and to be known as an accessible, affordable and world-class wine tourism destination. To achieve this goal, the WA Wine Tourism Council should be the lead organization in the development and marketing of wine tourism. For the state to be successful it needs to have in place the necessary infrastructure for developing wine tourism throughout the state's wine regions, including a critical mass of tourist-oriented wineries, visitor interpretive centres, wine routes, wine villages and wine-related events. Another goal is continuously to improve a full range of visitor services for wine tourism, including information, inbound and regional tour companies, educational and interpretive services, and related packages.

All of WA's wine regions and affiliated attractions and services should undertake co-operative marketing with other regions and states in order to ensure that the benefits of wine tourism accrue to wine and tourism industries, host communities and the regions. Wine tourism should remain a high-yield niche market, and should not generate the volume of visitors or scale and types of development that could threaten its sustainability.

CONCLUSIONS

The future of wine tourism looks bright. It is in a phase of growing recognition and consumer interest. Central to this continued evolution of the industry at the start of the third millennium are a number of key tasks. These include the close co-operation amongst all of the various sectors of the wine and tourism industries, hospitality and food services. Countries and states or provinces should establish major wine interpretation and visitor centres with direct linkages to smaller centres in the surrounding wine regions. Each region should implement a signage policy to ensure that wine routes are attractive to independent travellers. Each region is linked with the others, but tourists are encouraged to explore fully one at a time.

Wine events should form a major part of the calendar of regional and local celebrations. Cities near wine-growing regions could establish major centres of food and wine. Events concentrated in the shoulder seasons will bring in new visitors. Multi-site wine festivals encourage exploration of groups of wineries, while community-based festivals invite visitors into the regional towns and villages. Each wine region should be successfully positioned through at least one wine occasion as its 'hallmark' event, attracting publicity nationally, and in some cases internationally, to the region.

Enterprising wine regions will have sufficient accommodation, dining and information services to house wine tourists. Some of the regions will remain very rural with dispersed wineries. In these areas key sites will be designated as wine villages and the appropriate level and types of services will be concentrated in them. Wine village planning will proceed beyond the conceptual and basic services stages to incorporate heritage restoration and architectural design, streetscaping and landscaping. Success will be realized in developing related attractions and services in these villages.

Research will have been completed to define the country's, state's and/or region's wine tourist markets and segmentation studies to illustrate the range of wine tourists will have been carried out and will underpin the marketing effort. Some regions will be recognized internationally as ones of high quality and will attract high-yield wine tourist visitors. As planning progresses, the targeting and attainment of specific benefits will become more refined and effective. Some regions will stress employment creation, others the development of new infrastructure.

Finally, wine tourism planning and management committees will have been established in each region, bringing together local authorities, industry associations and the interested public. Impact studies will have been completed and periodic visitor surveys and analysis will be undertaken regularly. Communities and regions will have taken ownership of the wine tourism planning and management process.

ACKNOWLEDGEMENTS

We wish to acknowledge the information obtained from the WA Draft Wine Tourism Strategy which was prepared by the authors in collaboration with Jane Ali-Knight, Jack Carlsen and Steve Charters of Edith Cowan University for the Western Australian Tourism Commission and the Wine Industry Association of WA.

REFERENCES

Australian Bureau of Statistics (1996) *1995 Australian Wine and Grape Industry Compendium*. Cat. 1329.0. Canberra: Australian Bureau of Statistics.
Australian Wine Foundation (1996) *Strategy 2025: The Australian Wine Industry*. Adelaide: Winemakers Federation of Australia.

Cambourne, B. (1999) 'Wine tourism in the Canberra district'. In R. K. Dowling and J. Carlsen (eds)
    Wine Tourism: Perfect Partners. Proceedings of the First Australian Wine Tourism Conference,
    held at Margaret River, WA, 7–9 May 1998. Canberra: Bureau of Tourism Research, pp. 171–83.
Carlsen, J. and Dowling, R. K. (1999) 'Acquiring a taste for wine tourism research'. In J. Molloy and
    J. Davies (eds) *Tourism and Hospitality: Delighting the Senses 1999*, Part Two. Proceedings of
    the Ninth Australian University Tourism and Hospitality Research Conference, Adelaide,
    Australia, 10–13 February. Canberra: Bureau of Tourism Research: 100–8.
Carlsen, J., Getz, D. and Dowling, R. K. (1999) 'The wine tourism industry'. In R. K. Dowling and J.
    Carlsen (eds) *Wine Tourism: Perfect Partners*. Proceedings of the First Australian Wine Tourism
    Conference, held at Margaret River, WA, 7–9 May 1998. Canberra: Bureau of Tourism Research,
    pp. 267–76.
Choisy, C. (1996) 'Les points du tourisme viti-vinicole'. *Espaces*, **140**, 30–3.
Commonwealth Department of Tourism (1993) *Tourism – Australia's Passport to Growth: A
    National Tourism Strategy*. Implementation Report No. 1, December. Canberra: Commonwealth
    Department of Tourism.
Dodd, T. (1995) 'Opportunities and pitfalls of tourism in a developing wine industry'. *International
    Journal of Wine Marketing*, **7**(1), 5–16.
Dodd, T. and Bigotte, V. (1997) 'Perceptual differences among visitor groups to wineries'. *Journal of
    Travel Research*, **35**(3), 46–51.
Dowling, R. K. and Carlsen, J. (eds) (1999) *Wine Tourism: Perfect Partners*. Proceedings of the
    First Australian Wine Tourism Conference, held at Margaret River, WA, 7–9 May 1998. Canberra:
    Bureau of Tourism Research.
Dowling, R. K., Carlsen, J., Charters, S., Ali-Knight, J. and Getz, D. (1999) *Draft Western Australian
    Wine Tourism Strategy*. Report for the Western Australian Tourism Commission and the Wine
    Industry Association of WA. Perth: School of Marketing, Tourism and Leisure, Edith Cowan
    University.
Getz, D. (1999) 'Wine tourism: global overview and perspectives on its development'. In R. K.
    Dowling and J. Carlsen (eds) *Wine Tourism: Perfect Partners*. Proceedings of the First
    Australian Wine Tourism Conference, held at Margaret River, WA, 7–9 May 1998. Canberra:
    Bureau of Tourism Research, pp. 13–33.
Getz, D., Dowling, R. K., Carlsen, J. and Anderson, D. (forthcoming) 'Critical success factors for
    wine tourism'. *International Journal of Wine Marketing*.
Global Tourism and Leisure (1998) *Draft National Wine Tourism Strategy*. Sydney: Global Tourism
    and Leisure.
Hall, C. M. and Johnson, G. (1999) 'Wine and tourism: an imbalanced partnership?' In R. K. Dowling
    and J. Carlsen (eds) *Wine Tourism: Perfect Partners*. Proceedings of the First Australian Wine
    Tourism Conference, held at Margaret River, WA, 7–9 May 1998. Canberra: Bureau of Tourism
    Research, pp. 51–71.
Hall, C. M. and Macionis, N. (1998) 'Wine tourism in Australia and New Zealand'. In R. Butler, M.
    Hall and J. Jenkins (eds) *Tourism and Recreation in Rural Areas*. Chichester: Wiley,
    pp. 197–224.
Howley, M. and van Westering, J. (1999) 'Wine tourism in the United Kingdom'. In R. K. Dowling and
    J. Carlsen (eds) *Wine Tourism: Perfect Partners*. Proceedings of the First Australian Wine
    Tourism Conference, held at Margaret River, WA, 7–9 May 1998. Canberra: Bureau of Tourism
    Research, pp. 73–80.
Kennedy, F. (1998) 'Vignerons sniff out the tourist appeal'. *The Australian*, 13 May.
King, C. and Morris, R. (1999) 'Wine tourism: costs and returns'. In R. K. Dowling and J. Carlsen
    (eds) *Wine Tourism: Perfect Partners*. Proceedings of the First Australian Wine Tourism
    Conference, held at Margaret River, WA, 7–9 May 1998. Canberra: Bureau of Tourism Research,
    pp. 233–47.
Reilly, A. (1996) 'A marketing approach for small winemakers in regional areas'. Unpublished thesis,
    Master of Business Administration, University of Adelaide.

Robins, P. (1999) 'Potential research into wine tourism'. In R. K. Dowling and J. Carlsen (eds) *Wine Tourism: Perfect Partners*. Proceedings of the First Australian Wine Tourism Conference, held at Margaret River, WA, 7–9 May 1998. Canberra: Bureau of Tourism Research, pp. 81–96.

Shapiro, L. (1998) 'A glass half empty'. *Newsweek*, 5 October, pp. 74–6.

Shelmerdine, S. (1999) 'The Victorian Wineries Tourism Council'. In R. K. Dowling and J. Carlsen (eds) *Wine Tourism: Perfect Partners*. Proceedings of the First Australian Wine Tourism Conference, held at Margaret River, WA, 7–9 May 1998. Canberra: Bureau of Tourism Research, pp. 159–61.

South Australian Tourism Commission (1997) *Wine and Tourism: A Background Research Report*. Adelaide: SATC.

WA Tourism Commission (1999) *Research Brief on Tourism, April 1999*. Perth: WATC.

Winemakers' Federation of Australia Inc. (1998) *National Wine Tourism Strategy Green Paper (Draft)*. Magill Adelaide: WFA.

CHAPTER 5

Short Break Markets – from Product Positioning to a Value-Based Approach

David Edgar

> The rise of the Short Break market has been one of the most dramatic changes in tourism since the advent of paid holidays and is widely seen as the salvation of domestic tourism. (Beioley, 1999)

This chapter explores the changing nature of short break holidays. The discussion draws on a range of published sources to provide an indication of the characteristics and changing nature of demand as well as using primary research to explore supply-side issues and determine the changing nature of the competitive dynamics.

The primary data was gathered from three phases of research and represents a longitudinal study into the competitive dimensions of supply in short break markets. Since 1991, leading hotel companies have been sampled to determine their perspectives of the nature of the short break market and their competitive actions, both current and future. This chapter implicitly draws upon the wealth of knowledge to provide the reader with an alternative perspective to that of the popularized demand studies, for understanding the dynamics of the short break market.

DEFINING SHORT BREAKS

Despite the fact that the short break phenomenon is not new, and not restricted to the UK (Loverseed, 1992; Cockerell, 1989; Potier and Cockerell, 1992), there is still no standardized definition for short break, short holiday, short holiday break, short break holiday or bargain break. What can be stated with some confidence is that a short break is essentially characterized by two key elements:

(i) the duration of stay (Lohmann, 1991) and (ii) the form of accommodation used (BTA, 1989a).

Since the 1940s short holidays have been termed 'trips of up to three nights away from home, primarily for holiday purposes' (Beioley, 1991). While this duration of stay is the most commonly accepted for defining short break holidays (BTA, 1989a; UKTS, 1991; Law, 1990, 1991a; Beioley, 1991; Bailey, 1989; Davies, 1990), a more current stream of thinking is that short breaks are actually characterized by duration of stay of one to four or five nights (Schidhauser, 1992; MEW Research, 1994; Beioley, 1999).

These new definitions of short break holidays, while adding to the incomparability of data sources, do not fully establish why definitions have changed and may in effect represent the changing nature of the short break market from an off-peak market to a recognized market in its own right. As most secondary data is in the one- to three-night format, and considering the supply-side nature of the research, it is deemed that the duration of stay adopted for definition purposes should be 'stays of one to three nights duration'.

The vast majority of short holidays utilize friends' and relatives' (VFR) lodging for accommodation; however, the revenue value of this supply sector is minimal when compared to commercial accommodation. This difference in type of accommodation, i.e. commercial or non-commercial, forms the essential difference between the short holiday and the short break. Short holidays are commonly referred to as all holidays of duration one to three nights (BTA, 1989; Beioley, 1991, 1999; Bailey, 1989; Edgar, 1998; Edgar and Halcro, 1998) in all types of accommodation, while short breaks are referred to as holidays of one to three nights taken in commercial accommodation. Some definitions specify the type of accommodation as hotels (MSI, 1991; Davies, 1990), hotels and guest houses (Euromonitor, 1989) or simply paid-for accommodation (Bailey, 1989; Beioley, 1991; MEW Research, 1994).

Definitions of short breaks or short break holidays therefore vary considerably from study to study, but any such analysis requires a clarity of definition to establish the exact parameters being examined either by location, time period, form of accommodation or product offering. This chapter uses sources of information encompassing a range of short break and short holiday definitions to provide background information from limited secondary data sources. The definition of a short break adopted for the purposes of this chapter is one that specifies accommodation type and time period.

This chapter therefore defines short breaks as *stays of one to three nights in commercial accommodation which for a single price together with accommodation include one or more of the following: meals; transport; entertainment; or a programme of activities.*

The evolution of short breaks

Having determined what a short break is it is useful to explore the evolution of short breaks before clarifying the specific characteristics. Understanding the evolution from both supply- and demand-side perspectives exposes the underlying logic of the market development and its resulting competitive dynamics.

Short breaks are often referred to as though they were a recent invention but in fact the phenomenon is not new. The concept was first introduced more than 30 years ago as a basic weekend package and has now evolved into a substantial market segment (particularly in Scotland). The growth of short breaks has been made possible by underlying socio-economic changes and stimulated by the way in which the tourism industry has adapted and developed the product. Therefore to appreciate fully the nature of this market an examination of the evolution of short breaks requires investigation of developments from both supply and demand perspectives.

The supply-side perspective

During the 1980s the short break sector of the UK holiday market experienced considerable expansion due to the market entry of a number of major players (Loverseed, 1992). Indeed, fifteen companies accounted for approximately 90 per cent of the total packaged short break supply in 1991 (MSI, 1991). With the fall in business travel induced by recessionary trends, many hotels looked towards leisure markets for custom. The result has been a short break concept, devolved from off-peak marketing efforts of hotel groups and associated intermediaries during the 1960s. During such periods of low demand, when premium rates for accommodation and service could not be achieved (BTA, 1989b) a philosophy was adopted that any room sold during off-peak periods was contributing to fixed costs, and with the importance of marginal pricing to boost occupancy, profitability could be enhanced (Hanks *et al.*, 1992).

As the market matured in the mid-1970s, the off-peak concept developed into a market in its own right, with accommodation providers, and intermediaries developing more sophisticated approaches to attracting market share. Indeed, in 1974 the English Tourist Board introduced its innovative and long-running 'Let's Go' campaign, designed to increase weekend occupancies in hotels and stimulate the short break market and by the late 1970s the same body was spending £750,000 a year on this campaign, with around 1000 hotels participating.

Companies actively attempted to compensate for low season trade by offering short breaks effectively to extend their operating week and seasons. Additional companies were formed serving specific elements of the short break concept, Superbreaks and Goldenrail, for example, providing booking, distribution and transport.

These developments continued throughout the 1970s and into the latter 1980s, when it became evident that a combination of economic boom, international crisis and the tendency to holiday two or three times a year, had resulted in major growth in the UK short break market, which by the end of 1989 accounted for around 90 per cent of the UK holiday demand of UK Hotels plc (Slattery and Johnson, 1991).

Suppliers were putting more effort into differentiating their product, seeking new markets and deliberately altering the off-peak image associated with short breaks (Greer, 1991). In addition, suppliers from other sectors of commercial accommodation began to exploit the emerging market opportunities. Center Parcs broke new ground in the late 1980s by bringing short breaks into the self-catering sector, and by the early 1990s the rest of the accommodation sector, including the cottage holiday groups, had followed suit.

As the market further matured so too did the means of marketing and distributing the concept. Thus suppliers have not only extended the variety and season of short breaks but have also increased the spread of market level and location, using a greater variety of distribution channels to raise awareness, and causing the emergence of new primary locations such as London, Manchester and Edinburgh, essentially utilizing the variety of activities available within major cities. Hence, while the long-haul markets have remained buoyant, the short break city market has also weathered the recession (Demetriadi, 1992).

The demand-side perspective

As the supply of short breaks is essentially related to monetary costs and fluctuation in utility rates, i.e. seasonality, it follows that demand for short breaks is determined by price, income and leisure time available. Research by Edgar and Nisbet (1997) highlighted close correlations between various socio-economic indicators and the growth and development of short breaks.

Such relationships are also highlighted by Beioley (1999), who supports these key areas by claiming that:

> Short holidays were clearly not an option for many when disposable incomes were low, the majority of people had two weeks' paid holiday and a 5 day week was the norm. Rising disposable income, increased paid holidays and more flexibility about when and how holidays could be taken have all helped fuel the demand for short holidays. Mass car ownership has made it easier to reach a greater variety of destinations, whilst increasing geographical mobility has meant more trips to keep in touch with friends and family. In the new work-driven, two-earner households of the 90s, getting away for a family break is seen as a reward for hard work and a way of creating time to be with each other.

It would therefore appear that the greater availability of disposable income among certain sectors of the population, the increase in leisure time and the experience of package holidays abroad and in the UK (Ryan, 1989; Tourism Intelligence Quarterly, 1991; Travel GBI, 1990c), combined with the need and desire to holiday more than once a year, has led to a group that is willing and able to try new holiday markets. This, combined with the tourism industry's willingness to capitalize on these changes by providing new products and increased availability of short breaks in number, variety and perceived quality, would make it reasonable to assume that the customers' knowledge would increase through experience, fuelling maturation of the short break market as consumers become more aware of alternatives, holiday more frequently and demand new, value-for-money experiences. Such developments have ensured a demand for short breaks into the 1990s and are in effect helping to shape the breaks of the future.

Such demand and supply developments act as a reference point only, as many different segments develop at different rates and in different ways, some demand-led, other supply-oriented. Whichever is the case, the size and value of the short break market is undisputed, with the gradual evolution of a short break concept away from the traditional off-peak image and representing a market in its own right.

GROWTH AND VALUE OF SHORT BREAKS

In reviewing growth, it is necessary to set the short break market within its industrial context, that is, its contribution to tourism as a whole, before exploring the specific nature of short break growth and value.

In 1997 the British took around 37 million short holidays in the UK, representing 54 per cent of all holiday nights taken by duration, with a total spend of £3,100m. Short holidays now outnumber long holidays and, as shown in Figure 5.1, represent the greatest growth sector since 1989, outperforming holiday tourism as a whole.

Clearly, from Figure 5.1 short breaks represent a market in their own right and can now be viewed as the norm for domestic UK tourism and not the exception. In this respect it is useful to profile the growth of short breaks and offer explanations for such growth.

Key factors influencing the growth of short breaks up to 1999

The short break market has been widely recognized as the fastest growth market in the UK (Beioley, 1991, 1999; Bailey, 1989; Davies, 1990; Teare, 1989; BTA, 1990b; Demetriadi, 1992; Middleton, 1991), in Europe (Potier and Cockerell, 1992; EIU, 1992a; Law, 1991b) and in North America (Loverseed, 1992).

Figure 5.2 has been compiled using figures from the British Travel Survey from 1980 to 1989, and then following on with figures from the UKTS from 1989 to 1997.

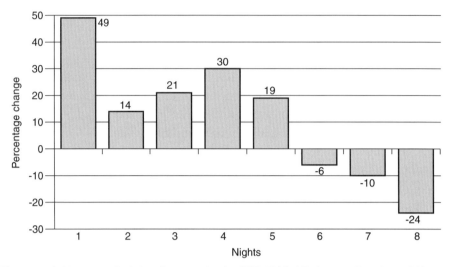

Figure 5.1 Change in holiday duration in the UK, 1989–97. *Source*: Beioley, 1999

The figure shows the growth of the UK short break market in terms of trips and nights.

It can be seen that the growth of the short break market in the UK has been consistent, reflecting patterns of boom and recession in the economy, often in an inverse manner. While the market may appear a little unsettled, if one considers the growth in spending as shown in Figure 5.3 it can be seen that the value of short breaks has grown steadily year on year even when volumes have fluctuated, essentially representing an acceptance of short breaks as a market in their own right and posing a major opportunity for short break suppliers and tourism destination managers.

The growth in value terms of this market is clearly evident. Such growth surely emphasizes the importance of the short break market to commercial accommodation providers, particularly if one considers the commercial accommodation providers' share of short break spend, and hotels' share of commercial accommodation spend.

While the growth in volume and value of short breaks in the UK is clearly evident, the nature of that growth is to a great extent hidden and unclear. By adding the dimension of long holidays, the other element of holiday tourism, some interesting conclusions can be drawn.

While short holidays indicated a decline in growth during certain periods of economic activity, long holidays also reflect decline in growth. This indicates that the total domestic holiday market had been in a state of decline, probably due to the boom in package holidays abroad (Ryan, 1989, 1991; Quiroga, 1990; Pearce, 1987) and the economic climate of the time. However, when the spending per trip and per night are

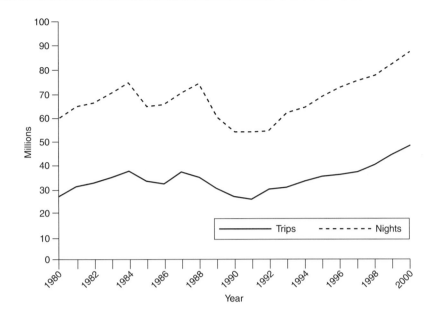

Figure 5.2 Growth of the UK short holiday market, 1980–2000. *Source*: UKTS and BTS

Note: e = estimates based on recent growth rate.

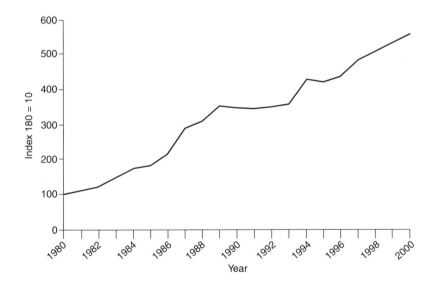

Figure 5.3 Growth in the spending of the UK short holiday market, 1980–2000. *Source*: UKTS and BTS

Note: e = estimates based on recent growth rate.

analysed, the considerable growth in spending indicated by the short break market has in essence been at the expense of the long holiday market and in fact does not represent organic growth but a shift in market share. This would appear to indicate that the short break market in the UK is growing in a mature holiday market through growth in market share, implying that operators in the market will essentially be subject to conditions that reflect a high degree of monopolistic competition (Chamberlin, 1962).

As no research has been undertaken into the nature of short break provision, this is an area that warrants further investigation to highlight implications upon the nature of competition and strategic activity within the UK short break market. As growth in the short break market has been at the expense of other market segments, to gain such growth and appeal to a range of consumers the market has developed a wide range of market segments. In this respect it is useful to explore further the demand for short breaks.

THE CHANGING NATURE OF DEMAND

The macroperspective of domestic short breaks in the UK

To examine the nature of the domestic short break market, this section looks at how the holiday is organized, what accommodation is used, what mode of transport is used, locations and geographic spread and seasonality (Beioley, 1999).

Most short breaks in the UK are DIY holidays, organized by the participants. In 1997, only 19 per cent booked their holiday through an intermediary such as a tour operator or travel agent and only 7 per cent were on an inclusive trip. Short breaks are more than twice as likely to be spent in some form of serviced accommodation as opposed to self-catering, with just over half (53 per cent) spent in hotels. Despite the dominance of the serviced sector, not all short breaks are spent in hotels. Short breaks are now an important sector of the market for many self-catering operators such as Center Parcs.

The pattern for short holidays is almost identical to that for holidays as a whole. The car is the dominant means of travel. Some form of public transport is used on 15 per cent of short breaks (trains account for 5 per cent of trips). This may be explained by the fact that many domestic short break programmes offer inclusive rail or coach travel. Short breaks are often seen as located either in major cities, historic towns or the countryside; however, one in three takes place at the seaside, representing a shift in dependence from such a destination for long holidays to short breaks. London and other major cities are important destinations for the packaged short break, accounting for a third of trips.

England accounts for 82 per cent of all short holidays in the UK and takes a slightly larger share of short holidays than holidays as a whole. This no doubt reflects the fact that people tend to venture less far on short breaks. These characteristics have major implications upon the nature of destination management into the twenty-first century.

Short holidays are more evenly spread throughout the year than long holidays and short breaks in particular show a tendency to peak in spring and autumn, although this is not as pronounced as one might expect. Indeed, the pattern from month to month is relatively consistent and provides suppliers with a less complex forecasting exercise as well as a baseline for business and portfolio development. Having determined the macroperspective of domestic short breaks it is useful to examine the nature of short breaks overseas, especially as this is an area for major development into the twenty-first century.

The macroperspective of international short breaks taken by UK travellers

Short breaks abroad have different characteristics from domestic breaks, reflecting the greater travel requirements and sociocultural differences.

There appears to be a much stronger reliance on the travel trade and other intermediaries for organization of overseas breaks. Sixty-two per cent of trips make use of some form of intermediary, resulting in a higher proportion of packaged short breaks (40 per cent sold as inclusive tours) and 93 per cent of breaks being taken in serviced accommodation. There is also a much stronger reliance on public transport, with two-thirds of short break takers using a sea crossing or the Channel Tunnel.

In terms of destination, France is the dominant destination accounting for 55 per cent of all short breaks in 1997, with Benelux accounting for a further 25 per cent. Only a minority of tourists travel further afield, although the trends are that as destinations widen and transport links improve this will change.

Cities and towns are the main destinations, comprising 80 per cent of trips, and city breaks are the main product in the packaged sector. Indeed, Paris and Amsterdam alone are estimated to account for 50 per cent of the city breaks market. However, Disneyland Paris has also established itself as a strong destination in the outbound market and is attracting ever-increasing numbers of visitors to its various forms of accommodation.

The microperspective of the short break taker

Around 60 per cent of the UK population took short breaks between 1989 and 1997, with around 20 per cent taking a break overseas (UKTS, 1998). Of the 60 per cent of short break takers, 18 per cent indicated that they are regular short break takers in the UK, with 32 per cent taking breaks from time to time and 10 per cent as a one-off event. Examining the socio-economic profile and the propensity to take short breaks, it is evident that short break takers are most likely to be drawn from the middle age groups (25–54 age group) and are more upmarket.

Having profiled the demographic and social nature of short break takers, it is useful to focus on the psychological aspects of taking short breaks, in particular the motives and expectations of the short break taker.

Table 5.1 highlights motivations for taking short breaks. From this it is evident that motivations for taking short breaks are clearly related to the changing nature of society and work with the main reason being an opportunity to relax or unwind from the day-to-day pressures of work or family commitments. Short breaks act as a sort of 'antidote to the pressures of modern living' (Beioley, 1999). This has implications for the future, especially in terms of how society and work may change in the twenty-first century. More working from home and mobility of work, for example, may mean a greater need to escape the home environment as well as the traditional work environment, which when combined with improved transport technology and the emerging power of e-commerce could mean more spontaneous longer-distance, greater-frequency breaks.

Other motivations for taking short breaks can be seen to be both related to quality of life and driven by emotion or special events. These are:

Table 5.1 Short break motivations. *Source*: Beioley, 1999

Attitudes to UK short breaks

'Which if any of these statements do you agree with?'	
Short breaks are good for:	%
Relaxing, treating myself	41
Visiting different parts of the UK	30
Visiting specific places	22
Specific occasions	16
Special events	14
Trying out new activities	9
Reasons for choosing short break	
Pursue special interest or hobby	13
Accommodation has good reputation for food	12
Good deals from big hotels	10
Go away without children	10
Health, fitness, sporting facilities	5

Note: Cross-section of British adults. Based on responses from 18 per cent who regularly take UK short breaks.

- They provide an opportunity to get out and about and appreciate the UK.
- A special anniversary or event will often provide the catalyst for a short break.
- Activity-related breaks form a small part of the total but are clearly important in stimulating some breaks.

Previous research and industry views support these findings. As such, it is clear that the development of short breaks has a close correlation with not only the changing nature of society but also of customers' values.

The changing consumers' value system for short breaks

To conclude the discussion of the nature of short break demand it is useful to introduce a qualitative dimension which represents the value system of the nature of demand. This is done with two key approaches, the transaction life cycle and the value system.

Figure 5.4 shows the transaction life cycle for short breaks. It can be seen that as breaks were introduced and formalized in the 1980s, they reflected packaged accommodation, with travel and a one-stop shop essentially geared towards educating the consumer. This phase can be seen as the system-buy phase. As buyers become more experienced they need less support in the purchase procedure and systems and seek more value and choice in the selection of breaks. This causes the competition to reduce differentiation and focus on one or two key areas, resulting in a product-buy from hotels focusing on a range of targeted packages and service-buy from the range of support services offered by the intermediaries such as Superbreaks.

As the short break concept developed further, differentiation was further reduced to allow management of the concepts. This developed briefly and evolved in the form of organizations creating short break brands, resulting in short breaks becoming a commodity-buy. In the 1990s, following patterns of consumer demand for flexibility and variety, organizations raised levels of differentiation essentially as a reaction to

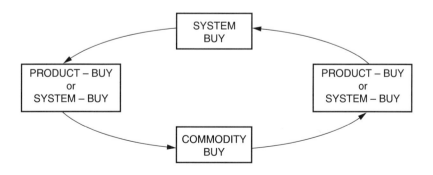

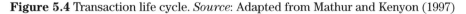

Figure 5.4 Transaction life cycle. *Source*: Adapted from Mathur and Kenyon (1997)

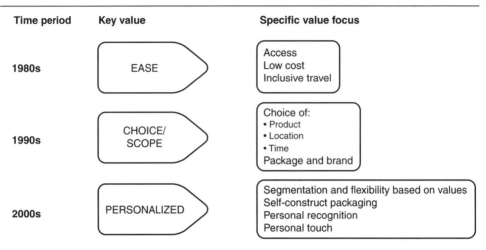

Figure 5.5 Value system of consumers

commodization and to develop themes and packages within the various brands while using Information Technology to help manage the complexity of packages (Crichton and Edgar, 1995).

In the later 1990s and undoubtedly into the next century, decommodization will continue to result in the product and service buyer perspective again. However, in the future, the impact of the Internet will be phenomenal. The system will speed up the transaction life cycle and will result in two streams of business in the future, the product stream and the service stream. These streams are likely to widen in their contribution and activities and may result in clear distinctions between the providers and service distributors.

In respect to the former developments it is useful to understand the value system of the consumer. Figure 5.5 shows the changing values of the consumer since the 1980s. From this figure it can be seen that, while the transaction cycle increases in speed and diversity, the values focus of the consumer shifts from ease and scope to personalized and flexibility as values of the break concept. How these are delivered is discussed after the supply perspective where the competitive dynamics are discussed.

THE CHANGING NATURE OF SUPPLY AND COMPETITION

The cost structure of hotels means that, like airlines, marginal pricing can be an important strategy to boost occupancy and increase profitability. Because hotels, being property-based businesses, have high levels of fixed to variable costs, marginal changes in occupancy may produce significant differences in profitability. This explains significant levels of discounting at certain times where occupancy may be low. Increased profitability may be gained from a contribution to fixed costs which would otherwise be lost, or by encouraging the lower-rated customer to increase consumption of supplementary hotel services such as meals, or by a combination of these two factors.

Low occupancy may be related to the location of particular units, meaning that hotels in resorts would need to fill certain months that were off-peak, while city centre hotels may need to fill beds during weekends. This differing seasonality results in a wider spread of available seasons for short breaks, as well as providing a higher standard of accommodation, especially in city centre locations. In addition, it gives rise to the concept of opportunity cost whereby developing in one market the operator must forsake another; these costs must be carefully considered, and the factors of production (land, labour and capital) correctly balanced for the selected market.

This reflects the logical progression of short breaks from a supply perspective. From a demand-oriented approach, short breaks are a logical progression in that they allow a marketing emphasis, identifying major price and activity segment differences, and forming a means of further segmenting and branding hospitality and tourism markets.

From both supply and demand approaches, the basic resource, a hotel, its services, location and tourism attractions conferred upon it are the same. What may change are the design and timing of the breaks, and the marketing methods used. To appreciate fully the nature of the short break market requires an understanding of the evolution of short breaks, an appreciation of the value, volume and growth of the market, and a model of industry structure, laying foundations for a structural analysis of the market relative to hotel groups.

The changing nature of the short break supply chain

The majority of the 17.6 million short breaks in the UK are self-organized, non-packaged and booked directly by the consumer. The sheer size of the market means that almost every accommodation operator is involved to some extent or other and destination brochures and the travel sections of newspapers are full of short break offers every week, largely from independents. A relatively small proportion of domestic breaks (UKTS suggests one in five) are booked through intermediaries such as travel agents, tour operators or the main commercial short break programmes.

To understand the changing nature of short break supply it is useful to understand how the short break supply chain is structured and how it may change in the twenty-first century. Figure 5.6 shows the supply chain for short breaks. The chain is composed of four key components, the consumer, distributor, producer and customer service/relations.

Table 5.2 has been constructed to show the changing nature of supply at each stage of the supply chain. From this it can be seen that the nature of short break

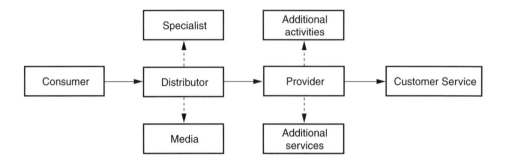

Figure 5.6 Short break supply chain

Table 5.2 Changing nature of supply chain

Period	Consumer	Distributor	Provider	Activities/ Services	Concept/ Approach
1980s	Leisure	Specialist	Hotels	Hotels	In-house
1990s	Leisure	Specialist Hotels Tourist Boards	Hotels Guest houses Holiday centres	Hotels Local attractions Special events Operational services	Packaging through strategic networks
2000s	Mix	E-commerce intermediaries	Wide range of commercial providers incl. Former plus type of short break providers	Individualized through strategic networks and relationship services	Flexibility and individuality with holistic solutions

supply has changed considerably since the 1980s. The consumer dimension of the chain has been discussed in the previous section but what should be considered further here is that the business consumer will become more of a key player in short breaks into the year 2000. In terms of distribution, the next century will see an explosion of e-commerce which will compete directly with the traditional intermediaries and will require a greater focus on the use of knowledge management to gain a competitive advantage and to allow focused relationship marketing to occur. While traditional providers have been hotel companies, the 1990s has seen a consolidation effect in terms of large hotel groups but also the development of the fragmented markets in terms of smaller hotels and guest houses using consortia and the development of niche markets in terms of holiday camps. The twenty-first century will see greater access for all suppliers especially when one considers the comments earlier regarding distribution – the result will be a massive selection of packages and breaks in various worldwide locations at a wide range of prices – the challenge is how to manage such complexity. In terms of activities, where the 1980s saw hotel companies creating the packages, the 1990s witnessed co-operation between hotels and local attractions or events. The twenty-first-century operators will need to focus on flexibility and personalized choices, which will require developing strategic networks and building relationships across a wide range of activity bases; ownership of such facilities will be uneconomical.

Figure 5.7 shows how such relationships have changed since the 1980s and how strategic networks will need to develop. From Figure 5.7 it can be seen that the approach to management varies across two key dimensions, the nature of ownership of the assets – common or no common ownership – and the approach – co-operative or non-cooperative.

The 1980s era with British Transport Hotels and Goldenrail saw an approach to management of the short break supply chain that reflected a vertically integrated company. This approach then split in the 1990s into two forms – the bureaucracy for larger hotel groups/chains attempting to concentrate, brand and gain critical

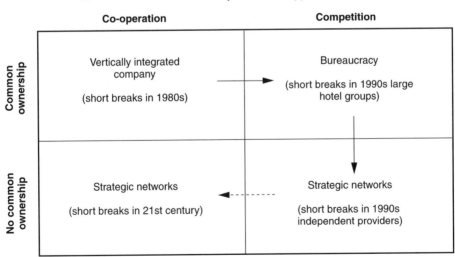

Figure 5.7 Strategic networks. *Source*: Adapted from Jarillo (1993)

mass of portfolios. The second form reflects a market approach which represents the independent sector for the 1990s short break supply. Strategic management of short breaks into the twenty-first century will be geared towards strategic management networking where organizations work in collaboration/co-operation to provide flexible and agile business concepts and information that allows a personalized approach to marketing, essentially reflecting relationship marketing.

The final element of Table 5.2 is that of the overriding supplier approach. While the 1980s was seen as an in-house operation focused upon asset ownership and using hotel facilities to gain a cost focus, the 1990s shifted towards attempting to package facilities around events and seasons resulting in a degree of strategic networking and brand marketing and providing a process focus. The twenty-first century will require more. Short break providers will need to invest heavily in developing knowledge management systems that link to both supply and demand to allow a highly personalized service to be offered to the consumer (from the demand perspective) and the management of a wide range of strategic networks to provide flexibility in product-buys, service-buys and distribution. The result for the twenty-first century is a need for a customer focus bounded by knowledge management and driven by innovation and personal service. This will be a major challenge for all sectors of the industry.

The key players

Having determined the nature of the supply chain, the challenges and strategic issues it is useful to understand who the key players in the industry are. Based upon the supply chain shown in the previous section a number of key players can be identified. The key players are divided into categories of supply.

The leading hotel groups

Hotel groups such as Forte were early pioneers in developing weekend breaks in the 1970s and what began as marginal business has developed into a core market for hotels. Forte estimate that short breaks now account for around a quarter of total business. All the main groups are active in this area and have leisure break programmes and brochures offering both special interest and general breaks. These are mostly distributed via direct mail and marketed through the hotels, although the bigger groups such as Forte are racked in travel agents. Two hotel groups, Thistle and Jarvis, have developed brands (Highlife and Embassy) which feature their own hotels but include others as well. These have a strong presence in travel agents and are offering a similar product to the independent short break operators.

Independent short break operators

Established in the early 1980s as a response to the growing short break market, short break specialists offer flexible packages of accommodation, travel and entertainment. They do not own their own accommodation and the product is largely sold via travel agents. London and theatre breaks have always been an important part of the product but a variety of themed breaks are offered all over the UK.

Superbreak Mini Holidays is the market leader, which together with Goldenrail is now owned by Eurocamp. These brands account for some 600,000 short breaks a year and are significantly ahead of the nearest competition represented by Highlife, Embassy and Rainbow. The latter, established in 1981, is a similar operation to Superbreak but with a much smaller market share.

Other accommodation sectors

Short breaks were initially seen as the preserve of hotels, with the self-catering sector locked into week-long stays. This began to change at the end of the 1980s. Center Parcs turned accepted wisdom on its head by only selling short breaks, although they now sell week-long stays during the school holidays and at Christmas. Their three sites probably account for in excess of 500,000 short breaks a year.

Warner Holidays (owned by Rank) have changed from holiday centres aimed at the family market to hotels and resorts aimed exclusively at adults, with 90 per cent of their business taking the form of three- or four-night breaks and achieving 90 per cent occupancy levels. The cottage holiday sector has also followed suit, and almost all the major operators now offer short breaks, usually with restrictions on how far in advance they can be booked. This is seen as crucial to extending the season and improving occupancy. Short break business is estimated to account for 10–15 per cent of total bookings at English Country Cottages. Almost all the major self-catering operators now offer short breaks.

The outbound short break operators

The outbound industry is rather different from the domestic industry and is much more dominated by tour operators and inclusive tours. Carriers also play a key role here. There is considerable overlap between carriers and tour operators, with operators using certain carriers for their programmes and carriers using operators to put together and manage their own branded holidays.

The two main outbound operators are Cresta and Bridge Travel, both now owned by Airtours. Together, it is estimated (Keynote, 1998) that these operators carry some 600,000 passengers a year. The next rival is Travelscene with a market share of around 100,000. Other significant players include Thomson, British Airways Holidays and Thomas Cook plus a whole host of small specialist independent operators. The best-selling product in the packaged market is still the city break.

FUTURE MARKET TRENDS

Key future changes

Despite the recession in the early part of the decade, the UK short break market has increased in size. In the period since 1989, UK residents have taken an additional 6 million short breaks (home and abroad) and spending has increased by 70 per cent in real terms. This growth of the short break market is part of a long-term trend, not just confined to the UK, which has been fuelled by lifestyle changes, increasing affluence and changes to the holiday product. The strong pound and falling transport costs have also played a part in stimulating breaks abroad.

Assuming no major economic disruptions, the trend should continue over the next decade as:

- There will be more money for spending on leisure and discretionary goods due to the economic well-being of the UK.
- The key segment for short breaks (45–59 age group) is projected to grow by 20 per cent, resulting in organic growth for short breaks.
- The short break has now become an accepted part of the lifestyle that people aspire to.
- There is considerable confidence in the industry about future growth.

Beioley (1999) estimates that the market will continue to grow at an average rate of around 5 per cent p.a. to 2005. However, if the nature of growth follows the current pattern, it will be at the expense of the longer holidays, which may result in suppliers seeking to capture a greater market share of short breaks and as such fuelling the dynamics of the market, making the market grow, stimulating additional demand quicker and simultaneously stimulating greater competition: this may overheat the short break market in pricing terms or is more likely to result in a consolidation and concentration of supply in larger networked organizations.

Given the former situation and as home markets become more saturated, it is likely that domestic operators will feature more overseas destinations in their portfolios (especially as organizations become more global). This will be stimulated further by overseas competitors tapping UK markets via the Internet and e-commerce.

Hence, in the twenty-first century there will be no room for complacency on the part of the domestic short break industry. The recipe for future success may lie in:

- continuing to invest in the product to improve standards and quality of service;
- becoming more responsive and flexible; and
- becoming more focused.

These changes and issues will have implications upon how suppliers will compete in the twenty-first century, some of which are worth highlighting.

Implementation issues

The former sections have argued that the future suppliers and management of short breaks will revolve around strategic networking, personalized concepts and innovation. The former principles can be generalized to many international operations with a caveat of different country markets being at different stages of the industry and transaction life cycle. To facilitate such a strategic networking approach three core management concepts will need to be developed: (i) the need for knowledge; (ii) a focus on value creation; and (iii) an understanding of competences.

Each of these is worthy of further research and is briefly defined below.

The need for knowledge

Organizations will need to be more aware of the principles and practices of knowledge management and the interlinkage with the learning organization. The overlap between people, process and technology will become critical for the management of the future in terms of both marketing and demand management, and the management of the supply chain.

A focus on value creation

While location and positioning have been traditional tourism management approaches, greater focus will be required on the nature of value creation in markets and organizations. Organizations will need to be aware of what components add value for consumers and be in a position to configure value packages for different forms of consumer.

An understanding of competences

While understanding value and using knowledge will allow a sustainable competitive advantage founded upon the organizational intangibles, the organization must also be aware of what its competences are. Understanding what an organization's competence is will allow resource allocation to be more effectively deployed. Considerable debate exists as to how one can measure a core competence and indeed whether competences can be quantified at all. The contention here is not that organizations must be able to measure a competence but more that organizations must be in a position to (i) recognize the difference between the threshold competence (i.e. the industry expected standard) and the core competence (the sustainable advantage) and (ii) understand what activities lead to their organizational strengths, i.e. what their specific competences are: these two concepts can then be compared to allow effective resource allocation.

While many areas for further research exist, the author believes the former three to be of critical importance to the management of short breaks in the twenty-first century.

CONCLUSION

This chapter has profiled the changing nature of short breaks. While the focus of the context has been upon the UK, the underlying principles influencing supply, demand and competition are universal in their nature. Clearly, given the discussion in the chapter and the nature of the change and issues raised, the short break markets of the future are going to be considerably more dynamic and complex than those of today. The result will be a need for better-quality information and a drive to ensure sustainable advantage through the use of innovative portfolios and better use of intangible assets. Given the growth and increasing contribution of the short break market, the strategic and marketing developments will need to be dedicated and recognize that short breaks are a distinct and valuable market segment.

REFERENCES

Bailey, J. (1989) 'Short holidays'. *Insights*, ETB / BTA, B1–B7.

Beioley, S. (1991) 'Short holidays'. *Insights* (September), B29–B38.

Beioley, S. (1999) 'Short and sweet – the UK short break market'. *Insights*, B63–B78.

BTA (1989a) 'The short break market'. BTA / ETB (November).

BTA (1989b) 'Holiday making in the British Isles'. *Insights*, A1–9–A1–15.

BTA (1990a) 'Holidays'. *Insights*, **6**, A127–A132, B61–B70.

BTA (1990b) 'British holiday intentions 1990'. BTA / ETB.

Chamberlin, E. H. (1962) 'Theory of monopolistic competition' (1st edn. 1932). London: Harvard University Press.

Cockerell, N. (1989) 'The short break market in Europe'. *EIU Travel and Tourism Analyst*, **5**, 41–55.

Connell, J. (1992) 'Branding hotel portfolios'. *International Journal of Hospitality Management*, **4**(1), 26–32.

Crawford, P. (1992) 'Short breaks in Scotland'. *Glasgow Herald*, 23 June, p. 25.

Crichton, E. and Edgar, D. (1995) 'Managing market complexity for competitive advantage: an IT perspective'. *International Journal of Contemporary Hospitality Management*, **7**(2/3), 12–19.

Davies, B. (1990) 'The economics of short breaks'. *International Journal of Hospitality Management*, **9**(2), 103–6.

Demetriadi, J. (1992) 'Taking a break'. *Hospitality* (June), 10–15.

Edgar, D. (1992a) 'Commercial short holiday break markets in Scotland'. Unpublished report for the STB, Napier Polytechnic, March.

Edgar, D. (1992b) *A Model for Analysing the Commercial Short Holiday Break Market in Scotland*. CHME Research Conference proceedings, Birmingham Polytechnic, April.

Edgar, D. (1993) *Commercial Short Holiday Breaks – An Analysis of Market Provision and Supplier Strategies in Scotland.* CHME Research Conference proceedings, Manchester Metropolitan University, April.

Edgar, D. (1995) 'The strategic gap – a short break multi-site perspective'. In N. Johns (ed.) *Productivity Strategies for Service.* London: Cassell.

Edgar, D. (1998) 'Strategies for optimising revenues from short breaks: lessons from the Scottish hotel markets'. In E. Law, B. Faulkner and G. Moscardo, *Embracing and Managing Change in Tourism.* London: Routledge.

Edgar, D. and Halcro, K. (1998) *Tangiblising the Intangibles.* EuroChrie Conference, Lausanne, Switzerland.

Edgar, D. and Litteljohn, D. L. (1994) 'Strategic clusters and strategic space: the case of the UK short break market'. *International Journal of Contemporary Hospitality Management,* **6**(5), 20–6.

Edgar, D., Litteljohn, D. L., Allardyce, M. and Wanhill, S. (1994) 'Commercial short holiday breaks: the relationship between market structure, competitive advantage, and performance'. In A. V. Seaton (ed.), *Tourism: The State of the Art.* Chichester: John Wiley & Sons, pp. 323–42.

Edgar, D. and Nisbet, L. (1995) 'A matter of chaos: strategy for hospitality industries'. *International Journal of Contemporary Hospitality Management,* **8**(2/3), 6–9.

EIU (1991) 'UK visitor forecasts to 1995'. *Travel Industry Monitor,* 20 November, 8.

EIU (1992a) 'Short breaks still growing'. *EIU Travel Industry Monitor,* 24 March, 2–4.

EIU (1992b) 'The French short break domestic leisure market 1991'. *EIU Travel Industry Monitor,* 31 October, 3.

ETB (1993a) 'Tourism by UK residents in 1992'. *Insights* (September), F11–F17.

ETB (1993b) 'Holiday tourism of UK residents in 1992'. *Insights* (July), F1–F9.

Euromonitor (1987) 'Short break holidays'. *Market Research G.B.* Euromonitor Publ. Ltd (April), **26**, 15–22.

Godfrey, K. (1992) 'In search of identity'. *Caterer & Hotelkeeper,* 6 April, 56–7.

Goulding, P. (1992) *Britain's Leisure Industry.* Bristol: Jordan and Sons Ltd., p. 23.

Greer, S. (1991) 'Off peak targeting'. *Leisure Management,* **11**(5), May, 32–3.

Hanks, R. D., Cross, R. G. and Noland, R. P. (1992) 'Discounting in the hotel industry: a new approach'. *The Cornell HRAQ,* February, 15–23.

Hoseasons (1992) 'Hoseasons holiday survey'. *Travel GBI* (June), **164**, 6.

Hunt, J. (1991) 'Prospects for international tourism 1992'. *EIU Travel and Tourism Analyst,* **6**, 77–93.

Jarillo, C. J. (1993) *Strategic Networks – Creating the Borderless Organization.* Oxford: Butterworth-Heinemann, p. 131.

Key Note (1998) *Hotels: A Market Sector Overview.* Hampton: Key Note Publications.

Law, J. (1990) 'Short breaks'. *Travel Trade Gazette* (1931), November, 27–30.

Law, J. (1991a) 'UK short breaks'. *Travel Trade Gazette* (1950), March, 51–5.

Law, J. (1991b) 'European short breaks'. *Travel Trade Gazette* (1956), May, 43–9.

Litteljohn, D. L. and Goulding P. (1994) 'International tourism reports: Scotland'. *EIU Travel and Tourism Analyst,* **2**, 62–81.

Lohmann, M. (1991) 'Evolution of shortbreak holidays'. *Tourist Review,* **2**, 14–22.

Loverseed, H. (1992) 'The North American short break market'. *EIU Travel and Tourism Analyst,* **4**, 48–65.

Mathur, S. and Kenyon, A. (1997) *Creating Value – Shaping Tomorrow's Business.* Oxford: Butterworth-Heinemann, p. 184.

MEW Research (1994) 'Short break destination choice'. *Insights* (January), A77–A94.

Middleton, V. T. C. (1987) 'Marketing holidays to Wales – responding to market changes'. *Tourist Review,* **2**, 27–30.

Middleton, V. T. C. (1991) 'British tourism : market prospects for the next 12 months'. *Insights,* **4**, A71–A76.

MSI (1991) 'Databrief : short break holidays'. *Marketing Strategies for Industry.*

Muller, T. E. (1991) 'Using personal values to define segments'. *International Marketing Review*, **8**(1), 57–70.

Pearce, D. G. (1987) 'Special patterns of package tourism in Europe'. *Annals of Travel Research*, **14**(2), 183–201.

Porter, M. E. (1979) 'The structure within industries' and companies' performance'. *Review of Economics and Statistics*, **61**, 214–27.

Potier, F. and Cockerell, N. (1992), 'The European international short break market'. *EIU Travel and Tourism Analyst*, **5**, 45–65.

Quiroga, I. (1990) 'Characteristics of package tours in Europe'. *Annals of Tourism Research*, **17**(2), 185–207.

Ryan, C. (1989) 'Trends past and present in the package holiday industry'. *Service Industry Journal*, **9**(1), 61–78.

Ryan, C. (1991) 'UK package holiday industry'. *Tourism Management*, **12**(1), 76–7.

Schidhauser, H. (1992) 'The distinction between short and long holidays'. *Tourist Review*, **2**, 10–17.

Slattery, P. (1991) 'Hotel branding in the 1990s'. *EIU Travel and Tourism Analyst*, **1**, 23–35.

Slattery, P. and Johnson, S. (1991) *Quoted Hotel Companies: The World Market*. London: Kleinwort Benson Securities Limited (February).

Teare, R. (1989) 'The operational challenge of hotel short breaks'. *Contemporary Journal of Hospitality Management*, **1**(1), 22–4.

Tourism Intelligence Quarterly (1990) 'The British on holiday 1990'. *Tourism Intelligence Quarterly*, **12**(4), 53–65.

Travel GBI (1989) 'Christmas and winter breaks'. *Travel GBI*, 132 (October), 8–10.

Travel GBI (1990a) 'Christmas and winter breaks'. *Travel GBI*, 144 (October), 20–21.

Travel GBI (1990b) 'Short Breaks – the crystal ball gazers are right'. *Travel GBI*, 145, (November), 22.

Travel GBI (1990c) 'UK package holidays'. *Travel GBI*, 145 (November), 12–13.

Trinity Research (1989) *The Short Break Package Holiday Market*. London: Trinity Research Ltd.

TTG (1991) 'Travel Trade Gazette UK'. *Travel Trade Gazette*, 24 October, p. 21.

UKTS (1991) *The UK Tourist Statistics 1991*. London: ETB / STB / WTB / NITB.

PART 2

Trends and Issues in Tourism Industry Management

Edited by Eric Laws

In the opening chapter of *Tourism in the Twenty-first Century: Reflections on Experience*, the editors presented an overview of the changing nature of tourism. Part 1 has focused on the impacts of these changes on tourists' activities and on the tourists themselves. The chapters in Part 2 consider current aspects of the changing operations and environment of tourism organizations, tracing trends from antiquity. The chapters analyse industry relationships, those with customers, with destination communities and between the main players – other businesses – and with governmental agencies. The authors interweave into their chapters debate about the future pattern of tourism, with attention paid to the rapidly developing impacts of the Internet and World Wide Web (the Web), and speculate on the potential for two emergent forms of tourism, virtual and space tourism, which a century ago were the preserve of fiction writers.

Bruce Prideaux opens the discussion with a critical review of the 'Links between Transport and Tourism – Past, Present and Future'. He traces the development of transport from antiquity and identifies significant gaps in both transport studies and tourism studies, noting particularly the need to develop further understanding of causal links between transport and tourism. The chapter adopts a systems framework to explore and simplify the relationships of the two industries, and the impacts of changing transport technologies on the operation of the tourism system.

The authors of 'Tourist Attractions: Evolution, Analysis and Prospects' note that attractions and tourism have been inextricably linked throughout the history of the industry, but they challenge the validity of one of the most familiar metaphors in the tourism literature, the notion that the magnetism of key attractions lures visitors to a specific point. Philip Pearce, Pierre Benckendorff and Suzanne Johnstone propose instead that tourist regions function as a dynamic force field within which researchers can focus their attention on competition between attractions, and the roles of attractions in customer choice. Nell Arnold examines the trend to regard community festivals as tourist attractions. 'Festival Tourism: Recognizing the Challenges; Linking Multiple Pathways between Global Villages of the New Century' summarizes her extensive research into the roles and functions of festival tourism. The chapter focuses attention on issues such as authenticity and economic sustainability in managing community festivals as tourist events and it introduces a discussion of the transformational potential on communities of festival tourism.

Dimitrios Buhalis discusses 'Tourism in an Era of Information Technology'. He examines the roles of the Internet and the Web in revolutionizing business transactions with customers and suppliers, enhancing the transparency of organizational information and decision-taking, and democratizing human communications. Xinran You, Joseph O'Leary and Daniel Fesenmaier consider the need for a new marketing paradigm. They discuss the ways in which National Tourist Organizations are using the Web as an effective communications channel to disseminate destination information. The three authors of 'Knowledge Management through the Web: A New Marketing Paradigm for Tourism Organizations' argue that the Web provides the potential for organizations to improve their knowledge of customers' shifting travel preferences and behaviour. The integration of customer knowledge management strategies into marketing strategy will therefore become one of the most challenging and promising issues for NTO managers.

The next chapter in this section is in the form of an action-based case study, 'Destination Management: Co-operative Marketing, a Case Study of the Port Douglas Brand'. The chapter demonstrates how two hotels and the State Tourist Organization pooled their knowledge of visitor motivations in order to create more distinctive images for each hotel within the overall brand values for the destination. Noel Scott, Nick Parfitt and Eric Laws argue that destination level co-operation between tourism organizations can provide mutual benefits harnessing the self-interests of operators with disparate objectives and operational styles, but point out that co-operative marketing or destination development programmes depend on effective leadership. Part 2 concludes with a review of 'Issues in Public Sector Involvement'. Stephen Wanhill points to the resilience of the tourism industry and its significance as a mechanism for economic development as rationales for public sector involvement. He evaluates the limits to the roles of governments within a contemporary framework, which favours the primacy of markets to determine the allocation of resources, and advocates a more pragmatic approach to intervention, emphasizing international collaboration.

CHAPTER 6

Links between Transport and Tourism – Past, Present and Future

Bruce Prideaux

Transport and tourism are interwoven in a complex relationship that has been barely recognized by tourism researchers. Most research ignores the impact that transport can exert over the shape and viability of the tourism industry. However, the transport industry is continually undergoing change as new technologies are adopted. The resulting increases in speed and comfort as well as reductions in the cost of travel have significant implications for tourism. As in the past, the tourism industry will need to adapt to these changes and alter its product mix to take advantage of the new opportunities that will be created. Should tourism operators fail to recognize that vast changes may occur with the adoption of new transport technologies, they face the danger of extinction in much the same way as the 1950s' ocean liners were scrapped in the face of overwhelming competition from jet airliners.

Until the late 1830s, transport was based on a bimodal system comprising roads and sea. With few exceptions, these modes operated independently of each other and were rarely competitors. The introduction of railways in the 1830s changed this situation, as rail competed with both road and sea for freight and passengers and set in place a process of evolution that has resulted in the emergence of a competitive multimodal transport system. The quest for new and more efficient transport technologies has directly benefited the tourism industry in areas such as speed, price, safety and comfort. This chapter will trace the development of the transport system from antiquity, identifying those innovations that have aided the development of travel and which in time laid the foundation for the current transport system. It is this transport system that largely underpins the operation of the modern tourism industry.

Analysis of the interaction between transport and tourism using a systems approach is a major theme of this chapter. A systems approach can be defined as research methodology that is both capable of identifying the complex web of relationships between the many elements involved and, concurrently, is able to rationalize and simplify these links into a number of relationships and components that can be studied individually or as a group. In this way it is possible to study the relationship between tourism and transport in a manner that enables identification of the impact of changing transport technology on the operation of the tourism system. A systems approach is capable of accommodating these requirements because it does not presume to have a predetermined view (Gilbert, 1990). The systems approach, by its nature, is able to accommodate a multiplicity of relationships and connections between participants in the industry. A further advantage of viewing both transport and tourism as systems, rather than as a specific industry, is the ability to study changes in the morphology of the relationship between transport and tourism from a multi-sector perspective. Change is dynamic and once instigated has a tendency to impact on every part of a system in ways that include unanticipated effects.

TRANSPORT AND TOURISM

Although the link between tourism and transport is fundamental in nature, research into the transport aspects of tourism is a neglected field of study. While Casson (1974) and Maczak (1995) have published insightful studies into the relationship between travel and transport in earlier times, research into the modern tourism phenomenon has generally neglected to explore the connections that exist between tourism and transport. This has occurred even though a number of authors (Gilbert, 1939; Gormsen, 1991; Gunn, 1994; Hall, 1991; Inskeep, 1991; Mill and Morrison, 1985; Pearce, 1987; Robinson, 1976) have acknowledged that there are substantial links between transport and tourism. Causal relationships have yet to be systematically investigated. Leiper (1979), for example, developed the often cited model of the transit zone that exists between tourism-generating regions and destination regions, while Miossec (1976) proposed a model of tourism growth that incorporated a strong transport element. Neither author further explored the notion of tourism development being inextricably linked to the continuing development of transport systems. In the recent literature, useful discussions of the relationship between tourism and transport have been written by Page (1999) and Prideaux (2000). Significant gaps continue to exist, particularly in relation to the operation of the transport system as the link between origins and destinations, the study of the role of individual modes and the contribution of transport to destination development. The lack of investigation into the relationship between tourism development and transport is also evident in the transport literature.

The relationship between tourism and transport has been built on the continual introduction of new transport technologies that have enabled travellers to move between origin and destination either faster, safer or for a lower cost. In the modern era, rail initiated the first transport revolution (Chew, 1987) and laid the foundation for the development of the modern tourism industry. In the twentieth century, the automobile and the aeroplane largely supplanted rail, creating their own revolutions in opportunities for tourism development. It is unlikely that the rate of introduction of new technology will abate and technological innovations will continue to improve all aspects of the provision of tourism transport into the future. The likely impact of new transport technologies on the operation of the tourism industry can be measured against a set of criteria that includes safety, speed, range, price, comfort and carrying capacity. Of these, range, safety, speed, comfort and capacity relate to the incorporation of new technologies into the design of the transport vehicle regardless of mode. Price, or more precisely the cost of individual travel, is an outcome of both technological

Table 6.1 Relationship between new transport technologies and travel

	Technological advance in transport	**Component of tourism**
Sumeria	Wheeled wagons, domesticated animals, roads	Currency, travel made more comfortable with wagons and roads
Minoans and Mycenaeans	Limited paved roads	
Assyrians	Domesticated horses, extensive road system	Increased speed of travel
Greek City States		Travel writing, tours, attractions, currency exchange
Roman Empire	Extensive paved roads	Annual holidays, itineraries, seaside resorts
19th Century	Railways, first cars	Development of modern resorts, organized tours
20th Century	Mass-produced cars, air travel, first space travel	Development of mass tourism

innovation and the level of economic development. Collectively, these criteria determine the cost of travel via a specific class of transport vehicle. In many instances, cost and perhaps time are the major factors in consumer acceptance of specific transport modes. For example, the Concorde is able to halve travel times between Europe and the United States of America although at a considerable cost premium. Most travellers, faced with paying the additional cost of higher speed, opt for cheaper subsonic aircraft. The degree of substitution between modes based on price and other factors is significant and in many circumstances may determine the suitability of specific transport modes for a particular route.

Before assessing the impact that current transport technology has had on twentieth-century tourism this chapter will briefly explore the relationship between the introduction of new transport technologies and their impact on travel in the past. Table 6.1 summarizes the impact of transport technologies on the development of travel. In the following discussion a significant distinction is made between the use of the terms 'travel' and 'tourism', reflecting the passage of time and changes in the reasons for undertaking a journey. In antiquity, travel was undertaken for a specific purpose including, administration, trade, to engage in battle, to escape natural dangers, to flee from invaders, for religious pilgrimage or perhaps just because of the promise of unsettled territory. People usually had little time, or ability, to engage in travel for the purpose of pleasure. Conversely, while travel for purposes of commerce, administration and war continues to occur in the modern era, travelling for the purpose of pleasure, entertainment, recreation or just indulgence has expanded considerably and now constitutes the main purpose for undertaking travel. For the purposes of this chapter, travelling for pleasure is broadly defined as tourism. A more precise definition of the term *Tourist* is a visitor who travels to a destination other than his/her usual residence for a period not exceeding one year and whose main purpose of visit is other than the exercise of an activity remunerated from within the place visited (WTO, 1994). This definition is not adopted for this chapter because it fails to include the historical perspective necessary to show how tourism has evolved from travel.

TRAVEL AND TOURISM IN ANTIQUITY

Human migration, perhaps spanning a period measuring hundreds of thousands of years, saw the spread of *Homo sapiens* and earlier groups from the region where they originated to almost every part of the earth. Travelling by foot, domesticated animal and sea, in migrations that are still the subject of academic debate concerning details of time and technology, our early ancestors conquered rivers, deserts, forests and oceans. Recent, though disputed, evidence suggests that about 840,000 years ago *Homo erectus* migrated from Java to Flores using some form of purpose-built water craft (Brook, 1999). For whatever reason travel was undertaken in the past, many dangers and hardships had to be expected and endured. Indeed the term travel has its origins in the word 'travail' which describes the conditions that often confronted travellers in the past. The concept of travelling for pleasure is a more recent innovation, perhaps beginning on a small scale in Egypt about 1500 BC when travellers of the New Kingdom era were recorded as visiting the pyramids built over a millennium before (Casson, 1974). It was not until the twentieth-century phenomenon of mass tourism that travel for pleasure gained relatively wide appeal and acceptance.

Military necessity, trade and administration created the structures that facilitated travel in the ancient world of the Middle East and the Mediterranean. Over a period of nearly three millennia the various components of a functional transport system were developed or redeveloped and merged to create a system of travel that by Roman times comprised roads, domesticated animals, chariots and wagons, currency, currency exchange, itineraries, seaside resorts, accommodation and the concept of annual holidays. Thus by Roman times it was possible to identify a small-scale tourism system where emphasis was placed on pleasure travel versus other forms of travel.

In the ancient world three transport technologies transformed land travel: domestication of animals (particularly the horse); construction of roads; and development of animal-drawn wagons. Development and adoption of these technologies was slow, occurring over a period exceeding two thousand years. The earliest evidence of the systematic development of a transport system designed to transport passengers and goods over considerable distances along some form of road system appeared in Sumeria where the first wheeled vehicles appeared about 3000 BC (Casson, 1974). The Sumerians developed heavy four-wheeled wagons, drawn either by oxen or onagers, a type of wild ass (Casson, 1974), to undertake travel within their empire. The Sumerian transport system based on roads, domesticated animals and animal-drawn wagons became the prototype for the transport systems adopted by later empires. Sumeria is also credited with the invention of currency which is an essential component of the development of travel. After the rapid technological advances made by the Sumerians, progress in later centuries was relatively slow and incremental as demonstrated by the time that elapsed from the first use of the horse as a draught animal to its use for individual transport. The first horses appeared in the Middle East about 2300 BC and were initially used only as draught animals. Several centuries later they began to be used to pull light carts and about 1600 BC the horse-drawn chariot appeared (Casson, 1974). Adaptation of the horse for riding did not become widespread for almost another five centuries.

Development of roads also occurred slowly. Although there is some evidence of roads in Sumeria as early as 2100 BC, the widespread construction of paved roads did not appear until much later. The Bronze Age Greek civilizations of the

Minoans centred on Crete (1700 BC to 1450 BC) and the Mycenaeans (about 1600 to 1250 BC) also built paved roads in the latter part of their existence (Eoley, 1975). The great expense of building and maintaining paved roads prevented further expansion of this technology until Roman times when many of the engineering problems of road and bridge-building were solved.

Travel by water also developed during this period, commencing in Egypt where the first sturdy wooden rivercraft were introduced about 2700 BC (Casson, 1974). Later, larger boats powered by oars or sails were developed for commerce in the Mediterranean.

As is often the case in history, the Minoan and Mycenaean civilizations fell (about 1200 BC), overwhelmed by the 'Sea Peoples' of obscure origin. Initially, travel for commerce and pilgrimage declined but as bronze was replaced by iron new opportunities for trade and conquest emerged and with it new components of transport technology were developed. The emergence of the Assyrian Empire (900 BC to 612 BC) saw the development of an extensive road network based on packed earth surfaces and sparing use of stone bridges. Roads were signposted and controlled by guard posts sited about 10 kilometres apart (Casson, 1974). Perhaps the greatest contribution of the Assyrians was the adoption of the horse for riding rather than for use only as a draught animal. Although popularized by the Assyrians and used with great effect for cavalry warfare, the actual development of riding techniques may be traced to the nomads of the southern Russian steppes.

Assyria eventually collapsed under the weight of attacks from Persia and was incorporated into the Persian Empire (sixth to fourth centuries BC). To maintain control over its large empire, the Persians constructed a large road network including the 'royal road' stretching nearly 2400 kilometres from Sardis on the Mediterranean coast to the Persian capital of Susa. Although built for military use and the administration of the empire, the 'royal road' included rest houses and inns at regular intervals and was secure enough for ordinary travellers using donkeys. Trade was encouraged by the construction of roads and the introduction of a standard currency throughout the empire. Persia's drive to the west stalled in Greece (at the battles of Salamas and Plataea) and, after Persia's defeat by Alexander the Great, the centre of gravity of the ancient world moved westward from Persia to the Mediterranean, ushering in a lengthy era of transport development.

The Greek city states established colonies throughout the Mediterranean stimulating trade and in its wake travel. Although Greece was never a unified state, citizens of the independent Greek states often travelled to religious festivals, sporting events such as the Olympic Games and to visit other cities, particularly Athens. Herodotus, a citizen of the fifth-century BC Greek city state of Halicarnassus (then a vassal state of Persia) and the world's first recorded travel writer, wrote that 'A great many Greeks went to Egypt, some as might be expected, for business, some to serve in the army, but some just to see the country itself.' Apart from Herodotus' accounts of contemporary and earlier travel, the major contribution of the Greeks to the later development of tourism was the introduction of currency exchange. Previously, travellers carried goods for exchange, but the introduction of convertible currency in the Hellenized world allowed travellers to carry coin that could be readily converted to local currency, making travelling for pleasure a much easier proposition. By the time Herodotus had written his account of travel and history in the Hellenized world of the fifth century BC, most of the elements of a transport system able to sustain pleasure travel had been established. Only the widespread acceptance of the concept of annual holidays was lacking. During this period travellers used horses, horse-drawn wagons or donkeys, travelled on roads and overnighted at inns. On the seas, ships regularly traversed the Mediterranean, conveying travellers from city to city or state to state for trade, pilgrimage, administration and in limited instances for pleasure. On the open waters of the Mediterranean, sails and oars competed with each other as the main form of propulsion. On arrival in a new port travellers could convert coin into the local currency and stay in purpose-built inns.

The fall of the Greek states to the armies of Rome did little to inhibit the continued development of the concept of travel for pleasure. Diocletian (AD 245–313) described 372 Roman roads with a total length of 84,742 kilometres (Kraul, 1985). Roads were often paved, patrolled by military units, and rivers were spanned by stone bridges. Inns were sited at regular intervals to provide for the needs of travellers. Such was the extent of travel in Roman times that the seven wonders of the ancient world (the Pyramids, the Hanging Gardens of Babylon, Phidia's statue of Zeus at Olympia, the Temple of Artemis at Ephesus, the Mausoleum, the Colossus of Rhodes and the Lighthouse at Alexandria) became the must dos of the Roman traveller. The drawing up of the list of the seven wonders probably occurred in the third century BC undertaken by an unknown scholar who apparently lived in Alexandria (Casson, 1974). Many other sites attracted the Roman traveller, including the cave in Greece where Zeus was born, the stone at Salamis where Telamon sat watching his sons Ajax and Teucer sail off to Troy, the remains of the clay from which Panopeus moulded the first humans and the graves of Ajax and Achilles at Troy (Casson, 1974). Also on the traveller's list were museums, including the Baths of Caracalla (one of Rome's principle museums), tours of Greece (following a centuries-old itinerary of Delphi, Athens, Corinth, Epidaurus, Olympia and Sparta), Asia Minor (Troy, Cnidus, Ephesus and Smyrna) and Egypt (Alexandria, the Pyramids and up the Nile to Thebes), and holidays at seaside villas. Casson observed that during the era of the Greek city states the five basic motives for travel were: people going on business (either their own or for the government); for their health; to go on a pilgrimage to a shrine or oracle; to attend festivals; or, in a few cases, to see the world. To this list the Roman elite added the concept of the holiday, an annual departure from home to the seaside or mountains. The acceptance of the idea of holidays added the final component required to develop the concept of travel for pleasure as the embodiment of tourism. During the Roman Empire the volume and extent of travel increased substantially and resort towns such as Pompeii and Herculaneum were built to service Roman tourists. The ability of Rome's citizens to travel to all areas of the empire and participate in a tourism industry that in some respects resembles that of our time, rested on the ability of the empire's transport systems to convey travellers from generating regions to destination regions by road or sea in transport vehicles that were acceptably safe and comfortable for travellers living during this period.

The ordinary Roman citizen made few journeys but when required he or she usually travelled by foot or beast along roads that were paved, if they formed part of the administrative and military road system, or earth, if of lesser importance. Indeed the first millennium AD commenced with one of the great recorded stories of travel. The Gospel of Luke in the Christian Bible records the journey of Mary and Joseph from their home in Nazareth to Bethlehem in the Roman Province of Judea to participate in a census: after travelling by road with Mary riding on a donkey (according to tradition) the travellers were unable to find accommodation at an inn and their first son Jesus was born in the inn's stable. By the fourth and fifth centuries AD, religious tourism to view sites associated with Christianity had become a major industry involving travel by land and sea, accommodation provided by inns, guided tours and purchase of souvenirs.

In Asia, travel also became a feature of the various empires and kingdoms centred on China and India. On reaching India, Alexander the Great found an extensive network of well-developed roads serviced by regular guest houses. Travellers rode in chariots, bullock carts and palanquins or on elephants, camels and horses (Kraul, 1985). Further east in China travel was also common and a system of roads radiated out from major cities into the countryside. Unlike Roman roads, Chinese roads were never built in straight lines and featured numerous sharp curves designed to protect travellers from evil spirits which were supposedly capable of only travelling in straight lines (Kraul, 1985). Chinese roads featured tea shops and inns at frequent intervals. Many of Asia's great rivers including the Ganges, Indus, Yangtze and Yellow River were also used as transport corridors for travel for business, administration or pilgrimage.

DARK AGES (500–1100 AD) TO MIDDLE AGES (1100–1500 AD)

The collapse of the Western Roman Empire in AD 476 under the combined weight of internal decay and attacks from tribes in the east and north (including the Vandals, Visigoths, Goths and Huns) resulted in Western Europe descending into a long era of decline where travel almost ceased. During this period the freedom of travel enjoyed by the citizens of Rome was lost and a new political order based on feudalism emerged. Trade declined, as feudal society was generally self-sufficient. Where commerce occurred, traders generally banded together in caravans for protection from bandits and travel was largely confined to commerce between town and countryside, pilgrimages or for making war. Monasteries became centres of learning in Europe and often fulfilled a secondary task of providing shelter for travellers. The Church's spiritual control over the lives of Europeans resulted in pilgrimages becoming the dominant non-trade form of travel particularly during the early Middle Ages.

The second millennium commenced much as the first in respect to transport technology. The principle methods of land travel were by domesticated animal, animal-drawn wagon or foot, often using the remnants of road network built during the Roman Empire. On the seas, propulsion by sail or oars had improved little in the preceding thousand years.

Although large-scale commerce ceased during the Dark Ages, a trickle of silks, spices, porcelains and other luxury goods continued to reach Europe via the Silk Road which linked China and Europe via a network of land and sea routes. Caravans of traders took years to carry their cargoes along the Silk Route, following a tortuous route over deserts and through the interior of Asia via remote cities such as Samarkand and Xian. According to Gartner (1996), the fleas that were carriers of the bubonic plague may have also travelled with the silk caravans. On reaching the crowded towns and cities of Europe the plague spread quickly and between 1347 and 1351 killed up to 25 million people, about one-quarter of Europe's population. Believing that the plague was caused by the bad air of the towns and cities, wealthy citizens fled to the seaside for fresh sea air. This phenomenon saw the re-establishment of seaside resorts (Gartner, 1996).

The Renaissance

As the Renaissance pushed aside the conservatism and inward-looking perspectives of the Middle Ages, trade flourished although war remained an important tool of the trading empires of Portugal, Spain, England, France and Holland. The journeys of Marco Polo (AD 1254–1324), undertaken at the behest of the Doge of Venice, renewed interest in re-establishing contacts between Europe and the Orient that had been lost with the collapse of the Roman Empire (Roman traders ventured as far east as Malaya, Sumatra and Java in the second century AD). A desire to develop trading monopolies based on commodities such as spices, cotton and silk lay behind much of the exploration embarked upon by fifteenth- and sixteenth-century Europe. Advances in navigation, cartography and shipbuilding culminated in the burst of exploration sponsored by Portugal's Henry the Navigator (1394–1460) and King John II (1455–95). During this time Portuguese caravels and trade ships rounded the Cape of Good Hope (1487) and reached India (1498) before opening sea routes to China (1513) and Japan (1543).

The success of the Portuguese traders stimulated further voyages of exploration in Asia as well as westward to the Americas. The process of trade established the infrastructure of travel between the Old World and the New World of the Americas and between Europe and the Orient, laying the foundations for increased travel and eventually migration from Europe.

In contrast to the epic voyages of discovery and conquest undertaken by Portugal, Spain, Holland and England, land travel changed little during the Renaissance. The fifteenth-century traveller in England, as in other parts of Europe, had a limited choice of road transport. According to Kraul (1985, p. 487) the traveller could 'walk; he could ride on horseback; he could have himself carried in a litter or he could travel in a springless wagon. Riding on horseback was the quickest means and, very often, the next quickest was walking.'

RECENT TRANSPORT ADVANCES

The great Industrial Revolution that transformed agrarian Great Britain and later Western Europe and the United States of America laid the foundations for the technological breakthroughs that produced the steam train, iron-hulled steam-powered ships and later, automobiles and aeroplanes. If the new transport technologies of the nineteenth century transformed society, the technological breakthroughs of the twentieth century revolutionized society in the way it organized itself, creating opportunities for travel never imagined by earlier generations.

The modern tourism industry is of recent origin and is usually acknowledged as commencing in 1841 when Thomas Cook organized the first excursion by train. The significance of Cook's first excursion is its incorporation of many of the elements of today's tourism industry, including organized group travel, marketing, a common fare, an itinerary, use of specialized passenger transport, albeit in a converted open railway carriage fitted with chairs. Later, Cook introduced overseas package tours and traveller's cheques.

The twentieth century began with most tourists travelling by rail because the roads had not yet experienced the automobile revolution. The skies were empty save for a few hot-air balloons and, on the sea, sailing ships continued to fight a rearguard action against the encroachment of the steam-powered liners introduced many decades before. Yet by the close of the century, people were able to watch the grainy video replays of the first steps by mankind on the Moon some 30 years before and travel between continents in passenger jets. The roads were full of cars and passenger trains travelled at speeds approaching 350 kph with the promise of even greater speeds in the near future. The popular press contained articles about sub-orbital space planes

(*The Sunday Telegraph*, 1999) and other new transport technologies. At the cinema, grand spectaculars of future space travel attracted large audiences. Films such as *Star Wars Episode 1 – The Phantom Menace* speculated on the political intrigues and methods of warfare of civilizations many millennia in the future. Other features including *Deep Impact* and *Meteor* looked at the possibilities of space travel in the near future, echoing earlier science fiction writings of travel to the moon by Jules Verne.

The close of the twentieth century marks the end of history's greatest 100-year period of transport development with the potential for even greater change in the twenty-first century. The technological advances of the twentieth century provided the foundation for the emergence of the global tourism system where even the remotest corner of the planet is connected to the most urbanized area via the global transport system. The structure of the global transport system consists of an interconnected web of rail, road, sea and air travel modes which are in a constant state of change made possible by the almost continual introduction of new technologies. The following sections will examine technological advances in each mode and highlight possible implications for tourism in the near future.

Roads

Road-building technology remained almost static from Roman times until the late nineteenth century when all-weather roads were built using asphalt surfaces. Henry Ford's mass production of the Model-T Ford initiated a revolution in individual mobility. Freed of the need to rely on public transport with its inherently inflexible routes and timetables, the car has enabled travellers to set their own travel parameters, travelling when and where they liked. On the land, cars competed with rail for supremacy for some decades, eventually winning when the network of all-weather roads surpassed rail in its geographic spread and increasing national wealth facilitated widespread car ownership in developed economies.

Aside from relatively minor engineering improvements to vehicle design and engine efficiency, the technology used in cars remained relatively static for many decades until the widespread inclusion of computer technology commencing in the late 1980s. In the near future a number of new technologies may be incorporated into vehicle design to reduce reliance on fossil fuels and improve efficiency. This will be particularly important as non-renewable energy resources become scarce and therefore more expensive. Fuel cells appear to be one promising technology. In a recent demonstration of the potential of fuel cell technology, William Clay Ford, the grandson of Henry Ford, unveiled the P2000 hydrogen-powered saloon developed at Ford's plant in Aachen, Germany. Fuel cell technology produces electricity by mixing hydrogen with oxygen, creating an exhaust of pure water. Capable of speeds of 150 km/h and a range of 120 km, the P2000 is scheduled to begin mass production in 2004 (Massey, 1999), perhaps initiating a second automotive revolution. Significant improvements have also been made in the engineering aspects of road design and traffic control. Freeways and motorways have been built to allow high-speed travel, particularly in North America and Europe and increasingly in Asia and Latin America. Future development of automotive design may see a shift to automated highways where computer-controlled autopiloting will allow substantial increases in speed and safety (Davies, 1995; Rillings, 1997).

The introduction of high-speed highway systems, new automotive technologies and advanced computer-assisted traffic control will have significant implications for tourism. The dominance of the private car as the preferred mode of travel for short journeys has exerted a powerful influence on the design and location of tourism infrastructure. Where roads form the main transport arteries, they usually become the location of a substantial proportion of the infrastructure that supports the tourism industry. In Australia, for example, 78 per cent of domestic tourism was undertaken by car in 1996/97 (Bureau of Tourism Research, 1998) and caravan parks and motels represent a significant proportion of the nation's stock of tourism accommodation. Similar patterns may be observed in North America and many European countries. Despite the apparent supremacy of the car as the preferred form of short-distance travel at the close of the twentieth century, its dominance may be short-lived unless emission of pollutants are reduced or alternative propulsion systems are adopted.

Automobiles are a significant contributor to global pollution and global warming (Bureau of Transport and Communications Economics, 1996) and as signs of global warming become apparent considerable pressure will be placed on governments to control auto emissions and encourage greater use of public transport. New engine technology, improved car design and automated highways will lead the fight by automobile manufacturers to retain their current supremacy. Oil companies, however, will face enormous financial problems if new engine technologies such as fuel cells become feasible and widely accepted. The outcome of any future car versus public transport debate will have significant implications for tourism. Should the car in its present form lose the battle, there will be a considerable reorientation of transport and tourism infrastructure particularly in areas where the car is the primary mode of tourism transport. Road-dependent businesses such as motels and caravan parks will suffer, as will many attractions accessible only by road.

Sea

After roads, water is the oldest form of transport and, until the introduction of passenger jets, the only form of intercontinental travel. The relatively slow speed of ships greatly restricted their use for tourism because of lengthy passage times except across the Atlantic. For a relatively short time (1900 to the early 1960s), fast passenger liners sustained a buoyant travel and tourism industry embracing both

North America and Western Europe. The introduction of jet passenger aircraft, including the Comet, Boeing 707 and Douglas DC8, in the late 1950s caused the demise of the scheduled passenger liner during the 1960s. In its wake cruising emerged as a means of harnessing the tourism potential of the oceans. Cruising has grown in popularity, particularly in the Mediterranean and Caribbean, and resulted in the construction of a new generation of large luxury cruise ships. Although its role in intercontinental travel has been lost, sea has retained its popularity for short-haul ferry type services and short coastal voyages between islands and the mainland. Services of this type remain a popular mode of tourism transport in many regions including the Mediterranean, Baltic, Caribbean and in many parts of Asia.

Recent technological advances may enable the relatively leisurely speed of ships to be increased by new propulsion systems and new hull designs. These might include substitution of conventional propellers by water jets driven by gas turbines, use of multi-hull designs and new propulsion systems based on electromagnetic propulsion. Size might also increase and one recent proposal outlined plans for a super cruise boat capable of carrying up to 115,000 people and weighing 2.7 million tonnes. The proposed vessel, named *Freedom*, will circle the earth every two years, operating as both a residential tax haven and a cruise boat (Wilson, 1998).

Although new technology may produce increased speed and carrying capacity, it is unlikely that the future enhancement of capabilities will be sufficient to alter the current balance between sea and other modes used for tourism transport. Perhaps the only circumstances where new technology might make some impact on the existing passenger mix between modes is if coastal passenger services and ferry services can capture a larger share of the passenger markets in which they operate.

Rail

Railways ushered in the modern tourism era in the 1840s yet, within a period of a little over a hundred years, rail had lost its dominance, surrendering to the flexibility of the automobile and the speed and comfort of the jet plane. Introduction of new technologies in recent decades has allowed rail to recapture some passenger traffic from road and air transport. Development of Very Fast Trains (VFT) has enabled rail to compete with other modes on the basis of speed, comfort, safety and importantly, price. Recent progress in research into maglev technology may lead to even faster trains in the future. In Europe, a number of high-speed train networks have been constructed including the German InterCity Express (ICE), French train à grande vitesse (TGV) and the Anglo-French Eurostar which links Paris and Brussels with London via the English Channel Tunnel (Kemp, 1995). In Japan, the Shinkansen network, first introduced in 1964, continues to expand. High-speed trains are also planned for Australia, Korea, Poland, Turkey, Hungary and Russia.

Continuing research into new methods of propulsion, track technology, signalling and train design may enable future high-speed trains to cruise comfortably at speeds of up to 400 kph (Raoul, 1997), although at speeds above 350 kph the high energy consumption of VFTs compares unfavourably with air travel.

In the future, maglev technology may replace current electrically powered Very Fast Trains and in some cases road and air transport, particularly on short-haul routes. Maglev uses high-strength magnets to lift and propel a train several centimetres above a monorail guideway (Stix, 1997), giving it the potential to achieve higher speeds than current systems. Various techniques to achieve levitation include electromagnetics on the train to achieve lift (electromagnetic), electromagnets on the guideway to levitate the train (electrodynamic) and permanent magnets over passive coils to achieve lift (inductrack) (Gourley, 1998). Speeds of up to 500 kph are anticipated. Although the technology remains experimental despite 30 years of research, a future long-distance maglev network could increase pressure on airlines by offering a viable alternative transport mode (Miller, 1995).

Very fast rail has already altered travel patterns in Europe, capturing tourist traffic from both road and air. Further increases in speed either of the VFT class of fast train or a future commercial maglev train will create new opportunities for the tourism industry by reducing travel times yet offering a level of comfort comparable to planes.

Travelling by train has also developed into a growing niche market. The nostalgia and romance of rail travel epitomized by train journeys such as the Orient Express has caused a resurgence in demand for rail as a tourism experience (Prideaux, 1999). The renewed interest in rail has encouraged railway companies to market new train journeys and created a growing interest in historical rail journeys operated either as commercial ventures or by non-profit rail preservation societies.

Aviation

The introduction of long-range jet passenger aircraft has made mass inter-continental travel possible and has greatly assisted remote countries, including Australia and the Pacific Island nations, to develop significant inbound tourism industries. Aviation began to exert a significant impact on the tourism industry with the introduction of passenger jets in the late 1950s. In ensuing decades the introduction of new technologies has caused air fares to fall while safety and comfort levels have risen. Except for the limited operation of the Concorde, speed has not increased due to the high cost of developing and operating this class of aircraft. In the future, the options for aviation development are, supersonic aircraft, larger subsonic aircraft and/or sub-space planes. Based on the operation of the Concorde and the accumulated expertise of aircraft manufacturers and operators over the last four decades, it appears that the main factor likely to determine the technology to be adopted will be operating costs. Technically, a new generation of supersonic transport (SST) aircraft is feasible and a number of designs have been proposed in recent decades, including the Boeing supersonic 280 passenger High-Speed Commercial Transport project. The research and development costs of aircraft of this type are enormous and their introduction will depend almost entirely on the ability of the SST to compete with subsonic aircraft including future super jumbo aircraft such as the proposed 656 seat Airbus A3XX-200 (Carman, 1999). While it is theoretically possible to develop a space plane, a substantial amount of engineering refinement and testing will be required to build a production model (Davis, 1995). Space planes similar to the proposed Hypersonic Systems Technology Program (HySTP) funded by NASA (Pope, 1994) will reduce travel times by flying into sub-orbital space. To achieve the speeds required, new engine technologies, including the proposed scramjet (fuelled by a blended mix of hydrogen fuel), would be required. Ultimately, the cost of flying by space plane versus subsonic aircraft will be a major determining factor on when rather than if it is built.

A major impediment to the introduction of both SSTs and space planes is the need for the private sector to fund the research and development costs of commercializing the technology required. In the past, much of the funding for research and development of new aviation technology has been provided by governments as part of their military budgets. Unless there is a military need for aircraft of this type the high research and development costs may preclude their early introduction. It is therefore likely that in the foreseeable future commercial aviation will continue to rely on incremental development of large subsonic aircraft.

The introduction of either a space plane or SST will have a significant impact on the tourism industry by reducing the travel times to current long-haul destinations. Asia and Australasia, currently long-haul destinations for Europeans, will become medium-haul destinations if SSTs are developed or a short-haul destination if the space plane is introduced. The implications for tourism are enormous. New markets will be opened and traditional markets will face new competitors.

Space

The major impediment to space travel has been the high cost of launch vehicles principally because of their expandable nature (Space Tourism, 1999). This problem will be solved if reusable single-to-orbit launch vehicles can be developed. Currently, NASA and Lockheed Martin are preparing to launch the X-33 technology demonstrator to confirm systems necessary for single-to-orbit operations and, if successful, a new launch vehicle able to be flown like an airliner will be built as a possible space shuttle replacement (Mattingly, 1997). A number of new propulsion technologies are currently under development or are under consideration, including scramjets, Ion engines, a linear aerospike engine and nuclear fission propulsion. If the cost per kilogram of launching passengers and cargo into space can be substantially reduced, the way would be open for the introduction of commercial passenger flights. As in the past, the commercialization of space is following the historical model of war (spy and military communications satellites), followed by trade (commercial satellites) and finally by travellers (commencing with the crews of space ships including the Space Shuttle and Soyuz series). The commercialization of space has progressed rapidly and by 1996 space was generating estimated revenue of US$77 billion per annum (Beardsley, 1999).

The intriguing possibility of the commercialization of space with tourism flights is still some way off. Current chemical combustion engines are expensive to operate and until replaced by newer and cheaper technologies will inhibit the commercialization of space for tourism. Other hurdles that will need to be surmounted prior to the commercialization of space for tourism include the problem of weightlessness, possible risks to health, safety and the high g-forces encountered on blast-off. Once in space, travellers will face a range of lifestyle challenges as a consequence of weightlessness as well as restrictions on movement and limited opportunities for participating in the type of activities usually associated with earthside tourism. Perhaps the first tourists into space will follow the pattern of the first aeroplane travellers and participate in space travel for its novelty value. Mass space tourism will follow but the time-frame is unknown and most likely many decades into the future. Overall, the impact of space on the world's tourism industry will be small for many decades into the future, in the same manner that aeroplanes were essentially a novelty for their first 40 years. However, when developments in space are viewed as the newest component of the transport system, it is apparent that current technological hurdles will be surmounted in much the same way as earlier scientists and engineers developed the jet engine and radar in the 1940s.

CONCLUSION

In the past, changes in the operation of the transport system were a product of the supply side in that new technologies were adopted as they became available, primarily to service military requirements. In the future, this trend may change and introduction of new technologies may become more demand-oriented with the ability to pay being the major factor in determining which technologies are ultimately adopted. It is also possible that space travel may be the final new transport mode, unless exotic technologies such as teleporting and interstellar travel via some unknown technology are developed at some time in the future.

The advantage of viewing the impact of transport technology on tourism from the standpoint of history is that it enables observations to be made of the impact of technological change on the processes moulding the development of the tourism industry. With the aid of an historical perspective, questions about the future interaction between transport and tourism can be approached from a more informed basis and 'what if' questions answered with some degree of certainty. For instance, in the same way that the slower trains of the 1950s were superseded by cars, will the new generation of fast trains see travellers turn back to rail? Will rail retain its newly won markets if new technology allows the average speed of road travel to increase? Will SSTs replace jumbo jets in the near future? For the tourism industry, the question of technological change in transport will shape future planning and investment. If space planes are introduced at some future date, will the blurring of the boundaries between short- and medium-haul increase competition and weaken the loyalty of existing visitor sectors? Will new transport systems make some currently viable businesses obsolete? These types of question cannot be answered with a high degree of accuracy given the speculative nature of forecasting but it does enhance management's ability to plan for and cope with foreseeable change.

In the foreseeable future the transport industry will follow an evolutionary path rather than the revolutionary path observable over the last 160 years. Even with the slow commercialization of space it is unlikely that mass space tourism will become a regular feature of travel agencies' brochures in the near future. Each mode is undergoing technological development and creating a see-saw effect between modes. Thus rail might regain many of the passengers it lost to the car as the speed of rail increases and the cost of operating a car increases.

The tourism industry will benefit from future technological improvements to the transport system, principally in the areas of lower price and greater speed. Following the patterns of the past, falling cost and increased speed will increase the propensity for people to travel. New tourism destinations will open although increasing numbers of tourists will create problems of sustainability in all destinations.

ACKNOWLEDGEMENT

I wish to acknowledge the assistance of my daughter Jillian Prideaux, who helped with the research undertaken for this chapter.

REFERENCES

Anon. (1987) 'Tourism in Space'. *Tourism Management,* **7**(3), 222.

Anon. (1999) 'Rocket off to Europe'. *The Sunday Telegraph,* 29 August, 55.

Beardsley, T. (1999) 'The way to go in space'. *Scientific American,* **10**(1), 58–75.

Brook, S. (1999) 'Homo Erectus walking, talking and boating some 840,000 years ago'. *The Australian,* 6 July, 6.

Bureau of Tourism Research (1998) *Domestic Tourism Monitor 1996/97.* Canberra: Bureau of Tourism Research.

Bureau of Transport and Communications Economics (1996) *Transport and Greenhouse Costs and Options for Reducing Emissions Report 94.* Canberra: Bureau of Transport and Communications Economics.

Carman, G. (1999) 'Grappling with reality, not a dream'. *Aircraft & Aerospace,* **78**(6), 10–15.

Casson, L. (1974) *Travel in the Ancient World.* London: John Hopkins.

Chew, J. (1987) 'Transport and tourism in the year 2000'. *Tourism Management,* **8**(2), 83–5.

Davies, P. (1995) 'The intelligent highway: into the twenty-first century'. In G. B. R. Feildon, A. H. Wickens and I. R. Yates (eds) *Passenger Transport After 2000 AD.* London: Spoon, pp. 199–208.

Davis, R. A. (1995) 'From physics to customers: the Jet Age Phase II'. In G. B. R. Feildon, A. H. Wickens and I. R. Yates (eds) *Passenger Transport After 2000 AD.* London: Spoon, pp. 137–43.

Eoley, M. A. (1975) *Lost World of the Aegean.* Nederland: Time-Life International.

Gartner, W. C. (1996) *Tourism Development Principles, Processes, and Policies.* New York: Van Nostrand Reinhold.

Gilbert, D. C. (1990) 'Conceptual issues in the meaning of tourism'. In C. P. Cooper (ed.) *Progress in Tourism, Recreation and Hospitality Management,* Vol. 2. London: Belhaven, pp. 4–27.

Gilbert, E. W. (1939) 'The growth of inland and seaside health resorts in England'. *The Scottish Geographical Magazine,* **55**(1), 16–35.

Gormsen, E. (1981) *The Spatio-Temporal Development of International Tourism: Attempt at a Centre Periphery Model.* La Consommation d'Espace par le Tourisme et sa Preservation. CHET, Aix-En-Provence: Centre des Hautes du Tourisme.

Gourley, S. R. (1998) 'Tracks to the future'. *Popular Mechanics.* http://popularmechanics.com/popmech/sci/98

Gunn, C. A. (1994) *Tourism Planning Basics Concepts Cases.* Washington: Taylor & Francis.

Hall, C. M. (1991) *Introduction to Tourism in Australia: Impacts, Planning and Development.* Melbourne: Longman Cheshire.

Inskeep, E. (1991) *Tourism Planning. An Integrated and Sustainable Development Approach.* New York: Van Nostrand Reinhold.

Kaiser, C. and Helber, L. E. (1978) *Tourism Planning and Development.* Boston: CBI Publishing, p. 144.

Kaspar, C. and Laesser, C. (1994) 'Systems approach'. In S. F. Witt and L. Mountinho (eds) *Tourism Marketing Handbook.* Hertfordshire: Prentice-Hall.

Kemp, P. (1995). 'The European High Speed Network'. in G. B. R. Feildon, A. H. Wickens and I. R. Yates (eds) *Passenger Transport After 2000 AD.* London: Spoon, pp. 63–83.

Kraul, R. N. (1985) *Dynamics of Tourism: A Trilogy, Vol 111 Transportation and Marketing.* New Delhi: Sterling Publishers.

Leiper, N. (1979) 'The framework of tourism: towards a definition of tourism, tourist, and the tourism industry'. *Annals of Tourism Research,* **6**, 390–407.

McKinlay, R. M. (1995) 'Airbus and future passenger aircraft'. In G. B. R. Feildon, A. H. Wickens and I. R. Yates (eds) *Passenger Transport After 2000 AD.* London: Spoon, pp. 163–75.

Maczak, A. (1995) *Travel in Early Modern Europe.* Cambridge: Polity Press.

Massey, R. (1999). 'Car without a choke'. *The Courier Mail,* 17 June, 5.

Mattingly, T. K. (1997) 'A simpler ride into space'. *Scientific American,* **277**(4), 88–93.

Mill, R. C. and Morrison, A. M. (1985) *The Tourism System: An Introductory Text*. New Jersey: Prentice-Hall.

Miller, L. (1995) 'High Speed Maglev Systems'. In G. B. R. Feildon, A. H. Wickens and I. R. Yates (eds) *Passenger Transport After 2000 AD*. London: Spoon, pp. 101–27.

Miossec, J. M. (1976). *Elements pour une Théorie de l'Espace Tourisque*. CHET, Aix-en-Provence: Les Cahiers du Tourisme, C–36.

Page, S. J. (1999) *Transport and Tourism: 'Themes in Tourism' Series*. London: Addison Wesley Longman.

Pearce. D. (1987) *Tourism Today: A Geographical Analysis*. London: Longman.

Pope, G. T. (1994) 'Scramjets get serious'. *Popular Mechanics*.
http://popularmechanics.com/popmech/sci/9411STTRBM.html

Prideaux, B. (1999) 'Tracks to tourism: Queensland Rail joins the tourism industry'. *International Journal of Tourism Research*, **1**(2), 73–86.

Prideaux, B. (2000). 'The role of the transport system in destination development'. *Tourism Management*, **21**(1), (forthcoming).

Raoul, J. C. (1997) 'How high-speed trains make tracks'. *Scientific American*, **277**(4), 68–73.

Rillings, J. A. (1997) 'Automated highways'. *Scientific American*, **277**(4), 52–7.

Robinson, H. (1976) *A Geography of Tourism*. London: MacDonald and Evans.

Space Tourism (1999) http://www.spacefuture.com/tourism/tourism.shtml (30 August).

Stix, G. (1997) 'Maglev: racing to oblivion?' *Scientific American*, **277**(4), 77.

Wilson, J. (1998) 'City at sea'. *Popular Mechanics*.
http://popularmechanics.com/popmech/sci/9802STRSAM.html

World Tourism Organization (1994) *Recommendations on Tourism Statistics*. Madrid: World Tourism Organization.

Wouk, V. (1997) 'Hybrid electric vehicles'. *Scientific American*, **227**(4), 44–8.

CHAPTER 7

Tourist Attractions: Evolution, Analysis and Prospects

Philip Pearce,[1] Pierre Benckendorff and Suzanne Johnstone

INTRODUCTION

The attraction literature in tourism is dominated by the metaphor of magnetism. This image, reoccurring in tourism writing for at least one hundred and fifty years, sees key tourism sites as luring tourists to a specific point. Examples of the 'magnetic' power of key attractions to shape the travel experience are richly featured in travel writing from Mark Twain to John Steinbeck, and from Clive James to Umberto Eco. Visitors, according to this view, are much like iron filings drawn inexorably to a positive magnetic pole. Since such metaphors can overly structure (and limit) our creative thinking, perhaps it is time at the start of a new century to draw some new tourism attraction analogies. In itself this is not a novel suggestion. Leiper (1995) expressed dissatisfaction with the literal interpretation of the term attraction and has explicitly emphasized visitors' needs and the relative qualities of home and visited sites to explain travel flows. Additionally, a diversity of writers in problem-solving, scientific thinking and the creative reformulation of problems has suggested that periodically we need to refresh our metaphors and analogies to stimulate better analysis (Nadler *et al.*, 1999; Gilovich, 1993; Langer, 1989).

It is perhaps desirable to suggest that attractions in a region might be thought of as analogous to a dynamic matrix of force fields affecting bodies with varying degrees of susceptibility. Such an analogy directs attention to the competition between attractions in a finite area, addresses management and marketing influences which can shape the power of the fields and highlights audience receptivity and choice.

Armed with this new analogy, the present chapter reviews tourist attraction development and classification and, through select examples, profiles empirical studies of attractions varying in their success. Further, the chapter will also consider some key concepts to understand attraction success better and note emerging trends from recent studies of attractions. The work reported here undertakes these reviews in order to establish the nature of the influences which have, are and are likely to work in the force fields of the attraction sector. In conclusion, the chapter will direct attention to emerging technologies and evolving management responses which are likely to produce new attraction products.

HISTORY AND EVOLUTION OF ATTRACTIONS

The history of attractions has often been inextricably linked with the development of the travel industry as a whole. It can generally be said that older attractions are either natural attractions or man-made attractions that were not designed principally to appeal to travellers. Some of the best examples include Niagara Falls and the Pyramids at Luxor. Conversely, most modern attractions have been purpose-built for visitors, such as Disney World in Orlando or the themed gambling palaces of Las Vegas (Swarbrooke, 1999). Towner (1995) argues that the history of tourism, and thus the history of attractions, is fundamentally presented from the perspective of Western culture. For example, an Asian perspective on attractions might emphasize a multiplicity of motives such as feasting, fasting or cultural celebrations and thus give rise to a different evolutionary story in attraction development. It is wise, perhaps, for attraction researchers not to be trapped by a local or parochial cultural view. In the following overview the reader's attention is directed towards the changing social definition of attractions, the global diversity of attraction products and the persistence of some of the earliest attraction types and sites through to modern times.

Attractions of the Ancient World

Casson (1994) provides an insightful and definitive analysis of travel between 3000 BC and AD 600 and identifies a number of key attractions and motives for travel during this period. The Ancient Egyptians were attracted to religious festivals several times a year. During the New Kingdom in Egypt (1600 to 1200 BC) a number of prominent monuments such as the Sphinx and the great pyramids of Giza were already over 1000 years old and graffiti left by curious sightseers can be found on the walls of these attractions (Feifer, 1985; Casson, 1994).

In Ancient Greece such attractions as the Parthenon, the Oracle at Delphi and the athletic competitions at Olympia were prominent (Casson, 1994). A noteworthy collection of attractions includes the seven wonders of the world identified by an unknown scholar in the third century BC. These include the Pyramids, the Hanging Gardens at Babylon, the statue of Zeus at Olympia, the Temple of Artemis at Ephesus, the Mausoleum, the Colossus of Rhodes and the Lighthouse at Alexandria. Certain natural features, such as springs, caves and mountains, also became attractions because of their association with literary, religious, historical and military events (Casson, 1994).

The Roman calendar boasted a huge number of public holidays, allowing Roman citizens the opportunity to visit attractions such as the Colosseum which offered chariot racing, boxing, theatrical performances and gladiatorial shows (Casson, 1994). The Roman Empire also gave rise to a number of early coastal resorts such as the Bay of Naples, whilst the health-giving properties of mineral springs or *aquae*, such as Bath in Britain, proved to be fashionable attractions in their own right (Feifer, 1985; Casson, 1994). Ancient museums, usually housed in religious sanctuaries, also existed in Greece and Rome. All centres of the Roman Empire were linked by an extensive network of roads which allowed travellers safe access to popular Roman attractions (Feifer, 1985). The key motives for visiting attractions during ancient times thus appear to involve the gratification of needs associated with health, curiosity and the expression of culture and religion.

Attractions of the modern world

The disintegration of the Roman Empire and the advent of the Dark Ages resulted in what Laistner (1930, p. 19) describes as 'the decay of geographical knowledge and the decline of exploration'. The deterioration of a common currency and language and the loss of a reliable road network prevented people from travelling to attractions in any great numbers. It was only during the medieval period that certain attractions once again began to flourish. During this time religious pilgrimages were actively encouraged by the Church and destinations such as Jerusalem, Rome, Canterbury and Santiago de Compostela became popular (Rinschede, 1992; Smith, 1992). The attractions at these destinations included religious artefacts and shrines, such as the shrine of St Thomas à Becket in the Cathedral at Canterbury. As Chaucer's *Canterbury Tales* suggest, these religious pilgrimages evolved into more than just the pursuit of religious fulfilment. Pilgrim hostels en route to religious attractions were replaced by inns which provided opportunities for entertainment, social gatherings, matchmaking, gambling and illicit activities (Sumption, 1975; Smith, 1992).

During the rule of Elizabeth I of Britain (1558–1603) travel to a wider range of attractions became popular. The growth in travel was fuelled partly by a special type of attractions-based exploration known as the *Grand Tour*. The Grand Tour was designed as an educational experience for the young men of European aristocracy. The tour itinerary included important historical and cultural sites and ranged from 40 months in the mid-sixteenth century to 4 months in the early nineteenth century (Towner, 1985). Towner suggests that the decline in tour length is due to several factors, including a change in the nature of the tour, a greater influx of the middle classes with limited time and money and the unsettled conditions created by the French Revolution and Napoleonic Wars. Gentlemen participating in the Grand Tour were motivated by a desire to experience and learn about the wonders and cultures of both the modern and ancient worlds. Attractions commonly included continental universities and scholars, art galleries, museums and collections, and architectural marvels.

The seventeenth century saw the re-emergence of the hot springs and spas originally used by the Romans (Pimlott, 1947). These spas were reputed to have numerous health-giving properties. Key destinations included Bath and Buxton in Britain, Wiesbaden and Baden-Baden in Germany and Vichy in France. Visitation to these spa towns also triggered the development of a number of secondary attractions to provide visitors with a range of activities. Pimlott (1947) draws attention to the fact that Bath was one of the first towns outside London to boast its own public theatre. Other supplementary attractions included parks and gardens, assembly rooms, pumping rooms and dancing halls (Pimlott, 1947; Towner, 1996). Clearly, by the end of the eighteenth century attractions were not only based on heritage sites but had started to expand to purpose-built facilities to suit tourist needs and activities. Several travelling fairs also started to move between towns during this period (Walsh-Heron and Stevens, 1990).

The Industrial Revolution sparked a number of social and technological changes which ultimately enhanced the demand for attractions. Demand for an affordable method of transporting increasing numbers of travellers from industrial centres to holiday areas led to the development of rail networks in Europe and North America. Concurrently, the concentration of populations in large industrial centres created the need for holidays as a means of maintaining health and efficiency (Pimlott, 1947).

Burgeoning seaside resorts emerged in the mid-eighteenth century amidst claims that bathing and drinking of sea water offered numerous health benefits (Walton, 1983). In Britain, resorts such as Brighton and Scarborough grew rapidly and soon challenged the status of Bath as fashionable holiday destinations (Towner, 1996). Like spa resorts, seaside resorts also sought to offer a diverse range of tourist activities through attractions such as tea gardens, aviaries, aquaria, winter gardens, pier promenades and open-air entertainment (Walton, 1983). In the latter part of the nineteenth century seaside pleasure gardens and travelling fairs began to evolve into more static fair parks, which were to become the forerunners of modern theme parks (Walton, 1983). During this period a number of casinos also emerged as attractions on the French Riviera and ski resorts developed in both Europe and North America to meet the growing demand for skiing and mountaineering activities (Swarbrooke, 1999).

By the end of the nineteenth century the history of attractions leads us out of Europe and to the emergence of major environmental and cultural sites on other continents. In particular, the declaration of the great national parks of North America characterizes renewed interest in natural attractions (Jakle, 1985; Swadling, 1992).

The early twentieth century saw the rise of event-based attractions such as the re-emergence of the modern Olympic Games and other sports events (Swarbrooke,

1999). The advent of Henry Ford's motor car and the proliferation of paid annual holidays led to greater flexibility and increased demand for attractions that offered relaxation, adventure and amusement (Pimlott, 1947; Belasco, 1981). The growth of small local attractions was fostered by this new breed of independent travellers. Interest in exotic destinations and wildlife led to the creation of modern zoological gardens and safari parks in Africa, Europe and North America. Holiday camps offering self-contained accommodation, communal dining, organized amusements, dance halls, bathing pools and sports fields emerged near urban centres (Pimlott, 1947). While these camps provided lodging for several thousand visitors, they also became attractions in their own right. Seaside resorts, health spas and health resorts also continued to develop with a greater range of activities and facilities (Towner, 1996).

The continuing trends of increased leisure time, greater mobility and higher disposable income heralded a boom in the attractions sector after the Second World War. For the first time attractions were being purpose-built specifically for recreation and entertainment. Many businesses not traditionally associated with tourism began to develop themed tourist attractions. The entertainment industry embraced the concept of theme parks to create mass entertainment venues such as Disneyland and the Six Flags theme parks. Parallel attractions quickly emerged throughout the world, such as Dreamworld in Australia, Gardaland in Italy and Gold Reef City in South Africa. In the late twentieth century Asian countries also enthusiastically developed theme parks, such as Singapore's Sentosa Island, Japan's Disneyland and Korea's Lotteworld. A number of shopping centres and waterfront developments have also become tourist attractions in their own right (Judd, 1995; Swarbrooke, 1999).

The consideration of the evolution of attractions heightens awareness of the social and technological changes which continually reshape visitor demand for leisure opportunities. The review suggests strongly that attractions are continuously being identified, discovered and created to suit changing national and international tastes, motives and purchasing power.

MULTIPLE EMPHASES

Following a generic evolutionary examination, attention will now be focused on a multiple emphases approach which examines specific levels of contemporary attraction definition and analysis.

Defining attractions

Attractions have been defined with both generic and specific aims in mind. Pearce (1991) provided a generic definition, which encompassed many settings and circumstances. He suggested:

Table 7.1 Some classifications of tourist attractions

Classification Emphasis

1.	*Natural* (Scottish Highlands, Yosemite)	*Purpose-built* (Universal Studios, Six Flags parks)
2.	*Outdoor* (San Diego Zoo)	*Indoor* (Smithsonian Museums)
3.	*Heritage-based* (not purpose-built for tourism) (English cathedrals)	*Purpose-built for tourism* (Stockman's Hall of Fame, Australia) (Jorvic Viking Centre, UK)
4.	*Special global events* (Olympics)	*Local festivals/events* (Local parades, exhibitions)
5.	*Drawing power (high)* (Great Barrier Reef, Australia)	*Drawing power (low)* (local recreation sites)
6.	*Ownership* (Star City Casino)	*Stewardship* (Banff World Heritage Area, Canada)
7.	*Content themes:* Historical (Sovereign Hill, Australia), Cultural (Amish communities), Music (Branson, Nashville, USA), Sporting (events, museums, Halls of Fame), Military (Gallipoli, Culloden), Art (the Prado/Louvre), Marine (aquaria), Animals (zoos, sanctuaries).	

> A tourist attraction is a named site with a specific human or natural feature which is the focus of visitor and management attraction. (1991, p. 9)

Similarly, Middleton (1988) in Swarbrooke (1999) argued that a tourist attraction is:

> A designed permanent resource which is controlled and managed for the enjoyment, amusement, entertainment and education of the visiting public. (1999, p. 3)

These broad definitions are supplemented by a number of classifications. Table 7.1 sets out a selection of classifications that have evolved over the last decade.

Emphasis on management

It is clear from an historic view that tourist attractions are inextricably linked with the growth of travel and leisure. Initially classification emphasis revolved around the attraction itself, with little importance given to the needs and motives of people travelling to the attraction, and the roles of the attraction managers (Lew, 1994). Some recent shifts in classification emphases can be noted here. There has been an increase in the need for specific classifications, taking into consideration not only the attraction itself but other factors such as marketing activities and the style of management. This marketing and management emphasis can provide an understanding of trends in different attraction classifications thus promoting a transfer of knowledge from attraction sectors which do not usually communicate with each other (Pearce, 1998).

Emphasis on visitors

While it has become increasingly common to identify the management directions for attractions, it is just as important to identify the motives and activities of the people who visit the attraction. The growth and continued development of organizations such as the Visitor Studies Association is testimony to the need to build a cumulative research base for enhanced attraction design, management and evaluation (Screven, 1999). This rapidly growing topic area is rich in market appraisals and interpretation research and provides an important source of information as we identify future attraction trends in a later section of this paper.

PATHWAYS TO THE FUTURE

A consideration of the tourist attraction history and tourist attraction classification needs to be augmented by a consideration of some conceptual approaches to tourist attraction study. While description and classification are worthwhile, an understanding of the force fields at work in any tourism attraction space is likely to be enhanced by ideas which integrate and synthesize the descriptive database (Dann *et al.*, 1988). Four such mechanisms can be outlined: Gunn's model of tourist attractions zones; an adapted form of Canter's model to describe places; a marketing model built on Kotler's ideas; and a stages model from the sociological writing of MacCannell (Gunn, 1985; Canter, 1977; Kotler, 1994; MacCannell, 1976, 1990).

The concentric rings model

According to Gunn (1985) tourist attractions can be understood by a concentric ring model (see Figure 7.1). This model presents tourist attractions as having a nucleus which is the core attraction. Successful attractions should have an inviolate belt which provides a context in which the nucleus or core attraction can be appreciated. Further, Gunn argues that an outer ring labelled the zone of closure is a necessary part of a well-planned tourist attraction.

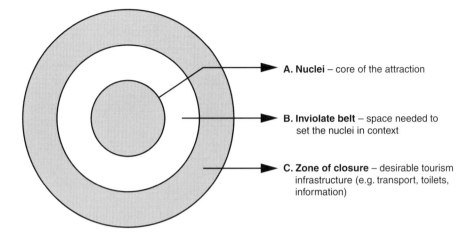

Figure 7.1 Gunn's model of a tourist attraction. *Source*: Gunn, 1985

All visitor services and facilities, but particularly transport, toilets, kiosks and souvenir shops, should be in the zone of closure. Gunn does not discuss whether information services should only be in the zone of closure or whether they are permissible in the inviolate belt or close to the nucleus, but since no particular mention is made of information and interpretive services it is, perhaps, best to assume that they should be found in the zone of closure.

Gunn's model implicitly argues that any tourist attraction missing one of these zones will be incomplete, possibly hard to manage and likely to attract visitor criticism. That is, attractions where the core is poorly defined, where there is limited context in which to experience the attraction or where visitor services are poorly developed will be unsatisfactory. Gunn's model is more applicable to single site tourist attractions, as opposed to features which have multiple nuclei (such as a collection of restored houses). There may be a need to consider each attraction in the multiple nuclei case as a separate item with its own inviolate belt and zone of closure.

A sense of place model

A second approach which helps collate the range of ideas about tourist attractions can be developed from Canter's work on the psychology of place (Canter, 1977; Pearce, 1988). Canter summarized a considerable body of literature in psychology, geography, planning and the design field to present a concise Venn diagram summary of the components necessary to gain a 'sense of place'.

The three elements presented in Figure 7.2 – the physical attributes of a setting, the activities one performs in a setting and the conceptions people bring to a setting –

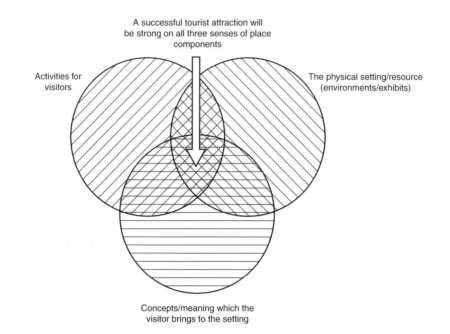

Figure 7.2 Canter's 'place' model applied to a tourist attraction. *Source*: Pearce, 1991

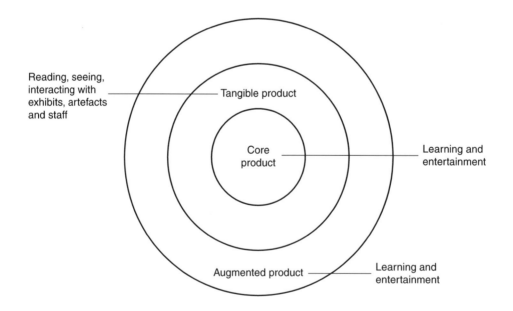

Figure 7.3 Kotler's adapted model. *Source*: Swarbooke, 1995

are all required if one is to understand fully and experience the unique sense of a specific location. In extending the general place mode to tourist attractions, the same three elements are all required. A good tourist attraction, according to this deductive approach, is one in which the public has clear conceptions of what the place is about, and is one where the activities in the setting are understood, accessible and excite public imagination. Furthermore, the physical elements which comprise the setting should be distinctive and aesthetically pleasing.

Levels of product approach

Kotler (1994) argues that the planners and marketers of tourist attractions, like other industry personnel, need to think about their products at three levels. The first of these levels is labelled core product (largely human needs or services), the second tangible product (purchases to meet the psychological needs) and the third augmented product (the functional elements needed to make the other product levels work). Swarbrooke (1999) applies Kotler's idea to one specific form of attraction, the theme park. In Figure 7.3 the application of Kotler's ideas to a museum are illustrated.

Kotler's model emphasizes the importance of translating the core product (here the visitor's need for learning and entertainment) into a tangible product (appealing, effective displays and accessible staff, supported by good functional services).

Staged development

A sociological account of the development of tourist attractions is provided in the work of MacCannell (1976, 1990). MacCannell argues that there is an orderly development process which transforms sites from simple places to sacred and worthy attractions. The five stages he suggests are:

1. *naming the site:* providing a clear label and location
2. *framing and elevating:* effective promotion and control of admission
3. *enshrinement:* specifying peculiar and unique features of the setting
4. *social reproduction:* where a group or region identifies with the attraction
5. *mechanical reproduction:* souvenir or artefact manufacture.

MacCannell's stages are visible in such tourist attraction claims as the 'biggest', 'smallest', 'oldest' style of promotions (enshrinement) as well as in social reproduction ('Gateway to', 'Home of') and mechanical reproduction (commercial production of copies, miniatures and artefacts). The whole process is referred to as 'site sacrilization' and can be seen as equally applicable to such diverse attractions as Gracelands (Elvis Presley's mansion) and Aboriginal art sites.

One limitation of this approach is that it merely describes a possible ordered sequence in the development of tourist attractions rather than providing any sustainable tourism management guidelines. Nevertheless, an awareness that these processes are likely to take place or are developing forces in tourist attraction growth and change may assist managers in thinking about how to frame, enshrine and have people own and profit from the attraction.

Interpretation and markets

The presentation of conceptual models in the attraction field largely directs attention to the attractions or the attractions and services surrounding them. In building an understanding of the attractions sector, two further components of the system warrant attention. First, as mentioned in the classification sector, the nature of the audiences to attractions needs to be considered for each setting. Since this factor is generically powerful and pervasive it will be illustrated in the present chapter only in relation to the three specific 'success' case studies. Nevertheless, as we attempt to understand attraction history and attraction futures it remains a key issue for inclusion.

The final element to be included in any analysis of attractions is the special role of interpretation. In Kotler's terminology interpretation is a tangible product, in Canter's system it contributes to part of the concepts and meanings people bring to the situation, in Gunn's formulation it is an activity in both the ancillary and core zone and in MacCannell's evolutionary model it is central to the framing, elevating and enshrinement of the attraction.

In the current metaphor of tourist attractions as force fields, interpretation is effectively the shaping of the attraction's force field so that the visitor can connect to the experiences on offer. It is the 'high touch' element of attraction design and management which can ensure an attraction's success. Moscardo (1999), following the theoretical formulation of Langer (1989), suggests that good interpretation consists of making the visitor mindful, that is mentally active and involved in understanding what is being experienced. Table 7.2 itemizes some good practice practices for enhancing tourist attraction appeal through interpretation.

Table 7.2 Principles for effective interpretation. *Source:* Moscardo, 1999

1. *Vary the interpretive experience:* repetition of any communication style reduces effectiveness.
2. *Provide personal connection for visitors:* relate what is being described to the visitors' life experience.
3. *Practise participation:* a multisensory experience improves satisfaction.
4. *Organize orientation:* reduce the difficulty of wayfinding with clear maps and signs.
5. *Provide clear content:* make messages accessible and oriented to users.
6. *Allow for alternative audiences:* build in layers of information and opportunity to meet diverse audience needs.

CASE STUDIES: VARYING SUCCESS STORIES

This section considers three Australian tourist attractions where detailed analyses of visitors and attraction performance have been made. The purpose of considering these cases in some detail is to develop further our understanding of some of the forces at work in shaping contemporary tourist attractions. The cases will be described and reviewed and a cumulative view will then be provided of how they inform attraction futures.

The first case is that of the Skyrail Rainforest Cableway. This attraction in Far North Queensland, near Cairns, consists of an elevated transport system above the canopy of the World Heritage Rainforest. Visitors travel in six-person cabins or gondolas just above the treetops. In addition to ticketing and shopping facilities at the two ends of the cableway, there are two stations along the route. The lower station offers a rainforest boardwalk and the second station an interpretive centre and several lookouts over the adjacent gorge and waterfalls. Moscardo and Woods (1998) and Pearce and Moscardo (1998) have provided detailed reports on visitors to the attraction using both survey and detailed observation methodologies. On multiple indicators, this attraction is a key success story in the Australian tourist attractions scene. The business is profitable and has expanded in its short four-year history through the addition of extra gondolas on the cableway (K. Chapman, personal communication, May 1999). There is a high level of visitor satisfaction with the experience and a key component of the satisfaction was the effectiveness of the visitor interpretation. Moscardo and Woods (1998) report that the interpretive programmes offered at the visitor centre and on the boardwalk were 'successful at increasing independent travellers' rainforest knowledge' and further that the attraction lessened pressure on other nature-based sites which have more limited capacity to cope with intense tourism use.

The Tjapukai Cultural Park is a second North Queensland site immediately adjacent to the lower level entrance station of Skyrail. This cultural park concentrates on the history, cultural beliefs and dance performances of the Tjapukai people, the name for the local Aboriginal community of this part of the Wet Tropics rainforests. The attraction is a relocated attraction, being a larger, more expansive cultural presentation of the Tjapukai story than an earlier attraction located in a small rainforest village and operated as a dance performance only. Like its neighbouring attraction, Skyrail, the facilities are modern, purpose-built and well designed, attending to the principles of providing zones of closure, augmented products and enshrinement as suggested by the theoretical literature. The success story here is more modest than that of Skyrail. The Tjapukai cultural park is having some difficulty in building up the visitation level needed to service the infrastructure costs (D. Freeman, personal communication, May 1999). Detailed visitor satisfaction studies and analyses of ethnic tourism markets indicate that visitors who do experience the product are well satisfied (Pearce and Moscardo, 1999). Part of the problem appears to lie in the difficulty of communicating exactly what the attraction offers (in fact there are three key components: a history theatre, a laser cultural storytelling explanation and live dance performances) amid the appeal of other attractions in the region, notably rainforest experiences and reef tours and trips. The modest success of Tjapukai is testimony to the competitive context of regional tourism and the customer receptivity to different styles of products and offerings.

The case study also illustrates the applicability of components of Carter's approach to defining tourist places, since some of the limitations of Tjapukai in attracting and satisfying visitors is explained by an unclear conception of the product and experience and a weakly defined image of available activities.

The third case study reviews a detailed report by Leiper (1997) which examines the Big Banana, an early icon of Australian tourism. Essentially a large replica of the basic regional produce of the Coffs Harbour district in Northern New South Wales, this roadside attraction was a rest area stop, providing easy public access and financially dependent on souvenir and refreshment opportunities. The core market was the family and senior self-drive market. A redesigned 'Big Banana' converted the roadside attraction into a mini theme park with an entrance fee, hillside train ride and more expensive and expansive visitor facilities. Leiper links the failure of the attraction with inflated and inaccurate perspectives of the market. The eventual outcome resulted in the operators scaling down the expanded version of the site and returning to a basic roadside rest stop.

Conclusions from the case study approach

The three case studies direct attention to a number of dominant forces. These include clear communication to the target market of the attraction's offerings, a realistic assessment of market demand, the importance of assessing the spatial context in which attractions operate and the ease with which visitors can relocate their preferences. There is much cross-referencing here with the basic conceptual models, notably the work of Canter on the unique sense of place which attractions must strive to create. One way of summarizing this issue from the three case studies is to suggest that attraction managers must maintain a 'high-touch' style with their customers. That is, there must be a close scrutiny of how well the attraction communicates with and responds to the needs of the changing visitor market.

Another perspective on appraising the success of tourist attractions is the issue of value for money for the customer. In this view the core issue in understanding tourist attraction visitation would focus less on markets, communication and context, and more on price. Expressed briefly, this view contends that if the facility was seen as above some standard value for money curve it would be unappealing and ultimately non-profitable.

Benckendorff (1999) established some groundwork with a sample of 213 leisure and tourist attractions in the Australian context which helps to address the feasibility of this price-dominated interpretation. The base admission prices for adult and child entries, defined as the lowest cost of entry that did not include specials or discounts, were obtained. The amount of time spent by patrons at each establishment was estimated, based on responses from a number of establishments contacted.

The study focused on the relationship between time spent and entry prices. If a reductionist approach to tourist attractions is at all feasible, then at least there should be some linear relationship between these variables, as rational economic behaviour suggests that longer visitation should justifiably result in higher prices. Regression analysis indicates a medium to strong positive relationship between adult prices and time spent (accounting for 67.3 per cent of variance), and a reasonable positive relationship between children's prices and time spent (accounting for 58.2 per cent of variance).

This kind of analysis represents an important but not fully complete view of how to proceed with understanding tourist attractions. The approach could be developed further by considering different market segments or it could link entry price to the infrastructure value of the attraction, the number of visitors or the age of the attraction (Benckendorff, 1999). As the analysis of tourist attractions proceeds in the twenty-first century, the marriage between this kind of empirical approach to attraction analysis and the more holistic conceptual models already discussed may offer an important research pathway.

FUTURE TRENDS AND PROSPECTS

The final section of this chapter examines some future attraction trends based on the forces already discussed in historical and contemporary appraisals of the sector.

The noted author and commentator on life systems, Stephen Jay Gould, cautions against a particular mistake in reasoning about trends. He argues that there is

> An extensive fallacy in reasoning about trends – a focus on particulars or abstractions (often biased examples like the lineage of Homo sapiens), egregiously selected from a totality because we perceive these limited and uncharacteristic examples as moving somewhere – when we should be studying variation in the entire system and its changing pattern of spread through time . . . I shall illustrate a mode of interpretation that seems obvious once stated, but rarely enters our mental framework – trends properly viewed as results of expanding or contracting variation, rather than concrete entities moving in a definite direction. (Gould, 1997, pp. 15–16)

This thoughtful dissection of our propensity to think about trends as foreshadowing inevitable consequences of linear transition is paralleled in the tourism literature by the work on stages or phases of evaluation. For example, in the classic Butler tourism product life cycle model, each new stage of the cycle is seen as a progression, a shedding of the previous phases of being like a butterfly emerging from its chrysalid. It has been argued elsewhere that in human-based cultural systems such phases or stages of evolution are often overlapping and elements of earlier phases continue to coexist with new phases (Pearce *et al.*, 1991, 1996).

Gould's remarks represent a direct challenge to attraction trend spotters including some self-authored work (Pearce, 1998; Pearce *et al.*, 1998), commercial and academic writing on market trends (Mackay, 1995; World Tourism Organization, 1998) and some of the co-contributors to this volume and companion work (Laws *et al.*, 1998; Faulkner and Russell, 1997). It can be suggested that in the first two kinds of work there is an implied view that the market and management trends noted are a foretaste of the future. Even with the avowedly non-linear chaos view of change promoted by Faulkner and colleagues, tourism, and by implication tourist attractions, are seen as belonging to the category of dynamic systems which 'pass through phases involving transitions from one state to another'. Gould's views are therefore a timely reminder that systems have inherent variability and trends can usefully be seen as

> by products or side consequences of expansions and contractions in the amount of variation within a system, and not by anything directly moving anywhere . . . and [further] the reasons for expansion or contraction of a periphery may be very different from causes for a change in average values . . . we (should not) mistake the growth or shrinkage of an edge for movement of an entire mass. (1997, p. 33)

The prospects for tourist attractions described here are cast within these cautionary frameworks. As we note trends, we do so with the view that all attractions will not necessarily follow in this direction, nor do we maintain that tourist attractions will pass through predictable stages or phases of evolution in the simple product life cycle manner identified by Swarbrooke (1999). Instead, the view is that the trends discussed represent opportunities and possibilities for some tourist attractions. This view is congruent with the introductory metaphor to this chapter, where attraction systems were described as akin to force fields with their power and influence varying in time for target markets.

A distillation of much previous tourist attractions trend analysis can be summarized under two broad themes (cf. Ah-Keng, 1993; Boniface, 1995; Cox and Fox, 1991; Curtis and Camp, 1997; Hanna, 1997, 1998; Jacobsen, 1997; Martin and Mason, 1993; Moutinho, 1988; Pearce, 1991, 1998; Robinson, 1994; Stevens, 1991; Yale, 1990). There is both a contribution from *technology* in shaping attraction

Table 7.3 Prospects for tourist attraction futures

Area of Potential Influence	High Technology Contributions	High Touch Contributions
Management	• Computer-assisted financial, personal and customer records for knowledge-based decision-making.	• Better educated, highly skilled strategic attraction management staff.
Marketing	• Very precise, targeted, frequently evaluated marketing activities.	• New marketing roles to meet visitor needs.
Product development	• New technologies to simulate environments and experiences. • Better core of exhibits/resources.	• New roles for attraction personnel as experience facilitators, time managers and customer problem-solvers.
Interpretation and communication	• Major new uses of remote, controllable cameras, visual display for global, spatial and cultural performance access. • Massive data banks of interpretive information readily customized to individual biographies.	• Better pre-experience information off-site for visitor independence and effective staff-customer contact.

opportunities for the future and a contribution *from personal interaction and services*. The dual forces of this high-tech–high-touch power surge for tourist attractions is manifested in a number of areas as described in Table 7.3.

The use of high technology is already apparent in the development and transformation of attractions for the future. Some of these technologies can best be illustrated through the use of scenarios of attractions that may eventuate in the near future. It is clear from the historical review at the start of this chapter that travellers have always been drawn to places, people and objects which fascinate them. The only significant object of fascination that has not been touched by tourism is space. The development of affordable reusable rocket technology in the latter part of this decade has brought the prospect of space-based attractions one step closer. In the past few years a growing volume of research has been done on the subject and it is now clear that the establishment of commercial space tourism attractions is a realistic target for the next century (Ashford, 1997; Collins, 1999).

Recent estimates suggest that by 2020 about 1,000,000 passengers will travel to space annually at a cost of about $10,000 per person (Ashford, 1997). In an earlier analysis Ashford is clearly enthusiastic about the prospects of space as a tourist attraction:

> space tourism would expand rapidly, soon generating more revenue than any other commercial use of space, and eventually becoming a major sector of the tourism industry. (1990, p. 100)

It is conceivable that space tourists would explore their holiday options by consulting information presented on the Internet or on digital video disks (DVDs) rather than brochures. Once a desirable holiday has been selected visitors will board a reusable launch vehicle similar to the X-33 which is being tested by NASA in 1999 (NASA, 1999). After a short flight the vehicle would dock at a tethered docking station. From this point travellers will be transported to a space hotel by gondolas or lifts travelling skyward (Collins, 1999). The space hotel would offer some form of artificial gravity in addition to zero-gravity environments. Once on board the hotel guests will initially enjoy omnipotent views of Earth. Aided by digital technology, visitors will be able to zoom in on areas of the Earth's surface. For example, guests could enjoy viewing herds of wildebeest travelling across the Serengeti, or observing the hustle and bustle of New York from above.

As orbiting hotels become more sophisticated more advanced facilities will be developed. One direction of such developments will be to include larger rooms for guests to experience activities in zero gravity (Collins *et al.*, 1997). Guests will be able to take part in space sports which allow movement in a three dimensional stadium. Imagine, for example, participating in a game of basketball or viewing a ballet performance in a zero-gravity environment (Collins *et al.*, 1994). Other activities could include zero-gravity gymnasiums and artificial-gravity swimming pools (Collins *et al.*, 1997).

Guests from different nationalities will be able to communicate with each other through the use of universal translator devices. Similarly, guests will be able to use palm-sized devices to communicate with family and friends on Earth and to interact remotely with home appliances (Shafer, 1990). Space is clearly a viable attraction for a number of reasons and barriers of entry, such as the cost and technology constraints identified by Goodrich (1987), are slowly being eliminated.

For those who are unable to afford or stomach the thought of space travel, high technology offers further prospects. The refinement of virtual reality (VR) technology has the potential to alter drastically the nature of tourist attractions by simulating environments from our past, present and future. Virtual reality has been touted as 'a logical progression in the use of technology in tourism' (Cheong, 1995, p. 417). There are a myriad of applications for this technology, including the development of new attractions and the interpretation and communication of information. It is not beyond the bounds of imagination to conceive a high-technology theme park where visitors can experience simulations of high-risk recreational experiences such as skydiving, mountain climbing or underwater explorations. Furthermore, the use of 'Sensavision' televisions and simulators would allow tourist attraction patrons to experience elements such as temperature, humidity, smell and sight to create a truly unique interpretive and entertainment experience (Shafer, 1990).

SUMMARY

In conclusion, these vivid examples built on credible attraction trends suggest that future visitors will have much to engage their interest. Attractions, one can suggest, have historically been shown to expand and diversify as large social forces and specific market niches have emerged. In this century attractions have multiplied as independent travel has emerged. The blend of high-tech and high-touch trends to forge new attraction possibilities in the next hundred years is likely to see attraction growth further accelerate. Attention to attraction design and management may be in its early stages but a respectable literature and useful broad design models have emerged (Screven, 1999). Additionally there is a growing recognition that enhanced attraction management, like the better management of many tourism businesses, will be a combination of enhanced people skills and smarter use of technology. The twinning of these attraction trends has much to offer the future of sustainable tourism as attractions can be protectors, substitutes and educational aids for fragile resources and environments. Attractions in the future may no longer be simply a magnet for visitor attention but truly global force fields for sustainable tourism.

NOTE

1. Funding for this study was in part contributed by CRC-Sustainable Tourism and CRC-Rainforest.

REFERENCES

Ah-Keng, K. (1993) 'Evaluating the attractiveness of a new theme park'. *Tourism Management*, **14**(3), 202–10.
Ashford, D. M. (1990) 'Prospect for space tourism'. *Tourism Management*, **11**(2), 99–104.

Ashford, D. M. (1997) 'Space tourism: how soon will it happen?' Proceedings from the 1997 IEEE Aerospace Conference, Snowmass, Colorado, February 1–8.

Belasco, J. (1981) *Americans on the Road.* Cambridge, Mass.: MIT Press.

Benckendorff, P. J. (1999) 'The pricing of leisure attractions: a preliminary study of Queensland establishments'. Unpublished report. Tourism Program, School of Business, James Cook University.

Boniface, P. (1995) *Managing Quality Cultural Tourism.* London: Routledge.

Canter, D. (1977) *The Psychology of Place.* London: The Architectural Press.

Casson, L. (1994) *Travel in the Ancient World.* Baltimore: Johns Hopkins University Press.

Cheong, R. (1995) 'The virtual threat to travel and tourism'. *Tourism Management,* **16**(6), 417–22.

Collins, P. (1999) *SpaceFuture.* Available at: http://www.spacefuture.com

Collins, P., Fukuoka, T. and Nishimura, T. (1994) 'Zero-gravity sports centers'. Engineering Construction and Operations in Space 4. *ASCE,* **1**, 504–13.

Collins, P., Kuwahara, S., Nishimura, T. and Fukuoka, T. (1997) 'Design and construction of zero-gravity gymnasium'. *Journal of Aerospace Engineering,* **10**(2), 94–8.

Cox, L. J. and Fox, M. (1991) 'Agriculturally based leisure attractions'. *Journal of Tourism Studies,* **2**(2), 18–27.

Curtis, S. and Camp, D. (1997) 'Interactive science and technology attractions'. Insights: Tourism Marketing Intelligence Service 8, A189–94.

Dann, G., Nash, D. and Pearce, P. L. (1988) 'Methodology in tourism research'. *Annals of Tourism Research,* **15**, 1–28.

Faulkner, W. H. and Russell, R. (1977) 'Chaos and complexity in tourism: in search of a new perspective'. *Pacific Tourism Review,* **1**(2), 93–102.

Feifer, M. (1985) *Going Places: The Ways of the Tourist from Imperial Rome to the Present Day.* London: Macmillan.

Gilovich, T. (1993) *How We Know What Isn't So: The Fallibility of Human Reason in Everyday Life.* New York: The Free Press.

Goodrich, J. N. (1987) 'Touristic travel to outer space: profile and barriers to entry'. *Journal of Travel Research,* **26**(2), 40–3.

Gould, S. J. (1997) *Life's Grandeur.* London: Vintage.

Gunn, C. (1985) *Tourism Planning.* New York: Taylor and Francis.

Hanna, M. (1997) 'Sightseeing boom in 1996'. Insights: Tourism Marketing Intelligence Service, A77–45

Hanna, M. (1998) 'Sightseeing trends in 1997'. Insights: Tourism Marketing Intelligence Service, A89–98.

Jacobsen, J. K. S. (1997) 'The making of an attraction'. *Annals of Tourism Research,* **24**(2), 341–56.

Jakle, J. A. (1985) *The Tourist: Travel in Twentieth-Century North America.* Lincoln: University of Nebraska Press.

Judd, D. R. (1995) 'Promoting tourism in US cities'. *Tourism Management,* **11**(3), 175–87.

Kotler, P. (1994) *Principles of marketing* (6th edn). Englewood Cliffs, NJ: Prentice-Hall.

Laistner, M. A. (1930) 'The decay of geographical knowledge and the decline of exploration'. In P. A. Newton (ed.) *Travel and Travellers of the Middle Ages.* London: Percy Lund, Humphries and Company.

Langer, E. (1989) *Mindfulness.* Reading, MA: Addison-Wesley.

Laws, E., Faulkner, B. and Moscardo, G. (eds) (1998) *Embracing and Managing Change.* London: Routledge.

Leiper, N. (1995) *Tourism Management.* Melbourne: TAFE Publications Ltd.

Leiper, N. (1997) 'Big success, big mistake, at big banana: marketing strategies in road-side attractions and theme parks'. *Journal of Travel and Tourism Marketing,* **6**(3/4), 103–21.

Lew, A. (1994) 'A framework of tourist attraction research'. In J. Brent Ritchie and C. Goeldner (eds) *Travel, Tourism and Hospitality Research* (2nd edn). New York: John Wiley and Sons Inc., pp. 291–304.

MacCannell, D. (1976) *The Tourist*. New York: Schocken.

MacCannell, D. (1990) *The Tourist* (2nd edn). New York: Schocken.

Martin, B. and Mason, S. (1993) 'The future for attractions: meeting the needs of the new customers'. *Tourism Management*, **14**(1), 34–40.

Moscardo, G. (1999) *Making Visitors Mindful*. Champaign, Illinois: Sagamore Press.

Moutinho, L. (1988) 'Amusement park visitor behaviour – Scottish attitudes'. *Tourism Management*, **9**(4), 291–9.

Nadler, G., Hibino, S. and Farrell, J. (1999) *Creative Solution Finding*. California: Prima Publishing.

NASA (1999) *Welcome to the X33 Website*. Available at: http://stp.msfc.nasa.gov/stpweb/x33

Pearce, P. L. (1991) 'Analysing tourist attractions'. *Journal of Tourism Studies*, **2**(1), 46–55.

Pearce, P. L. (1998) 'Marketing and management trends in tourist attractions'. *Asia Pacific Journal of Tourism Research*, **3**(1), 1–8.

Pearce, P. L. and Moscardo, G. (1998) 'The role of interpretation in influencing visitor satisfaction: a rainforest case study'. In B. Faulkner, C. Tideswell and D. Weaver (eds) *Progress in Tourism and Hospitality Research*. Canberra: Bureau of Tourism Research, pp. 309–19.

Pearce, P. L. and Moscardo, G. (1999) 'Tourism community analysis: asking the right questions'. In D. G. Pearce and R. W. Butler (eds) *Contemporary Issues in Tourism Development*. London: Routledge.

Pearce, P. L., Morrison, A. M. and Rutledge, J. L. (1998) *Tourism: Bridges Across Continents*. Sydney: McGraw-Hill.

Pearce, P. L., Moscardo, G. and Ross, G. F. (1991) 'Tourism impact and community perception: an equity-social representational perspective'. *Australian Psychologist*, **26**(3), 147–52.

Pearce, P. L., Moscardo, G. and Ross, G. F. (1996) *Tourism Community Relationships*. Oxford: Elsevier.

Pimlott, J. A. R. (1947) *The Englishman's Holiday: A Social History*. London: Faber and Faber.

Rinschede, G. (1992) 'Forms of religious tourism'. *Annals of Tourism Research*, **19**, 51–67.

Robinson, K. (1994) 'Future for tourist attractions'. Insights: Tourism Marketing Intelligence Service, **5**, D29–40.

Screven, C. G. (ed.) (1999) *Visitor Studies Bibliography* (4th edn). Chicago: Screven and Associates.

Shafer, E. L. (1989) 'Future encounters with science and technology'. *Journal of Travel Research*, **26**(4), 2–7.

Smith, V. L. (1992) 'Introduction: the quest in guest'. *Annals of Tourism Research*, **19**, 1–17.

Stevens, T. R. (1991) 'Visitor attractions: their management and contribution to tourism'. In C. P. Cooper (ed.) *Progress in Tourism Recreation and Hospitality Management*. London: Belhaven Press, pp. 106–13.

Sumption, J. (1975) *Pilgrimage: An Image of Mediaeval Religion*. New Jersey: Bowman and Littlefield.

Swadling, M. (ed.) (1992) *Masterworks of Man and Nature: Preserving our World Heritage*. Sydney: Harper-McRae.

Swarbrooke, J. (1999) *Development and Management of Visitor Attractions* (2nd edn). United Kingdom: Butterworth-Heinemann.

Towner, J. (1985) 'The grand tour: a key phase in the history of tourism'. *Annals of Tourism Research*, **12**(4), 298–333.

Towner, J. (1995) 'What is tourism's history?' *Tourism Management*, **16**(5), 339–43.

Towner, J. (1996) *An Historical Geography of Recreation and Tourism in the Western World 1540–1940*. Chichester: John Wiley and Sons.

Walsh-Heron, J. and Stevens, T. (1990) *The Management of Visitor Attractions and Events*. New Jersey: Prentice-Hall

Walton, J. K. (1983) *English Seaside Resort : A Social History, 1750–1914*. Leicester: Leicester University Press.

Yale, P. (1990) *From Tourist Attractions to Heritage Tourism*. Huntington: ELM Publications.

CHAPTER 8

Festival Tourism: Recognizing the Challenges; Linking Multiple Pathways between Global Villages of the New Century

Nell Arnold

INTRODUCTION

During the past decade, a new surge in community and international festival tourism has been witnessed in Europe, Africa, Asia, Australia and the Americas. In Australia, 1300 festivals and events were reported over a twelve-month period from November 1995 to 1996. Only 31 of these events operated with a budget over $300,000, the remaining festivals were dependent on volunteer services and local partnerships (Australian Bureau of Statistics, 1996). In China the rebirth of festivals and cultural tourism welcomes international visitors to tourist festival-entertainment towns, to international festivals such as 'Pavarotti in the Forbidden City', or to the celebration of traditional events such as the 'Dragon Boat Races'. Festival tourism is being introduced in other areas of Asia as two new international festival theatre complexes, designed to support the increase in community festivals and to attract international events and festivals, have been undertaken in Taiwan and in Singapore (Ng, 1999).

Visitor attraction events, even in countries of Europe that have centuries of festival tourism practice, have tripled, with six out of every ten festivals in France being founded since 1980 (Frey and Busenhart, 1994). In America and Canada, as in 50 other countries, the indigenous people, in opening their cultural heritage celebrations to visitors, have begun to expand significantly the regional festival calendars and festival tourism options (Tables 8.1 and 8.2; Arnold, 1996–99).

Why the resurgence of festivals? When interviewed, three hundred contemporary festival directors in North America, Great Britain, Australia and several countries within the Asia Pacific Region responded by aligning contemporary festivals with tourism development; accordingly, they perceived that the increase in festivals corresponded to the ebb and flow of visitor market interests (Table 8.1; Arnold, 1997, 1999, 2000b, c, d). A review with festival directors from 44 original nations in the same countries confirmed this popular perception (Table 8.1; Arnold, 2000b, c, d). The perception may be warranted, for even community festivals, originally orchestrated by volunteers to celebrate community life, are being adapted in many urban centres to attract visitor markets. Issues of stakeholdership in community and in tourism festivals were companions to the challenges of authenticity, programme quality and economic sustainability.

During the descriptive, ethnographic and applied research processes of the two research teams, questions were raised about the roles, functions, purposes and challenges of festivals within and outside of tourism practice. In this chapter, attention is focused on three of the five major challenges perceived to be confronting festival tourism development at the turn of this century:

1.   the effect of ebb and flow patterns on festival tourism development and the introduction of festival tourism models responsive to the inherent challenges;
2.   the appearance of new sets of challenges in short term and long-term planning within changing environments; and
3.   the emergence of multiple festival themes, styles and directions.

The remaining two challenges, (4) the appearance of global villages and global theme festivals within regional areas orchestrated by population movements from urban centres and (5) the limited recognition by contemporary policy-makers for the transformational power of festival tourism, are recognized in brief as part of continuing research.

The discussion in this chapter is guided both by the summary of findings of the 1995–99 research projects and by the academic training and applied research of the teams, specifically over the past two decades as outlined in Tables 8.1 and 8.2. The author invites readers to reflect on the summary of findings and their implications in festival tourism design, direction and management in the new century.

THE RESEARCH PROCESS

From 1973 to 1993, as illustrated in Table 8.1, the author undertook descriptive and experimental research in festivals and tourism development in urban centres in the State of California and in urban centres of a number of countries. During this

Table 8.1 Schedule of action research projects in festival tourism development, 1979–1991

Year	Researchers	CountrY	Action Research Projects
1979	Arnold	USA	*Innercity Urban Youth Arts Project* in San Francisco, Sacramento, Los Angeles, San Jose, California;
			Incarcerated Youth Project in San Jose, California; Tapestry & Talent Multi-cultural Festival, San Jose Garlic Festival Regional Project, Salinas Valley
	Arnold/Dalis		San Jose Opera Project, San Jose
	Arnold		*Five Research Tours with artists and cultural anthropologists* through the state of California to identify cultural sites and histories of four nations of indigenous people within California, and cultural legacy of 82 cultural heritage immigrants
1980–83	Arnold with State of California Research Team	USA	*Cultural Festival Tourism Research Projects* for State of California: Historical Research, Design, Development, Testing of Cultural Festival Concepts in preparation for the 1984 Olympics:
			• Russian Festival of Northern California
			• Chinese Festival Series in Historic Parks of California: Sacramento Railroad Museum, Angel Island Immigration Station, Fishing Villages of Oakland and San Francisco
			• Mexican Historic Trails: California Railroads, California Missions
			• Black American History Trails: Los Angeles, San Diego, Allenstown
			• Japanese Gardens and History: San Francisco and Oakland
			• Spanish History Trails: Court Dances of Spain in San Juan Baptista, San Diego Old Town
			• Four Original Nations of California: Mission Trails in San Diego, San Jose, Sacramento, Northern California
			• Irish History Trail: California State Railroads
			• Pioneer Wagon Trails: Tahoe, Sacramento, San Jose, San Diego

Table 8.1 Schedule of action research projects in festival tourism development, 1979–1991 (cont.)

Year	Researchers	Country	Action Research Projects
1983	Arnold with Getty Museum and Hearst Castle Researchers	USA	*Ancient Art of Greece Gallery for the 1984 Olympics*-Concept Design, Development, Research and International Collection from the New York City Museum, Hearst Castle Museum, San Francisco Museum, London Museum and the Government of Greece
1983–84	Arnold with California State Architects, State Parks	USA	*Design and Development of Multicultural Park and Centre – Los Angeles; Renovation of Cultural Exhibitions in State Museums in the Olympic Park*-Los Angeles and throughout the State of California (State Parks Department, Arts Council, State Parks Foundation) 1983–84
1983–84	Arnold	Middle East, Malaysia, Hong Kong and India	*Research and Arts, Sports Development Tour* to research historic sites, arts and sports development programmes (sponsored by State Departments in each country and the USA Sports Academy)
1985–86	Arnold	USA	*Action Research Projects in Festivals and Youth,* Design and Development of Models for Youth at Risk and Women at Risk in Urban and Regional Communities (United Presbyterian Church, California State Arts Council, California State Society of Parks)
1986–91	Arnold with Feist	USA	*Cabrillo Opera Festival Tourism Training Project:* Design, development and testing of regional opera festivals with directors and artists from five regions in California (Cabrillo College, San Francisco Opera, Monterey Opera, San Jose Opera, Oakland Opera and Monterey Peninsula Opera)

era, festivals focused on the interests of multicultural people and their needs to define their traditional and immigrant pathways which had often been lost in the dynamic cultural revolutions of the past two centuries. The multicultural paths traced 82 new immigrant cultures beginning with the restructuring of boundaries of the four original nations of the land that became California as Mexican, Spanish, British, Americans, Irish, African Americans and then Chinese, Japanese and Middle Eastern immigrants established settlements.

From 1993 to 1999, the author revisited the California sites and festivals to record a major change as festival themes celebrated contemporary cosmopolitan life that mixed rather than highlighted the sounds, styles, rhythms and tastes of multiple cultures. Communities in urban centres rarely aligned their festivals with tourism practice. Events focused on community interests, shopping centres, tea–beer gardens, pony clubs, neighbourhood ethnic and multicultural dinners and street nights. Interviews with directors and observations in urban centres in the United Kingdom, Australia, France, and Germany confirmed a similar trend (Arnold, 2000b, c, d; Table 8.2).

Urban festivals for visitors were designed, funded and orchestrated by government or private enterprise. In these events, few attempts other than business seminars were undertaken to establish community/neighbourhood interaction with the tourism market. Exceptions were found in urban communities directly surrounding government events. In these instances, festival governance and economic issues were raised. Multiple small business enterprises anticipated and experienced political and economic benefits (Hall, 1992; Getz, 1986; Johnston and Deakin, 1993; Richards, 1992; and Sofield, 1994). Small businesses also experienced the challenges inherent in the ebb and flow of visitors to major international events such as the Commonwealth Games, the Olympics, the Asia Pacific Games or the Indigenous Games of North America.

Of particular interest uncovered during the interviews with festival directors from Europe, America and Australia, however, was the increased activity of festivals and festival tourism within regional communities. From 1993 through 1997, two research teams, one in regional development and one focusing on indigenous tourism, delved into the regional challenges. Festival directors from 50 countries participated in the Taabinga and Soil of Flame action research tours, seminars, conferences and experimental festival tourism projects undertaken in Queensland and the companion Four Winds Foundation projects in New South Wales (Arnold, 1995; Arnold and Thompson, 1995; Arnold, 1997, 1999b, c). During these projects, the researchers recorded the appearance of a number of festival dichotomies between urban and regional communities and the impact of change within rural communities as visitors introduced new ideas and marketing networks.

In 1997 the author extended the research comparing festival tourism development in three regions in Queensland with regional festivals in the United Kingdom. The continuing study attempted to determine the level of awareness of

Table 8.2 Schedule of action research projects in festival tourism development, 1995–1999

Year	Researchers	Country	Action Research Projects
1993	Arnold Feist, R	China	*Research Tour in China:* Interview Schedule with State Orchestra, Theatres, Conservatorium and Tourism Development Agencies in Beijing, Shanghai, Hong Kong and regional centres in five provinces
1994–95	Arnold	Singapore Thailand Malaysia Taiwan	*Pavarotti and World Festival Choir Tour in Australia* *Research Tour:* Interview Schedule with National and Regional Cultural Organizations in dance, theatre, music, sport and tourism development
1995–96	Arnold	Australia	*Taabinga Festival – Regional Training Project* with mayors, councillors, artists and performers from 20 communities (Councils of South Burnett–Queensland, Sunshine Coast, Fraser Coast)
1996–97	Arnold Iszlaub, A.	Australia	*Soil of Flame Festival – Regional Training Project* with international artists from 18 indigenous nations of America and arts organizations from Queensland in a 10-day festival tourism training project in regional Queensland *Pre-festival research, training and tours projects* were undertaken for two years in association with the Nanango Pioneer Festival, the Great Horse Ride, the Woodford-Maleny Festival, the Heritage Days of Maryborough, the Peanut Festival of Kingaroy. Tourism and arts directors from 25 countries participated in the regional research and action training projects
1996–97	Arnold	Australia	*Four Winds Foundation Indigenous Training Project* with indigenous artists and leaders from 50 countries
1999	Arnold Robert Dunlop OAM	Australia	*Mountain Glades Research Foundation Studios* Gallery for Arts, Innovations in Timber, Leather, Wool and Glass, Exhibitions, Technology (GLADES: Global Links, Associated Development, Education Services)
1999	Arnold Elsmore, P.	Australia	*Interviews with 100 Festival and Tourism Policy-Makers and Directors in Queensland* Interviews with 100 tourism policy-makers in UK

public policy agencies in the community transformation values of festival tourism and, thereby, the potential for use of festival tourism as a tool for new industry development in regional communities. In-depth interviews were undertaken with 100 tourism and development leaders in regional Queensland. The interviews began with policy-makers in Commonwealth and state agencies responsible for planning and development in tourism, environment, arts and culture. The interviews continued at the regional level of governance in three different regions. The final set of interviews was undertaken with community leaders of organizations representing community voice within the arts, environmental interests and governance within each of the three regions.

The study was repeated in three different regions within the United Kingdom, in a comparative analysis between regional festival and tourism development values and decision-making structures, processes and personalities (Arnold, 2000c, d). A companion study began to study the evidence of cultural and power transformations within indigenous communities as observed by cultural teachers and leaders from the original 50 countries of the festival tourism action research (Table 8.2).

The research and action research projects outlined in Tables 8.1 and 8.2 were under the supervision of the author and undertaken in co-operation with regional communities and their councils. The action research was designed to identify and clarify cultural presentation and learning challenges which, due to sensitivity of cultural protocol, had not been defined in the literature.

CHALLENGE I: REFLECTIONS ON SIX EBB AND FLOW PATTERNS OF FESTIVAL TOURISM

Analysis of the responses of the festival directors from 50 countries during the experimental projects undertaken in Queensland from 1996 to 1999 (Arnold, 2000b) recognized the important role festivals played at the community level. The responses also confirmed the challenges the directors were confronting, as well as the sociocultural and economic benefits attained, when these festivals aligned with tourism development. Particular attention was given to the general concern of festival directors' perception of 'ebb and flow' patterns in festivals. For example, festival directors focused on the changes in market interests, attributing the ebb and flow patterns to visitor boredom in a plethora of festivals with redundant themes, or a divergence between visitor expectations and quality of visitor experiences. At risk, in directors' perceptions, was the sustainability of the festival tourism endeavours and, thereby, the garnering of an economic return on investments in infrastructure, human resources and community expectations.

The concept of festival ebb and flow interests and patterns, however, is not new.

A reflective scan of the history of the arts disciplines, whether visual or performing arts, architecture or theatre, uncovers at least six different ebb and flow patterns (Arnold, 1998). The issues of stakeholdership, authenticity, quality, responsibility and protocol also appeared as a result of these ebb and flow patterns. Contemporary researchers of cultural history who participated in the Soil of Flame Training Festival Project, 1996–97 (Arnold, 1997b, 1999a, b) and the Four Winds Foundation, 1996–97 (Table 8.2; Arnold, 2000b, c, d) traced both touring and community festive activities to the earliest people. The reasons for festival tourism have been continuous through the centuries. For instance, as civilizations formed, communities developed festive activities initially to entertain and communicate with each other (community festival). Over time villages sought opportunities for social exchange with other villages (marriage celebrations and intercommunity festival) and in some countries, to attract trade caravans and their entourage of explorers and travellers (trade festival). As armies formed to protect the trade caravans, the games festivals were introduced to display through festival competitions the athletic and military skills of the villages and the visitors (McNeill, 1973; Arnold, 1998).

Two ebb and flow patterns and festival styles, recognizably different, were attributed to these early community and tourism festivals. Community festivals, in celebrating the harvests, births, marriages and deaths, and other events or rituals which held meaning for the community followed a pattern of ebb and flow with the harvest and planting seasons. The festival style valued community participation in all aspects of the festival games, cultural events and social activities (Table 8.2).

As families sought to 'captivate' both marriage and trade partners, however, festival performances were designed by the community to display their wealth, skills and attractiveness through body adornment, dancing and singing. The visitors reciprocated and also entertained their hosts with gifts of foods, craft, music and dance, thus beginning a two-way exchange of cultural interests and craft skills. The ebb and flow of the visitor market interests followed a pattern that, over time, became part of a routine trade calendar. In contemporary times, these patterns continue in the 'Thursday Farmer Markets', the 'Sunday Craft Fairs' and the quarterly, annual or biannual national or international trade conferences of many countries. The style of festival incorporated both participatory and performance activities, thus introducing games, competitions and the qualification or ranking of athletes, performers and their arts.

Twenty-two festival activities evolved around the visual and performing arts, home-making crafts, horticulture, viniculture, sports and martial arts, many of which were developed into art forms and presentation styles to attract or accommodate the interests of various trading and visitor markets. Examples of these diversified visitor programmes continue in the form of military parades and martial arts displays; athletic games; circus and trade exhibitions; religious pageants and enactments; gipsy, folk or court dances; or camel, boat and horse races (Arnold,

1998). The ebb and flow patterns of the visitor (tourism) festival aligned with the trade exhibition schedules of the towns and villages rather than with the harvest or community celebrations. This ebb and flow pattern was perceived to introduce new challenges as the economic benefits of trade dominated the events and therefore market size and interests became important. Different styles of festivals emerged in response to different interests of the military, court or religious markets.

A third pattern of festival ebb and flow appears in history as artisans, artists, performers and their touring ensembles formed. Community and tourism festivals and exhibitions incorporated the portfolio of the visiting artists' portfolios. The early ebb and flow pattern of gipsy carnivals and nomad circus, originally attached to seasonal weather patterns, changed as tents, cathedral squares and trade exhibition centres provided covered performance areas. The diversity in performance styles and interests increased and annual or biannual schedules of the touring artists and exhibitions became features of the festival. Over the centuries, the guest performance festivals were organized into five art programme seasons revolving around the dance, opera, symphony, theatre and circus or shows to accommodate market interests and artists' schedules (Arnold, 1998).

It is interesting to note, that with this ebb and flow pattern, multiple styles in music, dance, art and theatre also evolved as artists, while touring, learned from each other and exchanged skills and cultural rituals. Artists, historians and critics, in attempting to define the arts festival and classify activities into original, traditional, cultural, ethnic and classic performance styles, raised the issues of authenticity and quality. As artists developed performance skills and individual interpretive styles, and designers, composers, choreographers, writers and lyricists established themselves, the art of criticism found a new vocabulary to express views on originality, creativity, innovation, adaptation and transformation. The issues continue into contemporary times.

With the emergence of artisans and performing artists, traced in most cultures to the evolution of dynasties (McNeil, 1973), a fourth ebb and flow pattern was introduced. The pattern follows the award of funds, grants or investment by the patron, ruling family or government to underwrite the cost of the 'attraction', whether artists, athletes, circus or military show. This donation, undertaken for sociocultural–political reasons, often supported the celebration of religious holidays or traditional ritual experiences.

In contemporary times, the ebb and flow of patron resources has continued in the form of small grants for community celebrations or more substantial commercial investment for festival tourism development. This ebb and flow pattern introduced a number of challenges as sponsors, often political leaders or aspirants, focused on mass-market interests and inherent economic strength. A dichotomy in investment patterns appeared between regional and urban centres, with urban centres supporting the infrastructure required for mass-market conventions and performances. In many cases, regional communities that have centuries of experience in patron support now must apply for grant and sponsorship underwriting in competitive bids to continue their harvest festivals and festival tourism endeavours. The application and accounting processes, although still revolving around political party and patron interests, now often follow a complicated two- to four-year schedule of developing and implementing public policy, application procedures, approval processes and follow-up reporting systems.

It is interesting to note that on some continents, the history of this ebb and flow pattern is erratic. Accordingly, many of the festival directors who participated in the research had a wide range in experience and diverse views regarding portfolio festivals and their ebb and flow patterns. For example, just as there were long periods in the Middle Ages when festivals, dancing and merriment were forbidden in European communities, in more recent history there were long periods of world wars in which festival activities were curtailed by survival needs. In contemporary times, some indigenous nations in Africa, South America and Australia have only experienced community festival activity and therefore this ebb and flow pattern of artists schedules is yet to be realized. In some countries the peace missions introduce artist portfolios in the building of the peace effort, for example as in eastern Europe with the Suzuki Theatre and John Noad Productions 1999. In other countries, communities attempt to recover without this festival support, as discussed by researchers from countries in South-East Asia and Africa.

The fifth ebb and flow pattern appeared in more recent history to follow the family holiday markets. School holiday and family vacations of European and American markets are scheduled during the June through to August calendar months. In many Asia Pacific countries, however, the heat seasons and slower paced months were registered to be in December through to February. Accordingly, as international travel, holidays and trade conventions increase around the world, two tourism seasons are emerging, with festivals being designed to accommodate market interests of southern hemisphere countries and other festivals prepared to attract the northern hemisphere seasonal holiday markets (Arnold, 1998).

The sixth ebb and flow pattern is recognized in the dual lifestyle of patrons, seniors and, more recently, the technology 'rich', who move between urban and regional residences. For instance, the patrons, more readily the wealthy, maintained seasonal residences in both urban and regional centres. The patrons escaped urban life to rest, relax and entertain in regional retreats. As greater numbers of people around the world developed higher standards of living, they also afforded a holiday retreat. Holiday flats in beachfront towns and country villas in regional settings in most countries bear witness to this international trend. Rapid transport, weather responsive technology and year-round work schedules have also encouraged individuals or families to take more frequent but shorter breaks throughout the year. As regional communities experienced the fluctuating demographics of these part-time residents, more community festivals have been designed to undertaken the challenge of accommodating the interests of the more frequent, long weekend visitor or other part-time residents. The adjustments are witnessed for example in the extension of the San Juan Bautista-California theatre and mission festival programme from an annual event to several seasons of festival activity. The expanded festival tourism strategy has increased the social, cultural and economic wealth of the community (Tables 8.1 and 8.2).

Another major part-time resident found in this ebb and flow pattern is the senior market; participants extend their regional visits to avoid poor weather in their own part of the country. In some cases their visit helps them determine whether or not the hosting community also offers the sense of place to which they would retire. Regional festivals are encouraged by many of the retirees who seek the social outlets as well as opportunities to invest in and develop 'hobby tourism' projects (Arnold, 1995a).

A more recent example is witnessed in the high-tech families who, in valuing the flexibility of lifestyle and their global links, re-establish their sense of community in regional centres. Their technology prowess enables them to work from home centres and to commute to clients around the world. As more high-tech residential 'visitors' settle in regional communities, a reversal of the rural to urban migration pattern is witnessed. The flow into regional communities introduces the benefits of new social and economic resources as well as the challenge of increased complexity in lifestyles and entertainment requirements in regional communities.

What are the implications of these six ebb and flow patterns to contemporary festival tourism development? The ebb and flow patterns, specifically the longer-term residential pattern, suggest that many regional communities are either experiencing or anticipating increased complexity in their socio-economic evolution. The increase in community festivals in some countries may in fact be a reflection of the need for regional centres to adjust to changing demographics within their communities rather than a desire in communities to establish festival tourism for economic reasons. If this is the case, community festivals will continue to serve as a vital community development function to integrate new residents and their interests into the community while at the same time assisting former residents to adjust within their changing social and cultural landscapes. If the urban to regional settlement trend continues in the new century, festivals designed to re-establish a community's sense of place and future may require new resident and patron investment and be undertaken with greater independence from festivals designed to attract, retain and build tourism markets and industries.

The festival directors concluded that, whether focusing on community or visitor interests, festival directors should:

Activities   **Monthly calendar**

Dec Jan Feb Mar April May June July Aug Sept Oct Nov

Southern hemisphere holidays
Northern hemisphere holidays
Religious holidays
Trade conventions
Touring artists
Summer schools
Harvest activities
Community activities
Festival tourism activities

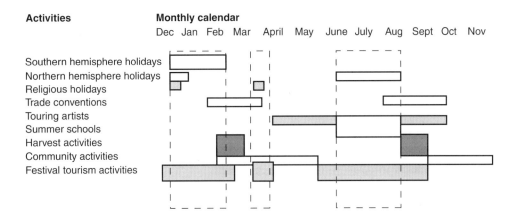

Figure 8.1 Potential festival calendar in rural Queensland

- Recognize and chart the multiple ebb and flow patterns and, in so doing, determine both the impact of these patterns on community evolution and the implication for longer-term festival tourism development in their region.

  In charting the actual and potential visitor flow patterns, the communities should be able to establish regional festival calendars and identify windows of opportunity for joint venture efforts in both community and tourism festival endeavours. The joint venture efforts should reduce intercommunity competitive behaviours and focus communities toward attracting, integrating and managing the sponsors and volunteer workforce within a co-operative and sustaining effort of festival tourism development. During the off-season the communities may better enjoy local activities, festival training programmes, product development and other value-adding practices in preparation for the peak visitor season.

  Figure 8.1 presents an example of a potential festival calendar for regional Queensland that experiences two planting and harvest seasons. As many as 26 festival activities each year in 3 small communities dissipated the resolve of the volunteer workforce (Arnold, 1998). Restructuring activities into two major festival tourism seasons would focus the efforts of volunteers and establish events on which tour operators could depend.

- Identify the players, structures and decision-making processes required for effective festival regional tourism development and, in so doing, determine which festival tourism development efforts should be integrated. In undertaking this activity, communities should identify areas of conflict between six levels of regional festival tourism management, specifically,

- management teams for each community's festival activities;
- agents of the visiting artists;
- festival tourism operators;
- managers of the sponsorship funds or grants;
- directors of the festival schools, exhibitions and competitions; and
- co-ordinators of the festival tourism calendars and integration of events.

- Determine the design of festival orchestration structures to ensure that the focus, quality and integrity of activities meet the expectations of the visitors, performers, sponsors and community hosts.

For example, the action research in festival tourism development in regional Queensland identified a number of challenges in festival development structures, processes and personalities. Four festival tourism-training models were designed to assist regional communities in planning with the ebb and flow patterns (Arnold, 1999a, b). The training models helped communities build festival design, planning, marketing, business development and tourism and hospitality skills in preparation for external visitor and new resident markets. Each of the festival structures concentrated on a specific focus. For example:

- *Model I: The Trade Anchor Model*, designed around the ebb and flow of harvest seasons of the rural communities, focuses on the trade fair. Community festival races, parades, games, dances and entertainment are designed to attract and retain regional visitors over the weekend. During the trial festivals, visitors remained for a week to two days of training activities thus increasing the revenues in hotels, restaurants, shopping centres and leisure clubs.
- *Model II: The Portfolio Model* features touring artists of the theatre, ballet, opera and symphony and accordingly accommodates the ebb and flow of government-funded or corporate sponsored touring programmes. The intent of the touring portfolio is to outreach the arts to regional communities. During the training festivals, portfolio performances attracted visitors from several regions. A festival training school, attached to the portfolio model, helped communities build presentation skills, encouraged young artists in the region, extended the festival season and initiated efforts to build future arts markets in the region. Festival training programmes and camps introduced a longer-term source of funds into the communities that hosted the young artists, their parents and grandparents. The portfolio model is illustrated in Figure 8.2.
- *Model III: The Festival Games Model* introduces competitions in 22 festival sport and art forms, confirming and preserving social and cultural patterns of the region as exampled in the Highland and Scottish Games and the Indigenous Cultural Sports and Dance Competitions of North America. The

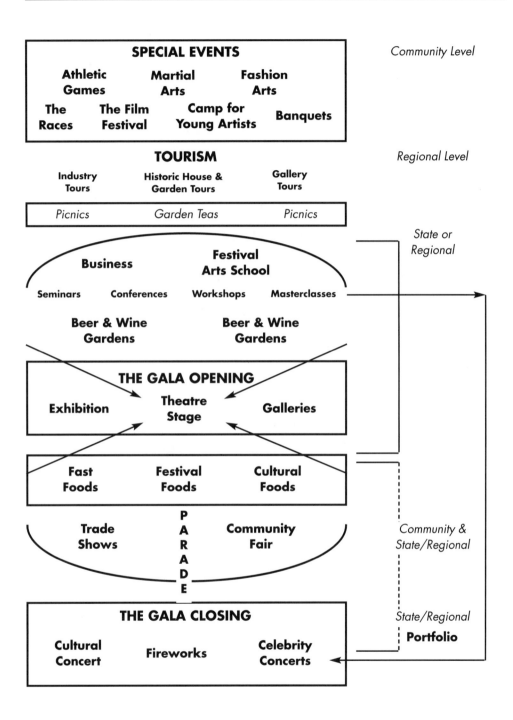

Figure 8.2 Model II: Portfolio festival model

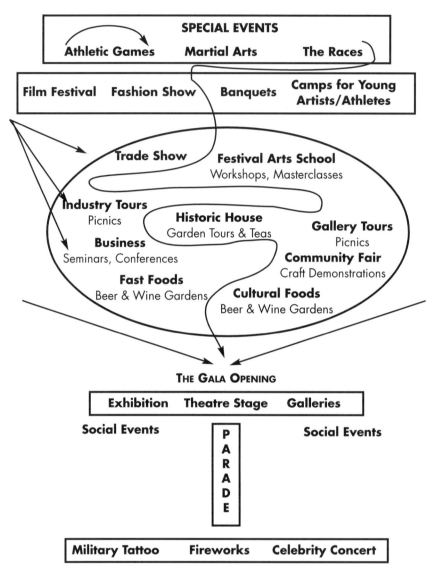

Concept Design, N. Arnold, 1996–7 Research Process

Figure 8.3 Model IV: The Pathway Festival Model

model enables communities to schedule a series of cultural festivals throughout the year with task forces from each cultural cluster dedicated to the festival training, management and presentation.

- *Model IV: The Pathway Model* incorporates all of the other festival models to host international festival artists, festival training programmes, export seminars, business development conferences, industry tours, community fairs and regional trade shows with the benefits garnered by participating communities as visitors take multiple pathways into the major festival. This model requires interregion co-operation and planning around all ebb and flow patterns, and accordingly takes five years of development to achieve a level of success (Arnold, 2000b) The pathway model, as structured during the action research in regional Queensland, is found in Figure 8.3.

CHALLENGE II: REFLECTIONS ON LONG-TERM PLANNING WITHIN A CHANGING ENVIRONMENT

Closely aligned to the concerns raised by the research team about the ebb and flow patterns of festivals were the issues surrounding long-term planning. On reflection on the research experience and findings, the multiple issues clustered around three common areas of challenge, specifically

- dichotomies affecting long-term development of festival practice;
- change within the macro environment; and
- micro level problems in establishing decision-making structures and processes responsive to the multiple players and personalities involved in festivals and tourism development.

The dichotomies

Analysis both of the findings from interviews of festival directors from 50 countries and the results of the action research projects confirmed that, although not all festival directors confronted all of the same challenges, five dichotomies appeared to be affecting contemporary festival projects. For example, festival directors from countries in Asia Pacific, Africa, Eastern Europe and Australia perceived a move by governments to take over major urban community festivals, placing them under professional management with the mandate to attract international visitors. As grants and sponsorships focused on building selected festivals, many of the other urban community-based efforts disappeared, for people were leaving their neighbourhood activities to attend the bigger events 'downtown'.

One challenge led to another as, in several instances, government restrictions and in some cases censorship, investment and leadership were perceived to confine the exploratory nature of festival artists and activities. The festival directors were witnessing a reduction in the expressions of originality as sponsored festivals were orchestrated repeatedly to meet politically correct presentations designed for a mass visitor market. As events became commercialized, the festival activities became repetitive.

On the other hand, festival directors active in regional communities registered a lack of government interest and funding, in comparison to urban centres, for regional festival tourism development. The issues raised by the regional festival directors focused on an increasing social, cultural and economic complexity as leaders in many communities, in an attempt to attract funding, visitors and the economic benefits of tourism, copied urban festival tourism development patterns. Accordingly, indigenous and other regional communities began to commercialize their cultural and social legacy to compete for the urban and international visitor market. Communities advertised their artefacts and cultural images within time capsules of the past, promoting their history rather than their technologies and innovations over time or their potential for industry development in the future. The markets that were being attracted were often local seniors seeking to recall memories and socialize in the process. International visitor markets, however, without a link to the social history of regional communities, rarely ventured in large numbers beyond a two-hour coach ride from urban centres or seafront towns.

In regional communities attractive to investors, government agencies had deployed external festival tourism developers to orchestrate the festival tourism events. During this regional festival tourism developmental process, the dissolution both of the community sense of ownership of festivals and the volunteer workforce was witnessed in many countries. Issues of cultural protocol, authenticity, ownership, leadership responsibility and funding dominated the responses of directors from both indigenous communities and regional arts or historic societies. In some cases, efforts were undertaken either to access the economic benefits or to regain control of their heritage as local cultural and social organizers began competing for the limited number of government grants and private sector donations. The competitions fuelled intercommunity rivalry within most regions and in some cases communities boycotted the professional, portfolio festival tourism endeavours as exampled in the Soil of Flame Festival experiments of 1997 (Arnold, 1998, 1999a, b).

The second dichotomy, rising between the state-funded, professionally managed festivals and the experimental projects of young artist festivals and ethnic festivals, was noted in a number of countries. Sponsors and government agencies viewed young artists as niche market activity and experimental projects as being 'on the fringe' of market interest. Festival directors registered concern that youth and ethnic artists were not receiving adequate opportunities to express their cultures or to build artistic and presentation skills. In recognizing the importance of participatory expressions, directors were seeking to establish festival schools, workshops, extemporaneous performance opportunities, experimental development spaces and audience participation options attached to festivals as exampled in the Soil of Flame projects undertaken from 1995 to 1997 (Arnold, 1999a, b).

The third dichotomy appeared between those who can or cannot access technology. For instance, the effects of advancements in transportation technologies are witnessed in the increased ability of some countries not only to mobilize military forces but also to transform the technology for transporting mass markets. Accordingly the evolutionary pace of history that intermittently mingled cultures at the rate of caravan-styled trade, war and tourism, changed pace with the inventions that enabled the world to engage in transcontinental wars. Following two world wars and decades of multinational military activities, many more countries now house multinational immigrants. Cultural festivals, initiated originally to celebrate centuries of heritage and lineage, now celebrate, in many countries, multicultural and transnational themes. A cultural dichotomy is appearing between visitors in search of lost heritage and cultural traditions, and those communities who, having integrated their diverse cultural base to such an extent, now enjoy cosmopolitan and new age festival experiences. The dichotomy is witnessed as international visitors look without success for traditional cultural expressions in cosmopolitan festivals that rarely reflect on past culture but enjoy the blending of tastes, sights, sounds and dance rhythms and styles. Cosmopolitan age festivals are exemplified in the Brisbane River Festival, the New Age Jazz Festival of Monterey and the Contemporary Music Festival of Santa Cruz, California.

The festival directors interviewed expected to continue celebrating a diversity of culture in some countries. However, most events organizers recognized a contemporary severance from the slow pace of cultural evolution and the appearance of a dichotomy between the technology-rich and the technology-neglected artists and their markets. The technology dichotomy aligned at times with the economic dichotomy defining the markets by those who could or could not afford global travel and communication options.

Analysis of the history of civilizations chronicles the uneven advances in technology in some countries. Early examples included the introduction of irrigation, animals for transport, printing press for communication, artificial substances for construction, medical instruments and procedures and many others (McNeil, 1973). Modern history's intermingling of advancements in two technologies, transportation and communication, has had profound effects on festivals and tourism development. For example, television has enabled audiences both to view the intimacy of community celebrations of original cultures and to participate vicariously in the opera, dance and symphonic festivals of Europe, Asia and the Americas. Festivals designed for television markets have increased over the past four decades to introduce cyberspace festivals linking closed circuit or mass-market cabled television channels and computers.

Through commercialization of communication and transportation technology, mass markets now enjoy both the tourism and arts experiences previously reserved for the economically advantaged social classes. Accordingly, the television audience of the past four decades is able, through rapid transport, to seek out the experiences they viewed originally through satellite systems. In addition to attending the festival programmes, designed specifically for visitor markets in urban centres, international visitors may experience in person the traditional cultural experiences and the intimacy of community celebrations they witnessed on television.

In some countries these dichotomies persist, polarizing (1) urban and regional communities; (2) young artists from professional artists; and (3) those who can or cannot access technology. The result witnesses the urban community internationalizing through their conventions, festivals and enterprises as festival services advance to meet the requirements and global interests of their guest markets. On the other hand, many regional communities, previously isolated by access and singular cultural settlements, remain stoic in attempts to save their evaporating sense of community.

Changes in the macroenvironment

Although the festival directors' concerns focused on micro-management challenges, the cause of the concern could be traced to changes within the macroenvironments, specifically in the uneven geographic and demographic distribution of government or ruling family support. The macroenvironments are recognized in marketing literature (Kotler, 1999) and are designated as

- natural (vista, climate, geography);
- economic (economic infrastructure, human resource, natural resources);
- technology (ability to develop ideas, production systems and products);
- political/legal (processes for decision-making and governance);
- demographics (the breakdown of lifestyles and habitats of people within a region);
- social and cultural (education, religious, heritage patterns and psycho-graphics of a community) (Kotler, 1999).

Prior to planning for festivals, environmental scans should be undertaken to determine existing and potential macro level evolution that may initiate change and either influence government, business and market decision-making processes or support the continuation of festival development dichotomies.

Australia offers an example of interaction between the political and economic environments at the macro level and the effect of that interaction on the socio-cultural environment of communities across Australia. Although statistical records of festivals may be viewed as estimates rather than actual attendance, the national festival profile over a twelve-month period starting November 1995 (Australian Bureau of Statistics, 21 Sept. 1999) recorded 1300 festivals. The dichotomies appear as the main arts festivals (urban) were awarded $11.5 million in funding and received $16.6 million in receipts and $10.7 million in sponsorships. These festivals attracted 58.7 per cent attendance with an additional 15.4 per cent of the market visiting popular music festivals and another 13.2 per cent attending exhibitions and film festivals. Regional festivals, on the other hand, were awarded $1.8 million and attracted 12.7–15 per cent of the market. Ticket receipts and sponsorship in these regional festivals was not even registered.

The Australian Bureau of Statistics did not record the capital investment in performing arts centres, museums, libraries, sports centres, arts centres and other festival, sport or arts venues in urban centres. Nor does the research record whether or not the urban festivals run at a profit or loss; and consequently, whether or not the government is required to continue investing in the urban festival tourism infrastructure and programmes. Operating budgets for Queensland festivals and arts and sports events, for example, registered considerable loss and called for financial rescue packages for orchestra, ballet, opera, film, sports and theatre festival activities as noted in the Board of Director's Reports for Warana Festival, Queensland Philharmonic Orchestra, Winter Carnival Races and Indy Motor Races, 1995–98.

Expenditures in urban centres may be rationalized on demographic realities of urban centres and the social needs of the urban mass markets. Accordingly, the benefits of the festival tourism investment were perceived by sponsors and government agencies to reach greater numbers of small businesses who are either contracted for festival service or experience increased revenues from visitor traffic. An opposing view, registered predominantly by regional festival directors, questioned this past practice. The point of their argument did not call for a reduction in investment in urban festival tourism. Instead, regional festival directors called for a discussion of whether or not the urban investment should continue to the exclusion of investment in festival tourism development in regional communities also seeking the economic and social benefits associated with visitors (Arnold, 1995a, 1997a, b, 1999a, b).

The issues of the debate are not new and remain complex as noted in tourism and leisure development conferences of the past three decades (Arnold: UN-INTERCALL Conference and Task Force Research/Training Programs 1974 (Sapora, 1978; Arnold, 1980)). These reports reviewed during research undertaken by the author (Arnold, 2000b Tables 8.1 and 8.2), and research undertaken by the Four Winds Foundation (Arnold, 1997–9), shed light on the real challenge. Specifically, over four decades, rural and regional communities have experienced not only the accumulated loss of economic opportunity, but also the opportunities afforded through sociocultural and political exposure to new ideas, technologies and the building of joint venture enterprises to support new industries and export practices. The ensuing dilemma of the dichotomies appears to be revolving now around three broad challenges:

- the encroaching economic dissolution of communities unable either to attract or to develop new industries, specifically those aligned with changing technologies responsive to the directions of international or global enterprises;
- the capabilities of rural communities to change their mindsets either to welcome the international market or to compete within a global economy; and
- the poor management of tourism development in many regional areas, and the outcome on regional economies and community practice in preserving sites of ritual, historical or ecological significance.

The issues of sustainability and progressability were raised in the discussions on each challenge. Economic *sustainability* issues appeared to revolve around the ebb and flow pattern of tourist market interests. The companion challenge of *progressability*, however, related to the community's capabilities and motivation to change to meet market interests.

The ethnographic and action research projects undertaken in regional Queensland recorded the appearance of change within each of the macro-environments and the profound effect of that change on festival tourism development (Arnold, 1995–99). For example, many regional communities had experienced directly or indirectly the effects of long-term drought. As rural communities lost crops, cattle and associated industries, their towns and other economic and social support infrastructure dissipated. Government restructuring changed many of the service boundaries, introducing layers of decision-making processes at the Commonwealth, state, regional and community levels. Each layer of governance retained different boundaries so festival directors had to seek support and approvals for health, transportation, communication, education, emergency services and arts funding from multiple councils and government agencies spread across eleven regions. Communication technologies had not been updated, thus distance and obsolete technology increased the sense of isolation of rural families and communities. In these settings, efforts to develop festival tourism were stressed, as visitor markets became acutely aware of the compounding economic, natural, political and technology challenges and their effect on the changing demographics and social–cultural landscapes of the communities.

In delving into these challenges, two research teams, one in regional development and one focusing on indigenous tourism, undertook action research in rural communities from 1995 to 1997 in regional Queensland and regional New South Wales. Festival directors from 50 countries participated in the action research tours, seminars, conferences and experimental festival tourism projects. The research teams recorded the impact of change within communities as visiting artists and tourism development specialists introduced new ideas and marketing networks during ten-day training festivals.

Micro level challenges

The research process confirmed that all of the macro level challenges could be identified and addressed through research and strategic planning (Arnold, 1997a, b). The greater challenge during the festival tourism trials, however, was found at the microcosm level as several people thwarted community efforts to build festivals designed to attract visitors to their community. The disruptive personalities, in each of the 23 communities involved in the festival tourism projects, were found to be new residents who perceived the festival tourism enterprise would compete with their own efforts to establish business or hinder their progress in becoming political leaders in the community. In attempting to influence political decision-making structures such as regional councils, the new residents insisted on introducing new health, security, traffic control and signage policies and fees on all festival tourism endeavours (Arnold, 1998).

In some instances, the efforts to control or discontinue festival tourism did have effect as community volunteer groups were confronted with newly imposed fee structures on what had previously been free public service. Elaborate festival tourism decision-making processes were also imposed, replacing the community club planning system. For example, a year of multiple public hearings and council approvals was required for each festival tourism activity. When members of the community did not comply, whether wittingly or unwittingly, the local media were advised and thus community volunteers and their festival tourism efforts were afforded unexpected, investigative reporting from the media. Festival administrators and community leaders supporting the new industry received frequent calls to report to councils to explain their actions and activities.

Over a five-year period of these unorganized efforts and at times disruptive behaviours, however, the regional festival tourism efforts began to transform community opinion. Festival cottage industries developed new products for export, refurbished historic homes and designed nature, industry and historic trails. Tour buses were witnessed as gallery and vineyard tours were introduced. The rate of adoption of festival and tourism practice within the communities built momentum, spreading to most communities within each of the twelve regions participating in the action research projects (Arnold, 2000b).

Similar challenges were met in the indigenous communities (Arnold, 2000b, c, d). In these instances, the micro level challenges were also witnessed in decision-making structures, processes and personalities as various indigenous councils co-operated in their efforts to establish festival tourism. Establishing the protocols required consensus-building exercises. During these prolonged discussion periods, many of the planning activities lost their momentum. As the festival training activities began, however, the international artists were able to provide examples and models from which the indigenous communities could evolve joint venture festival experiences. The extemporaneous flow of the festivals enabled the participating communities to exchange, experiment and progress their ideas. As noted earlier in this chapter, the festival youth initiated and continued the festival learning experiences by studying their own and others' cultural dances and by organizing performing tours to several countries.

Implications from the action research suggest that festival tourism planning should take into account the effect the macro and microenvironments on the festival tourism endeavours, and the effect that both the festival experiences and the visitors will have on hosting communities in the long term. In recording the changes in the communities over a five-year period, the research team recommended that regional festival tourism directors should:

- anticipate and plan both for shorter-term responses of the hosting communities, specifically for reactions that may develop longer-term challenges or opportunities between the hosting and visiting people of the festival experience;
- realize that festival dichotomies have evolved over many years of political and economic structuring of festivals and tourism practice without, in many instances, consideration by governments for the longer-term effects on the mindsets of people;
- recognize that the orchestration of tourism festivals within many regional communities may initiate a series of dynamic reactions within the community;
- recognize planning processes that continue the dichotomies, specifically those festival development processes that neglect to undertake either analysis of macroenvironmental challenges or projections of the evolutionary and induced changes. For example, in the past, the investing of government funds induced change within the economic environment of a community and created a catalyst for change in the political and social–cultural environments of that community. In some instances, the projected economic benefits were destroyed as the social and cultural values of the community were changed from volunteer practice into a pattern of charging fees for public or voluntary services;
- monitor the changes in attitudes and sociocultural patterns in the community as these patterns can foreshadow whether or not the community intends to restrict, sustain or progress the new industries introduced through festival tourism.

CHALLENGE III: FESTIVAL THEMES

A third area of interest appearing in the interviews and action projects encompassed five festival themes which returned during the two decades: Space Age, Traditional Ritual, Heritage, Innovation and Invention and Community Sense of Place.

The Space Age festival theme is not surprising. Four generations around the world have witnessed the launch of manned rockets and the beginning of space exploration. These images have become part of the popular culture that celebrates through film and 'energy art' festivals the science fiction literature of the past century. For example, the television comedies of the 1960s introduced space *martians* into television families. *Dr Who* and the *Star Trek* television series and the *Star Wars* movies picked up the momentum, encouraging youth to emulate popular images of youth in space suit festivals; their parents participated by bridging the gap between the future and the past in *New Age Happenings* in the 1980s.

The popular festival celebration at the close of the twentieth century witnessed both youth and seniors, whose world transverse experiences enabled them to write the preface of new century manuscripts and the technology enhanced musical scores. Space Age themes appearing in film, music, art, dance and fashion paid tribute not only to the creators of new images, sounds and styles, but also to the audience preparing to explore new limits in space and energy technology. The Space Age festivals at the close of this century, moving away from subject and theme materials, are electronic competitive rather than culture specific. As films and video games follow suit, some of the indigenous and heritage festivals directors called for the recognition of multiple pathways forging into an internationalizing voyage and a globally conscious celebration of a new century. Other directors of indigenous, settlement heritage and classical festivals expressed concern with the festival focus on technology. In the kaleidoscope of vibrant colours and sounds, entertainers are dwarfed and silhouettes of the bemused are glimpsed as they search for fragments of original and settlement cultures.

A second festival theme was dedicated to original people. The traditional celebrations and tours appeared as part of the spiritual, social and education practice of the original people on all continents. The festival directors in the research projects aligned modern indigenous festivals with the routines of the earliest human inhabitants that celebrated the hunt and shared, through enactments, their sense of community. Beyond the dances and songs, early communities participated in rituals, reinforcing their responsibility of stewardship of landscapes that held special meaning for them. Tours across the land to these landscapes and the celebrations and experiences of ritual continued through the centuries. Over the centuries, many of the original nations have merged, losing their lifestyles and language and, accordingly, many of the ancient rituals have also lost meaning over time.

At the turn of the century, indigenous festival tourism directors are welcoming efforts towards the recovery of original languages, rituals and festival practice; the process of rediscovery, however, introduced multiple challenges (Arnold, 2000b, c, d). Centuries of transformation of traditional cultures have made this task of relearning difficult. The disintegration of culture, caused both by external and internal drivers, was recognized as issues raised revolved around the relocation of indigenous people, cultural authenticity, the introduction of social class systems within their societies and the breaking down of the sense of community. Accordingly, indigenous community leaders have begun preparing for indigenous festival tourism as a cultural revitalization effort and a social transformation process as much as for economic development reasons (Table 8.1).

The major indigenous visitor market at the turn of the century comprises scholars, leaders, artists and cultural interpreters of the indigenous communities of 50 countries. Authenticity, ethnicity, ownership and right of presentation of the language, symbols, music, arts and rituals are significant issues to be discussed and resolved (Arnold, 2000b, c, d). These learning needs draw the indigenous community to Australia, New Zealand and to some communities in Africa and South America where traditional rituals are still practised. International interest in indigenous traditions and people has drawn response for restoration of indigenous communities also in Taiwan, China, Tibet, Malaysia, Indonesia and Thailand (Arnold, 1995, 1997).

A companion issue raised by some indigenous artists was the right, as contemporary people, to be recognized as artists within a contemporary world. The desire by indigenous leaders and the visitor market to rediscover lost civilizations and culture has placed pressure on many artists and youth to be strictly traditional rather than contemporary artists (Arnold, 1997). At the individual level, artists were experiencing a challenge in maintaining a sense of balance as a traditional and contemporary person; at the community level, the challenge appeared in establishing a sense of balance between individual rights and cultural community responsibility was witnessed during the Soil of Flame projects (Table 8.2; Arnold, 2000b, c, d) and in the previous decade during the cultural tourism development projects in California (Table 8.1; Arnold, 1997).

The consensus of the participants in seminars, tours and festival training sessions in these trail projects confirmed a festival practice that treasured the traditional practice through ritual openings, and then followed with interpretation of traditional dress, dance, foods, medicine and other routine life. As the concerts and exhibitions unfolded, the audience was drawn into new century entertainment, fashions and art of indigenous people. Many of the traditional leaders embraced the young performers who extended the history theme (Arnold, 2000b, c, d). Caught between a desire to treasure their legends and a need to call world attention to the responsibility of earth's stewardship, some indigenous leaders now share their traditional festivals with the visitor market. The decision to approve the practice of releasing youth for contemporary expressions and international travel remains unresolved, however, for leaders in some communities, particularly in communities in which the issues of cultural protocol and disclosure of traditional stories and practice are yet to be settled.

Paralleling the traditional cultural experiences are the *Heritage Festivals Trails* of Europe that trace multiple threads of cultural difference. This multi-dimensional pathway, which initially meandered in an evolutionary pace through the centuries, has begun to fuse with the assist of dynamic advancements in communication and travel technologies. For example, European heritage trails appear not only in Europe but also in Africa, America, Australia and many islands that hosted the venturers, invaders, pioneers, military, artists and others who established settlements. The European trails are mirrored in nineteenth-century trails through Africa and in the twentieth-century Chinese 'paper' trails following the 1910 revolution.

As the history of the world at war unfolded in the twentieth century, immigrants and multinational governing bodies transported their traditional and classical cultures to many continents. The continuing flight of refugees, their artefacts and the festival tourism practices, while expanding community awareness of diverse cultural practices, has also increased the challenge of preserving historic festival trails. Through the intermingling of the resident and immigrant cultures over several generations, new era cultures now celebrate multiracial heritage and mingle with enthusiasm the ingredients of foods, music, dance, art, styles and philosophies.

Between the future focus and the historical treks is a mass festival market *Celebrating Innovation*. These travellers explore inventions outside of their industrial experience. Innovations in healing and art within the original gathering and harvesting communities are as fascinating as the technologies that transformed the industrial age into time periods earmarked by electronic, communication, information and new energy discoveries. Trade shows, conventions, exhibitions, conferences and industrial showcases and tours are the dominant features of these festive learning and trade environments. The festival activities are electronic designed for mass and popular cultural interests.

Coexisting with, and in some cases, despite these tourism market events, community festivals survive. *Celebrating A Sense of Place*, community festivals are organized within a social or cultural construct of a region. Referred to as 'Inward Based Tourism' (Brohman, 1997; Crompton, 1995; Jamal and Getz, 1995; Lenzi, 1996; Mayfield and Murphy, 1985; Oppermann, 1997; Selin and Chavez, 1995; and Somerset, 1995), the festival activities tend to be exclusive to one or more social or cultural conclaves of a community. In efforts to increase cash flows into their neighbourhood arts programmes, historic societies and social charities, community festivals attach to local fairs, trade shows and tourism ventures. The affiliation introduces multiple leadership personalities, structures and decision-making processes, adding a level of organizational *complexity* to both the festivals and to tourism endeavours.

Implications of these continuing festival themes suggest

- people will continue to participate in festival tourism for the same reasons; how they celebrate and who celebrates, however, has changed over time with improved travel and communication technology;
- the dichotomies of festival tourism may lessen as greater numbers of people gain access to mass communications and mass transportation;
- traditional and heritage festival tourism will increase as more cultural groups seek opportunities to learn about their original cultures, and the reasons behind the sets of values, rituals, symbolism and artistic styles of their festivals;
- the case for regional festival tourism development is significant as many of the original and immigrant cultures of traditional and heritage trails reside in rural communities.

CONSIDERING THE FUTURE

In this chapter, the author has reflected on only three of the challenges in festival tourism which appear to have confronted festival tourism development over the past two decades:

1. the effect of ebb and flow patterns on festival tourism;
2. the appearance of new sets of challenges in short-term and long-term planning within changing environments; and
3. the emergence of multiple festival themes, styles and directions.

In pondering over the past, the research team reviewed the ebb and flow patterns that induced change and established dichotomies or introduced opportunities. In so doing, they recognized the exponential rate of change in travel and communication technology during the last century that has underwritten the multicultural flow of people into urban centres around the world. As the generations that follow experience cosmopolitan life in the new century, their festivals are expected to celebrate the 'high-energy–high-tech' innovations of a space age.

As the team of researchers reflected on communication and transportation advances and the dichotomy issues that prevailed in contemporary research literature and festival practice, they glimpsed a change on the horizon. The change is occurring both at the village level and in some communities in the Highlands of Scotland, in the Andes Mountain Range, in Alaska and in the desert communities of North America, as residents link into a global communication corridor. Communities of 100 or a 1000 people are participating in discussions with scientists, philosophers and artists around the world. In this festival of cyberspace, ancient villages are celebrating a sense of global community.

Further research found interactive 'indigenous' arts sales from Tibet through Australia to the United States. Fifty-two indigenous nations are using technological enhanced communication to go on-line to sell art and other cultural products. Interactive communication technology between indigenous people and the 'virtual markets' of the world offers the economic advantage of tourism without intrusion of visitors in the village.

Not to be outdone, indigenous youth with and without the consent of their communities have also begun to travel. For example, within six months following the Soil of Flame Festival trial projects (Arnold, 1997b) in which indigenous youth in Queensland worked with indigenous Americans artists, they had boarded aeroplanes in search of cultural tourism development examples in Canada and the United States of America. During this venture, they performed in the opening and closing ceremonies of the World Indigenous Games in Canada. Within another six months, as cultural tourism performers, they toured Japan, France and Russia, and then returned for performance tours to Canada and America. In each instance the youth, unable to raise grants or sponsorship funds, saved money from their after-school jobs to pay for transatlantic transport. Their efforts were endorsed by the indigenous communities who hosted the youth as artists in residence.

In observing these global link festival tours and the endeavours of youth, the research team gained greater insight into the history of cultures and the reasons for their festival and tourism practice. Festivals offered not only outlets for celebration, but also encouraged a desire to exchange ideas, to test skills, to explore one's senses, to interact with people who share common or different values and lifestyles and to renew cultural ties within the microcosm of the community.

In the new century, the research teams anticipated community festivals would continue to increase, fulfilling a need both for maintaining a sense of place within a rapidly changing environment and for establishing opportunities for continual learning in order to keep up with the changes. The research teams also considered that even as communication and travel technology continues to extend the global reach of many more communities, festival tourism will continue to serve as a process for expanding community insight. Beyond the celebration, festival tourism will link, in time, multiple pathways between global villages of the new century.

REFERENCES

Arnold, N. (1976) *The Integrated Arts in Leisure: Perceiving and Creating.* Mosby Times Mirror Publishing House, St. Louis

Arnold, N. (1980) *Proceedings and Papers.* The Second World Conference of Experts on Leadership in Leisure, INTERCALL-UN, New York.

Arnold, N. (1992) Reports for Queensland Health Department and for the Queensland Department of Sport, Tourism and Racing.

Arnold, N. (1995a) *Building a Regional Tourism Development Strategy.* Queensland, Office of the Premier: Regional Export and Investment Consultative Group.

Arnold, N. (1995b) *Queensland Cultural Strategy: Draft for the Queensland Olympic Task Force.* Queensland: Department of Tourism, Sport and Racing.

Arnold, N. (1996) 'Opportunities offered by the Olympics 2000'. *Queensland Trade & Investment Bulletin*, Department of the Premier, Economic and Trade Development, **5**(1) Jan–March.

Arnold, N. (1997a) 'In search of economic sustainability: turning twentieth century legacy into twenty-first century opportunity'. *Globalisation and Regional Communities: Geoeconomic, Sociocultural and Security Implications for Australia.* USQ Press.

Arnold, N. (1997b) *Festival Tourism in Rural Australia.* Canberra: Commonwealth Department of Science, Industry and Tourism.

Arnold, N. (1997c) *Research in Progress.* Sydney: Four Winds Foundation (unpublished).

Arnold, N. (1998) *Festival Tourism Development in Rural Australia.* Canberra: Commonwealth Department of Science, Industry and Tourism.

Arnold, N. (1999a) *Marketing and Development Models for Regional Communities: A Queensland Experience.* CAUTHE Research Conference – Refereed Proceedings, Feb.

Arnold, N. (1999b) *Festival Tourism Development in Regional Queensland: Explorations Beyond Hypothetical Dialogue.* CAUTHE Research Conference – Refereed Proceedings, Feb.

Arnold, N. (2000a) 'Festival tourism'. In W. Faulkner, G. Moscardo and E. Law (eds) *Tourism in the Twenty-first Century.* London: Continuum.

Arnold, N. (2000b) 'Macro environment affecting youth at risk', Academy of Marketing Sciences Conference Proceedings, Refereed, June 20–4, Montreal, Canada.

Arnold, N. (2000c, d) 'Culture and power in regional community transformation', Papers 1 & 2 Refereed Conference Proceedings, 18th Annual SCOS Conference, July, Athens, Greece.

Arnold, N. and Blatto, M. (1996) 'Rural innovation: twenty-first century technology'. Formal paper presented to Brisbane's International Business Week. Italian Chamber of Commerce, Oct. Used in 1997 for Queensland Government Seminar for the World Congress for Investment in Tourism in Milan, Italy.

Arnold, N. and Thompson, N. (1995) *Assessment of Economic Indicators in the Development of Business through Arts, Culture and Sport: Sunshine Coast Region Leading into Year 2000.* Sunshine Coast 2000 Inc. Mooloolaba. Commonwealth Regional Development Study.

Australian Bureau of Statistics (1994) *Cultural Trends in Australia No. 1: A Statistical Overview ABC Catalogue No. 4172.0.* Canberra: Commonwealth of Australia.

Australian Bureau of Statistics (1996) *Cultural Trends in Australia: Business Sponsorship of Arts Activities 1993–1994.* Canberra: Department of Communications and the Arts.

Australian Bureau of Statistics (1999) *Cultural Trends in Australia: Festivals.* Canberra: Department of Communications and the Arts.

Australian Heritage Commission (1996) 'A national future for Australia's heritage'. Discussion paper. Canberra: Australian Government Publishing Service.

Australian National Commission for UNESCO (1976) *Entertainment and Society.* Melbourne: Advocate Press. Australian Heritage Commission.

Australian National Commission for UNESCO (1996) *A National Future for Australia's Heritage.* Discussion paper. Canberra: Australian Government Publishing Service.

Bailey, K. D. (1982) *Methods of Social Research* (2nd edn). New York: Tue Free Press, A Division of Macmillan Publishing Co. Inc.; and London: Collier Macmillan Publishers.

Bartlam, J. (1993) 'CQ company ploughs new furrow in overseas market'. *Central Queensland Journal of Regional Development*, **2**(3).

Biswas, Tapan (1997) *Decision-Making Under Uncertainty*. London: Macmillan.

Black, T. R. (1996) *Evaluating Social Science Research*. London: Sage Publications.

Blank, U. (1989) *The Community Tourism Industry Imperative: Its Necessity, Opportunities, and Potentials*. State College: Venture Publishing.

Boydan, R. and Taylor, S. J. (1975) *Introduction to Qualitative Research Methods: A Phenomenological Approach to the Social Sciences*. New York: John Wiley & Sons Inc.

Britten, S. and Clarke, W. (1987) *Ambiguous Alternatives: Tourism in Small Developing Countries*. Suva, Fiji: University of the South Pacific.

Britton, R. A. (1977) 'Making tourism more supportive of small state development: the case of St. Vincent'. *Annals of Tourism Research*, **6**, 269–78.

Brohman, J. (1997) 'New directions in tourism for Third World development'. *Annals of Tourism Research*, **23**(1), 48–70.

Brokensha, P. and Guldber, H. (1991) *Cultural Tourism in Australia*. A study commissioned by the Department of the Arts, Sport, the Environment, Tourism and Territories. Canberra.

Burns, R. B. (1995) *Introduction to Research Methods* (reprinted 2nd edn). Melbourne, Australia: Longman Australia Pty Ltd.

Bush Problems–Bush Solutions (1991) Longreach Conference Report. Queensland Department of Business, Industry and Regional Development.

Cameron, N. (1995) *Maleny Folk Festival: The Art of Celebration*. Queensland: Mimburi Press.

Central Queensland Journal of Regional Development (1993) University of Central Queensland, **2**(3).

Cohen, J. (ed.) (1999) *Unconventional Wisdom*. Huntington, CT: The Sloan Institute of MIT Publications.

Commonwealth Department of Tourism (1994) *National Rural Tourism Strategy*. Canberra: Australian Government Publishing Service.

Compton, J. L. and McKay, S. L. (1997) 'Motives of visitors attending festival events'. *Annals of Tourism Research*, **24**(2), 425–39.

Copleston, P. (1991) 'Qualitative research answers, HRM's "law" and "why"'. *HR Monthly*, February, 11–12.

Cornish, E. (1978, 1999) *The World of Tomorrow: Selections from the Futurist*. Washington DC: World Future Society.

Chur, C.-N. (1992) *Thick Face, Black Heart*. NSW: Allen & Unwin.

deKadt, E. (1979) *Tourism: Passport to Development?* Oxford: Oxford University Press.

Dent, H. S. (1998) *The Roaring 2000s*. New York: Simon and Schuster.

Denzin, N. K. (1989) *The Research Act: A Theoretical Introduction to Sociological Methods* (3rd edn). Englewood Cliffs, New Jersey: Prentice-Hall.

Dychtwald, K. (1999) *How the 21st Century Will be Ruled by the New Old*. New York: Tarcher/Putnam.

Dyson, R. and O'Brien, F. (1998) *Strategic Development Methods and Models*. New York: John Wiley and Sons.

Elsmore, P. (2000) 'Culture and power I: an investigation of the arena in the context of the tourism industry'. Refereed Conference Proceedings, Eighteenth Annual SCOS Conference, July, Athens, Greece.

Fabun, D. (1967) *Dynamics of Change*. Englewood Cliffs, NJ: Prentice-Hall.

Fabun, D. (1971) *Dimensions of Change*. California: Glencoe Press.

Fetterman, D. M. (1989) *Ethnography: Step by Step*. Newbury Park, California: Sage Publications.

Fisher, H.-D. and Melinik, S. R. (1979) *Entertainment. A Cross-Cultural Examination*. New York: Communication Art Books, Hastings House Publishers.

Fisher, H.-D. and Merrill, J. C. (1976) *International and Intercultural Communication*. New York: Hastings House Publishers.

Frey and Busenhart (1994) 'Special exhibitions and festivals: culture's booming path to glory'. Paper presented at the Eighth International Congress on Cultural Economics. Association for Cultural Economics International, Witten, Germany, 24–27 August.

Getz, D. (1986) 'Models in tourism planning: towards integration of theory and practice'. *Tourism Management*, **7**(1), 21–32.

Golembiewski, R. (1967) *Organizing Men and Power: Patterns of Behavior and Line-Staff Models*. Chicago: Rand-McNally Series in the Organization Sciences.

Hall, C. M. (1992) *Hallmark Tourism Events*. UK: Belhaven Press.

Hamilton, G. G. (ed.) (1996a) 'The organisational foundations of western and Chinese commerce: a historical and comparative analysis'. In G. G. Hamilton (ed.) *Asian Business Networks*. Berlin and New York: Walter de Gruyter, pp. 43–58.

Hamilton, G. G. (ed.) (1996b) The theoretical significance of Asian business networks'. In G. G. Hamilton (ed.) *Asian Business Networks*. Berlin and New York: Walter de Gruyter, pp. 43–58.

Hammersley, M. and Atkinson, P. (1995) *Ethnography Principles in Practice* (2nd edn). London and New York: Routledge.

Hawkins, D., Neal, C. and Quester, P. (1994) *Consumer Behaviour: Implications for Marketing Strategy*. Sydney: Irwin.

Henry, S. T. (1990) *Practical Sampling, Applied Social Research Methods Series*, Volume 21. Newbury Park, London and New Delhi: Sage Publications.

Hong, L. (1998) 'Old linkages, new networks: the globalisation of overseas Chinese voluntary association and its implications'. *The China Quarterly*, **155**, 582–609.

Hughes, C. C. (1973) *Make Men of Them*. Chicago: Rand McNally College Publishing.

Hunt, S. D. (1991) *Modern Marketing Theory, Critical Issues in the Philosophy of Marketing Science*. Cincinnati, Ohio: South Western Publishing Com.

Jamal, T. B. and Getz, D. (1995) 'Collaboration theory and community tourism planning'. *Annals of Tourism Research*, **22**(1), 186–204.

James Cook University (1989) *Expo 88 Impact, The Impact of World Export 88 on Queensland's Tourism Industry*. The National Centre for Studies in Travel and Tourism, James Cook University.

Johnson, G. and Scholes, K. (1993) *Exploring Corporate Strategy* (3rd edn). Hertfordshire: Prentice-Hall International (UK) Ltd.

Johnston, C. and Deakin, E. (1993) *Sydney Olympics 2000 – Approaches and Issues for Management of Social Impacts*. Report for the Office on Social Policy, Social Policy Directorate, Sydney.

Kotler, Phillip (1999) *Marketing Management*. New York: Prentice-Hall.

Ladki, S. M. (1993) *An Evaluation of Tourists' Experiences in Rural Northern West Virginia*. Proceedings of the Society of Travel and Tourism Educators Conference, **5**, 90–102.

Lenzi, R. C. (1996) 'The entrepreneurial community approach to community economic development'. *Economic Development Review*, **14**(2), 16–20.

McClymont, A. (2000) *Notes on Rural Debt in Queensland*. QRAA. Regional Development Queensland Survey of 1998. Unpublished Notes.

McNeill, W. H. (1973) *Ecumene: The Story of Humanity*. New York: Harper and Row.

Magala, S. (1998) *The Velvet Cage*. Paper presented at Modernity and Post-modernity Seminar, East London Business School, December.

Marris, T. (1987) 'The role and impact of mega-events and attractions on regional and national tourism development: resolutions'. *Revue de Tourisme*, **4**, 3–10.

Marsden, D., Oakley, P. and Pratt, B. (1994) *Measuring the Process. Guidelines for Evaluating Social Development*. UK: INTRAC.

Mathieson, A. and Wall, G. (1982) *Tourism: Economic, Physical and Social Impacts*. New York: Longman.

Maude, A. J. S. and van Rest, D. J. (1985) 'The social and economic effects of farm tourism in the United Kingdom'. *Agricultural Administration*, **20**, 85–98.

Mayfield, T. L. and Crompton, J. L. (1995) 'Development of an instrument for identifying community reasons for staging a festival'. *Journal of Travel Research*, **33**(3), 40–5.

Moore, C. M. (1994) *Group Techniques for Idea Building, Applied Social Research Methods Series.* Vol. 9. London: Sage Publications.

Murphy, P. (1985) *Tourism, a Community Approach.* New York: Methuen.

National Board of Employment, Education and Training (Australian Commonwealth) (1994) *Cultivating the Human Factor: Employment and Skills in Australia's Rural Industries. Small Business Employment and Skills Supplementary Report.* Canberra: Commonwealth Department of Education and Training.

Newman, W. L. (1994) *Social Research Methods Qualitative and Quantitative Approaches* (2nd edn). Boston, London, Toronto, Sydney, Tokyo, Singapore: Allyn and Bacon.

Ng, N. L. P. (1999) 'An analaysis of the perceived objectives, benefits and contemporary marketing challenges facing the Esplanade – theatres on the Bay (Singapore)'. Unpublished Honours Thesis, Queensland University of Technology.

Nystrom, H. (1998) *Entrepreneurship and Innovation.* Paper presented at Modernity and Post-modernity Seminar, East London Business School, December.

Oppermann, M. (1997) 'Rural tourism in Southern Germany'. *Annals of Tourism Research*, **23**(1), 86–102.

Pearce, P. L. (1990) 'Farm tourism in New Zealand, a social situation analysis'. *Annals of Tourism Research*, **17**, 337–52.

Perry, C. with Robinson, E. and Seabrook, J. (1993) 'Regional development bodies in Queensland: analysis of four case studies'. *Queensland Economic Forecasts and Business Review*, **2** (new series) (2), 59–70.

Queensland Department of Tourism, Sport and Racing (1993) *Reports on Queensland Olympic Forums: Tourism Think Tank and Sports Forum.* Queensland Tourism Development Task Force.

Queensland Department of Tourism, Sport and Racing (1994) *Queensland Tourism Strategy: Draft Issue Paper – Product Development and Marketing.* Queensland Tourism Development Task Force.

Queensland Events Corporation (QEC) (1997) *Market Research 1996–1997 Woodford/Maleny Folk Festival: Strategic Facts.* Queensland: Queensland Folk Federation.

Raybould, M. (1996) *A Report on the Visitor Survey Conducted at the 1995/96 Woodford/Maleny Folk Festival to Department of Business, Industry and Regional Development.* Queensland: Centre for Tourism and Hotel Management research, Griffith University.

Richards, B. (1992) *Tourist Attractions, Festivals, and Special Events.* Harlow: Longman Group UK Limited.

Robinson, A. and Noel, J. G. (1991) 'Research needs for festivals: a management perspective'. *Journal of Applied Recreation Research*, **16**(1), 78–88.

Samovar, L. A., Porter, R. E. and Jain, N. C. (1981) *Understanding Intercultural Communication.* California: Wadsworth Publishing Company.

Sanderson, K. (1998) 'Assumptions underpinning training models for hospitality supervisors'. Unpublished doctoral thesis, Queensland University of Technology, pp. 181–397.

Sapora, A. V. (1978) *Proceedings and papers: the First World Conference of Experts on Leadership for Leisure.* New York: World Leisure and Recreation Association.

Sarantakos, S. (1993) *Social Research.* Melbourne, SA: Macmillan Education Australia Pty Ltd.

Selin, S. and Chavez, D. (1995) 'Developing an evolutionary tourism partnership model'. *Annals of Tourism Research*, **22**(4), 844–56.

Senge, P. M. (1990) 'The leader's new work: building learning organizations'. *Sloan Management Review.* MIT Sloan School of Management, Fall.

Sofield, T. (1994) 'From cultural festival to international sport – the Hong Kong Dragon Boat Races'. *Journal of Sports Tourism*, **1**(3).

Somerset, G. (1995) *Rural Tourism Australia: Rural Tourism – Suggestions and Information, Industry Paper*.

Spradley, J. P. (1979) *The Ethnographic Literature Review*. Orlando, Florida: Harcourt Bruce Jovanovich College Publishers.

Spradley, J.P. (1980) *Participant Observation*. New York: Holt, Rinehart & Winston.

Suzuki, T. (1991) *SCOT, History of Suzyki Scompany of Toga*. Japan: SCOT Publication.

Terpstra, V. and David, K. (1985) *The Cultural Environment of International Business*. New York: South Western Publishing.

Tidd, J., Bessant, J. and Pavitt, K. (1997) *Managing Innovation*. New York: John Wiley and Sons.

Toffler, A. (1970) *Future Shock*. New York: Random House.

Vayda, A. (1969) *Environment and Cultural Behaviour*. Garden City, New York: The Natural History Press.

Wanhill, S. R. C. (1996) 'Local enterprise and development in tourism'. *Tourism Management*, **17**(1) February. Washington, DC.

CHAPTER 9

Tourism in an Era of Information Technology

Dimitrios Buhalis

INTRODUCTION: ORGANIZATIONS IN THE NETWORKED ERA

Recent developments in information technologies (ITs) and in particular the introduction of the Internet and the World Wide Web (WWW) in the early 1990s introduced a new era in human communications and revolutionized the entire range of business transactions. Multimedia protocols enabled the instant distribution of media-rich documents (such as textual data, graphics, pictures, video and sounds), effectively revolutionizing the interactivity between people, consumers and organizations (Buhalis *et al.*, 1998; Buhalis and Schertler, 1999). The Internet established an innovative and user friendly platform for efficient, live and timely exchange of ideas and products providing unprecedented opportunities for communication and interaction. The pace of development demonstrates that the Internet restructures the lives of people and business processes worldwide and introduces new practices such as home shopping, tele-entertainment, tele-working, telelearning, telemedical support and telebanking. Eventually the electronic/interactive/intelligent/virtual home and enterprise will emerge, facilitating the entire range of communications with the external world and supporting all functions of everyday personal and professional life through interactive computer networks. The Internet also influences global political life, as it introduces a democratic, transparent, uncontrollable and difficult to dominate way of communication, where everyone is more or less able to broadcast his/her views, regardless of hierarchical rankings and political power. The Internet 'has the capacity to change everything – the way we work, the way we learn and play and even maybe the way we sleep or have sex' (Symonds, 1999).

The *Internet* is particularly relevant to tourism as it facilitates interactivity between the enterprise and the external world, however distant. Thus it is re-

TOTAL INTERNET

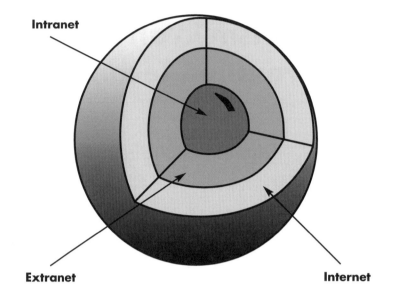

Figure 9.1 The ITs nucleus in operations

engineering the entire range of process and transactions undertaken by organizations to communicate with their partners, customers and suppliers, and provides unique opportunities for interactive marketing to all service providers. Once the communication protocols were established, similar methodologies were used to re-engineer internal processes and communication with trusted and valuable partners. *Intranets* emerged to operate as closed or secured networks within organizations and transformed their interactivity and internal processes. By using a single controlled, user-friendly interface, organizations can distribute all relevant data to employees by using multimedia representations. This empowers their function and supports the formulation of close partnerships with other members of the value chain for the production of goods and services. More recently, *Extranets* use the same principles and computer networks to enhance interactivity and transparency between organizations and trusted partners. By linking and sharing data and processes they formulate low-cost and user-friendly electronic commerce arrangements. Automation of standard procedures supports the effectiveness of business networks and encourages closer collaboration. The combination of all three systems constitutes the networking environment which will increasingly determine the competitiveness of organizations around the globe.

Networking is therefore the most important element of the contemporary information technology revolution. Synergies and interoperability between processes, departments, external partners and the entire range of functions enable organizations to reduce their labour cost, increase efficiency, exercise flexible specialization and differentiation and support their decision-making processes. Developments on software and integration of entire processes reduce work duplication, whilst enhancing transparency of information and decisions within organizations, empowering employees to improve their performance. Networking is experienced within organizations, between organizations and their partners as well as between the entire world of individuals and enterprises. As illustrated in Figure 9.1, the Internet as well as Intranets and Extranets provide the nucleus of operations and strategies for the entire range of organizations globally.

TOURISM AND INFORMATION TECHNOLOGY

During the last decade, researchers have begun to illustrate how ITs will affect tourism. Sheldon (1997) suggests that 'information is the life-blood of the travel industry', and therefore effective use of ITs is pivotal for its competitiveness and prosperity. Tourism is also inevitably influenced by the business process re-engineering experienced in other sectors due to the technological revolution. Therefore 'a whole system of ITs is being rapidly diffused throughout the tourism industry and no player will escape its impacts' (Poon, 1993). ITs developments represent a revolution for the tourism industry, whose impact is perhaps only paralleled by the introduction of the jet engine. As with other industries (Tapscott, 1996; Tapscott and Caston, 1993; Hammer and Champy, 1993), the re-engineering of business processes in tourism generated a paradigm shift, altering the structure of the industry and developing a whole range of opportunities and threats for all stakeholders.

ITs empower the emerging globalization of tourism demand and supply experienced worldwide. At the same time they propel it by providing effective tools to consumers for identifying and purchasing suitable products and to suppliers for developing, managing and distributing their offerings on a global scale. ITs therefore become an imperative partner as they increasingly determine the interface between consumers and suppliers (O'Connor, 1999; Vlitos-Rowe, 1995). More importantly, ITs will be determining the competitiveness of tourism destinations and enterprises as they will influence their ability to differentiate their offerings as well as their production and delivery costs (Buhalis, 1998a and 1998b).

Tourism demand and information technology

In the late 1990s, the proliferation of the Internet revolutionized communications as it enabled organizations to demonstrate their offerings globally using multimedia interfaces (Smith and Jenner, 1998). Consumers are empowered through the new

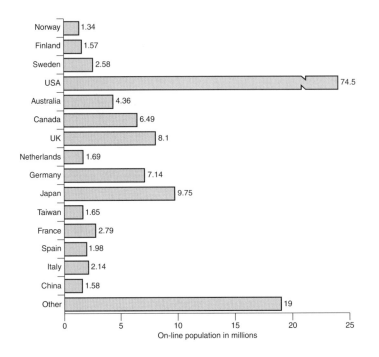

Figure 9.2 On-line population in millions. *Source*: Taylor, 1999

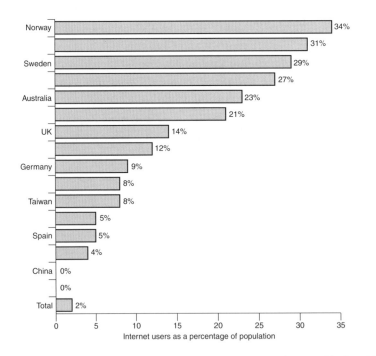

Figure 9.3 Internet users as a percentage of population. *Source*: Taylor, 1999

tools to search for information and to undertake on-line reservations. The availability of information on everything conceivable enables consumers to package their own bundles of tourism products and to purchase only the most suitable products for their own individual needs. Suppliers on the other hand have an unprecedented opportunity to communicate with their target markets globally, to develop their global presence and to establish direct relationships with consumers. Nobody really knows how many consumers are currently connected to the Internet and how many of them buy products electronically. Figures 9.2 and 9.3 illustrate the latest estimates of the on-line population in certain countries. It is estimated that 150 million people or 2 per cent of the global population use the Internet currently (Taylor, 1999). Most Internet users are well-educated professionals who travel frequently and therefore should have a higher disposable income, as well as a higher propensity to spend on tourism products (Smith and Jenner, 1998). On-line surveys clearly demonstrate this point (www.nua.com). These markets are targeted by most destinations and tourism organizations and hence the industry has to reflect on their needs and abilities in order to take advantage of the emerging tools. The rapid growth rate and the expeditious increase of on-line revenue experienced in most industries, including tourism, illustrates that electronic commerce will dominate by the year 2005. This justifies massive investments by organizations to develop their electronic presence.

The usage of ITs is also driven by both the development of the volume and complexity of tourism demand. The WTO (1988) argues that 'the key to success lies in the quick identification of consumer needs and in reaching potential clients with comprehensive, personalised and up-to-date information'. Consumers not only require value for money, but also value for time for the entire range of their dealings with organizations. This reflects people's shortage of time, evident in Western societies. Increasingly, ITs, and the Internet in particular, enable travellers to access reliable and accurate information as well as to undertake reservations in a fraction of time, cost and inconvenience required by conventional methods. ITs can also improve the service quality and contribute to higher guest/traveller satisfaction by providing additional information, in-flight and in-room entertainment as well as by differentiating products according to individual tastes at an affordable cost.

The Internet is revolutionizing flexibility in both consumer choice and service delivery processes. Every tourist is different, carrying a unique blend of experiences, motivations and desires, often as a result of previous experience, background and social status. Increasingly customers become much more sophisticated and discerning as they have experienced high levels of service and they enjoy advanced facilities in their everyday environment. Tourists become demanding, requesting high-quality products and value for both their money and perhaps more importantly their time. Having experienced several products, the new, experienced, sophisticated, demanding travellers rely heavily on electronic media to obtain information about destinations and experiences, as well as to be able to communicate their needs and wishes to suppliers rapidly. Tourists are increasingly frequent travellers, linguistically and technologically skilled and can function in multicultural and demanding environments overseas. The Internet has empowered the 'new' type of tourist to become more knowledgeable and to seek exceptional value for money and time. New consumers are more culturally and environmentally aware and they would often like a greater involvement with the local society. Using the Internet not only provides information about the tourism products they can consume but also a whole range of additional data about the resources, history, social and economic structure of destinations. In this sense certain consumer groups are better equipped to engage in social interaction with locals and to use their travels as an educational experience. Tourists therefore will tend to participate in the experience by being active and spending their time on their special interests. Leisure time will increasingly be perceived as an exploration as well as for both personal and professional development (WTO, 1999). Thus, consumer satisfaction will increasingly depend on the accuracy and comprehensiveness of specific information on destinations' accessibility, facilities, attractions and activities. ITs enable tourism enterprises to develop and deliver complex offerings to satisfy specific interests. This supports the segmentation function to specific niche segments. Increasingly success will depend on the quick identification of consumer needs and interaction with prospective clients by using comprehensive, personalized and up-to-date communication media for the design of products. Speed of acknowledging and satisfying enquiries may even be more important than product attributes as increasingly consumers make emotional decisions, under time pressure. Although competition will be more fierce as consumers have access to endless numbers of suppliers, providing value for time will be at least equally important to value for money.

Although many consumers currently use the Internet for collecting information and building their itinerary, the majority still use traditional intermediaries to book their tourism products. Research has demonstrated that several factors discourage people from booking on-line, as illustrated in Table 9.1. Although these factors deter on-line purchases in the short term, it is estimated that consumers will familiarize themselves with the new tools and take increasing advantage of the Internet. Progress is also evident in the design and interactivity of Internet pages as well as the speed, security and reliability of funds transfers. Tourism organizations also realize their benefits and change their business practices to take advantage of the on-line bookings. As a result they offer special discounts to on-line bookers, distribute their excess capacity on-line for a fraction of the cost and include telephone numbers with support operators should consumers require assistance.

Table 9.1 Reasons discouraging people from purchasing tourism products on-line.
Source: Adapted from PhoCusWright, 1998; Forrester, 1999

User/Client factors	Internet/Business factors
Safety and security	Not enough selection
Navigation difficulty	Internet too slow
Cannot see or touch the product	Internet chaotic and difficulty in
No trust, unfamiliar name	finding suitable information
Prefer regular travel agency	Higher prices
Afraid of making mistakes	Cost of telephone calls
Did not realize that could make reservations	

Challenges and opportunities for the tourism industry

The recent technological developments have a major effect on the operation, structure and strategy of tourism organizations and destinations, mainly by enabling efficient co-operation between partners for the provision and distribution of seamless tourism products and by offering strategic tools for global expansion. The ability of enterprises to communicate and co-operate efficiently with remote branches, destinations, principals, agencies and to control their operational elements support the expansion of their activities. Both operational (e.g. schedule planning, pricing, inventory handling and reservations) and support (e.g. payroll, accounting, marketing) functions are improved considerably. Based on the Internet and other IT tools, they can reduce both communication and operational costs and at the same time enhance their flexibility, interactivity, efficiency, productivity and competitiveness.

As well as expanding geographically and penetrating new markets, perhaps more importantly they can expand their activities through horizontal, vertical and diagonal integration. ITs have a dramatic impact on the travel industry because they force this sector as a whole to rethink the way in which it organizes its business, its values or norms of behaviour and the way in which it educates its workforce (Vlitos-Rowe, 1995; Poon, 1993; Buhalis, 1995). Entrepreneurs often develop innovative practices, which if successful can be adopted by others. The competitiveness both of enterprises and regions is therefore redefined, based on the conditions of utilization, development and application of new technologies.

The revolution of ITs is leading to a shift from product-oriented organizations to a flexible and responsive market place, where success depends on sensing and responding to rapidly changing customer needs, using ITs for delivering the right product, at the right time, at the right price, to the right customer. ITs become the backbone of the tourism value chain and are critical in defining the competitiveness and prosperity of enterprises and regions by either improving their cost or differentiation advantage. A comprehensive re-engineering of the market place propels new best management practices to take advantage of the new ITs tools (Werthner and Klein, 1999; Kärcher, 1997; Minghetti and Mangilli, 1998).

Distribution is one of the few elements of the marketing mix which can still improve the competitiveness and performance of enterprises. ITs support the achievement of competitive advantages by increasing the unique characteristics of products, as well as enhancing efficiency throughout the production and distribution processes. ITs transform distribution to an electronic market place, where access to information is achieved, while interactivity between principals and consumers provides major opportunities. It also enables the design of specialized products and promotion in order to maximize the value-added for individual consumers, and to enhance the total quality of product (fitness to purpose) (Hawkins *et al.*, 1996; Buhalis, 1995; Mutch, 1995). Packaging tourism is becoming a much more client-based activity and, thus, a certain degree of disintermediation of the channel is inevitable, offering opportunities and threats for partners.

The Travel Industry Association of America predicts that by the year 2002 airline tickets purchased on-line will account for $6.5 billion. Airline tickets accounted for 90 per cent of all on-line travel sales, generating $243m in revenue in 1996. Although in 1996 only less than 1 per cent of all airline ticket revenue came from on-line sources, it is anticipated by that by the year 2002 it will increase to 8.2 per cent and will be the leading travel purchase on the Internet (TIA, 1997). ITs are also instrumental in the globalization of the industry. In airlines, global alliances, such as the 'One World', 'Qualiflyer', 'Star Alliances' and others, are only possible because of the co-ordination that can be achieved through harmonized IT systems or through effective interfaces. In effect, consumers receive a seamless service, collect frequent flyer miles and enjoy privileges from different carriers in all continents simply because ITs provide the 'info-structure' for close collaboration. Similarly, the expansion of hotel groups globally are facilitated by uniform electronic systems which allow the head office to monitor the progress and operational functions of remote properties. Hence, ITs not only influence most elements of the marketing mix of tourism enterprises, but they also determine their strategic directions, partnerships and ownership.

Innovative organizations which respond to current and future challenges by designing new processes and adapting to new trends, will take advantage of the emerging opportunities and increase their market share. Corporations need to convert their operations from business functions to business processes, as well as redesign their distribution channels strategy. Even more significantly, this implies changes to long-term planning and strategy. Rational management will need to ensure that organizations reach their optimum capacity and achieve sustainable competitive advantage. Human resources are also becoming critical for the success of tourism organizations of the future as they will need effective and innovative users of ITs who can lead change in a dynamic and uncertain environment. Intellect therefore becomes a critical asset for the competitiveness of enterprises and continuous education and training will need to support all levels of organizations. In contrast, enterprises and destinations which fail to take advantage of the emerging opportunities and address these issues, can jeopardize their market share, competitiveness, prosperity and even existence.

INDUSTRY PIONEERS

Several success stories are quoted in the tourism industry of pioneers who use Internet-based interfaces to develop and distribute their products. A new breed of intermediaries and enterprises have emerged to take advantage of the new capabilities of the Internet (e.g. TravelWeb, Internet Travel Network, Expedia, Travelocity) as illustrated in Table 9.2. In addition, a number of discount and auction specialists undertake electronic auctions as well as sell distressed capacity and discounted travel products (e.g., www.priceline.com; www.previewtravel.com; www.select.com; www.a2btravel.com; www.bargainholidays.com; www.cheap flights.com; www.lastminute.com) (TIA, 1997; Wardell, 1998).

Success stories include new types of intermediaries such as the TravelWeb (www.travelweb.com) which represents 18,000 hotels belonging to 90 chains. About 17,000 are bookable on-line and TravelWeb attracts 6.5m page accesses per month, while their predicted on-line travel sales by the year 2000 is expected to reach $4.7 billion (Hart, 1998). Preview travel (www.previewtravel.com) reached 6.4 million subscribers on 31 December 1998, up 145 per cent from the

Table 9.2 Tourism electronic intermediaries emerging in the electronic market place in 1998. *Source*: Adapted from Sileo, 1998

	Expedia.com	ITN	Preview Travel	Travelocity
Registered users	2m	4m	3.4m	2.5m
Page Views/month	NA	15m	NA	40m
Unique Visitors/month	2,341,000	NA	1,608,000	2,441,000
Visits per month	NA	7.5m	6.3m	NA
Estimated gross bookings/month	$12m	$10m	$12m	$16m

previous year. Expedia (expedia.com) (the Microsoft on-line travel agency) has emerged in the top 25 travel agencies in the USA in less than 3 years. Some of the Expedia figures clearly illustrate the trends: $8.5 million per week in travel related sales; more than $430m in sales in October 1998; 1 million airline tickets sold already; 3 million visitors per month and 3 million registered users (Nell, 1998; Hart, 1998).

Principals also take advantage of the Internet by bypassing agencies and thus reducing commission costs. Although most of the people use web sites for information and then book through conventional channels, innovative principles take advantage and sell an increasing percentage of their capacity on-line. Marriott Hotels already enjoys '13,000 visits per day and is now conducting well over $1.5 m of business every month over the net'. In 1998 it took more than $50m in on-line reservations, an increase of 213 per cent over the 1997 figures with 80 per cent of the business coming directly from their Internet site (www.marriott. com). Traffic to the site increased by 367 per cent over the same period equating to almost ten million new visitors. This performance not only increased the revenue and market share of the company, but it also reduced its distribution, promotion and marketing costs contributing directly to the bottom line (Dennis, 1998). British Airways' Internet site (www.british-airways.com) currently achieves 1.5m visits per month, while the average growth of on-line bookings has been 11 per cent per month. BA estimates that by the year 2003 more than 50 per cent of its bookings will be coming through the Internet (Skapinker, 1999). Small carriers with limited financial resources already see the benefits through direct bookings. As illustrated in Figure 9.4 easyJet (www.easyjet.com), having launched its site in September 1997 and having started electronic commerce in April 1998, already sells between 25 and 35 per cent of its seats electronically and sales often exceed 30,000 tickets per week. easyJet uses the slogan 'the web's favourite airline' and gives a £1 discount (almost equal to the incentive commission paid to staff) to all passengers booking on-line (Rosen, 1999). The figures often quoted for American carriers are significantly greater as a result of the penetration of the Internet. It is evident therefore that only tourism organizations and destinations that prepare their presence in the emerging electronic market place will be able to gain some of the projected benefits and achieve competitive advantages.

Small and medium-sized tourism enterprises

Although larger organizations seem most likely to capitalize on the new tools, the vast majority of tourism enterprises are small and medium-sized tourism enterprises (SMTEs) which are often independent, seasonal, peripheral and family-run organizations. Research into the marketing and management of SMTEs suggests that growing concentration and globalization increasingly threaten them. Their future is also jeopardized by internal weaknesses, namely lack of

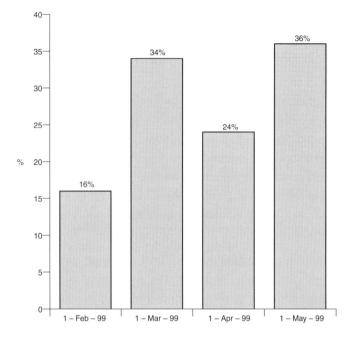

Figure 9.4 EasyJet web sales percentage for week ending as shown. *Source*: Rosen, 1999, p. 7

professionalism, inadequacy of management and marketing skills. They also lack economies of scale available to larger, often chain-based accommodation establishments in terms of access to necessary capital, human resources, marketing expertise and technology and are frequently overdependent on few distribution partners. Insufficient formal education or training also means that proper business practices and skills are often absent, placing SMTEs at a competitive disadvantage. As a result, they are unable to market their products adequately and suffer a wide range of deficiencies, which have dramatic effects on their profitability and ability to survive in the emerging global competition era (Buhalis and Cooper, 1998; Cooper and Buhalis, 1992).

SMTEs often fail to use the emerging tools, as a result of several factors illustrated in Table 9.3. SMTEs are getting increasingly marginalized as they tend to lack both resources and expertise to take advantage of the emergent technologies. Hence, SMTEs and independent properties are the weakest and most vulnerable part of the tourism and hospitality hotel industry as they are at risk of losing a substantial slice of their business. As a result, they continue to lose market share and fail to attract new target markets and SMTEs are placed at a major disadvantage and jeopardizing their future existence (Buhalis, 1999; Buhalis and Main, 1998; Go and Welch, 1991; Chervenak, 1993; Go, 1992).

Table 9.3 Factors affecting ITs' penetration to SMTEs

- ITs literacy of entrepreneurs
- the cost of ITs is often perceived as prohibitive for entrepreneurs
- inability to operate and control technological equipment
- perceived dependence on trained staff
- lack of standardization and often professionalism
- seasonality and limited period of operations in resorts
- lack of marketing and technology understanding
- insufficient training and established organizational practices
- small size multiplies the administration required by CRSs to deal with each property
- unwillingness of SMTEs to lose control over their property to agents or IT staff

As computers become smaller, quicker and cheaper, even the smallest companies can afford some basic systems. ITs equipment and expenses are becoming essential and are part of the core product and investment. Morrison (1994) explains that three types of participation expenses are required, namely economic in commission and fees; operational as a degree of autonomy to be sacrificed; and rules and sanctions which reduce their flexibility and individuality. Unless SMTEs develop their Internet presence and interactivity as part of their marketing strategy, they will lose market share, increase their dependence on intermediaries and jeopardize their profitability and existence. SMTEs have no other alternative than to understand their markets and initiate changes in their management and technology in order to serve their new markets adequately. SMTEs cannot afford to continue watching the rapid developments of ITs with apathy as the future of those which will be unavailable on the electronic market place and thus inaccessible to consumers and intermediaries will be questionable.

Nevertheless, there is evidence suggesting that innovative small operators increasingly take advantage of the situation and profit. Small properties, which advertise and offer on-line bookings, are reported to achieve as much as 60 per cent of their reservations through the Internet. Although there is an element of replacement of media in this figure, there is an emerging new market which will only search for products and services on-line and this can assist SMTEs to attract new business. The Corisande Manor Hotel in Cornwall is an example of best practice in IT usage. Not only does it receive 90 per cent of its bookings through the Internet but it has also developed a new part of the business where it assists other SMTEs to develop their Internet presence for a fee. David Grant bought the hotel in 1997 and realized that advertisements in the Sunday press were ineffective as they were very expensive but yielded low results. He taught himself a Web authoring package and developed his Internet domain (www.cornwall-calling.

Table 9.4 Cost and benefit analysis for developing Internet presence for SMTEs. *Source*: Buhalis, 1999

Costs

- Cost of purchasing hardware, software and communication package
- Training cost of users
- Design and construction of Internet presence
- Cost of hosting the site on a reliable server
- Ongoing maintenance and regular updating
- Marketing the Internet service and registration of domain
- Development of procedures for dealing with Internet presence
- Commissions for purchases on-line by intermediaries
- Advertising fees for representation in search engines and other sites
- Interconnectivity with travel intermediaries such as TravelWeb, ITN, Expedia

Benefits

- Direct bookings, often intermediaries and commission-free
- Global distribution of multimedia information and promotional material
- Low cost of providing and distributing timely updates of information
- Global presence on the Internet, 24 hours a day, 365 days a year
- Durability of promotion (in comparison to limited life of printed advertising in press)
- Reduction of promotional cost and reduction of brochure waste
- Great degree of attention by visitors to web site
- Reduction of time required for transactions and ability to offer last-minute promotions
- Low marginal cost of providing information to additional users
- Support of marketing intelligence and product design functions
- Development of targeted mailing lists through people who actively request information
- Greater interactivity with prospective customers
- Niche marketing to prospective consumers who request to receive information
- Interactivity with local partners and provision of added value products at destinations
- Ability to generate a community feel for current users and prospective customers

co.uk). He decided that instead of showing pictures of the hotel he should provide destination content and attract people to Cornwall. In each page a slogan appeared: 'If you come to Cornwall why not stay at the Corisande Manor?', offering a link to his hotel with plenty of information and pictures demonstrating a home feel. As a result, 90 per cent of bookings currently come through e-mails. Following this success David Grant developed the Soft-Options Internet company (www.soft-options.co.uk) which registered Internet domains for all the UK regions (such as www.greatbritain.co.uk; www.capital-calling.co.uk; www.wales-calling.co.uk). He offers a package solution for small properties where the design and management of their web presence is charged £950 for the first year and less during consequent years. He suggests that a minimum of one to two hundred hits per day is needed to provide a critical mass for SMTEs to make the Internet a valuable generator of bookings. Based on his experience, Grant suggests that around 1 per cent of browsers normally e-mail hotels for information and 50 per cent of those book a room, depending on the speed in replying to e-mails and the quality of the site and the hotel.

A careful cost and benefit analysis can demonstrate that developing an Internet presence can be affordable and much more effective than other promotional and communication tools. Table 9.4 illustrates a comprehensive framework of all cost and benefit elements for developing an Internet presence for SMTEs.

Most costs and benefits are management and marketing-based, rather than IT based. Hence it is evident that competent and innovative entrepreneurs will find the Internet more beneficial than their counterparts who lack marketing or management skills, abilities and knowledge. Costs can be reduced by intensive management, marketing and IT training for SMTEs which will enable them to develop a comprehensive marketing strategy and use ITs as a strategic tool for their long-term development (Buhalis, 1999; Buhalis and Keeling, 1999).

Destinations

In addition to individual efforts, SMTEs should also establish collaborative ventures at the destination level, which would enable small firms to pool resources and share development and operation costs. Partnerships between private and public sectors as well as close collaboration are critical for the success of such schemes (Buhalis and Cooper, 1998; Buhalis, 1998a). Networks of shared costs–resources–information can assist small hotels to alleviate some of the constraints of being small sized and to assist them to obtain more benefits from scale economies. This co-operation needs support by public tourism organizations as well as associations of local tourist enterprises. 'There will be no place for the small stand alone participants, but the world can become the oyster for the small, innovative, flexible and net-worked enterprises' (Poon, 1988).

SMTEs' co-operative participation on the Internet and electronic market place through the development of Destination Management Systems (DMSs) is therefore suggested as a strategic direction (Sheldon, 1993, 1997; Archdale, 1993; Buhalis, 1993, 1994 and 1997). DMSs revolutionize destination marketing as they 'combine a radically improved and rapidly evolving methodology [computing] with new or better communications [telecommunication networks] in order to satisfy a growing private sector market [tourism]' (Archdale *et al.*, 1992). It is estimated that 200 destination-oriented systems of various kinds emerged in the early 1990s. As these systems facilitate the dissemination of information and reservation functions for destinations, DMSs are emerging as a major promotion, distribution and operational tool for both destinations and SMTEs. Buhalis (1994) has taken the DMS concept a step forward, to Destination Integrated Computerised Information Reservation Management Systems (DICIRMSs). DICIRMSs are ideal systems based on integration of technologies, for the integration of the local tourism industry and the integration of regional economies. DICIRMSs ultimately empower the strategic management and marketing of destinations and integrate both micro and macro functions at the destination level. Their contribution is to strategic management and marketing, which is demonstrated by their ability to co-ordinate and manage destinations as well as increase the intra-channel power of principals within the distribution channel, elevates them to strategic tools. This can support the achievement of long-term prosperity for indigenous people, maximization of returns of investments for tourism enterprises and can also enhance the quality of products and satisfaction of consumers/tourists. DICIRMSs are expected to benefit the prosperity of both local enterprises and destinations by facilitating the tourism value chain and by creating a system of wealth creation for all stakeholders at the destination level (Buhalis, 1995).

However, despite the conceptual developments on DMSs, the majority of public tourism organizations' projects have a high failure rate, as they often fail to attract the support and commitment required from the private and public sectors as well as funds for their development. DMSs hitherto have also failed to attract a critical mass of tourism demand to break even. Two systems, Gulliver, the Irish DMS, and the Tyrolean TIScover in Austria, are widely seen as an exception to the rule. Both systems have followed a very dynamic development and adopted their technological basis and ownership status. They remain as the few operational and successful systems in the world (O'Connor and Rafferty, 1997; Frew and O'Connor, 1998, 1999; Werthner and Klein, 1999).

SYNTHESIS – TOURISM IN THE NETWORKING ERA

Technology presents an opportunity and a challenge for the tourism industry. Although there is a degree of uncertainty over future developments of information technology, the only constant will be change. In this environment, organizations which need to compete will need to compute. IT developments and the proliferation of the Internet has introduced a new networking era which is changing not only 'best' managerial practices but also the way of life in most Western societies. ITs stimulate radical changes in the operation, distribution and structure of the tourism industry. Consequently, a paradigm shift is transforming business practices and introducing great benefits in the efficiency, differentiation, cost reduction and response time of organizations. ITs re-engineer both tourism operations and distribution channels. In the future, the visibility of principals in the market place will be a function of the technologies and networks used to interact with their individual and industry customers. Tourism enterprises will need to understand, incorporate and utilize ITs, in order to be able to serve their target markets, improve their efficiency, maximize profitability, enhance services and maintain long-term prosperity for themselves and for destinations.

Consumers are increasingly able and confident to browse through the Internet and identify a rich variety of offers in order to make travel choices suited to their personal requirements. Although the majority of users still 'look' but do not 'book', there is evidence that the percentage of on-line bookings is increasing rapidly. The focus is thus shifted towards individual travel and dynamic packages, enabling enterprises to target mini-segments and specialized interests. Technology empowers consumers to seek the best option, which satisfies their needs and wants, and thus it serves best a new type of sophisticated customer.

Although IT developments introduce a wide range of opportunities for innovative players, there is also a plethora of threats for members of the industry who will fail to change their practices and benefit from the new tools. A wide range of new players are attracted to the industry and larger organizations which have resources and expertise may increase their market share. Small and independent enterprises should therefore use innovation, differentiate their products and develop cost-effective interfaces with their markets and partners. Destinations can emerge as major beneficiaries of the ITs developments, as they can take advantage of new strategic tools for management, planning and marketing through co-ordination of local product as well as increasing their power in the distribution channel. In order to achieve the above benefits, a closer partnership and co-operation is required throughout the tourism industry. The provision of seamless travel experiences requires the development of virtual corporations and platforms for interactive product design and service before, during and after the travelling experience. Training and education of human resources in new technologies are becoming even more critical in order to empower the tourism industry to strengthen its competitiveness. Hence, adaptation and innovation will enable the tourism industry to develop its organizational competitiveness and assist them to take the opportunities and avoid the threats which will emerge as the ITs revolution continues in the twenty-first century.

REFERENCES

Archdale, G. (1993) 'Computer reservation systems and public tourist offices'. *Tourism Management*, **14**(1), 3–14.

Archdale, G., Stanton, R. and Jones, G. (1992) *Destination Databases: Issues and Priorities.* San Francisco: Pacific Asia Travel Association.

Buhalis, D. (1993) 'Regional integrated computer information reservation management systems as a strategic tool for the small and medium tourism enterprises'. *Tourism Management,* **14**(5), 366–78.

Buhalis, D. (1994) 'Information and telecommunications technologies as a strategic tool for small and medium tourism enterprises in the contemporary business environment'. In A. Seaton *et al.* (eds) *Tourism – The State of the Art.* Chichester: John Wiley & Sons, pp. 254–75.

Buhalis, D. (1995) 'The impact of information telecommunication technologies on tourism distribution channels: implications for the small and medium sized tourism enterprises' strategic management and marketing'. Guildford: University of Surrey PhD thesis, Department of Management Studies.

Buhalis, D. (1997) 'Information technologies as a strategic tool for economic, cultural and environmental benefits enhancement of tourism at destination regions'. *Progress in Tourism and Hospitality Research,* **3**(1), 71–93.

Buhalis, D. (1998a) 'Strategic use of information technologies in the tourism industry'. *Tourism Management,* **19**(3), 409–23.

Buhalis, D. (1998b) 'The future of tourism: information technology'. In C. Cooper *et al.* *Tourism: Principles and Practices.* Wokingham: Addison-Wesley Longman, pp. 423–65.

Buhalis, D. (1999) 'The cost and benefits of Information Technology and the Internet for small and medium-sized tourism enterprises'. In D. Buhalis and W. Schertler (eds) *Information and Communications Technologies in Tourism.* ENTER 1999 Proceedings. Wien: Springer-Verlag.

Buhalis, D. and Cooper, C. (1998) 'Competition or co-operation: small and medium sized tourism enterprises at the destination'. In E. Laws, B. Faulkner and G. Moscardo (eds) *Embracing and Managing Change in Tourism.* London: Routledge, pp. 324–46.

Buhalis, D. and Keeling, S. (1999) 'Distributing B&B accommodation in York, UK: advantages and developments emerging through the Internet'. In D. Buhalis and W. Schertler (eds) *Information and Communications Technologies in Tourism.* ENTER 1999 Proceedings. Wien: Springer-Verlag.

Buhalis, D. and Main, H. (1998) 'Information technology in small and medium hospitality enterprises: strategic analysis and critical factors'. *International Journal of Contemporary Hospitality Management,* **10**(5), 198–202.

Buhalis, D. and Schertler, W. (eds) (1999) *Information and Communication Technologies in Tourism.* Wien: Springer-Verlag.

Buhalis, D., Tjoa, A. M. and Jafari, J. (eds) (1998) *Information and Communication Technologies in Tourism.* Wien: Springer-Verlag.

Chervenak, L. (1993) 'Hotel technology at the start of the millennium'. *Hospitality Research Journal,* **17**(1), 113–20.

Cooper, C. and Buhalis, D. (1992) 'Strategic management and marketing of small and medium sized tourism enterprises in the Greek Aegean islands'. In R. Teare, D. Adams and S. Messenger (eds) *Managing Projects in Hospitality Organizations.* London: Cassell, pp. 101–25.

Dennis, P. (1998) 'Marriott International on the Internet: a success story'. Presentation at the ENTER'98 Conference, Istanbul.

Forrester (1999) 'On line travel bookings' [http://www.forrester.com].

Frew, A. and O'Connor, P. (1998) 'A comparative examination of the implementation of destination marketing system strategies: Scotland and Ireland'. In D. Buhalis, A. M. Tjoa and J. Jafari (eds) *Information and Communications Technologies in Tourism.* Wien: Springer-Verlag, pp. 258–68.

Frew, A. and O'Connor, P. (1999) 'Destination marketing system strategies: refining and extending an assessment framework'. In D. Buhalis and W. Schertler (eds) *Information and Communications Technologies in Tourism.* Wien: Springer-Verlag, pp. 398–407.

Go, F. (1992) 'The role of computerised reservation systems in the hospitality industry'. *Tourism Management,* **13**(1), 22–6.

Go, F. and Welch, P. (1991) *Competitive Strategies for the International Hotel Industry*. Special report No. 1180. London: The Economist Intelligence Unit.

Hammer, M. and Champy, J. (1993) *Re-engineering the Corporation: A Manifesto for Business Revolution*. London: Nicholas Brealey.

Hart, P. (1998) 'Travel servers on the Internet'. Presentation at the ENTER'98 Conference, Istanbul.

Hawkins, D., Leventhal, M. and Oden, W. (1996) 'The virtual tourism environment: utilization of information technology to enhance strategic travel marketing'. *Progress in Tourism and Hospitality Research*, **2**, **3** and **4**, 223–39.

Kärcher, K. (1997) *Reinventing Package Holiday Business*. Berlin: DeutscherUniversitätsVerlag.

Minghetti, V. and Mangilli, V. (1998) 'InTRAsystem: an advanced Internet-based information system for managing business travel'. *Information Technology and Tourism*, **1**(1), 33–44.

Morrison, A. (1994) 'Marketing strategic alliances: the small hotel firm'. *International Journal of Contemporary Hospitality Management*, **6**(3), 25–30.

Mutch, A. (1995) 'Destination information and the World Wide Web'. *Insights*, September, D.5–9.

Nell, L. (1998) 'Changes in the tourism market place: the effect of the Internet'. Presentation at the ENTER'98 Conference, Istanbul.

O'Connor, P. (1999) *Electronic Information Distribution in Tourism and Hospitality*. Oxford: CAB.

O'Connor, P. and Rafferty J. (1997) 'Gulliver–distributing Irish tourism electronically'. *Electronic Markets*, **7**(2), 40–5.

PhoCusWright (1998) 'The Travel eCommerce Survey' [www.phocuswright.com/].

Poon, A. (1988) 'Tourism and information technologies'. *Annals of Tourism Research*, **15**(4), 531–49.

Poon, A. (1993) *Tourism, Technology and Competitive Strategies*. Oxford: CAB International.

Rosen, N. (1999) 'Smart firms should follow easyJet's lead'. *Revolution*, July, 7.

Sheldon, P. (1993) 'Destination information systems'. *Annals of Tourism Research*, **20**(4), 633–49.

Sheldon, P. (1997) *Information Technologies for Tourism*. Oxford: CAB.

Sileo, L. (1998) 'Preview travel post IPO: why Wall Street loves Internet travel'. *The PhoCusWright Insighter*, **1**(5), 11 May [www.phocuswright.com/ptstory.htm].

Skapinker, M. (1999) 'BA to make new cuts in fleet expansion plan'. *The Financial Times*, 26 February, p. 15.

Smith, C. and Jenner, P. (1998) 'Tourism and the Internet'. *Travel and Tourism Analyst*, **1**, 62–81.

Symonds, M. (1999) 'The net imperative: business and the Internet'. *The Economist*, 26 June, pp. 8–44.

Tapscott, D. (1996) *The Digital Economy: Promise and Peril in the Age of Networked Intelligence*. New York: McGraw-Hill Inc.

Tapscott, D. and Caston, A. (1993) *Paradigm Shift: The New Promise of Information Technology*. New York: McGraw-Hill Inc.

Taylor, P. (1999) 'Business urged to get a connection as web turns out to be more than a fad'. *The Financial Times*, 6 July, p. 14.

TIA (1997) *Travel and Interactive Technology: A Five-Year Outlook*. Washington, DC: Travel Industry Association of America.

Vlitos-Rowe, I. (1995) *The Impact of Technology on the Travel Industry*. London: *Financial Times* Management Reports.

Wardell, D. (1998) 'The impact of electronic distribution on travel agents'. *Travel and Tourism Analyst*, **2**, 41–55.

Werthner, H. and Klein, S. (eds) (1999) *Information Technology and Tourism: A Challenging Relationship*. Wien: Springer-Verlag.

WTO (1988) *Guidelines for the Transfer of New Technologies in the Field of Tourism*. Madrid: World Tourism Organization.

WTO (1999) *Changes in Leisure Time: The Impact on Tourism*. Madrid: World Tourism Organization Business Council.

CHAPTER 10

Knowledge Management through the Web: A New Marketing Paradigm for Tourism Organizations

Xinran You, Joseph O'Leary
and Daniel Fesenmaier

INTRODUCTION

The rapid advancement of information technology, especially the Internet and the World Wide Web, is having a profound impact on the information-intensive travel and tourism industry. With electronic travel information available in a convenient and timely fashion and booking and reservation capabilities directly accessible for consumers, Internet technology is substantially altering the role of each player in the value-creation process of the industry. From a marketing perspective, the Web is giving rise to a new and very effective market communication channel, a 'marketspace' instead of the traditional market place (Rapport and Sviokla, 1995). The digital revolution changes the way in which companies collect, store and process data on consumer behaviour and the way marketers define price, promote and distribute their products.

Travel and tourism is the Internet's second largest commerce area after computer technology (Sheldon, 1997). The industry is very well represented on the WWW. A wealth of travel products and services and travel-related businesses are easily available over the Web. Government tourism offices and travel suppliers from destinations to airlines, hotels, car rentals, travel agencies, tour operators and attractions all over the world have home pages on the Web. The metamorphosis that the industry finds itself in poses challenges for tourism destinations and calls for a new paradigm to cope with the changes that are reshaping the industry and consumption patterns. The leading role in marketing a destination as a package to the rest of the world is usually played by National Tourism Organizations (NTOs), the national tourism authority in each country. NTOs are facing new challenges as well as new opportunities in the era of the information technology revolution. The Internet and the Web provide NTOs with a very effective market communication channel to disseminate information and knowledge about a destination to the public. Meanwhile, the Web also provides an excellent opportunity for NTOs to capture customer knowledge, such as shifting preferences towards travel products and destinations and varying travel behaviour patterns. Integrating them into a destination marketing strategy and product development is going to be paramount for these organizations. The key to achieving these goals is to make effective use of available information technology, especially the Internet, and embrace a new but very important management tool: knowledge management. NTOs can use this mechanism to create an environment where information and knowledge about a destination are disseminated and shared with customers while knowledge about potential and actual travellers is captured, utilized and provided to other players in the industry.

The purpose of this chapter is to examine the possible mechanism for NTOs to use over the Web to disseminate destination knowledge effectively, capture customer knowledge for marketing purposes and evaluate the current status of NTOs to embrace customer knowledge management.

KNOWLEDGE AND KNOWLEDGE MANAGEMENT

What is knowledge?

The importance of knowledge and knowledge management has been emphasized increasingly as a result of the explosion of information technology. Knowledge has been regarded as the most important corporate asset for companies. Increased realization of knowledge as the core competence coupled with recent advances in information technology such as the World Wide Web has kindled keen interest in the subject of knowledge and knowledge management. Prominent authors such as Peter Drucker and Alvin Toffler herald the arrival of a knowledge economy or society. Drucker (1993) argues that, in the new economy, knowledge is not just another resource alongside the traditional factors of production – labour, capital and land – but the only meaningful resource today. Toffler (1990) proclaims that knowledge is the source of the highest quality power and the key to the power shift that lies ahead. These authors agree that the future belongs to people and organizations endowed with knowledge.

What is knowledge? Knowledge, according to Drucker (1993) is 'information that changes something or somebody – either by becoming grounds for actions, or by making an individual (or an institution) capable of different or more effective action.' Machlup (1980) suggests that knowledge can also be categorized as descriptive, procedural, reasoning, linguistic, assimilative and presentation. Descriptive knowledge is 'know-what', procedural knowledge is 'know-how', while reasoning knowledge is 'know-why'. The remaining three categories are ancillary types of knowledge that can be used either to interpret incoming observations, to alter the contents of a knowledge storehouse or to package outgoing messages. According to Nonaka and Takeuchi (1995), knowledge is more than just necessarily explicit – something formal and systematic. They draw on Polanyi's (1966) distinction between tacit knowledge and explicit knowledge. Tacit knowledge is personal, context-specific and therefore hard to formalize and communicate. Explicit or 'codified' knowledge is transmittable in formal, systematic language. Nonaka and Takeuchi explain that tacit knowledge and explicit knowledge are mutually complementary entities which interact with and exchange into each other in the creative activities of human beings.

What is knowledge management?

There is not yet a common consensus on the concept of knowledge management. Newman's (1996) definition is that knowledge management is the collection of processes that govern the creation, dissemination and utilization of knowledge. Skyme (1996) explains that knowledge management has several categories: knowledge creation, knowledge accumulation, knowledge dissemination, knowledge sharing and knowledge use. He proposes that the major processes of a knowledge life cycle are: (1) creation/gathering/identifying; (2) organizing/ assimilating; (3) applying/using; (4) diffusing/disseminating; and (5) protecting. Newman (1996) added another dimension to Skyme's knowledge life cycle: the continuum of data, information, knowledge and intelligent behaviour. Malhotra (1998) emphasizes that knowledge management

> caters to the critical issues of organizational adoption, survival and competence in the face of increasingly discontinuous environmental change. Essentially, it embodies organizational processes that seek a synergistic combination of data and information processing capacity of information technologies, and the creative and innovative capacity of human beings.

Knowledge management and activities can occur in both a traditional market place and the new on-line market environment. Researchers and practitioners have recognized the importance of a conscious strategy for businesses to encourage knowledge activities and effectively capture customer knowledge through the on-line environment and put it to utilization for possible value creation. Davenport (1994) notes that to maximize the potential for value creation, management needs to develop effective marketing communication channels and explicit customer knowledge capture strategies as part of their broader on-line agenda. These strategies should address a broad range of issues regarding targeting, capturing, leveraging and competing for information and knowledge about consumers. Once there is a clear focus on the information that is most valuable to the business, the next step is to assess the relative importance of on-line environments in facilitating customer knowledge capture and the specific approaches best suited to exploit the potential of on-line environments as a capture medium. Another challenge to face the organization, Davenport points out, is to make use of the knowledge captured or readily available for capture and the actual use of this information/ knowledge to create economic value. Knowledge management embodies organizational processes that seek synergistic combination of the data and information-processing capacity of information technologies, and the creative and innovative capacity of human beings.

Skyme (1996) predicted that the challenge of the future is to learn to manage the 'mechanics' of knowledge. These mechanics will allow an infinite variety of 'knowledge connections' as in the Internet today, out of which individuals will carve their own knowledge spaces in global communities. These spaces will reflect their interests and personal values. Malhotra (1996) sees the future role of knowledge management as helping individuals make effective connections to like-minded people, to specific information and to problem-solvers/helpers as well as to opportunities. Organizations of the future will overlap these communities and industries and seek opportunities to evolve their businesses with these networks of interest.

NTO and its new marketspace

Virtually every country has a national tourism organization, either as part of a federal government agency or as a quasi-governmental entity. It is usually the official body with a network of overseas, state or city tourist offices, responsible for the development and marketing of the country as a tourism destination to the rest of the world in conjunction with the private sector (Mill and Morrison, 1992). Other tasks include (Pearce, 1992) information provision to potential travellers, travellers and travel intermediaries; and the collection and analysis of tourism statistics and assessment of the size and economic impact of tourism in the destination. Marketing and promotion of the country as a destination would nevertheless seem to be the dominant function (Middleton, 1988).

NTOs are usually considered the official government-backed provider of destination information and, therefore, are often considered as less biased compared with other tourism commercial sites. Traditionally, NTOs have distributed information by mailing printed materials and brochures in response to mail, fax and phone inquiries or have delivered destination marketing messages through TV commercials. Through provision of information, they also collect data on consumers and try to establish an effective communication channel with the consumers. However, comparing the traditional marketing communication approaches with what the Internet can offer for NTOs as a marketing communication channel, the latter has much more efficiency, effectiveness and timeliness, especially when taking into account the huge growth potential of the Internet user market. This is due to the unique nature of this electronic communication channel that other marketing channels cannot match.

NTOs have numerous options to disseminate destination information electronically and the World Wide Web has provided an excellent way for information provision (Sheldon, 1997). According to Shaw and Gaines (1996), web technology provides a new knowledge medium in which artificial intelligence methodologies and systems can be integrated with hypermedia systems to support the knowledge processes of a variety of communities worldwide.

Many NTOs are already distributing information about their destination, travel products and services over the Web. However, the implications of using the Web as an information channel go far beyond information provision. The network-based NTO is strongly positioned to create value by aggregating people and resources on networks, thereby developing rich profiles of consumers and integrating these into both destination marketing strategy and travel product design and management. The interactive features of the Web have provided enormous opportunities for these groups to organize activities such as travel itinerary planning assistance, travel experiences and destination knowledge sharing in the market place. This in turn leads to opportunities for NTOs to understand consumer behaviour, build on-line virtual communities, influence consumer destination decision-making and ultimately influence customer loyalty, even using the Web as a word-of-mouth marketing tool.

NTOS' USE OF THE WEB AS A KNOWLEDGE ACTIVITY FACILITATOR

The emergence of a new marketing paradigm

Today, consumers are well travelled, sophisticated and demand quality and value (Poon, 1996). As a result, the interaction between the product and the market in order for the product to comply with market conditions and exigencies is paramount. To sustain an effective strategy, a better understanding of the shift in consumer tastes and demand would definitely serve as the preliminary step to launch effective marketing programmes and give direction and guidance to industry players in travel product planning and packaging.

In today's business environment, on-line marketing activities facilitate on-line knowledge creation, sharing and utilization. Customer knowledge management on-line will become a critical issue for NTOs. In fact, on-line customer knowledge management may become a new marketing paradigm for NTOs. A knowledge management system seems to be the right solution.

To provide examples, we undertook a study of National Tourism Organization's web site in the context of knowledge activities and management. It attempted to see how NTOs use the web environment to facilitate and manage knowledge activities, optimize their on-line destination marketing communication efforts and investigate the potential for further developments. More specifically it was intended to find out: (1) what are the explicit knowledge presentation or dissemination facilitation features over the web sites of NTOs; (2) what are the mechanisms that NTOs use over the Web to acquire customer knowledge and facilitate travellers or potential travellers in their information searching and destination knowledge acquisition; (3) what are the mechanisms that NTOs use to encourage and facilitate on-line knowledge sharing activities; (4) what are the efforts from NTOs to encourage visits and revisits of their web sites to create more opportunities for knowledge creation and sharing; and finally, (5) what are the potential opportunities for on-line knowledge utilization.

The organizations that were chosen for the study are the national tourist offices or agencies of the top fifteen tourism destinations of the world in terms of tourism receipts. The selected fifteen countries are the United States of America, France, Italy, Spain, the United Kingdom, Austria, Germany, Hong Kong, China, Thailand, Singapore, Switzerland, Canada, Poland and Australia. Due to the fact that USA, China and Poland did not have a national tourist office general web site at the time of the study, these three countries were dropped from the survey. The selection of the subjects does not imply that the chosen subjects maintain a higher level of knowledge activities or command a higher level of sophistication in on-line knowledge management. These twelve web sites are simply places to start. The data used in this study were collected between 15 February and 25 February 1999. All observations were made based on the main web site of each NTO and any modifications made by the NTOs after 25 February 1999 were not taken into consideration.

Explicit knowledge/information dissemination through the Web

In terms of explicit knowledge/information distribution and dissemination, NTO web pages were studied in their application of presentation formats such as text, images, audio, video and employment of dissemination facilitation features such as language media choices, hyperlinks, search functions, list/drop boxes, etc. It is found that all web sites are text and hypertext based, with static images. The United Kingdom, Hong Kong and Switzerland have attempted to offer audio programmes such as music and narratives on-line on the Web. More countries use digital video programmes as a means of disseminating destination knowledge or information.

Some are non-interactive (pure video per se) while others are interactive (such as virtual tours), where the viewers can have control over pace and content.

As to the knowledge dissemination facilitation features, most countries seem to have taken into consideration the fact that their audiences are people from all over the world with different language backgrounds. Almost all NTO web sites provide language choices to facilitate better comprehension of their web site content. English is the most commonly used language medium. There are variations as to the number of language versions provided by each destination. Countries that tend to be most advanced in using multi-language presentation strategies are the United Kingdom, Switzerland, France, Hong Kong and Spain, each with at least four different language choices.

Most NTOs are aware of the need for users to be able to do further search for relevant information or knowledge. To function as a bridge and facilitate users' further search of related information or knowledge, almost all web sites use a hyperlink feature linking the user with related web sites. Links are usually made to NTO branches or overseas offices, industry partners such as travel agents, hotels, airlines or service-related industries such as restaurants, retailing or wholesaling, or other information sources such as an embassy that will provide general information about the country, immigration, weather, etc.

Search functions based on an NTO's own web site aim to help the user conveniently to locate certain information or knowledge from the current web site. As an NTO's web site gets more data intensive and multidimensional, this function appears to ease the anxiety of aimless searching and improve the efficiency of knowledge dissemination. The most commonly used search function is keyword search or site map search. Other search facilitation features such as list box or check box or drop box are commonly employed by most web sites.

Customer knowledge acquisition on-line

Customer knowledge is a very important ingredient that every NTO seeks, since it is vital in effectively marketing their destinations. It appears that almost all NTOs realize the importance of it and attempt to set up mechanisms to acquire knowledge about their customers. However, the level of sophistication varies. The twelve web sites utilize both direct and indirect mechanisms for customer knowledge acquisition. The direct approaches are usually through asking the user/customer to provide demo-graphic or psychographic information by filling out structured forms. In return, customers benefit from incentives such as free brochures or travel pamphlets, free on-line electronic card services, memberships or opportunities to express emotions about travel issues through feedback. Indirect customer knowledge acquisition is realized in more subtle ways such as through tracking customer on-line searching activities, or through aggregating unstructured information while providing facilities in the form of a search function, on-line chatting or bulletin board message posting.

Countries such as Spain, the United Kingdom, Austria, Hong Kong, Singapore, Switzerland and Australia offer direct on-line brochure or pamphlet request opportunities to customers. Hong Kong, Singapore, Switzerland and Australia are among countries that offer on-line E-card service. Some countries request only name and e-mail address, but some make the consumers fill out more information such as their home address. Another example could include free membership in a travel club. This serves as another means to collect data by offering sign-up benefits like receiving a weekly/monthly travel newsletter, best deals, last-minute discounts, etc. Some ask for the address or demographic information; some even put up a travel preference survey or travel history survey together with the sign-ups.

Feedback is another approach for inputs from customers. Customers can either give feedback to the design and content of the Web or feedback about the pros and cons of the travel products or services that they have received from the destination. Knowledge created from a feedback loop definitely helps in web site fine-tuning and travel products or services improvement. For instance, a destination may realize through the feedback loop that travel information they provide is mismatched with what the targeted travellers are looking for. Therefore they can make necessary adjustments or modifications of their site accordingly. Eight out of twelve web sites provide feedback mechanism for consumers through special on-line programs such as 'write-to-us', 'tell us what you think', either using a free message style or using a structured check box survey format. Search functions, chat rooms and bulletin boards are some indirect means of getting feedback for the customers. By tracking down the search trail, the NTO can learn what the user is looking for. The chat room has been used to link people with similar interests and the exchange of ideas on-line in real time in many web sites of other industries. Since this is freestyle chatting, casual and subjective, it can provide NTOs a means to gather subjective opinions and feedback from the customers and identify opportunities for improvement. By monitoring what is happening in the chat room, the NTO will be able to gain greater insight into how people look at their destination. Bulletin boards provide mechanisms for people to post information, knowledge, opinions or questions for people to interact. The chat room is still not commonly used. Singapore, Switzerland and Spain have bulletin board mechanisms where people can post their messages. None of the twelve web sites provided a chat room mechanism.

Knowledge and experiences sharing on-line

Knowledge and experience sharing is an important component of on-line knowledge activity for NTOs. Parties involved in this activity are consumers, i.e., travellers or potential travellers, and NTOs as travel experts. There are different types of message-posting methods: post message with no feedback, post message with synchronous feedback, such as on-line chatting, and post message with asynchronous feedback such as is found with a bulletin board (Table 10.1).

Table 10.1 Mechanisms of knowledge sharing activities on-line

Parties involved	Post Message on Web (no feedback)	Post Message with Synchronous Feedback	Post Message with Asynchronous Feedback
(Potential) Consumers Expert(s)	Consumer posts his/her experience to share with other (potential) consumers	On-line chat among other consumers	Bulletin board for (potential) consumers to interact
	Expert posts advice/suggestions to travellers	On-line chat with expert(s)	Expert–customer exchange box; general feedback from consumers regarding their preferences, or complaints that need to be dealt with by NTO

Posting messages with no feedback can include mechanisms for consumers to send messages on the Web to share destination-specific travel experiences, either negative or positive, subjective evaluations of the experiences and recommendations or criticisms about the destination's travel products. This is a one-way knowledge/experience from the consumer, but all parties benefit from the process. For the contributors, it is a way to express emotions and experiences. For fellow consumers, it is useful peer evaluation about a destination. This is subjective knowledge sharing but also serves as a potentially convincing message. From a destination or NTO's perspective, it promotes and encourages knowledge and experience exchange among customers or between the customers and travel experts. The NTO could benefit from these 'conversations' or communications to gather consumers' preferences for target marketing. Even in the case of negative comments, they help NTOs identify possible problem areas either in products or services and look for means to improve. This is a window that an NTO can either passively observe through studying the messages posted by consumers or where an active role can be taken to influence consumers' choices by posting travel suggestions. They can also actively engage in on-line discussion groups to exchange views with consumers, communicate with them and share their expertise and knowledge about the destination that may eventually influence them. In some web environments such as the European Union, where there is legal liability for information providers, this form of spontaneous feedback may be inhibited. Additionally, NTOs can provide tailor-made services in itinerary planning. Finally, this is also a channel to improve a destination's image. By handling complaints or negative feedback, they may find ways to improve travel experiences. This knowledge/experience sharing process is an important marketing communication tool that NTOs cannot afford to neglect. It is a very good application of persuasive marketing communication theory which brings the consumer and the destination closer. Another important application is to employ this as a mechanism to develop on-line travel communities, eventually building up customer loyalty, and using it as a word-of-mouth marketing tool. This is a very efficient and cost-effective way to promote the destination (Hagel III and Armstrong, 1997).

While posting messages without feedback seems to be the most popularly used approach for knowledge/experience sharing among the web sites, some NTO web sites use mechanisms similar to the travel expert's suggestion box. In this example, travel experts actually share their expertise and knowledge about the destinations and provide one-way suggestions or ideas in itinerary planning, sometimes giving out general or situational advice. Among the twelve web sites studied across the world, ten have devices such as itinerary suggestions, travel tips, trip planners and answers to frequently asked questions, etc. Posting messages with synchronous feedback such as on-line chatting among consumers or on-line chatting with experts seems to be uncommon. Overall, there are few interactive mechanisms employed by NTO web sites. However, both Singapore and Switzerland's sites provide customers with limited expert interaction. Users can submit basic information such as when they plan to visit, length of stay, activity categories of interest, etc. Expert systems can, in real time, suggest a customized itinerary based on the customer's on-line input. This is an application of a travel expert system, which allows limited on-line two-way interaction between the customer and the expert.

Web page visit and revisit

Another feature looked at in these web sites is the provision of extra benefits such as free on-line post card services. Recreational uses of the medium, manifested in the form of non-directed search behaviour, can be an important benefit to consumers intrinsically motivated to use the medium (Hoffman *et al.*, 1995). Value latent benefits that are linked to free fun activities or services allow NTOs to benefit from customer information that comes from creating a critical mass. The variety of fun choices offered over the Web is not necessarily connected with knowledge activities. However, the entertaining effects created keep users on a particular site for a longer period and certainly play a positive and important role in encouraging visit and revisit. This in turn improves potential opportunities to enhance knowledge activities on the Web such as knowledge sharing and creation.

For example, the Hong Kong Tourist Association 's web site has the largest collection of titbits to encourage visits and revisits. The list is long: games, video clips and virtual tours, interesting animations, downloadable wallpapers, screen savers, Ecards where the user can personalize messages and customize personal animation designs, a Chinese horoscope, etc. Other countries that are at the forefront in providing value latent benefits include the British Tourist Authority and the Singapore Tourism Authority which offers free post card services, a learning English programme and learning Singlish (English blended with local Singapore flavour).

The level of technology factor should be taken into consideration. A fully loaded home page with sophisticated or large database supported functions may significantly increase the browsing waiting time and run the risk of losing the patience or interest of the intended user. This may become a major deterrent. A lot of technically sophisticated functions may appeal to computer enthusiasts or web masters; however, they may not be as desirable to the travellers or potential travellers. It is important to bear in mind that the design of a NTO web page should attempt to fulfil the organization's mission and strategic goals rather than winning a technical reward for sophisticated programming.

DISCUSSION

Knowledge management as a means to achieve effective marketing communication

The result of the exploratory study of NTOs' web site efforts in knowledge management indicates that there are different strategies to organize on-line knowledge activities. Figure 10.1 illustrates that each communication channel level leads to a different knowledge management process and marketing effect. As the level of the communication mechanism changes, the sophistication level of the knowledge management process is also altered, leading to higher intensity marketing effects. Marketing communications perform three functions: to inform, to remind and to persuade (Anderson and Rubin, 1986). The traditional marketing communications model for mass media, which took the form of one-to-many and was passive, is giving way to many-to-many and being interactive. This was supported by the Internet, through distributed computing and interactive multimedia (Hoffman *et al.*, 1995). As the communication channel moves forward toward being many-to-many and interactive, knowledge activity moves from dissemination to active knowledge sharing while the marketing effect intensifies. This includes going from 'to inform' customers to 'educate/remind' and, ultimately, to 'influence/persuade'.

Knowledge management as an ecological system

The NTOs' knowledge activities on-line can take the form of multiple elements. Five key processes are identified and proposed: (1) knowledge dissemination; (2)

knowledge acquisition; (3) knowledge sharing; (4) knowledge embedding; and (5) knowledge utilization and embodying. Knowledge embedding refers to the process of the individual traveller or NTOs' acquired knowledge being absorbed and becoming part of the individual or organization's knowledge base. Knowledge embodying refers to the process of knowledge being utilized and represented in forms such as a decision, a new product or strategy. Figure 10.2 shows a layout of knowledge-related activities in a web environment for both NTOs and customers. For NTOs, the knowledge system is a self-enhancing system. Knowledge about customers that is embedded within the organization will help the process of embodying the knowledge in new marketing strategies, products and services, and the improved products and services can lead to improved knowledge dissemination.

The Web is an attractive medium for disseminating destination knowledge. It meets the knowledge demand of the customer and at the same time serves as a promotion channel to inform customers what a destination can offer. The ideal situation is that the web site is itself an informed action based on an NTO's understanding of what the destination can offer and the interests of the targeted audience. Different target markets may vary in their activities of interest or travel products. The level of sophistication also makes a difference: first-time visitors or prospective travellers differ from repeat visitors in what they are looking for in a destination. An 'Expert's' suggestion box provides a mechanism to deliver knowledge about a destination as well as influencing behaviour and destination choice: seasonal activities, highlight attractions, new development, suggestions for different demographic groups or segments or suggestions about what to see and do for new and repeat visitors. This is an excellent channel to provide a theme for a destination's products. Using a travel expert's knowledge about a destination and his or her authority makes it easier to convince and influence travellers. Based on persuasive communication theory, one of the key elements for effective marketing communication is the source factors (McCarville et al., 1992). The most frequently studied source factors are the communicator's credibility and attractiveness. Persuasion is generally assumed to increase with credibility. This refers to the perceived expertise and trustworthiness of the communicator. As a governmental entity, NTOs have the advantage in being perceived as an authoritative source for destination information and knowledge and travel advice.

Knowledge acquisition on-line has two elements: travellers and potential travellers who seek travel/destination knowledge on the one hand and, on the other, the NTOs and the industry players who seek customer knowledge in terms of travel behaviour, travel motivation, travel destination decision-making process, expenditure patterns and travel product preferences. The interactive nature of the Web and the hypertext environment allow for deep, non-linear searches initiated and controlled by customers but traced and researched by NTOs. In communication theory, receiver factors, the characteristics of the receiver or audience to whom

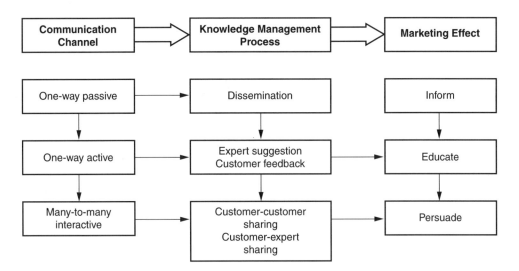

Figure 10.1 Levels of communication channel sophistication and performance intensity

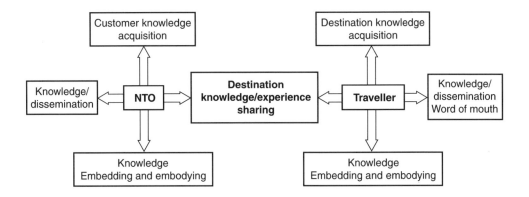

Figure 10.2 On-line knowledge activity layout

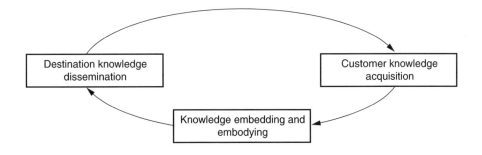

Figure 10.3 NTO ecological knowledge system

the message is addressed, cannot be ignored (Anderson and Rubin, 1986). Any attribute or combination of attributes of the receiver may provide a context contributing to the effectiveness of the message. As a result of receiver factors, a good understanding of the targeted markets would assist in delivering the destination marketing message. In facilitating the knowledge quest of the customer, the NTO creates an excellent opportunity to acquire customer knowledge.

Knowledge sharing among customers and between customer and expert leads to several implications. The organization can use mechanisms such as chat rooms, discussion groups or an expert/customer exchange box as channels for word-of-mouth destination promotion. Of course, word of mouth can be positive or negative. However, the negative comments or experiences can be changed into positive inputs if the NTO takes action on what people are complaining about. These can also be channels for travel product and service enhancement after identifying and knowing better where the weaker linkages lie in the whole tourism system that brings negative experiences to the customer. The positive comments can lead to elaboration and further refinement. A third opportunity is a way to communicate with the customers and provide personalized services. Finally, this is an opportunity to build an on-line traveller community: a group of people with common interests gathered to share their experiences.

Knowledge embedding and embodying is another crucial part of knowledge management that has not been studied in depth. However, this is a link in the NTO's knowledge system that must be enhanced. It is a vital part of an ecological knowledge system as shown in Figure 10.3.

From embedded to embodied knowledge: the new focus on knowledge management in product development

Knowledge management is not an end in itself but a means to fulfil multiple goals. One goal is to assimilate on-line customer knowledge, embed the knowledge into travel product planners and travel marketers and ultimately embody them in the form of new or enhanced travel products/services or marketing programmes. Nonaka and Takeuchi (1995) pointed out the major strategy for Japanese companies such as Honda to bring about continuous innovation and to stay competitive is their active implementation of a knowledge input–output model. These companies have continually turned to their suppliers, customers, distributors, government agencies and even competitors for new insights. What is unique about the way these companies bring about continuous innovation is the link between the outside and the inside. Knowledge that is accumulated from the outside is shared widely within the organization, stored as part of the company's knowledge base and utilized by those engaged in developing new technologies and products. A conversion process takes place – from outside to inside and back outside again in the form of new products, services, systems or targeted segments. This is exactly the ecological knowledge model that would benefit NTOs: to anticipate change constantly, take informed action and come up with innovations – a new technology, a new product or service design, a new marketing approach, a new form of distribution or a new way of servicing customers. The knowledge embedding and embodying process is an issue that relates to how NTOs should create an ecological environment where knowledge sharing and creation can be well facilitated, thus bringing out increased productivity and efficiency.

The knowledge input–output model applies to consumers as well. Application, a process of knowledge embedding and embodying, also takes place. People are no longer passive receivers of information and knowledge; this makes interactive features important. Travellers usually act on the information or knowledge presented to them, integrating it and constructing interpretations of their own. After assimilating outside knowledge (embedding), the consumer would be engaged in forming his or her own opinions, drawing inferences and making decisions on issues such as preferred travel plans (embodying).

From one-to-many to one-to-one: knowledge activities as a means to relationship marketing

Another important implication for the NTO is that the on-line knowledge environment provides a natural channel for one-to-one relationship marketing, a preferred mode and a continuing trend in marketing. The Web as a medium for marketing communications has made one-to-one marketing possible and plausible due to its interactive nature and the tremendous growth of the Internet and particularly the WWW. This has lead to a critical mass of consumers (Hoffman *et al.*, 1995).

Newsgroups, electronic bulletin boards and chat rooms are important services on the Internet that allow travellers to research travel products and destinations in a less formal medium. That focus can be a particular destination or a given type of travel such as ecotourism or cultural tourism. One characteristic unique to chat rooms is that the information exchange is in real time. Experts on travel may be invited into chat rooms to share their subjective expertise on a given topic or destination. Users can send requests to them and receive responses on-line, as if chatting. The on-line nature of chat rooms is closer to interacting with people personally and frequent side conversations bring together people with like interests. General travellers using the services can expect the shared knowledge to be more subjective and ad hoc, yet valuable. All three are mechanisms for building virtual travel communities. According to Hagel III and Armstrong (1997), virtual communities can be highly effective at stimulating word of mouth allowing a company to leverage its most effective sales force: its own customers. Virtual communities are the mechanism that can bring the vision of relationship-based, individually tailored marketing to reality. This capability of the medium offers unprecedented opportunities to tailor communications precisely to individual customers.

By engaging travellers in a personal relationship with the NTO and helping to build up on-line traveller communities, on-line knowledge sharing activities can serve as important and effective means to facilitate relationship marketing that takes tourism organizations into the twenty-first century.

REFERENCES

Anderson, P. M. and Rubin, L. G. (1986) *Marketing Communications*. Englewood Cliffs, NJ: Prentice-Hall, Inc.

Davenport, T. H. (1994) 'Reengineering: business change of mythic proportions?' *MIS Quarterly*, 121–7.

Drucker, P. F. (1993) *Post-Capitalist Society*. New York: Harper Business (a division of Harper-Collins).

Hagel III, J. and Armstrong, A. G. (1997) 'Net gain: expanding markets through virtual communities'. *McKinsey Quarterly*, **1**(2), 140–53.

Hoffman, Donna L., Novak, Thomas P. and Chatterjee, Patrali (1995) 'Commercial scenarios for the Web: opportunities and challenges'. *Journal of Computer-Mediated Communications*, Special Issue on Electronic Commerce, **1**(3). <http://shum.huji.ac.il/jcmc/vol1/issue3/vol1no3.html>

McCarville, R. E., Driver, B. L. and Crompton, J. L. (1992). 'Persuasive communication and the pricing of public leisure services'. In M. J. Manfredo (ed.) *Influencing Human Behavior: Theory and Application in Recreation, Tourism, and Natural Resources Management*. Champaign, Ill: Sagamore Pub. Inc.

Machlup, F. (1980) 'Knowledge: its creation, distribution, and economic significance'. In *Knowledge and Knowledge Production*. Princeton, NJ: Princeton University Press.

Malhotra, Y. (1996) 'Organizational learning and learning organizations: an overview'. <http://www.brint.com/orgLrng.htm>

Malhotra, Y. (1998) 'Knowledge management, knowledge organizations and knowledge workers: a view from the front lines'. <http://www.brint.com/interview/maeil.htm>

Manfredo, M. J. (1992) *Influencing Human Behavior: Theory and Application in Recreation, Tourism, and Natural Resources Management*. Champaign, Ill: Sagamore Pub. Inc.

Middleton, V. T. C. (1988) *Marketing in Travel and Tourism*. Oxford: Heinemann Professional.

Mill, R. C. and Morrison, A. (1992) *The Tourism System: An Introductory Text*. Englewood Cliffs, NJ: Prentice-Hall.

Newman, B. (1996) 'The knowledge management forum'. <http://www.km-forum.org/htm>

Nonaka, I. and Takeuchi, H. (1995) *The Knowledge-creating Company*. New York: Oxford University Press.

Pearce, D. (1992) *Tourist Organizations*. New York: John Wiley & Sons.

Polanyi, M. (1966) *The Tacit Dimension*. London: Routledge & Kegan Paul.

Poon, A. (1996) *Tourism, Technology and Competitive Strategies*. New York: CAB International.

Rapport, J. and Sviokla, J. (1995) *Managing in the MarketSpace*. Harvard: Harvard Business School.

Shaw, M. L. G. and Gaines, B. R. (1996) 'Distributed knowledge modeling through the WWW'. <http://penta.ufrgs.br/edu/telelab/10/kmwww.htm>

Sheldon, P. J. (1997) *Tourism Information Technology*. New York: CAB International.

Skyme, D. J. (1996) 'The knowledge management forum'. <http://www.km-forum.org/htm>

Skyme, D. J. (1997) 'Knowledge management: oxymoron or dynamic duo?'. *Managing Information,* **4**(7), 24–6.

Toffler, A. (1990) *Powershift: Knowledge, Wealth, and Violence at the Edge of the 21st Century.* New York: Bantam Books.

URL of NTO web sites surveyed:

Canada: <http://www.canadatourism.com>

Thailand: <http://www.tat.or.th>

Britain: <http:// www.visitbritain.com>

Singapore: <http://www.travel.com.sg>

Austria: <http://www.austria-tourism.at>

Australia: <http://www.aussie.net.au/>

France: < http://www.maison-de-la-france.fr/>

Italy: <http://www.enit.it>

Spain: <http://www.tourspain.es>

Hong Kong: <http://www.hkta.org>

Germany: <http://www.germany-tourism.de/>

Switzerland: <http://www.switzerlandtourism.ch/>

CHAPTER 11

Destination Management: Co-operative Marketing, a Case Study of the Port Douglas Brand

Noel Scott, Nick Parfitt and Eric Laws

INTRODUCTION

This chapter addresses the question of how operators and destination authorities work within a destination region, illustrating how the problems resulting from different geographic scales and the objectives of business units and government agencies can be tackled through co-operative marketing within a strong destination image. The market positioning of Tropical North Queensland (TNQ) provides the basis for strategies to develop tourism opportunities and is a framework for promotion by local businesses and communities. The State Tourist Organization (TQ – Tourism Queensland)[1] is thereby providing a leadership role as the overall manager of this process.

Destination marketing is increasingly demanding with rising customer expectations and intensifying competition between destinations and between tourism and alternative purchases. In response, more sophisticated marketing is used including product development (packaging of holidays), enhanced promotional imagery and targeting of specific market segments. However, in tourism because of the fragmented nature of the 'product', in order to be effective the destination structure (the network of business relationships) itself requires enhancement. The development of cohesive destination image and the development of cohesive destination organizations go hand in hand.

The traditional approach to destination management strategy (both in terms of development and marketing) has been derived from the literature on organizational strategy. However, there is a fundamental weakness in an approach to destination management which relies on the assumption of strong leadership and clear goal-driven decisions to which all participants adhere (at least in the short term). Destinations are conglomerates of attractions, operators and agencies which each have individual objectives. Often these are in direct conflict, and managers may regard competition with local organizations as their main policy concern, resulting in attempts to position themselves uniquely in the market place and in price competition. In contrast to the classical organizational strategy paradigm of clarity and consensus based on a rational process of analysis, destinations experience tension between operators, they seldom have strong leadership and lack cohesion in the way in which the area promotes its image externally.

Within this setting, the following case study examines an image repositioning study of two hotels in Port Douglas, Tropical North Queensland. The development of these hotel positions was done in relation to the destination images of Port Douglas and Tropical North Queensland. The case presents a study of the domestic (Australian) market, illustrating how the optimization of destination image is related to enhancements in destination organization.

This chapter considers the policy implications of the findings for State Tourist Organizations and for operators involved in destination image management and discusses the need for further research into collaboration in the management of destinations.

CASE SETTING

Tourism in Queensland is an important part of the state economy with an overall contribution of tourism to Gross State Product (GSP) of around 10 per cent in 1997. Tourism Queensland (previously the Queensland Tourist and Travel Corporation (QTTC) is a Queensland Government Owned Enterprise. Its role is defined by an Act of Parliament as 'promotion of Queensland as a Tourist Destination'. As a result of its marketing activity, Queensland has very strong, positive perceptions in the domestic (Australian) market as a destination offering sun, fun, warmth, activity and friendliness.

In 1995, changing consumer buying behaviours and sophisticated competitor promotional campaigns led to a new approach to Queensland's tourism marketing. After a review of the marketing strategy, TQ shifted from the promotion of Queensland with one destinational image to the development of a portfolio of 'destinational images'. It focused promotion to Australian markets on its main destination hubs. This was especially important for newer destinations such as Tropical North Queensland based in Cairns with its World Heritage Daintree rainforest and Great Barrier Reef attractions.

By branding Queensland's five developed destinations, TQ has taken a sophisticated consumer goods approach to tourism marketing – the first time such an approach has been applied to tourism marketing in Australia. The process involved extensive market research and industry consultation at every stage. All organizations undertaking destination marketing were involved, including the Far North Queensland Promotion Bureau, Tourism Queensland, the Australian Tourist Commission (ATC) and industry operators.

The process involved the following steps:

- Market research (market audit, focus groups and in-depth interviews)
- Identification of target markets
- Definition of a distinctive positioning for each brand
- Development of a joint marketing strategy
- Development of appropriate communication messages for the new creative campaign.

The resulting 'destination image' provides the basis for co-ordination of promotional activities for each destination. TQ in taking a co-ordination role has also been expected to develop advertising creative for particular campaigns. The current strategy is to develop destinational image advertising and not directly promote individual operators. TQ does, however, contribute to the individual operator price leader advertising by developing brand reinforcement messages that tie in to stand-alone advertising by operators. The positioning was developed to link to that of Australia developed by the Australian Tourism Commission.

Thus a multi level co-ordinated approach to destination image development at destination, state and national level has been developed. This case study describes how this multi level approach was extended to sub-destinations and individual operators.

THE STRATEGIC PROMOTION OF DESTINATION AREAS

Governments have increasingly recognized the economic significance of tourism and its role as a tool for regional development (Wanhill, 1999). One consequence of this has been the active development and promotion of towns, regions and countries, as if they were tourism place-products (Kotler *et al.*, 1993). Hall (1994) has highlighted the need for more research into the political and administrative dimensions of tourism, and Wilkinson (1997, p. 13) states that 'little attention has been paid in the tourism literature to the analysis of tourism policy and its subsequent implementation.' A key issue arising from the complex range of destination attractions and services is the way in which the destination is presented to visitors. It is not 'the totality of all possible or potential elements . . . it is a packaged selection. If it is the package that is the product then the two basic questions of definition and identification concern the nature of this packaging process and who performs it' (Ashwood and Voogd, 1994, pp. 5–19). They note that the packaging role is performed either by tour operators or government agencies.

It is generally assumed in the tourism literature that National or State Tourist Organizations exercising quasi-governmental powers and deploying a budget funded at least in part from public sources should take the initiative in setting strategy for a destination area. However, attempts to manage destinations based on organizational models of strategic thinking and action are inadequate. The heart of the problem for destinations is their complex nature, resulting in policy/implementation conflicts between operators. Typically, the destination experience for visitors comprises the products of a wide range of organizations of differing scales and levels of business sophistication presented within a general ambience derived from a combination of the area's primary attractions and the ways in which tourists perceive its image (Laws, 1995). Not only are destinations complex, but they lack the formal relationship frameworks between operational departments which enable large enterprises to act consensually. Approaches to strategic management differ on two dimensions, the outcomes of the strategy (profit maximizing or pluralistic) and the processes by which strategy is made (deliberate contrast with emergent styles).

Crompton (1979) defined vacation destination images as being 'the sum of beliefs, ideas and impressions that a person has of a destination'. The crucial role of image in marketing strategies for destinations has been noted in many studies (Bramwell and Rawding, 1996; Chon, 1990; Echtner and Ritchie, 1993; Goodall, 1998; Illiewich et al., 1997; Mayo, 1973). A recent review of the literature on destination image confirms it as a critical component in the traveller's destination selection process (Balgolu, 1997).

Dellaert et al., (1998, p. 314) note that most studies of travel decisions are concerned with destination choices. 'In some studies, this element is combined with decision-making processes.' They comment that the two main factors investigated are the activities that may influence consumer choice, and the attributes of the destination itself, but note also that traveller characteristics can influence travel choices and report their findings that 'more attention might be paid to interrelate tourists' choices of various components of travel decision-making, which jointly affect tourists' ultimate travel choices.'

PACKAGING THE DESTINATION CONCEPT

The effectiveness of image management techniques depends on an understanding of potential visitors' interests in and attitudes towards the holiday destination. Appropriate images can establish a meaningful position for the destination in the minds of selected segments of the public as being a place which is different from other destinations offering similar primary attractions (Ahmed, 1994). The significance of imagery in tourism marketing has been summed up by Buck (1993,

p. 179): 'Tourism is an industry based on imagery; its overriding concern is to construct, through multiple representations of paradise, an imagery (of the destination) that entices the outsider to place himself or herself into the symbol-defined space.'

Tourist destinations can be differentiated by mapping the structure of destination images in perceptual space, recognizing that 'places evoke all sorts of emotional experiences', (Walmesley and Young, 1998, p. 65). Selecting which aspects of a specific destination to feature in the market place where tourists choose their holiday destination depends on two steps:

- identifying the destination's special advantages (its attributes); and
- understanding how to entice those visitors which the destination hopes to attract (its benefits).

The second point is critical. Lack of knowledge of the destination's appeal from potential visitors' perspectives is an impediment to development and implementation of a strategic view of a destination's image. A further impediment is that the tourist sector at destinations is characterized by fragmentation and a preponderance of small businesses. Gunn (1988, p. 108) argues that resorts are 'complexes providing a variety of recreations and social settings at one location'. Some of the constituent businesses do not even regard themselves as operating within the tourism sector, while many trade seasonally. This can lead to a lack of specific functional knowledge within a destination, a divergence of aims between the public and commercial sectors and a short-term planning horizon which in part is driven by public sector, twelve-monthly budgeting cycles, but also by the tactical operating horizon of small businesses (Athiyaman, 1995). The lack of direct involvement by destination marketing bodies in the area's products and the marketing mixes which they use has been noted as a common problem by McKercher (1995).

The difficulties of co-ordination and control have the potential to undermine a strategic approach to marketing based on destination branding because campaigns can be undertaken by a variety of tourist businesses with no consultation or co-ordination on the prevailing message or the destination values being promoted. As a result of their structural complexity there are relatively few destinations in which one major commercial organization can take this leadership role. Furthermore, most tourist businesses lack the resources required for extensive mass marketing, and those which can afford to, often promote a variety of destinations as they are members of international chains or are domiciled in origin markets. Examples include hotel chains and airlines, which have significant power in their market places; their communications emphasise the features of their services, with local destination features being accorded a secondary role. Furthermore, a number of major tourism organizations may promote a particular destination, but emphasizing different or even conflicting place attributes. Laws (1991) has shown how one Hawaiian island was variously promoted as 'the Volcano Island', 'the Orchid Island' and 'the Big Island' at one time despite the efforts of the Hawaii Visitor Bureau to give each of the islands a unique and clear brand image within the image of the State of Hawaii.

DESTINATION BRANDING

The purpose of branding is to differentiate the goods or services of one seller or group of sellers from those of competitors (Kotler *et al.*, 1993). Brand management is increasingly recognized as a strategic management tool rather than as an abstract concept (Lawson and Balakrishnan, 1998). Kim and Chung (1997, p. 366) have argued that the two key variables in the success of global brands are brand popularity and country image. 'Brands originating from a particular country seem to create intangible assets or liabilities that are shared by those brands originating from the same country.' In the context of destination and hotel co-marketing, this point might have relevance in that the perceived attributes of the place are the broad context for motivations towards staying in a particular property in that destination.

Prichard and Morgan (1998, p. 147) note a general agreement that branding can be applied to tourist destinations, but comment that there is 'less certainty about how the concept translates into practical marketing activity . . . destination managers face three unique challenges in (branding) initiatives: a lack of control over the total marketing mix; relatively limited budgets and political considerations.'

The essential advantage of branding is that it creates a favourable position for the destination and its integral products, enabling clients to distinguish it from competitors on attributes which are significant to their motivations. This can be expressed as the destination's brand personality: branding provides a way of building an emotional link between product and consumer, appealing to holiday-makers' self-image and lifestyle concepts. Destination branding is a process that can be likened generically to destination image management, requiring development of a destination image that is well positioned in relationship to the needs and wants of the target market, the image of competitor destinations and of course the deliverable attributes of the destination.

Market positioning in turn enables the destination organization to develop a detailed marketing mix for its product, based on research to establish the visitor's buying behaviour and alternative destinations in the visitor's consideration set. Brand advantage is obtained by image building which emphasizes specific benefits and contributes to an overall impression of one brand's superiority. The goal is to position a brand in the visitor's mind as occupying a unique and desirable market niche. The imagery used to promote the destination has to be consistent with the self-image of the target customers: to become branded, a place must offer added values which match tourists' needs closely, and are different from those promoted by competitors (De Chernatony and McDonald, 1992).

Branding is carried out to influence the consumer's choice. Peterman (1997) found that the desire to achieve goals guides people's approach to acquiring information. Van Raaij and Francken (1984) introduced a generic 'vacation sequence' model in which five steps (generic decision, information acquisition, decision-making, vacation activities and satisfaction or complaints) provide the framework for consumer choice and behaviour. Woodside and Sherrell (1977) looked at the sets of alternative products consumers consider along a spectrum from evoked to inert. Van Raaij (1986, p. 7) argued that consumers can be classified along a number of dimensions according to their behaviours to 'discover a natural grouping of tourists into segments'. The purposes are essentially operational, that is, to identify how to influence that segment's behaviour. Jenkins (1978) postulated that consumers first select the destination and then choose a hotel. The present study confirms this pattern in holiday decision-making, and investigates how the two decisions are linked.

COLLABORATION IN DESTINATION MARKETING

Destinations generally operate under a co-ordinating body to which only some of the local tourism operators belong, raising the issue of leadership in promoting destination areas through marketing partnerships, as noted above. Given the variety of businesses operating from a particular destination, and the geographic dispersion of source markets, co-operative marketing arrangements are quite common. Palmer (1998) has observed that these occur at various levels from local to national, or supranational. Nevertheless, the preponderance of small businesses in resorts and the diversity of objectives of the larger organizations is an impediment to the implementation of strategic destination marketing.

Interest in the collaborative relationships between organizations operating in a defined market place is increasing, exemplified by theories of relationship marketing (McKenna, 1994), and organizational networking (Gummesson, 1995). These approaches have been applied to the functioning of tourist destinations (Laws, 1997; Poon, 1993). Poon advocated new forms of tourism based on an understanding of the contribution which various types of business can make to the tourism value chain. She argued that strategic alliances can lead to improvements in productivity and profits.

It has been noted that, in many mature destinations, the authorities are taking proactive decisions about their product and market portfolios. This involves choosing facilities to offer, anticipating the demands and changing tastes of their visitors and attempting to influence the nature of their experiences (Laws and Cooper, 1998). This proactive approach contrasts to the often ad hoc, opportunistic entrepreneurial responses which characterized the early development of many resorts (Laws, 1995). A strategic approach has become increasingly common where decisions are taken in terms of the direction of the product offering and the markets to target. Strategic market planning provides an effective framework for the consideration of these issues, while also providing clear advantages for resorts (Cooper, 1995). 'The process of goal setting provides a common sense of ownership and direction for the many stakeholders in the resort, whilst at the same time sharpening the guiding objectives. The coherence provided by the approach provides a framework for joint initiatives between the commercial and public sectors and demands the clear identification of roles and responsibilities' (Laws and Cooper, 1998, p. 341).

A CONCEPTUALIZATION OF CO-OPERATIVE DESTINATION AND HOTEL MARKETING

The research question addressed in this chapter is how several operators can co-operate in their marketing under one brand. Co-branding can 'command more power through customer awareness . . . than a single brand name operation' (Boone, 1997, p. 34). Her study of hotels which operate a leased or franchised restaurant indicated that customers are more likely to choose a familiar restaurant over one that is unknown, and that this has resulted in increased use of hotel restaurants once they are operated as franchises. In the context of the present research, this suggests that hotels located within a destination might benefit by linking their advertising imagery to the destination brand strengths.

Figure 11.1 conceptualizes the co-operative marketing approaches by operators and destination authorities. The shaded area, representing the range of clients which the destination authorities seek to attract, is broken into four notional motivational clusters or segments who will each be accessed using specialized appeals and media. The model indicates that operator A will seek to focus its advertising and use imagery attractive to only two market segments, while operator B will concentrate its resources on a narrower range of motivations.

1   Selected segments targeted by operator A
2   Segments targeted by operator B

Branding, imagery, positioning, market segmentation, target marketing and marketing mix are mutually dependent management decisions, but in typical destinations these decisions are taken independently by the managers of different

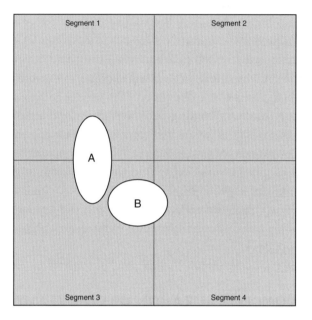

Figure 11.1 Collaborative destination and operator marketing

Note: Shaded area: a destination's four main client segments each targeted by the destination
   authority.

organizations based on their own operating criteria. It is important to note, however, that these organizations share benefits from the attributes of the place being marketed, the expectations raised in potential clients by marketing activities and the experiences of visitors attracted to the place. Research to establish brand strategies for destinations is therefore interactive, and open-ended. Furthermore, as the case study of Port Douglas demonstrates, it involves multiple stakeholders in the brand concept for the region.

DEVELOPING A DESTINATION IMAGE FOR
QUEENSLAND'S TOURIST REGIONS

Tourism Queensland (TQ) has recently begun to promote five key destination areas of Queensland to visitors as distinctive destinations. This strategy was initiated in response to the emergence of a number of regions of Queensland as tourist nodes, each with distinctive destinational attributes, target markets and a sufficiently developed tourist industry to warrant a portfolio (product line) approach to their management as destinations. These reflect the diversity and scale of Queensland,

Table 11.1 Queensland tourist destinations. *Source*: QTTC Brand and Advertising Style Manuals, 1998

Destinations	Positioning elements	Brand personality	% domestic visitors
Tropical North Queensland (TNQ)	Great Barrier Reef and tropical rainforest	Relaxed, friendly, natural, adventurous, active	57
Brisbane	Stimulating subtropical capital city experience	Plenty to see and do, relaxed fresh outdoors	75
Gold Coast	Beach and excitement/ nightlife, entertainment	Exciting, fast-paced, fun	70
Sunshine Coast	Beach and relaxation	Relaxed, simple, the way things used to be	90
Whitsundays	Aquatic playground	Relaxed, fresh, friendly, vibrant, natural	75

and translate into different destination image, target market, positioning and promotional programmes for each destination, summarized in Table 11.1.

TQ uses a variety of segmentation techniques (both a priori and post hoc) in developing an understanding of target markets and destination positioning and image. The a priori scheme is based on a combination of six household life cycle and income segments for each origin market (local, 400 km drive, interstate, short-haul and long-haul international). The rationale for this approach is that it can be applied readily to each destination and it has the advantage that the findings can easily be understood by the destination stakeholders. As with most demographic-based segmentation systems, however, these forms of segmentation tend to be limited when applied to marketing tourism destinations, since they take no account of the range of needs and motivations possible within each derived group.

TROPICAL NORTH QUEENSLAND AS A TOURIST DESTINATION

Tropical North Queensland (TNQ) offers an impressive array of attractions and, as well as being one of Australia's prime domestic destinations, it is also rapidly establishing itself as a major international destination area. The Queensland Visitor Survey (QTTC, 1997) reported that the TNQ area received a total of 1,408,000 overnight visitors staying in commercial accommodation. Of these 32 per cent were from Queensland, 25 per cent were from other Australian states and 43 per cent were from overseas. The major international markets are Japan, Germany and the United Kingdom.

The development of an agreed brand and destination image for TNQ provides an important reference point for tourism development and promotion by local businesses and communities. In facilitating this destination image development, the TQ is functioning in a leadership role and this raises the question of how operators work co-operatively to create this brand in TNQ. Within TNQ there are two major tourism nodes (Figure 11.2). Cairns City functions as a transport hub and accommodation centre while surrounding beach areas provide a tropical resort setting.

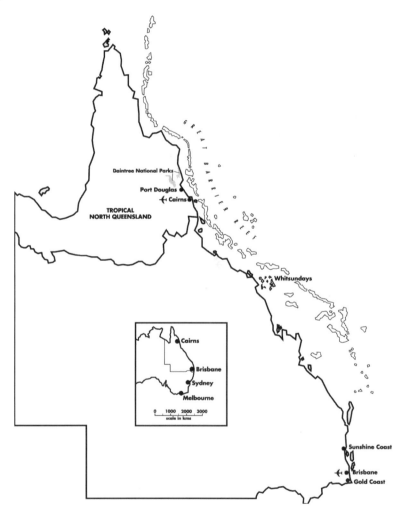

Figure 11.2 The location of Queensland's five key destination areas

SUMMARY OF THE PORT DOUGLAS RESEARCH

Port Douglas, located an hour north of Cairns by road, is a tropical resort town close to the World Heritage listed Daintree Rainforest, and it is also an access point for the Great Barrier Reef. Port Douglas's image has been developed around the relaxed tropical nature-based experiences it offers. Port Douglas has developed rapidly over the past fifteen years and now features several major hotels. This raises the issue of how several operators can co-operate within a defined area, and thus gain synergies in the competitive market place for holidays. The impetus to this research occurred when the two hotel properties in Port Douglas were brought together under the umbrella of one international hotel marketing organization. The objective of the research was to examine the relationship between these hotels' marketing images and that of the overall destination image developed for TNQ by Tourism Queensland.

The terms 'destination' and 'resort' are both sometimes used for geographic areas, but are also used to describe localized developments. 'Resort' can mean an established town which has a significant range of tourist facilities (NEDO/Tourism Society, 1992) or a region within which several holiday centres are located (Inskeep and Kallenbergher, 1992). Gunn (1988) has defined resorts as 'complexes providing a variety of recreations and social settings at one location'. Individual hotels sometimes promote themselves as self-contained resorts. In this chapter, the two properties are referred to as Hotel A and Hotel B. Hotel A is more expensive, and offers the upmarket ambience of a self-contained resort hotel. Hotel B also occupies landscaped grounds but is more intensively built-up and provides a single buffet catering outlet in contrast to the variety of more intimate and stylish restaurants in Hotel A. Thus, the two properties attract somewhat different client groups.

RESEARCH DESIGN

The research programme was multi-stage and involved three separate components. Since the overall purpose of the project was to examine the relationship between Tropical North Queensland, constituent tourist areas within the region (Cairns, Northern Beaches and Port Douglas) and accommodation within each area, the methodology was designed to be able to compare key issues across the various levels within the region by developing similar question and analysis formats. The research process therefore moved from detailed qualitative interviews to wider structured questionnaire research, and from a focus on the particular Port Douglas resort hotels to a wider regional study.

The first stage of the programme incorporated 70 qualitative interviews with guests at the two hotels. Australian-resident guests were approached randomly via the resorts' front office database, a letter from the General Manager and a follow-up telephone call from the researcher. The interviews took the form of 30-minute executive interviews and 90-minute focus groups, and were used to examine in detail issues of decision-making, reasons for choosing the destination and accommodation, overall attitudes towards vacations and motivation and imagery.

The semi-structured nature of qualitative interviewing allowed the use of indirect (projective) questioning, including mapping, creative pictorial techniques and repertory grid techniques to examine motivations and expectations (Durgee, 1986; Kelly, 1955; Reilley, 1990; Young, 1995). The information generated by this stage of the research was the basis for formulating a structured questionnaire for subsequent research. It also enabled TQ and the research partners to start to identify motivational groups, and devise appropriate advertising strategies as discussed below.

The findings of the executive interviews and focus groups were then quantified among a sample of 220 guests. Guests completing this questionnaire were again selected randomly from resort records. The third component of the research consisted of face-to-face interviews with 600 Australian visitors to Tropical North Queensland. This questionnaire included items common to those asked in the resort survey in order to enable comparisons of data to be made. Interviewing for this stage was conducted equally between the three main TNQ holiday centres of Cairns, the Northern Beaches and Port Douglas.

GENERAL FINDINGS

Profile of guests interviewed

The two hotels have different clienteles and as a result the demographics and the types of holiday chosen differ. The methodology described above enabled comparison of the profiles, needs, attitudes and behaviours of guests in both hotels with other visitors to Port Douglas and to the region overall. In comparison to regional visitors, hotel guests are more likely to be:

- older couples where the children have left home rather than families with children;
- higher occupational groups, although both resorts also show a higher proportion of retail and service workers as well.

Hotel A has a higher proportion of those living singly than B, and Hotel B has a higher proportion of the upper white occupational group. The profile of all visitors to the region tends towards people travelling (and living) singly rather than as a family and to be in manual and middle managerial/administrative occupational groups. The profile of people staying in Port Douglas tends to be closer to that of the region overall than to either of the hotels, with a high proportion of families staying in rental units in the Port Douglas area.

Compared to Port Douglas and Tropical North Queensland, both hotels have a lower proportion of people who are staying in the region longer than a week. The shorter length of stay reflects the higher standard of accommodation and costs of the hotels, rather than the location of stay. Hotel guests are also more dependent upon air travel into the region and upon coach services while in the region. They are more likely to be first-time visitors to the region. Almost all those staying at the two hotels flew to the destination, reflecting the distance from their homes. (Cairns, the nearest airport is a three and a half hour flight from Melbourne.) Almost none of the hotel guests toured the area by car, preferring coach tours, or using rented bicycles to get around Port Douglas.

SPECIFIC FINDINGS

The development of motivational groups

Qualitative research was used to establish why resort guests had decided to visit Tropical North Queensland on vacation and the decision-making process for so doing. A wide range of reasons emerged, and were measured quantitatively in the hotel guest self-completion questionnaires and the overall TNQ visitor study (Table 11.2). From the analysis of these specific motivations, four major motivational groupings were identified. These motivational groups are described in Table 11.3, but it should be noted that membership of one group does not necessarily preclude leanings towards another – they represent visitor tendencies rather than totally separate groups.

The four motivational segments were derived from a number of stages throughout the research process. Firstly, at the 'qualitative' stage, guests and visitors were asked directly their reasons for taking a vacation and the factors on which they distinguished between competitive destinations and different vacation styles. These verbatim comments were then used as the basis for nineteen statements which the sample of resort guests (217 interviews) and the broader sample of visitors to the region (600 interviews divided equally between Cairns, the Northern Beaches and Port Douglas) were asked to rate on a five-point scale (running from 'Very Important' to 'Not at all Important'). Cluster analysis was then used to establish the four major tendencies. The characteristics of each group is best represented through their motivational ratings. In Table 11.2, mean scores are shown where +2.5 is equivalent to a rating of 'Very Important' and −2.5 is equivalent to a rating of 'Not at all Important'.

Table 11.2 Motivations for TNQ visitors

Motivation factor:	Self-directed	Image-directed	Activity-directed	Other-directed
To relax	2.13	1.76	1.41	1.55
To spend time with my partner	1.47	0.89	0.0	0.90
To visit new places	1.38	1.76	1.71	1.60
To celebrate a special event or anniversary	−0.55	−1.25	−1.10	−0.60
To exercise my choice to do nothing	1.18	0.77	−0.19	1.05
To take the chance to think things over	0.30	−0.18	−0.23	0.45
To be pampered and waited on	0.07	−0.66	−1.09	-0.10
To indulge my senses	0.91	0.40	0.63	1.10
To feel fitter and healthier	0.77	0.52	0.51	1.35
To live life at a different pace	1.44	1.66	1.32	1.80
To feel warmer	1.25	1.63	0.69	2.20
To be active	0.53	0.53	1.90	0.78
To get close to nature	0.65	0.86	1.58	1.45
To travel as far north as possible	−0.19	−0.18	0.38	0.55
To be challenged	−0.46	−0.66	0.85	−0.03
To find out new things	0.41	0.64	2.10	1.02
To see somewhere that people have told me about	0.58	0.88	0.88	2.25
To visit a unique attraction	1.10	1.37	2.24	2.00
To have experiences I can tell other people about	0.83	1.13	1.41	2.05

Destination and hotel choice considered

The current research found a high degree of consistency in visitor decision-making processes which followed five stages:

1. the overall length, style, price and 'type' of vacation
2. overall destinational attributes likely to fulfil the criteria at (1.)
3. collection of advice/information to complement destinations known at (2.)
4. consideration of different areas within regions
5. consideration of different accommodation options

Table 11.3 Motivational groups

Motivational group	Summary description	Marketing implications
Activity-focused	This group goes on vacation and to particular destinations with clear objectives of undertaking particular activities or visiting specific locations, for example, observing coral on the Reef or viewing flora and fauna in the rainforests. The appeal of a holiday for them is marked by achievement and personal growth. This group tends to be well-informed, strong vacation planners and goal-focused.	Focus on detailed information in support of their particular interest, possibly using specialist media.
Image-focused	This group is motivated by general regional attributes since the primary motivation is to go somewhere different from home. They look for a different climate, different environments and lifestyles rather than specific activities. They are likely to consider a wide range of vacations since their criteria for choice is fairly broad.	They rarely have specific reasons for choice and are the group most amenable to overall regional imagery and marketing.
Other people focused	Members of this group choose their vacation based on what they have been told by other people. A primary motivation for them is then to relay back to the reference group their own experiences. In a sense this group might be referred to as 'snobs' although they occur across the range of socio-economic and income groups.	Marketing needs to generate the sense of a destination as 'the place to be'. They are particularly excited, for example, by the visits of President Clinton and various movie stars to Port Douglas.
Self-focused	For this group, a vacation destination is the backdrop to the fulfilment of their own needs and the expression of their own feelings. They may participate in specific activities but their motivations are based on what the experience means for them and what it can do for them (rather than on more outer-focused motivations of appreciation or learning). Elements of indulgence, service, relaxing and doing nothing, or being looked after are therefore strong among this group and the general resort promise is therefore of greatest appeal to this group.	Many places can offer them what they are looking for. Regional imagery and specific accommodation promises need to work in tandem to reassure them about all elements of their vacation.

However, it should be noted that the process followed is not always sequential. Consumer advertising by retailers may start visitors at stage 5 through a direct (usually price-based) promotion for accommodation; co-operative advertising may also move them to stage 5 by linking values at stage 2 to needs at stage 1.

One of the most important findings of the research was the high proportion of guests at the resort hotels who had considered alternative destinations and other accommodation within TNQ as part of their decision process. This group includes 70 per cent of Hotel A guests and 63 per cent of Hotel B guests. This places strong emphasis on understanding the decision-making process to ensure that the chances of 'losing' visitors is minimized. Kelly grid techniques were used to differentiate competitor destinations. This technique was considered appropriate to achieve understanding of the process since it identified the overall competitive context of TNQ and Port Douglas, the motivations which visitors seek to fulfil and the way in which different destination and holiday experiences are distinguished and clustered by visitors to establish segments in the market place.

Research into the process of selecting between regions and destinations and the consequent 'clustering' of destinations was based on a number of key bipolar criteria which emerged as significant during the first phase of the project:

* international versus Australian
* warm weather versus colder/temperate weather
* destinations requiring effort ('cultural' or sightseeing destinations) versus destinations not requiring effort (beach holidays)
* natural destinations versus 'developed' destinations

The sets of alternative destinations (Woodside and Sherrell, 1977), considered by guests varied, depending on their key holiday motivations as indicated in Table 11.4.

Given the importance of imagery to marketing and advertising, image perception was analysed for different locations. Figure 11.3 presents the image components for all visitors to the region mapped onto the four motivational clusters discussed above. All four groupings share a common and central motivation for relaxation, but they differ in the specific elements of their motivations. Similar image maps were constructed for Hotel A and Hotel B guests, Port Douglas visitors not staying in the resort hotels and regional visitors staying in other areas such as Cairns and Northern Beaches. This enabled the evaluation of the extent to which the contribution of 'components' to an image of the region differed for visitors to different locations. For example, the research indicates that, among visitors staying in four or five star resort accommodation, the image of the region as a whole is less strong than the image presented by the hotel. The seclusion which attracts guests to Hotels A and B is also a feature of the Port Douglas area; the resort style of hotel vacation may be seen as an end in itself when compared to visitors using lower-grade accommodation as a 'jumping off' point for access to the region as a whole.

Table 11.4 Motivational group and holiday preferences

Motivational group	Holiday preferences	
	Activity preferences	Alternative destinations considered
Activity-focused	Bushwalking, rainforest walks, Skyrail, diving, visiting Cape Tribulation, Cooktown	TNQ; Northern Territories; Fiji; Pacific islands
Image-focused	Visiting Cape Tribulation	Barrier Reef islands; Bali; Fiji; New Caledonia; Hawaii; Lord Howe; Norfolk Island
Other people focused	Reef cruising, visiting Daintree, Mossman, craft shops, Cairns	Barrier Reef islands; Noosa
Self-focused	Relaxation and indulgence	Warm area resorts; overseas islands; resorts in SE Asia; cruises; Europe

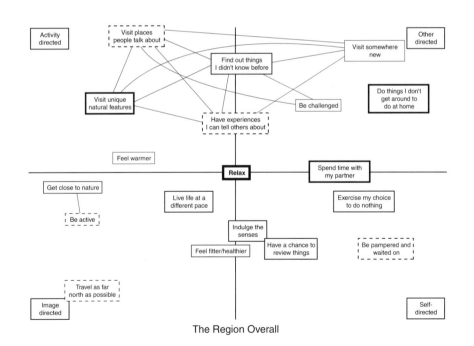

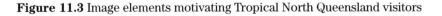

Figure 11.3 Image elements motivating Tropical North Queensland visitors

Implications for co-operative marketing

The key findings to emerge from this research are that the distinctive brand imagery of Port Douglas appeals to all visitor segments, but that guests need clear information about the two hotels to choose the property best suited to their holiday motivations and expectations. The research indicated a strong case for co-operative advertising based on consumers' needs for a mix of general information (about the attributes of the region as a whole) and accommodation-specific information. The fact that almost 75 per cent of resort guests had considered an alternative destination area indicates the importance of effective regional branding to be reinforced by information on specific accommodation suited to target markets.

The conceptual model presented earlier in this chapter (Figure 11.1) has been developed and applied to the Port Douglas case study. Figure 11.4 presents a positioning model based on plotting the current relative positions of the two hotels (A and B) and the destination (X). The corners of the model are formed from the four motivational groups identified in this research. Thus, the position of a hotel indicates the relative percentages of each of the four segments in its clientele. Also shown on this diagram are the target 'potential' groups for each hotel (A1 and B1). These groups have been drawn from the regional survey and they include, for each hotel, Australian visitors staying elsewhere in Tropical North Queensland who are financially capable of affording the hotel, who are already staying in a similar standard of accommodation, who are disposed to return to the region and who plan their accommodation in advance. Based on these criteria, the 'potential' market for Hotel A is around 18 per cent of TNQ visitors and that for Hotel B somewhat less at 15 per cent.

The figure should be read as indicative; however, it illustrates that in the current situation both hotels occupy similar spaces and away from the overall position of the region (X). Their primary appeal is based on 'self-directed' and 'image-directed' components in contrast to the region overall which appeals more broadly to a mix of motivations, in particular that for specific activities. This is perhaps to be expected of a situation where the hotels have been differentiated historically on the basis of price alone while still appealing to the 'resort market' (where the motivation to stay is based on each hotel's separateness from the surrounding region). The analysis of future target groups (A1 for hotel A and B1 for hotel B) indicates that, to maximize their potential to draw new markets, the following positioning steps need to be taken:

* to position themselves further from each other.

     In the case of A this means developing imagery based more on general regional attributes while continuing to appeal to images of self-fulfilment and actualization; for B this means a greater focus on specific activities which can be conducted from the resort.

- to position themselves closer to the region overall, as resorts within the region rather than separate from it.

    While the impact upon the region overall cannot be measured by this research, it can be hypothesized that, if the hotels were to pursue directions A1 and B1, this would pull the region overall closer to the midway point between the new resort positionings.

The research outlined here led to recommendations that future collaborative advertising campaigns undertaken jointly between TQ and the hotel group should feature pictures of the beach, and the town centre, with supporting imagery conveying feelings of freedom and comfort, a boat, a hammock, a deckchair and a sunset as imagery for the destination to achieve the emotional links between customers and the destination brand discussed earlier in this chapter. Specific images of the two hotels should include pools, lights and trees to emphasize their tropical, but safe, ambience, accompanied by information on accommodation, activities and prices to convey reassurance about the affordability of the region and the comforts it offers. A further recommendation was that print advertising should feature a map showing Cairns, the regional gateway in relation to Port Douglas, to emphasize the easy accessibility of the destination.

    The co-operative approach adopted in Tropical North Queensland can be seen as harnessing the self-interest of individual operators to reinforce and develop the

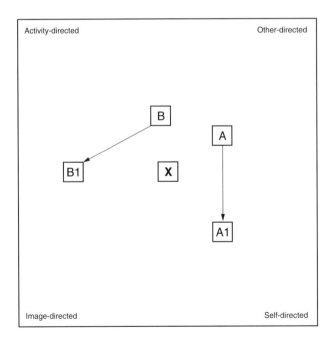

Figure 11.4 Port Douglas destination and hotel branding

common destination image of TNQ and at the same time maximizing the appeal of hotels to particular segments. The extent to which a particular operator uses the destinational image within its own marketing determines the extent to which Tourism Queensland can contribute to a co-operative marketing campaign.

IMPLICATIONS FOR FUTURE DESTINATION BRAND AND IMAGE RESEARCH

The research discussed in this chapter was action-based, and the findings are specific to the destination and the time-frame of the study. The collaborative approach to image management could be applied in other locations. However, if further studies follow, a number of challenges which were identified and addressed in this project need to be considered. (These have not been discussed due to issues of commercial confidentiality.)

- the identification prior to the study of rationales for collaboration between industry and public sector
- the need to specify appropriate boundaries for project partners and the research team
- a monitoring system to evaluate the results of any image management procedures implemented as a result of the research

There are also opportunities to extend the remit of such projects. In the evaluation phase in particular, it may be possible to study the spill over of brand-strengthening image management in terms of its consequences for the smaller destination-based operators such as excursion companies which do not have the resources to participate in the earlier motivational and image research phases. Other industry partners with developed brands, such as airlines serving the area, might be drawn into a further phase, both with respect to the match of their image components to the joint hotel and destination campaign, and in terms of better understanding the motivations underlying destination choice, particularly with respect to the set of destinations considered in the selection stage of holiday purchasing.

A series of studies similar to this, but based on a variety of destinations, might lead to a synthesis of co-operative destination branding issues. A number of key issues might emerge:

- a classification of destination-based businesses into those more and those less able to influence visitors' destination selection decisions;
- an extension of that typology to identify those organizations which are more or less central to the potential visitor's perceptions of the destination;

- effective and problematic research protocols when conducting collaborative studies where the objective is commercial and action-oriented.

Different forms of collaboration are possible from the co-operative marketing outlined here, and further case study research might help clarify the advantages of alternative approaches in the specific conditions of other destinations.

Research into destination branding processes, particularly those in which destination authorities collaborate actively with destination operators, is at an early stage of development, and a number of issues require more analysis. One point of concern is that the various organizations involved in providing services to a destination's visitors often hold different views of the area's attractions, and seek to attract different types of visitor. They therefore favour different ways to promote it. Further research is also needed to establish the nature of the links between destination marketing and the subsequent performance of individual destination-based businesses.

NOTE

1. In early 1999, the title of the State Tourist Organization for Queensland was changed from Queensland Travel and Tourist Corporation (QTTC) to Tourism Queensland (TQ). In this chapter, the organization is referred to as TQ, but documents produced prior to 1999 are ascribed to QTTC in the text and references.

REFERENCES

Ahmed, Z. (1994) 'Determinants of the components of a state's tourist image and their marketing implications'. *Journal of Leisure and Hospitality Marketing*, **2**(1), 55–69.

Ashwood, G. and Voogd, H. (1994) 'Marketing of tourism places: what are we doing?' In M. Uysal (ed.) *Global Tourist Behaviour*. New York: Haworth Press.

Ashworth, G. and Goodall, B. (eds) (1990) *Marketing Tourism Places*. London: Routledge.

Athiyaman, A. (1995) 'The interface of tourism and strategy research: an analysis'. *Tourism Management*, **16**(6), 447–53.

Baloglu, S. (1997) 'The relationship between destination images and sociodemographic and trip characteristics of international travellers'. *Journal of Vacation Marketing*, **3**(3), 221–33.

Boone, J. (1997) 'Hotel – restaurant co-branding, a preliminary study'. *Cornell Hotel and Restaurant Administration Quarterly*, October, 34–43.

Bramwell, B. and Rawding, L. (1996) 'Tourism marketing images of industrial cities'. *Annals of Tourism Research*, **23**(1), 201–21.

Buck, E. (1993) *Paradise Remade, The Politics of Culture and History in Hawai'i*. Philadelphia: Temple University Press.

Casson, L. (1994) *Travel in the Ancient World*. Baltimore: Johns Hopkins University Press.

Chon, K. (1990) 'The role of destination image in tourism: a review and discussion'. *The Tourist Review*, **2**, 2–9.

Cooper, C. (1995) 'Strategic planning for sustainable tourism: the case of the off-shore islands of the UK'. *Journal of Sustainable Tourism*, **3**(4), 1–19.

Crompton, J. (1979) 'Motivations for pleasure vacations'. *Annals of Tourism Research*, **4**(1), 25–35.

De Chernatony, L. and McDonald, M. (1992) *Creating Powerful Brands: The Strategic Route to Success in Consumer Industrial and Service Markets*. Oxford: Butterworth-Heinemann.

Dellaert, B., Ettema, D. and Lindh, C. (1998) 'Multi-faceted tourist travel decisions: a constraint-based conceptual framework to describe tourists' sequential choices of travel components'. *Tourism Management*, **19**(4), 313–20.

Durgee, J. (1986) 'Depth interview techniques for creative advertising'. *Journal of Advertising Research*, **25** (January), 29–37.

Echtner, C. and Richie, J. (1991) 'The meaning and measurement of destination image'. *Journal of Tourism Studies*, **2**, 2–12.

Goodall, B. (1998) 'How tourists choose their holidays'. In B. Goodall and G. Ashworth (eds) *Marketing in the Tourism Industry: Promoting Tourist Destinations*. London: Routledge, pp. 133–6.

Gummesson, E. (1995) 'Making relationship marketing operational'. *International Journal of Service Industry Management*, **5**(5), 5–20.

Gunn, C. A. (1988) *Tourism Planning*. New York: Taylor and Francis.

Hall, C. (1994) *Tourism and Politics, Policy, Power and Place*. Chichester: John Wiley & Sons.

Heath, E. and Wall, G. (1992) *Marketing Tourism Resorts*. New York: John Wiley & Sons.

Illiewich, S., Grabler, K., Jeng, J. and Fesenmaier, D. (1997) 'Deconstructing destination image'. *Proceedings of the TTRA Conference*. Virginia Beach, pp. 396–400.

Inskeep, E. (1993) *National and Regional Planning, Methodologies and Case Studies*. Madrid: WTO.

Inskeep, E. and Kallenbergher, M. (1992) *An Integrated Approach To Resort Development*. Madrid: WTO.

Jenkins, R. (1978) 'Family vacation decision making'. *Journal of Travel Research*, **16**(4), 2–7.

Kelly, G. (1955) *The Psychology of Personal Constructs*. New York: Norton.

Kim, C. and Chung, J. (1997) 'Brand popularity, country image and market share: an empirical study'. *Journal of International Business Studies*, Second Quarter, 361–85.

Kotler, P., Haider, D. H. and Rein, I. (1993) *Marketing Places*. New York: Free Press.

Laws, E. (1991) *Tourism Marketing, Service and Quality Management Perspectives*. Cheltenham: Stanley Thornes.

Laws, E. (1995) *Tourist Resort Management, Issues, Analysis and Policies*. London: Routledge.

Laws, E. (1997) *Managing Packaged Tourism, Relationships, Responsibility and Service Quality in the Inclusive Holiday Industry*. London: International Thomson Business Press.

Laws, E. and Cooper C. (1998, forthcoming) 'Inclusive tours and commodification: the marketing constraints for mass market resorts'. *The Journal of Vacation Marketing*, **4**(4), 337–52.

Lawson, R. and Balakrishnan, W. (1998) 'Developing and managing brand image and brand concept strategies'. *American Marketing Association*, Winter, 121–6.

McKenna, R. (1994) *Relationship Marketing, Successful Strategies for the Age of the Customer*. Reading, Mass: Addison-Wesley.

McKercher, B. (1995) 'The destination-market mix: a tourism market portfolio analysis model'. *Journal of Travel and Tourism Marketing*, **4**(2), 23–40.

Mayo, E. (1973) 'Regional images and regional travel behavior'. *Proceedings of the TTRA Conference*, Sun Valley, Idaho, pp. 211–17.

Morgan, N. and Prittchard, A. (1998) *Tourism Promotion and Power: Creating Images, Creating Identities*. Chichester: John Wiley & Sons.

NEDO (1992) *UK Tourism, Competing For Growth*. London: NEDO/Tourism Society.

Palmer, A. (1998) 'Evaluating the governance style of marketing groups'. *Annals of Tourism Research*, **25**(1), 185–201.

Peterman, M. (1997) 'The effects of concrete and abstract consumer goals on information processing'. *Journal of Psychology and Marketing*, **14**(6), 561–83.

Poon, A. (1993) *Tourism, Technology and Competitive Strategies*. Wallingford: CAB International Press.

Pritchard, A. and Morgan, N. (1998) 'Mood marketing – the new destination marketing stratetgy: a case study of "Wales the brand"'. *Journal of Vacation Marketing*, **4**(3), 215–29.

Queensland Travel and Tourist Corporation (1997) *Queensland Visitor Survey*. Brisbane: QTTC.

Queensland Travel and Tourist Corporation (1998) *Brand and Advertising Style Manual*. Brisbane: QTTC.

Reilley, M. (1990) 'Free elicitation of descriptive adjectives for tourism image assessment'. *Journal of Travel Research*, **28** (Spring), 21–6.

Van Raaij, F. (1986) 'Consumer research on mental and behavioural constructs'. *Annals of Tourism Research*, **13**, 1–9.

Van Raaij, F. and Francken, D. (1984) 'Vacation decisions: activities and satisfactions'. *Annals of Tourism Research*, **11**(1), 101–12.

Walmesley, D. and Young, M. (1998) 'Evaluative images and tourism: the use of personal constructs to describe the structure of destination images'. *Journal of Travel Research*, **36** (Winter), 65–9.

Wanhill, S. (1999) 'The economic aspects of location marketing'. In T. Baum and R. Mudambi (eds) *Economic and Management Methods for Tourism and Hospitality Research*. Chichester: John Wiley & Sons, pp. 159–96.

Wilkinson, P. (1997) *Tourism Policy and Planning: Case Studies from the Commonwealth and Caribbean*. Elmsford, New York: Cognizant Communications.

Woodside, A. and Sherrell, D. (1977) 'Traveller evoked, inept and inert sets of vacation destinations'. *Journal of Travel Research*, **16**(1), 14–18.

Young, M. (1995) 'Evaluative constructs of domestic tourist places'. *Australian Geographic Studies*, **33**, 272–86.

CHAPTER 12

Issues in Public Sector Involvement

Stephen Wanhill

INTRODUCTION

The undoubted growth in the economic prosperity of the major industrial countries together with the travel revolution brought about through holidays with pay, lower international transport costs in real terms and information technology, has seen world tourism grow to a truly global business. This growth has not been without fluctuations caused by shocks and cycles in the world economy, but what is remarkable is the resilience of the industry through troubled times and its ability to bounce back. Worldwide, the significance of tourism as a mechanism for economic development has meant that it is an investment opportunity that few governments can afford to ignore. As a rule, the greater the importance of tourism to a country's economy the greater is the involvement of the public sector, to the point of having a government ministry with sole responsibility for tourism. Beyond this governments are involved in supporting a variety of multinational agencies.

The official flag carrier for international tourism is the World Tourism Organization (WTO): it is an operative rather than a deliberative body, whose functions include helping members to maximize the benefits from tourism, identifying markets, assisting in tourism planning as an executing agency of the United Nations Development Programme (UNDP), providing statistical information, advising on the harmonization of policies and practices, sponsoring education and training and identifying funding sources. Elsewhere there are a number of other international bodies whose activities impinge upon tourism: these include the World Bank, the United Nations, the International Air Transport Association (IATA), the International Civil Aviation Organization (ICAO) and the Organization for Economic Co-operation and Development (OECD).

At a lower level, there are a variety of regional bodies such as the Organization of American States (OAS), the Pacific Area Travel Association (PATA) and the European Travel Commission (ETC). Most of their efforts are devoted to promotion and marketing, though they do provide technical assistance. Funds for developing the tourist infrastructure in low-income countries may be obtained from regional development banks such as the Asian Development Bank in Manila, the European Bank for Reconstruction and Development in London (for Eastern Europe) or the Caribbean development Bank in Barbados. Looking briefly at the structure in Europe, it may be found that, officially, tourism in the European Commission, situated in Brussels, comes under Directorate General XXIII, but the regional development work of Directorate General XVI also involves tourism projects as a means of overcoming regional differences. With the adoption of the Single European Act in 1987, there was a commitment by the European Union (EU) to promote economic and social cohesion through actions to reduce regional disparities and the Maastricht Treaty in 1992 acknowledged, for the first time, the role of tourism in these actions. The resources for mitigating regional differences are drawn from the Pan-European Structural Funds, which are made up of contributions from member states with the express purpose of: helping regions lagging behind, particularly rural areas, assisting the economic conversion of regions facing industrial decline, combating long-term unemployment and dealing with the very special problems of some of the sparsely populated Nordic regions. Alongside public moneys, commercial funding of tourism projects is obtainable from the European Investment Bank.

THE RATIONALE FOR INTERVENTION

In the last part of the twentieth century, the continuing globalization of competition and the classic failure of state planning (as has been witnessed in the appalling productivity record of the Eastern European countries), leading to the collapse of the Communist system, gave confirmation to the market-oriented view that questioned the role of governments in industrial policy. Globalization and reduced transport costs facilitated export-oriented strategies and the transfer of technology between countries in which there was little role for the state. The consensus arrived at, based on theory and experience, was that markets should be given primacy in the production and allocation of goods and services, but to obtain socially desirable outcomes it should be the task of government to provide an institutional infrastructure in which markets can function. Thus traditional demand management policies and state planning were abandoned in favour of macrostabilization policies to ensure sound money and micro policies to make markets work better. This was less so in less developed countries (LDCs) due to their political structure and the lack of private institutions to take on development. Concern was for action to remove the structural rigidities that gave rise to the dualistic nature of many LDCs, where the traditional and modern were located alongside each other. Bitter experience has shown that market-oriented projects in LDCs with inappropriate macroeconomic policies have struggled to survive. This acknowledgement heralded in an era of structural adjustment, dating from the 1980s, to build onto the characteristics of dualism already accounted for in the economic appraisal process (Wanhill, 1994). The purpose is to ensure a better economic climate, so new projects could function more efficiently, thus improving returns.

Role of government

With the rise in market power and the globalization of competition, it is becoming more difficult for the governments in the industrial democracies to meet their traditional obligations in terms of education, social security, health and pensions, because of resistance to high taxes by the electorate. This has led to cutbacks in public expenditure, privatization of infrastructure and the demand that some public merit goods such as museums, galleries and parks, which also form part of the tourist product, should charge for their services. The view is forming that, in an economy that has the appropriate institutional structure to ensure that markets perform as they are supposed to, then there should be no reason to have more than a small state enterprise sector. In sum, the state should fall back on its core tasks needed to run today's market economy:

- guarantor of macroeconomic stability;
- provision of defence and law and order, so as to include a sound regulatory framework for the conduct of business and finance;
- protection of the environment to preserve public health and well-being;
- the guardianship of future generations through sustainable development (World Commission on Environment and Development, 1987): natural resource depletion is considered sustainable if there is a more than compensating increase in the stock of other capital;
- providing access to welfare services, health, education and pensions: public merit goods that protect or enhance effective participation in a market economy, allow absorption of advanced technologies and provide a safety net. These can be a partnership between the state and private entities. In some cases the state provides the finance and production is left to the private sector; in others it involves itself in both finance and production;
- correcting for market failure so as to allow for external effects that cannot be internalized through private agreements. In this respect, industrial policy should not be about 'picking winners', but rather about providing the institutional arrangements to support private entrepreneurial success, such as

ensuring the efficient functioning of capital markets, accounting for project risk and long-time horizons, and the transfer and development of technology.

The tourism dimension

The increasing withdrawal of the state from matters to do with industrial development makes it necessary to query whether the public sector has any role in tourism. The case for government intervention in tourism can be made along traditional lines in terms of the:

- complexity of the tourist product;
- institutional structure;
- guardianship of the resource base;
- market failure.

Complexity of the tourist product

The complexity of the product is indicated by the characteristics of a tourist's journey, where it will be appreciated that the trip is not a single product, but rather it is made up of components supplied by a variety of organizations with different objectives and different economic structures. Furthermore, each offering may be considered unique, as visitors add their own preferences to the total experience. In this manner, the tourist becomes part of the production process.

Market success is the delivering of the right mix of components to satisfy the demands of the visitor, but this delivery requires co-ordination and co-operation. A critical difference between tourism and many other agents of development is that of inseparability, in that tourism is consumed at the place of production, thus involving itself with the host community, and requiring some commodification and sharing of traditions, value systems and culture (Cohen, 1988). Since the tourist industry does not control all those factors which make up the attractiveness of a destination and the impact on the host population can be considerable, then the essence of successful tourism development is the creation of a 'partnership' that is incentive compatible for the various stakeholders in the activity of tourism; central and local government, quasi-public bodies such as tourist boards, voluntary organizations and charitable trusts, the private commercial sector, the local community and the visitors themselves.

Institutional structure

As a rule, it may be observed that the greater the importance of tourism to a country's economy the greater is the involvement of the public sector, to the point of having a government ministry with sole responsibility for tourism. In this manner, the options concerning the development of tourism can be considered at the highest level of government. The ideal institutional structure is one that is compatible with the global market place in which the tourist industry finds itself, but offers the incentives for the 'partnership' to engage in socially and economically constructive activities, thus avoiding or resolving conflict and preventing actions which enrich one partner at the expense of another. Typically the emphasis is placed on trust, but this is commonly surrounded by a legal framework that gives powers of compulsion, something that is necessary for long-term agreements. What makes the public sector unique is that the state has a monopoly on the legitimate use of force to ensure compliance.

Guardianship of the resource base

The concept of sustainable development is infiltrating the policy framework of many government organizations and agencies, primarily through concern expressed for the natural environment as enshrined in the ' wise growth' policy of Agenda 21 (United Nations Conference on Environment and Development, 1992). But in tourism there is the broader relationship of visitors to the physical and social environment, and so sustainability may be summarized as development, which meets the needs of present tourists and host regions while protecting and enhancing opportunities for the future (WTO, 1993). It is evident that the public is becoming more aware of the perceived adverse effects of tourism on the environment and it has become fashionable to 'go green': Muller's 'green viruses' (1997) appear to be spreading. Some operators have consciously taken the decision to reduce their consumption of natural resources to the benefit of the organization and staff alike. Others have used the concept that green tourism is equated with 'soft' tourism, which has low impact and is therefore acceptable, as little more than a marketing tactic. But there has been generally a rise in the 'green' lobby and the number of 'green' products on offer, which in turn has encouraged both industry associations as well as tourist boards to issue examples of best practice and codes of conduct for their members. However, green tourism, ecotourism or alternative tourism (the words are often used synonymously) are in essence small-scale solutions to what is a large-scale problem, namely the mass movements of people travelling for leisure purposes. Thus, there is still a requirement to continue to create large 'resortscapes' capable of managing high-density flows. The challenge is to build sustainability into all aspects of tourism (Stabler, 1997).

If the institutional framework is to function in a manner that is socially compatible, then there is a prerequisite for local involvement in the development process to encourage discussion about future directions. This has generated interest in models of community tourism development (Murphy, 1985: Inskeep, 1991). Cultural conflicts need to be resolved through, say, staging development and using marketing communication channels to prepare guests better for their holiday experience. As a rule, the greater the difference in lifestyles between hosts and guests and the less the former has been exposed to visitors, then the longer should be the period of adaptation.

Market failure

The market failure argument follows on very much from what has gone before, namely that environmental protection and community ownership of the development process are not guaranteed by the free market. Those who argue for the market mechanism as the sole arbiter in the allocation of resources for tourism are ignoring the lessons of history and are grossly oversimplifying the heterogeneous nature of the product. The early growth of the seaside resorts during the latter half of the nineteenth century, as, for example, in the United Kingdom, was the result of a partnership between the public and private sectors (Cooper and Jackson, 1989; Cooper, 1992). The local authorities invested in the promenades, piers, gardens and so on, while the private sector developed the revenue-earning activities, which enhanced the income of the area and in turn increased property tax receipts for the authorities.

Thus, embodied in the tourist product are common goods and services, which are either unlikely to be provided in sufficient quantity if left to the market mechanism, or are available without cost, as is the case with natural resources. Hence, the value of their consumption to society is not reflected in their economic use. The principal concern for the environment is that indiscriminate consumption, without market regulation, will cause irreversible damage that cannot be compensated by increasing the stock of other capital. The upshot is that the single-minded pursuit of private profit opportunities within tourism may be self-defeating, as many older resorts have found to their cost (Plog, 1974).

In the past, as witnessed by the experience of a number of Mediterranean resorts, the lack of public involvement in tourism has resulted in overbuilding by the accommodation sector, since this tends to be the major revenue-earning activity where there are substantial short-term profits to be made during the early stages of development. Such building has often been at the expense of the aesthetic quality of the natural landscape and also, when it has been overlaid onto an existing town or village, it may severely disrupt the lifestyle of the local community (De Kadt, 1979). For example, the major hotel developments that took place in the resorts of southern Spain during the 1960s and early 1970s were completed under laissez-faire expansionism with little consideration given to planning or control. In general, the public infrastructure was overloaded and, since the second half of the 1980s, there has been a continual programme to correct this imbalance and to refurbish the resort centres to give more 'green' space in the form of parks and gardens.

INTERVENTION POLICY

It has been noted already that tourism is a multifaceted product: it includes accommodation, transport, restaurants, shopping facilities, attractions, entertainment, public infrastructure support and the general way of life of the host community. From a broad perspective, what is required is a balanced development of the many facilities so as to meet tourists' needs in a manner that is sustainable: for example, by ensuring that new developments are linked to and improve on other infrastructure, are located on public transport access routes, so as to counter car dependency, and are aesthetically attractive. What is clear is that the complex structure of the product lends itself to the fact that in any tourism development programme there is often a marked difference between private and social benefits and cost. It is right and proper that the private sector should concentrate on commercial criteria for their investment projects, but successful development requires there should be a partnership between the various stakeholders in the activity of tourism.

The role of co-ordinating the partnership approach towards achieving the desired level of tourism development invariably falls on the public sector. The exact nature of a country's position on tourism development is determined by the direction of emphasis given by the government, what the government sees as its core responsibilities and the extent of the development role it envisages for the private sector, which is considerable in terms of modern development thinking. The latter sees the overall objective of any strategy to be one of raising living standards. But this cannot only be seen through increasing levels of per capita GDP; it includes welfare, the environment and enhancing the opportunities for all citizens to participate in and benefit from the activities of society. This must include: the eradication of absolute poverty, provision of employment opportunities and the reduction of huge disparities in inequality, because of the political tensions that they generate and because egalitarian policies result in more citizens realizing their potential, thus enhancing social and economic efficiency. In a democracy, the difficult task of government is to build a consensus on these issues, drawn from shared values, traditions, cultures and a sense of belonging.

Table 12.1 presents a number of common strategic tourism policy objectives that may be found in development plans (Gunn, 1989). In most cases, economics forms the basis of development plans and the objectives shown in the table are commensurate with the broader concept of raising living standards expressed above. Within this framework there are three objectives that are normally given the central position:

- employment creation through spreading the benefits of tourism, both direct and indirect, to as many of the host population as possible;
- foreign exchange earnings to ensure a sound Balance of Payments;
- regional development, notably in peripheral areas, which, by their very nature, are attractive to tourists and often have few development prospects outside capitalizing on their natural surroundings to create tourism opportunities for the local economy. This is an objective that has already been shown to be a strong element in EU policy (Wanhill, 1997).

Table 12.1 Tourism policy objectives

Strategic Objective

1. Develop a tourism sector that, in all aspects and at all levels, is of high quality, though not necessarily of high cost.
2. Encourage the use of tourism for both cultural and economic exchange.
3. Distribute the economic benefits of tourism, both direct and indirect, as widely and to as many of the host community as feasible.
4. Preserve cultural and natural resources as part of tourism development. Facilitate this through architectural and landscape designs, which reflect local traditions.
5. Appeal to a broad cross-section of international and domestic tourists through sustainable policies and programmes of site and facility development.
6. Maximize foreign exchange earnings to ensure a sound Balance of Payments.
7. Attract high spending 'upmarket' tourists.
8. Increase employment.
9. Aid peripheral regions by raising incomes and employment, thus slowing down or halting emigration.

It is important that governments should not set objectives that may seriously conflict with each other. Too often governments talk of tourism quality yet measure performance in terms of numbers. Common examples of policy objectives, which are most likely to be at variance with each other, are:

- maximizing foreign exchange earnings versus actions to encourage the regional dispersion of overseas visitors;
- attracting the high-spend tourist market versus policies continually to expand visitor numbers;
- maximizing job creation through generating volume tourist flows versus conservation of the environment and heritage;
- community tourism development versus mass tourism.

However, it must be pointed out that, while it is no longer considered acceptable that the objectives shown in Table 12.1 should be at a cost to the environment or by adversely affecting elements of the host community, this is not always possible at the local level when jobs are at stake. The implementation of policy therefore becomes a process of maintaining the balance between the various objectives as opposed to trying to maximize any single one (Lickorish, 1991).

THE NATURE OF INTERVENTION

As stated earlier, deterministic or centralized planning models are no longer fashionable, because the reality is one of uncertainty in which the information is defective and the various economic agents are not under the planner's control. So what are needed are development instruments and flexible institutions that operate well under a wide set of relevant environments. In tourism, the range of policy instruments available to governments are considerable and enable the public sector to exercise varying degrees of influence over the direction of tourism development by acting on both the demand side and the supply side (Akehurst *et al.*, 1994; Charlton and Essex, 1994; Joppe, 1994). In situations where there is clear commercial profit potential, the public sector may only be required to demonstrate a commitment to tourism by stimulating the demand side through marketing and promoting the country, easing frontier formalities and initiating such aspects as liberal transport policies, particularly air access. Supply-side instruments are normally a mixture of incentives and control as well as ownership of the tourism plant by the public sector.

Specifically, the manner in which the governments have been able to influence tourism may be classified in two ways: demand and revenue management, and supply and cost management, as shown in Table 12.2. Demand management policies are aimed at guiding the tourist's choice, controlling the costs of stay or stimulating/regulating visitor numbers, whereas government activities on the supply side are concerned with influencing the providers of tourist facilities and services. It is evident from Table 12.2 that more instruments pertain to the supply side than the demand side, which is reflective of the traditional regulatory power of the state. But the move towards greater market orientation has left some of these instruments, such as ownership of the tourism plant, increasingly redundant.

Table 12.2 Public policy instruments

Demand and Revenue Instruments	Supply and Cost Instruments
1. Marketing and promotion	1. Land ownership and control
2. Information provision	2. Building regulations
3. Pricing	3. Research and planning
4. Controlling access	4. Market regulation
	5. Taxation
	6. Ownership
	7. Finance and development
	8. Manpower planning
	9. Education and training
	10. Investment incentives

Demand and revenue management

Marketing and promotion

Marketing is the principal function of the National Tourist Organization (NTO) and specific techniques have been widely discussed in the tourism literature (Jefferson and Lickorish, 1991; Middleton, 1994; Witt and Moutinho, 1994). It is sufficient here to point out that the key requirements for effective marketing are clear objectives, a thorough knowledge of markets and products and the allocation of adequate resources. Typically, with many other calls on the government's budget, treasury officials are naturally parsimonious with regard to expenditure on marketing because of difficulties in measuring effectiveness and they like to encourage co-operative venture with the private sector. As a rule, the amounts spent by governments and other public organizations on destination promotion are only a fraction of what is spent in total by the private sector. One of the main reasons for this is that private enterprises are competing for market share at the destination, whereas governments are interested in expanding the total market to the destination. In this respect, probably the most important task of the NTO is to build an image of the country as a tourist destination.

Information provision

The ability of tourists to express their demands depends upon their awareness of the facilities available, particularly attractions that are a key component of leisure tourism. The evidence suggests that the creation of trails or tourist circuits will enhance the visitor experience as well as regulating tourist flows. The establishment of a network of tourist information centres (TICs) and tourist information points (TIPs) at transport terminals and prominent tourist spots will both help the visitor and assist in dispersion. It is often not appreciated that it is the poorly informed visitor who is likely to contribute to crowding and traffic congestion due to lack of knowledge about where to go and what there is to see at the destination. Normally, visitors will first look for the main attractions and then 'spill over' into lesser attractions the longer they stay at the destination. Giving prominence to the variety of attractions available, restricting advertising and informing excursion operators of times when congestion can be avoided are examples of the way in which information management can be used to try and relieve pressure on sensitive tourist areas.

In some countries, NTOs use the provision of information to influence tourists' behaviour. This may come about through editing the information in the tour operator's brochure so that it does not generate unrealistic expectations about a destination and presents the tourist with an informed view of the culture of the host community. An alternative approach is a poster and leaflet campaign aimed directly at the tourist to explain the 'dos' and 'don'ts' of acceptable behaviour; for example, several island resorts offering beach holidays often produce leaflets on standards of dress and the unacceptability of wearing only swimsuits in shops, banks and so on. Such 'codes of conduct' are not mandatory, but are based on the presumption that it is lack of awareness that is preventing tourists behaving in a responsible way towards that society.

Pricing

There are several ways in which the public sector may affect the price the tourist pays for staying at a destination. The direct influence arises out of state ownership, notably in the case of attractions. Many of the most important attractions at a destination fall within the public domain and may be regarded as public merit goods that bestow recreational or educational benefits on the local population. For these reasons, admission has often been free or at a nominal price, but the trend in market economies is for governments to introduce charges for publicly owned attractions, although the public good argument still provokes political debate.

Governments own the majority of the world's airlines and it is not uncommon in LDCs to find state ownership of hotels and sometimes souvenir shops. Thus, in some countries, the key elements making up holiday expenditure are directly affected by the public sector, to the point of reaching total control in the situation that existed in the former centrally planned economies of Eastern Europe. However, many of these state-owned assets have become debt-ridden operations and, in an era of market liberalization, there is increasing pressure on governments to divest themselves of such responsibilities.

Indirect influences come from economic directives such as foreign exchange restrictions, differential rates of sales tax, special duty free shops for tourists and price controls to protect visitors. Exchange restrictions are commonly employed in countries where foreign exchange is scarce and the tourist is usually compelled to change money at an overvalued exchange rate, which serves to increase the real cost of the trip. Tourists are discouraged from changing money on the black market by threats of legal prosecution and severe penalties if caught. With the globalization of money markets, instances of exchange controls are becoming fewer and fewer.

The case for price controls is advanced in terms of promoting the long-term growth of the tourist industry and preventing monopolistic exploitation of tourists through overcharging, a practice which can be damaging to the reputation of the destination. There is no doubt that destinations are aware of their price competitiveness and some NTOs compile a tourist price index for their own country as well as others, in order to assess their relative market position. Where governments regulate prices, the objective is to set their level at a rate that is sufficient to encourage the long-run growth in supply and commensurate with market expansion. Producers, on the other hand, are prevented from making short-run excess profits.

Where price controls are enforced, they are normally a further stage in an overall market regulation package, which commences with the registration and licensing of establishments. In the case of hotels this will include classification and possibly a quality grading system. Price regulation can be found in almost all instances where the government manages capacity and therefore restricts competition. Worldwide, the most common example is the licensing and metering of taxis. Where competition exists then the argument for price controls hinges upon whether supply adjusts more quickly than demand. There have been many examples of Mediterranean resorts where the growth of bed capacity has outstripped demand and so the problem for the authorities has been more an issue of controlling standards than prices, as well as trying to prevent ruinous competition amongst hoteliers. In market economics, there is a basic ideology that is against regulating prices and, where opportunities for suppliers to make excess profits in the short term do arise, control is often exercised informally through exhortation that it will not be in the long-term best interests of the destination. It is reasonable to assume that firms themselves will be aware of competition from other countries, though they are often under considerable short-term pressures to increase profitability.

Controlling access

Controlling access is a means of limiting visitor numbers or channelling visitor flows. At an international level, the easiest way for a country to limit demand is by restricting the number of visas issued, but the trend is one of easing frontier formalities, with the imposition of visas being more to do with countering illegal immigration than tourism. Prohibiting charter flights is a means by which several countries have conveyed an image of exclusiveness to the market and, in some instances, have protected the national air carrier. At the destination, controlling access is usually concerned with protecting popular cultural sites and natural resources. Thus visitor management techniques may be used to relieve congestion at peak times and planning legislation invoked to prohibit or control the development of tourist infrastructure (particularly accommodation) near or around natural sites.

Supply and cost management

Land use planning and control

Control over land use is the most basic and arguably the technique that has the greatest influence on the supply of tourist structures. All governments have a form of town and country planning legislation whereby permission is required to develop, extend or change the use of almost every piece of land. As a rule, the controls are designed to protect areas of high landscape and amenity value. Zoning of land and compulsory purchase have been commonly used as a means of promoting tourism development. One of the key aspects of land control is that before any detailed site plans and future land requirements for tourism are published, the appropriate administrative organization and legislation is in place in order to prevent speculation, land division or parcelling. Dealings or speculation in land prior to legislative control have been a common cause of failure in tourism development plans.

Building regulations

Building regulations are used to supplement land use control and limit the impact of visual intrusion on the natural surroundings. Typically they cover the size of buildings, height, shape, colour, screening and car parking arrangements. The latter is a matter which is not always given the attention it deserves in some resorts. To private sector operators, car parks are often considered unproductive space and so there is a tendency to avoid having to provide them, leaving visitors little alternative than to park their cars in nearby streets. This may only serve to add to traffic congestion and the annoyance of local residents. In addition to structural regulations, many countries also have protective legislation governing cultural resources such as historic buildings, archaeological remains, religious monuments, conservation areas and even whole towns.

Research and planning

The tourist industry usually expects the public sector to collect statistical information and carry out market surveys. For their own part, governments are interested in monitoring changes in the industry and carry out research to identify the social benefits and costs of tourism. More recent developments have been in the field of local area statistics to enable communities to monitor tourist activity.

Market regulation

Governments pass legislation to regulate the market conduct of firms in matters of competitive practices and also to limit the degree of ownership in particular sectors of the industry to prevent the abuse of monopoly power. Governments may also regulate markets by imposing on suppliers, obligations to consumers. This does not have to be legislation; it could be industry-enforced codes of conduct of the kind laid down as conditions for membership of national travel trade associations, though in Europe such codes have passed into the legislation of member states as a result of the EU Package Travel Directive (European Community, 1990). The latter created a comprehensive scheme of consumer protection, the key features being a bonding and security regime to protect tourists in the event of insolvency by the travel organizer, and the organizer's contractual liability for proper performance of the elements of the package, whether provided directly by the organizer or other suppliers.

One of the economic criteria dictating the optimal workings of markets is that consumers should have complete knowledge of the choices open to them. For if consumers do not have the right to safety, to be informed, to choose or the right of redress and firms are not behaving according to the accepted rules of conduct, then resources will be wasted, which may be seen to be inefficient. The economic aspects of a consumer policy are essentially a trade-off in that, as the level of protection increases, so wastage or compensation payments decline, while at the same time the costs of protection increase. The optimum amount of protection is where the declining marginal costs of compensation just balance the marginal increase in protection costs. This is the economic rationale: on social or political grounds the state may legislate to ensure nearly 100 per cent protection. But the economic consequences of such an action could be to raise the supply price of the good or service to the point where the market is substantially diminished. At the consultation stage of the EU Package Travel Directive amendments were accepted to some of the proposals on the grounds that their compliance would significantly raise holiday prices.

Taxation

There are two main reasons why governments levy specific taxes on the tourism sector. The first is the classic argument for a tourist tax, namely to allocate to the supply price the external costs imposed on the host community through providing public amenities for tourists, including any environmental costs. The second is for purposes of raising revenue; tourists are seen as part of the overall tax base and, from a political perspective, they are not voters in the destination country. With the growth of tourism worldwide, there has been escalation in the number of countries levying tourist taxes and in the rates of taxation, drawing the inference that governments principally see such taxes as a source of revenue. It is not unreasonable that the tourist industry should pay taxes, but the World Travel and Tourism Council (Myers et al., 1997) has argued that such payments should be made in accordance with the following guidelines:

- Equity: the fair and even-handed treatment of travel and tourism with respect to the other sectors of the economy.
- Efficiency: the development of tax policies that have a minimal effect on the demand for travel and tourism, unless specifically imposed for the purpose of regulating tourist flows, to, say, environmentally sensitive areas (see Chapter 18).
- Simplicity: taxes should be simple to pay and administer, so as not to disrupt the operation of the travel and tourism system.

The most common forms of raising public income from tourism are airport departure taxes, ticket taxes and taxes on hotel occupancy. When it comes to raising revenue, casinos can be a very profitable source: governments have been known to take as much as 50 per cent of the 'drop', which is the amount of money taken in from the tables.

Ownership

Mention has already been made of state ownership of attractions, natural amenities and some key revenue-earning activities such as hotels, modes of transport (especially airlines) and souvenir shops. It is possible to add to this list conference centres, exhibition halls, sports and leisure complexes (including casinos) and the provision of general infrastructure. The latter may include: banks; hospitals; public utilities (water and energy supplies); telecommunications and road networks; transport terminals; and education and training establishments. The arguments for public ownership of these facilities rest on their importance as essential services for any economic development, the fact that outside investors would expect such provision and economies of scale in production. Traditionally, public infrastructure and transport networks have been regarded as natural monopolies; the minimum scale of production is such as to make it impossible for more than one firm to enjoy all the economies in the market, so that even if they were not publicly owned, these organizations would need to be publicly regulated.

Finance and development

Where the government envisages a particular direction for tourism growth or wishes to speed up the process, it may intervene extensively in the market place by setting up a Tourist Development Corporation (TDC) and assigning it the responsibility for building resorts. A well-known example of this process was the building of new resorts in Languedoc-Roussillon, France, but many countries have instituted TDCs at one time or another, for example, Egypt, India, Malaysia, New Zealand and a number of African countries. In theory, once the resort has been built, the development corporation's function ceases and the assets are transferred to the private sector (at a price) and the local authority. This is the general trend in market-oriented economies, but in countries where there is a strong degree of central planning, as in India, the TDC often maintains an operational role in running hotels and tours, but most recent directions have been towards privatization. Beyond this, governments may also establish a Development Bank with duties to provide special credit facilities for tourist projects and on lend funds made available by multinational aid agencies.

Manpower planning and education and training

The provision of an educated and trained labour force to meet the demands of a modern economy has been a task that has fallen to many governments. Actions that augment this may be the provision of low-cost housing for hotel and catering workers as well as immigration policies to manage the skills in the labour force.

Investment incentives

Governments around the world offer a wide range of investment incentives to developers. Their justification for them is the market failure argument, particularly in respect of regional development where the aim is to give the locality 'tourism presence' in the market place or to rejuvenate old resorts. They may be grouped under three broad headings:

- Reduction of capital costs: these include capital grants or loans at preferential rates, interest rate relief, a moratorium on loan repayments for, say, x years, provision of infrastructure, provision of land on concessional terms, tariff exemption on construction materials and equity participation.
- Reduction of operating costs: in order to improve operating viability governments may grant tax 'holidays' (5–10 years), give a labour or training subsidy, offer tariff exemption on imported materials and supplies, provide special depreciation allowances and ensure that there is double taxation or unilateral relief. The latter are government-to-government agreements that prevent an investor being taxed twice on the same profits.
- Investment security: the object here is to win investors' confidence in an industry that is very sensitive to the political environment and economic climate. Action here would include guarantees against nationalization, free availability of foreign exchange, repatriation of invested capital, profits, dividends and interest, loan guarantees, provision of work permits for 'key' personnel and the availability of technical advice.

The administration of grants or loans may be given to the NTO, a government-sponsored investment bank or the TDC. Tax matters will usually remain the responsibility of the treasury or the ministry in charge of finance. Less developed countries are often able to attract low-cost investment funds from multinational aid agencies, which they can use to augment their existing resources for the provision of development finance.

It may be taken that policies to ensure investment security are primary requirements for attracting tourism developers. The objective of financial incentives is to improve returns to capital in order to attract developers and investors. Where there is obvious market potential the government may only have to demonstrate its commitment to tourism by providing the necessary climate for investment security. Such a situation occurred in Bermuda during the early 1970s and so, in order to prevent overexploitation of the tourism resources, the Bermuda Government imposed a moratorium on large hotel building (Archer, 1995; Archer and Wanhill, 1980). On the other hand, there is no doubt that many countries have been forced by competitive pressures for foreign investment into situations where they become trapped in a bidding process to secure clients and as a result the variety of financial incentives multiplies together with an escalation of the rates of benefit, without evaluating their necessity or their true cost to the economy.

It is important to note that there are frequent instances where it is gross uncertainty, as in times of recession or where the concept is too new, rather than limited potential that prevents the private sector investing. In such situations the principal role of government intervention is to act as a catalyst to give confidence to investors. Thus public funds are able to lever in private money by nature of the government's commitment to tourism and enable the market potential of an area to be realized. The rejuvenation of inner cities and decayed harbour areas has often been achieved with the combination of establishing a development corporation and providing investment incentives for the private sector.

In implementing a tourism investment policy the government has to decide to what extent incentives should be legislated as automatic entitlements, as against being discretionary awards. Automatic incentives may give too much money away, when what is required to ensure that the treasury receives maximum benefit from its funds is the application of the concept of 'additionality'. The latter seeks to provide financial support or the equivalent benefits in kind to the point where the developer will just proceed with the project. This is the favoured approach amongst developed nations, where they have the ability to offer grants and loans, but LDCs are usually in a less fortunate position.

On a world scale, competition for tourism investment frequently requires countries to legislate for automatic financial help in order to attract investors in the first instance. Some countries may legislate for all the incentives discussed here; others for a subset of them. Several countries have been guilty of copying the incentive legislation of their neighbours without any real grasp of the meaning of this legislation.

The appropriateness of the various financial incentives available depends on understanding the nature of the business risk and the likely returns to the tourist industry, as well as the ability of the country to afford them. Thus developing countries may find themselves in no position to offer grants or cheap loans, which highlights the importance of contributions from aid agencies. One of the main sources of business risk in tourist enterprises is the tendency to have a high ratio of capital charges in relation to operating expenses. It is for this reason that incentives to reduce capital costs are the preferred form of assistance when the viability of the business is being considered.

MARKET SOLUTIONS OR CONTROL

Modern development practice gives emphasis to market solutions. The instruments examined above illustrate on the one hand less favoured policies of state control, either through legislative force or ownership, and on the other regulatory and co-operative agreements, incentives and infrastructure provision to help markets work. It would be convenient if there were only a few instruments or levers, which could be considered optimal from a policy perspective. Certainly, the tourist industry responds strongly to legislation and the availability of finance, but the tourist product varies so much around the globe that it has been customary for states to adopt a bundle of instruments and adjust them over time, in response to feedback information on their workings. This is the flexible institutional approach to conditions of uncertainty and throws light on the question of how the mechanism for sustainable development should work.

In market-oriented economies, the policy preference is based on the principle that the 'polluter' should pay, thus prices should reflect not only the economic costs of provision but also the social costs. The difficulty with market solutions is that many features of a destination have public good properties whereby consumption is non-excludable and there is an element of public resistance to charging for environments, which are presumed to belong to all. In such situations there is little choice other than to control visitor flows by influencing behaviour through visitor management schemes and/or to follow a programme of continual repair and maintenance. The significant aspect of many environmental matters is that the sheer number of agents involved in tourism, both public and private, with very different objectives and performance measures, makes it virtually impossible to achieve concerted action other than through a regulating agency that has the force of law, which leaves little scope for market economics. Where there are diverse agents, who share many goals in common, then it is possible to generate non-statutory agreements through trade associations, which act like clubs by devising a rule book of shared values for the benefit of their members.

As an example of this conundrum, the British experience has been that rarely have visitors or tourist businesses been charged directly for the social and environmental costs generated by their actions, because there is still debate on a common set of sustainable tourism development indicators (see Chapter 18). The money is paid indirectly through general taxation and most of the burden of coping with congestion, litter and visitor management falls on the public sector, particularly local authorities. To this extent the British Government tries to take account of the influx of visitors in its support grant for local provision of public services. This is not to say that the 'polluter pays principle' through the application of 'green' taxes may not be appropriate in certain circumstances. Thus the Australian authorities raise a specific charge on visitors to the Great Barrier Reef, a popular destination which is under considerable environmental pressure, and, more generally, governments are looking at a 'carbon tax' to try to limit emissions from car usage.

MONITORING INTERVENTION

Within Europe, the EU has developed tried and tested methods for evaluating its activities across member states and these are outlined here by way of an example of how monitoring procedures may be undertaken. The principle of subsidiarity, that is devolvement down to lowest competent authority, governs the monitoring and evaluation of projects within a regional funding package. This is carried out by Programme Monitoring Committees, which are normally made up of representatives of central and local government, public agencies and any other interested bodies. Targets are set for every project at approval stage and managers must submit returns, indicating progress against targets, every quarter. Failure to do this may result in the suspension of grant payments.

Under EU regulations, the appropriate central government department responsible for administering European programmes is required to make site visits to examine specifications and project development. Since EU assistance is normally a matching payment, other public moneys are usually involved, in which case it is customary for the government department concerned to undertake a post-evaluation study, via a questionnaire, to assess whether the project has lived up to its predicted performance. It is a member state responsibility to see that funds are correctly spent and yield good value for money.

The Commission and the European Court of Auditors have powers of examination and verification to establish that projects are:

- eligible for funds as specified;
- managed in accordance with Community rules with regard to technical and financial controls;
- claiming grants against justifiable expenditure.

Verification is carried out by one or two visits every year whereby a group of pre-selected projects are subject to detail checking. Thus the Commission's involvement is normally to do with accounting and administrative procedures, rather than overall programme direction. These procedures have revealed a number of fraudulent practices, but unfortunately for the Commission it is the press headlines concerning fraudulent behaviour that are drawn to the public's attention, rather than the Commission's success in catching the culprits.

CONCLUSIONS

With tourism set to be one of the major economic drivers of the twenty-first century, it has raised development and employment opportunities that few governments can afford to ignore. Modern development economics assigns a greater role to market power to determine the allocation of resources, with government being given the task of providing the institutional structure for markets to function. However, the complexity of the tourist product and the current emphasis on sustainable tourism indicates that, on the basis of past experience, uncontrolled commercial development is likely to create more problems than it solves. It is right and proper that the private sector should concentrate on commercial criteria for their investment projects, but successful development requires there should be a partnership between the various stakeholders in the activity of tourism.

The role of co-ordinating such a partnership, to achieve the desired level of tourism development, falls on the public sector. The economic theory suggests that targeting specific projects and concentration to ensure 'tourism visibility' is the most appropriate strategy. There is a whole range of instruments that can be used to influence the practical outcomes of such a policy. Given that tourist movements will increase both nationally and internationally, there will be a need for more regulation and improved management of tourism resources to prevent environmental and sociocultural degradation in the interests of 'responsible' tourism. The current approach is not to reverse the market changes that have taken place. Such a policy would now be difficult to implement, as the increasing globalization of economic activity has reduced the power of national governments to control their destinies. Rather, the move is one towards a more pragmatic approach to intervention and regulation, with an emphasis on international collaboration.

REFERENCES

Akehurst, G., Bland, N. and Nevin, M. (1994) 'Successful tourism policies in the European Union'. *Journal of Vacation Marketing*, **1**(1), 11–27.

Archer, B. (1995) 'Tourism in Bermuda's economy'. *Annals of Tourism Research*, **22**(4), 918–30.

Archer, B. and Wanhill, S. (1980) *Tourism in Bermuda: An Economic Evaluation*. Hamilton: Bermuda Department of Tourism.

Charlton, C. and Essex, S. (1994) 'Public sector policies'. In S. Witt and L. Moutinho (eds) *Tourism Marketing and Management Handbook* (2nd edn). Hemel Hempstead: Prentice-Hall, pp. 45–59.

Cohen, E. (1988) 'Authenticity and commoditization in tourism'. *Annals of Tourism Research*, **14**(2), 371–86.

Cooper, C. (1992) 'The life cycle concept and strategic planning for coastal resorts'. *Built Environment*, **18**(1), 57–66.

Cooper, C. and Jackson, S. (1989) 'Destination life cycle: the Isle of Man case study'. *Annals of Tourism Research*, **15**(2), 377–98.

De Kadt, E. (ed.) (1979) *Tourism – Passport to Development?* New York: Oxford University Press.

European Community (1990) *Council Directive on Package Travel, Package Holidays and Package Tours*. Brussels: EEC/314/1990.

Gunn, C. (1989) *Tourism Planning*. New York: Taylor and Francis.

Inskeep, E. (1991) *Tourism Planning: An Integrated and Sustainable Development Approach*. New York: Van Nostrand Reinhold.

Jefferson, A. and Lickorish, L. (1991) *Marketing Tourism: A Practical Guide* (2nd edn). London: Longman.

Joppe, M. (1994) 'Government controls on and support for tourism'. In S. Witt and L. Moutinho (eds) *Tourism Marketing and Management Handbook* (2nd edn). Hemel Hempstead: Prentice-Hall, pp. 60–4.

Lickorish, L. (ed.) (1991) *Developing Tourist Destinations*. London: Longman.

Middleton, V. (1994) *Marketing in Travel and Tourism* (2nd edn). Oxford: Butterworth-Heinemann.

Muller, H. (1997) 'The thorny path to sustainable tourism development'. In L. France (ed.) *The Earthscan Reader In Sustainable Tourism*. London: Earthscan Publications.

Murphy, P. (1985) *Tourism: A Community Approach*. New York: Methuen.

Plog, S. (1974) 'Why destinations rise and fall in popularity'. *Cornell H.R.A. Quarterly*, **14**(4), 55–8.

Myers, J., Forsberg, P. and Holecek, D. (1997) 'A framework for monitoring global travel and tourism taxes: the WTTC Tax Barometer'. *Tourism Economics*, **3**(1), 5–20.

Stabler, M. (ed.) (1997) *Tourism and Sustainability: Principles to Practice*, New York: CAB International.

United Nations Conference on Environment and Development (1992) *Agenda 21: A Guide to the United Nations Conference on Environment and Development*. Geneva: UN Publications Service.

Wanhill, S. (1994) 'Appraising tourism projects'. In A. V. Seaton *et al.* (eds) *Tourism: The State of the Art*. Chichester: Wiley.

Wanhill, S. (1997) 'Peripheral area tourism: a European perspective'. *Progress in Tourism and Hospitality Research*, **3**(1), 47–70.

Witt, S. and Moutinho, L. (eds) (1994) *Tourism Marketing and Management Handbook* (2nd edn). Hemel Hempstead: Prentice-Hall.

World Commission on Environment and Development (1987) *Our Common Future*. Oxford: Oxford University Press.

World Tourism Organization (1993) *Sustainable Tourism Development: Guide for Local Planners*. Madrid: WTO.

PART 3

The 'Researcher's Gaze' Towards the New Millennium

Edited by Bill Faulkner

INTRODUCTION

The reference to the 'researcher's gaze' in the title of this section of the book highlights the inevitability of a variety of different viewpoints being produced when we assemble a group of researchers to look at the new millennium in terms of research issues. Just as tourists, according to John Urry (1990), have different 'gazes' that structure the nature of their experience, the researcher's view of the world is coloured by the particular theoretical and methodological perspectives that drive their approach to research. Pearce *et al.* (1996) have emphasized that the gazes identified by Urry are themselves a reflection of different social representations produced by the social context of tourists' everyday lives. Similarly, it can be argued that researchers undergo a socialization process within their particular discipline or school of thought, and this has some parallels with social representations phenomena. This feature of scientific inquiry has been explicitly described by Thomas Kuhn (1962).

It has been noted (see Chapter 1) that, while tourism has been an element of human activity systems virtually since trade began, it was only since the second half of the twentieth century that this activity became a prominent part of the global economy and lifestyles. Tourism has therefore emerged as a distinct research focus relatively recently, and tourism researchers have used the foundations provided by a range of established social science disciplines to build what has essentially become a multidisciplinary field of study (Graburn and Jafari, 1991; Gunn, 1994). This aspect

243

of tourism research, however, may also be a reflection of the growing realization that the multifaceted and complex nature of most social phenomena demands such an approach (Faulkner and Goeldner, 1998). Whatever the reasons for the multi-disciplinary nature of tourism research, it does mean that we now have a range of perspectives at our disposal to inform the examination of tourism phenomena, and this is reflected in the collection of contributions contained in this part of the book.

In the selection of the following contributors and topics, we have been mindful of the constraints imposed by the overall organization of the book. Just as it would be very ambitious to compile a comprehensive overview of issues and trends affecting tourism in general within the covers of a single volume, it is not possible to do the same with respect to aspects of the research agenda within a part of the book. What we have endeavoured to do, however, is to provide a range of insights on the methodological traditions, challenges and innovations that will influence the research 'landscape', at least in the early years of the new millennium.

We begin with a chapter by Graham Dann and Joan Phillips, who note that the positivist tradition has become entrenched virtually as the modus operandi of tourism research. They attribute this to the growth in the influence of newer, business-oriented research disciplines (e.g. marketing and management), at the expense of more traditional social science disciplines (e.g. anthropology, psychology and sociology), and suggest that our capacity to understand tourism phenomena is circumscribed by the corresponding underutilization of qualitative methods. This point is reinforced by a clarification of the nature of qualitative research, a description of the advantages of such an approach and an indication of the situations where qualitative methods might be most effective. It is against this background that some thoughts about the future role of qualitative methods in tourism research are offered.

In one sense, Chris Ryan's chapter reinforces elements of the argument presented at the beginning of this section, at least to the extent that he emphasizes the subjectivity of tourism research. He also emphasizes that this is no less so in the case of the quantitative, positivistic method than it is with any other approach. After exploring the related issues of subjectivity and reflexivity in tourism research, he examines the potential applications of neural networks. The reference to neural networks provides a focus for highlighting a tourism research conundrum, which is not particularly new, but will nevertheless become as much a part of the research debate in the new century as it was in the old. That is, on the one hand, 'research into tourist behaviour involves an interaction of the researcher–researched with its respective subjectivities' and, on the other, there will be tools, such as neural network models, that in effect 'mimic tourist experiences', but shed little explanatory light because they are 'bound within an empiricist "black box"'.

Although it was inspired by the product life cycle model from marketing, the Tourism Destination Life Cycle (DLC) model developed by Richard Butler some 20 years ago (Butler, 1980) stands out as one of the few 'indigenous' theoretical schemas that have emerged in the tourism research field. Not only has it become one of the most influential and enduring heuristic frameworks for analysing the evolution of tourism destinations, but it has also been recognized as a useful organizational framework for destination development and planning (Cooper, 1994). In his chapter, Richard Butler reflects on the role his model has played in the development of tourism research 20 years on and considers its implications for research in the twenty-first century.

David Weaver's chapter examines the concept of sustainable tourism and some of the definitional and measurement problems associated with its applications to destination management. The relevance and importance of this issue to the research agenda springs from the universal acceptance, in principle at least, of sustainable development as a goal for tourism development. However, the identification of such goals in the planning and management process matters little without the development and utilization of indicators, so that progress towards the goal can be monitored. Thus, the establishment of planning and management regimes that are sensitive to sustainability principles in the twenty-first century hinges on the development of systems for measuring the parameters of sustainability.

With the trend towards the globalization of the ownership and control of productive capacity, and the likely continuation of this trend in the twenty-first century, national boundaries have become (and are becoming) less relevant as an organizational framework for economic activities. The implications of this with regard to the analysis of the economic impacts of tourism are explored by Trevor Mules, who, in the process, weighs up the relative merits of Input–Output (I–O) and General Equilibrium modelling approaches.

In the final chapter by Bill Faulkner and Roslyn Russell, Graham Dann and Joan Phillip's point regarding the positivistic orientation of tourism research in the recent past is noted and it is suggested that this reflects the dominance of the so-called Newtonian or Cartesian paradigm. The implication of this is that tourism research has tended to become more focused on central tendency in populations, rather than outliers, and it has been assumed that tourism systems are relatively stable equilibrium-seeking systems in which change can be generally understood in terms of linear or quasi-linear patterns. It is argued that, in order to develop a better understanding of change processes, more attention should be given to outliers because these often precipitate instability and fundamental change in tourism systems. It is also suggested that, during such phases, non-linear patterns of change are more prevalent and chaos theory (and the allied complexity perspective) provides a more meaningful basis for understanding the dynamics of change. Applications of chaos theory to the development of conceptual schema for analysing entrepreneurial activity and tourism disasters are then illustrated, with a view to providing a case for a new research focus on turbulence in tourism.

REFERENCES

Butler, R. (1980) 'The concept of the tourist area cycle of evolution: implications for the management of resources'. *Canadian Geographer*, **24**(1), 5, 5–12

Cooper, C. (1994) 'The destination life cycle: an update'. In A. V. Seaton, C. L. Jenkins, R. C. Wood, P. Dieke, M. M. Bennett, L. R. MacLellan and R. Smith (eds) *Tourism the State of the Art*. Brisbane: John Wiley and Sons.

Faulkner, H. W. and Goeldner, C. R. (1998) 'Progress in tourism and hospitality research: 1998 CAUTHE conference report'. *Journal of Travel Research*, **37**(1), 76–80.

Graburn, N. H. H. and Jafari, J. (1991) 'Tourism social research, special issue'. *Annals of Tourism Research*, **18**(1), 1–11.

Gunn, C. A. (1994) 'A perspective on the purpose and nature of tourism research methods'. In J. B. Ritchie and C. R. Goeldner (eds) *Travel, Tourism and Hospitality Research: A Handbook for Managers and Researchers*. New York: Wiley, pp. 3–11.

Kuhn, T. S. (1962) *The Structure of Scientific Revolutions*. Chicago: University of Chicago Press.

Pearce, P. L., Moscardo, G. and Ross, G. F. (1996) *Tourism Community Relationships*. Oxford: Pergamon.

Urry, J. (1990) *The Tourist Gaze*. London: Sage.

CHAPTER 13

Qualitative Tourism Research in the late Twentieth Century and Beyond

Graham Dann and Joan Phillips

INTRODUCTION

Every ten years or so tourism researchers seem to come to their methodological census. Over two decades ago, there was an important article by Cohen (1979) tracing developments in the sociology of tourism which included some very pertinent observations on the essential qualities of research. Then, in 1988, *Annals of Tourism Research* devoted a special issue to methodology which included another incisive paper by Cohen (1988) and a frequently cited editorial contribution by Dann *et al.* (1988). Eleven years later, *Tourism Management* carried out a similar state-of-the-art exercise (Faulkner and Ryan, 1999), which included a number of very useful articles demonstrating what progress had been made since tourism had become accepted as a legitimate domain of inquiry.

In between these various assessments, there has additionally been a number of published commentaries which provides food for methodological thought. Among these scattered offerings, there is a short essay by Ryan (1997, p. 4), which states that tourism as an academic subject 'is characterised by increasing debate and more sophistication in the methods used for analysis'. In spite of this seemingly rosy appraisal, however, Ryan (1997, p. 3) prefaces his remarks with the following cautionary observation:

> Until quite recently, I wondered if we were not entrenched in a positivist tradition that was blinding us, as a group of scholars, to developments in the other social sciences.

After citing works by Urry, Rojek, Nash, Dann and Selwyn as evidence of new approaches, he then rhetorically asks:

Do the methodologies these authors espouse impact upon the research being reported in the journals?

before supplying his own damning answer:

I would have to generally conclude 'no'! So much of published research is still dominated by conventional quantitative methods that are made all the easier by the wider spread of computer packages. (Ryan, 1997, p. 3)

A similar sentiment can be found in Riley (1996, p. 37), who argues that:

Despite a wide acceptance of qualitative methods in sociological and anthropological circles, the same acceptance has been limited in marketing and other disciplines that contribute to understanding tourism,

and in Burns and Holden (1995, p. 13), who maintain that:

Those who study tourism should not merely concern themselves only with that which is business or that which is easily quantifiable. While such an approach may provide a mark of respectability for tourism studies in a world dominated by quantitative method, neglect of qualitative issues will inevitably lead to a poorer tourism product for both the hosts and the guests.

The current chapter takes over from the foregoing positions. It attempts to develop them more fully under the following self-imposed tasks:

1. to examine the nature of qualitative research as it relates to tourism;
2. to supply examples of various topics to which qualitative tourism research may be appropriately applied;
3. to assess the major advantages of qualitative tourism research;
4. to provide a state-of-the-art model of qualitative tourism research that incorporates the main themes and principal players of contemporary tourism; and
5. to offer suggestions as to where late twentieth-century qualitative tourism research may lead in the future.

The first four stages of this account are retrospective; the fifth, together with a conclusion, is prospective. They collectively suggest that the days of pure quantification are numbered and that, when the counting stops, only quality will remain.[1]

THE NATURE OF QUALITATIVE TOURISM RESEARCH

Over twenty years ago, although admittedly from the standpoint of a single discipline, Cohen (1979) highlighted what he considered to be the hallmarks of research in the sociology of tourism, namely that it should be processual, contextual, comparative and emic. In other words, he was respectively claiming that investigations should be diachronic/longitudinal, explore various types of tourists and tourism institutions, be capable of generalization and be grounded in an insider perspective. Interestingly, whereas these attributes can apply to several other social science disciplines, they are more germane to qualitative research than to its quantitative counterpart. Needless to say, Cohen's pleas were largely disregarded at the time. Some nine years later, and no doubt sensing the need to restate his case, Cohen (1988) was more explicit in his comments. Referring now to what had become emerging traditions in the qualitative sociology of tourism, he identified a number of studies which had derived their inspiration from the theoretical insights of Boorstin, MacCannell and Turner. On this occasion, Cohen's point was that qualitative research had to be continuous, cumulative and case study transcendent. Even though he did not have a similar message for quantitative researchers, already a picture was beginning to develop.

In the same special issue of *Annals* in which Cohen's (1988) article appeared, guest editors Dann (a sociologist), Nash (an anthropologist) and Pearce (a psychologist) (1988) attempted to draw some of the methodological threads together and to apply them across tourism's multidisciplinary boundaries. They argued then that tourism research, in order to live up to its designation, had to demonstrate a satisfactory blend of high theoretical awareness and equally elevated methodological sophistication. However, and unhappily, they could only identify a few instances where such research met these basic requirements. Instead, it tended to fall into one of the three other categories occupied by quadrants resulting from the intersection of the two criteria.

The model generated by Dann *et al.* (1988) was later that year tested longitudinally by Dann (1988) in relation to developments in Caribbean tourism research. Here a similar conclusion was reached – that while some gains had been made in the literature over time (notably in the area of greater indigenization of authorship) – still only 5 per cent of the works surveyed reached the optimal situation.

According to Walle (1997), one reason for this sorry state of affairs has been the tendency in academia to equate scientific knowledge with quantitative techniques, in order thereby to reduce subjective bias and increase rigour (cf. Decrop, 1999, p. 157). Maybe the only rigour he has in mind is rigor mortis since Walle (1997, p. 529) maintains that, as far as tourism research is concerned, the very subject matter requires that 'an understanding of people in their own terms' of this highly experiential and interactive phenomenon should utilize some of the advances made in anthropology and allied fields which 'artistically' explore the life worlds of tourism's participants. In other words, if tourism is as multidisciplinary as claimed, should it not draw on the progress achieved by its qualitatively oriented constituent disciplines?

Hollinshead (1996, p. 68) anticipates this view with a complementary point when he argues that:

> The infixities of culture, of identity, of meaning and of representation do appear (at face value) to demand the kind of slow, exhaustive and ultrasuspicious practices that are generally offered by the qualitative researcher

rather than 'the heavy quantification of touristological studies'. For Hollinshead (1996, p. 69), tourism researchers should adopt the creative approach of the *bricoleur* (Levi-Strauss's inductive thinker, cf. Walle, 1996, p. 879), open to avenues of interpretation, introspection and the interactivity of gender and ethnicity. Indeed, he tellingly adds:

> Qualitative researchers always ought to think historically, interactionally, structurally, reflectively and biographically when they probe the lived experiences of the here and now in tourism matters of sun, sand and sensation as in any other social/human setting. (Hollinshead, 1996, p. 71)

Alternatively, and as stated by Babbie (1995, p. 307), the often quoted Master of Method:

> Like an investigative detective, the social researcher looks for clues, and clues of social behavior are all around you. In a sense, everything you see represents the answer to some important social scientific question – all you have to do is think of the question.

The 'all you have to do' is, of course, that vital element called 'theory' – the provision of understanding, the supplying of what Max Weber (1968, p. 99) refers to as 'adequacy at the level of meaning'.

What, then, is qualitative research? According to fellow expert Dooley (1984, p. 267), it is 'social research based on non-quantitative observations made in the field and analysed in non-statistical ways'. However, if there is a desire to go beyond a definition that merely describes something in terms of its opposite, it may be preferable to adopt Ali's (1998, p. 82) simple idea of 'getting close to data in their natural setting', or Riley's (1996, p. 38) somewhat longer version of 'An investigation that takes place in settings where subjects of interest exist, in an effort to bring meaning and understanding to different phenomena, as seen by the people who experience them.'

It is this 'naturalistic' attribute (cf. Denzin, 1989) of qualitative research which suggests a bottom-up approach to theory – or what Glaser and Strauss (1967) classically refer to as 'grounded theory'. Whereas quantitative research tends to follow the positivist requirements of deducing hypotheses from pre-existing theory, their subsequent testing, (in)validification of theory and prediction (Decrop, 1999), in qualitative research, theory is often as emergent as the culture it seeks to explore (Bruner, 1994). Hence the latter's association with constructivist and interpretevist paradigms (Bruner, 1994; Hollinshead, 1996).

VARIOUS TOPICS TO WHICH QUALITATIVE TOURISM RESEARCH MAY BE APPROPRIATELY APPLIED

To a large extent, the decision whether to opt for quantitative or qualitative methods (or maybe a mixture of both) is generally predicated on the nature of the topic at hand and the type of medium through which it is normally accessed.

Take the complex question of tourist motivation, for instance, and the largely unanalysed theme of escape (Moore, 1997). If one simply requires the validification of pre-existent theory (e.g., that of Maslow, 1954), or the replication of deduced and operationalized hypotheses, all that is needed is an application of the foregoing to a given population whose related attitudes can be scaled, measured and statistically tested. However, should one desire to go beyond a close-ended, standardized check list of items prepared by the investigator to more open-ended and unclassified issues raised by the research subjects, a more qualitative, multimedia approach becomes necessary. Thus, adopting the latter, reasons for travel may be gauged by analysing promotional material which has itself been produced in order to target the imputed motivation of persons and groups representing various niche markets. In such a manner, the brochures of tour operators, for example, have been explored by Dann (1996b), Selwyn (1993), Uzzell (1984) and Weightman (1987), travel advertising by Dann (1998a), Thurot and Thurot (1983), videos by Hanefors and Larsson (1993), guidebooks by Bhatta-charyya (1997) and maps by Dann (1996a) and Seaton (1994). However, if the inquiry wishes to go further and examine reactions to such material, it could well adopt a strategy employed by Dann (1995) in relation to the publicity disseminated by national tourist offices. Now it becomes possible to scrutinize the actual vocabulary of motive used by tourists (Pearce and Caltabiano, 1983) and to see how well this notoriously difficult realm of articulation corresponds to the language of tourism promotion (Dann, 1996a). Ancillary qualitative techniques might include the analyses of photographs taken by tourists (Chalfen, 1979; Markwell, 1997; O'Barr, 1994) or the content of their conversations (Fjellman, 1992; Ryan, 1995a). After all, word-of-mouth communication, a source for tourist decision-taking so frequently identified, yet so rarely investigated (Reid and Reid, 1993), is surely a vital component of the language of tourism.

Satisfaction is another hardy perennial and crucial dimension of the tourist experience (Ryan, 1995b). Examined quantitatively, it might simply comprise a numerical evaluation of various features of a holiday as they relate to the service offered by its components: travel, accommodation, activities, etc., that is to say, elements identified by the tourism industry as being important.

However, as Moore (1997, p. 14) has noted, the complexity and subtleties of the tourist experience cannot be adequately captured by satisfaction scales and questionnaires since the latter two techniques 'do not generally sit well with ambivalence, confusion or unease'. In fact, he adds, 'qualitative methods may be our only foothold into this area of interest.' Furthermore, there is the acknowledged difficulty of conducting cross-cultural studies in this domain (the Japanese, for example, are often found to be reluctant in voicing their criticisms to interviewers (Pizam, 1993)), just as there is the additional problem of uniformly and meaningfully quantifying what are essentially qualitative experiences. Alternative qualitative approaches might usefully encompass the study of positive and negative stories told (Jackson et al., 1996; Pearce, 1991) or written down (Small, 1999) by tourists, an examination of the diaries that they complete at the destination (Laws, 1998), the letters or postcards that they send home (Mellinger, 1994; Phillips, 1996), the complaints that they make to the authorities (Pearce and Moscardo, 1984) or to newspaper ombudsmen (Hannigan, 1980) and those they inscribe in visitor books or, via 'systematic lurking' (Dann et al., 1988, p. 25), overheard conversations conducted among themselves (Fjellman, 1992; Hanefors, 1994). In extreme situations, one might even wish to include tourist graffiti (Pearce and Moscardo, 1984) as indicators of utter dissatisfaction with a place which can act as warnings to fellow travellers, as one of us has found, for example, in the dire inscriptions adorning the toilet walls of Panama's central bus station (Dann, 1978, p. 43).

Imagery, too, is an area replete with possibility for qualitative tourism researchers, particularly those who accept the theoretical position that tourism is very much a postmodern phenomenon (Fjellman, 1992). Here, brochures, travelogues, advertisements and related publicity material come into their own, especially where they are open to different interpretation and readings (Dann, 1998a; Selwyn, 1993). More specifically, it is clearly both interesting and important to discover how destination people are portrayed (Dann, 1996b), either pictorially (Albers and James, 1988; Edwards, 1996) or textually (Dann, 1996c). On the other side of the coin, though comparatively neglected, are the various ways in which tourists are perceived by members of a host society. In this respect, there has been some innovative work on school children's drawings (Gamradt, 1995) and essays (Crick, 1989b; 1993). Such research is all the more fascinating with the appreciation that there is a greater methodological likelihood of obtaining less distorted versions of reality from uninhibited youngsters than are typically acquired from more cynical adults.

As to the actual behaviour of tourists, this facet of the vacational experience is strangely only occasionally monitored via the richly rewarding use of unobtrusive measures (Pizam, 1993; cf. Webb et al., 1966). More frequently, however, it is grasped through participant (Foster, 1986; Hanefors, 1994) and non-participant (Hartmann, 1988; Keul and Kuhberger, 1997) observational studies, sometimes in tandem with interviews (Bruner, 1994) which seek to capture respondents' explanations for their actions. Tours, for instance, are often joined by researchers (Fine and Speer, 1985; Seaton, forthcoming) in order to gauge reaction to 'sight sacralization' (MacCannell, 1989) and the selective way that history is interpreted by guides (Dahles, 1996; Katriel, 1994; Selwyn, 1996b). Geographers, in particular, are interested in touristic involvement with space and, in this regard, there have been several studies on cognitive mapping (Pearce, 1977; Walmesley and Jenkins, 1992). There has also been the odd ethnomethodological experiment which, via zany, candid camera type situations, has looked at the manner in which tourists live up to commonly held, though often incorrectly assumed, national stereotypes (Independent Television, 1998).

The list of topics is surely as endless as the fertile imagination of the researcher (Mills, 1959). The rather elementary point being made here, however, is that much of this creative research is more appropriately tackled by qualitative techniques than by pedestrian, quantitative methods.

THE MAJOR ADVANTAGES OF QUALITATIVE TOURISM RESEARCH

Returning once more to the earlier observation that research is only successful to the extent that it blends methodological sophistication with theoretical awareness (Dann *et al.*, 1988), perhaps the greatest advantage of qualitative methods is that they 'are particularly useful in theory construction', for exploring relationships and concepts rather than verifying existing hypotheses (Laws, 1998, p. 549), and in filling gaps in theory (Dooley, 1984, p. 268). Consequently, some argue (e.g. Peterson, 1987) that qualitative research is more suited to pilot investigations, the unstated implication being that quantitative methods will assume the senior role in the subsequent conducting of large sample surveys.

However, this rather limited view has been challenged by others (Jordan, 1997, p. 528) who argue that, since qualitative methods frequently yield more valid information than the reliable data typically yielded by quantitative techniques, they often can and should replace them. The crux of the matter thus turns on the importance attached to truth content or achieving what a study sets out to obtain, rather than the collection of similar responses to like stimuli.

In relation to the research process itself, qualitative methods may also be beneficial in gaining access to the field, particularly to 'hidden populations' who are perceived as deviant, carry a social stigma or represent 'a problem' to the host society (van Meter, 1990). A tourism example might include research conducted on bar girls in Thailand (Cohen, 1982; Phillips, 1996; Phillips and Dann, 1998). It would be patently quite meaningless to pass out questionnaires to these disadvantaged and marginalized young women, just as it would be to carry out a sample survey of drug users within a given destination population. Yet, the gradual establishment of necessary rapport can lead to the fruitful application of such qualitative techniques as conversation sampling and the analysis of correspondence. Relatedly, qualitative methods may be more appropriate for the examination of delicate topics. Jordan (1997), for instance, finds that discriminatory practices in tourism employment are far better handled through a small number of in-depth interviews than ever they might be via mailed questionnaires or a telephone survey. A similar conclusion could be reached regarding studies which seek to investigate questions of respondent identity. Rather than imposing a given theory on the subjects of investigation and then attempting to confirm or invalidate it, via qualitative methods, participant theory can be allowed to emerge through individual definitions of situations, an approach that is well suited to perspectives such as Symbolic Interactionism. This is the theoretical stance adopted by Phillips (forthcoming) and Karch and Dann (1981), for example, in relation to the issue of black masculinity as experienced by beachboys in Barbados.

Just as meanings are culturally constructed and contested, so too are they respectively assimilated or rejected diachronically. While quantitative techniques are more geared towards producing one-off snapshots of attitudes and activities within a determined period, or even on a particular day, qualitative measures are more processually oriented. They are thus quite appropriate for many longitudinal studies which require a focus on mental and behavioural development. In this connection, Pearce's (1993) notion of a travel career comes to mind, as also investigations that explore residents' reactions to tourists as they change along the course of the resort cycle.

Since many qualitative methods plan to capture the temporal dimension (and are therefore subject to the additional requirement of time sampling), it also follows that they can accumulate a greater depth of data than that customarily acquired via quantitative techniques based solely on sampling through space. Hence a simple 'yes' or 'no' answer obtained from the latter can be replaced by a greater sense of elaboration and distinction in the case of qualitative methods designed to trace evolution in thought. The ability to attain a more profound, and hence valid, level of meaning has acquired a number of designations from different qualitative researchers. Geertz (1973, p. 20), for instance, calls it 'thick description', while Denzin (1989, pp. 230–1) refers to it as 'subversive reading', Fjellman (1992, p. 284) as 'deep reading', and semioticians, such as Barthes (1984, p. 114) and his disciples, as 'second order' or 'connoted meaning'. Whatever the terminology, the underpinning approach is quite germane to the study of tourism promotion (Echtner, 1999) through diverse media (Dann, 1996a), as also to the various interpretations brought by different social actors to heritage attractions (Bruner, 1994).

Qualitative methods, too, since they are generally more freewheeling than quantitative techniques, are therefore more likely to alight upon instances of serendipity, unanticipated findings which may have the effect of modifying initial theory or even of refocusing an entire research project.

By the same token, qualitative methods, by virtue of their greater revelatory power, may also more tellingly highlight significant omissions than can quantitative methods. For instance, Bhattacharyya (1997) has relatedly discovered that popular guidebooks on India make little reference to the ordinary working lives of that country's inhabitants, and Urry (1990) claims that most of the pictorial content of tour operator brochures targeted at the British mass market tends to omit black persons, the elderly and those with physical disabilities. More ominously, perhaps, where particular groups are left out of a presentation (e.g., children in the publicity of some all-inclusive resorts), their significant omission may act as a covert form of social control, the message being that, if young couples really wish to enjoy themselves on holiday while in the company of fellow hedonists, they would be well advised to leave their tiresome offspring at home (Dann, 1996a). Qualitative methods tend to pick up these invisibles if only because the latter are incapable of discovery by the standardized anticipation of all outcomes so emblematic of quantitative techniques.

A STATE-OF-THE-ART MODEL OF QUALITATIVE TOURISM RESEARCH

In outlining an agenda that goes beyond the provision of mere typologies, Cohen (1988, p. 43) has proposed a tourism research programme 'which would simultaneously take account of and compare the tourist's psychological needs and experiences, the sociocultural features of tourist settings and the cultural symbols expressed in the touristic process'.

If these four basic elements are respectively translated into the main themes of motivation, satisfaction, impact/interaction and images of promotional communication (i.e., the essential ingredients of the field of tourism), and if they are further cross-tabulated with the principal players of contemporary tourism (tourists, the tourism industry and tourees (van den Berghe, 1994)), then Table 13.1 is yielded.

Here, it can be readily noted that cells 3, 5 and 9 are empty, indicating virtual absence of research in these areas. The remaining nine include typical examples of sources and techniques employed. Four of these cells (1, 2, 8 and 11) illustrate that many studies have been conducted. The other five (4, 6, 7, 10 and 12) show that, whereas some research has been carried out, there is still plenty of room for expansion.

Table 13.1 Qualitative tourism research: a state-of-the-art model

	Psychological Needs and Experiences		Sociocultural Features	Cultural Symbols/Images
Principal Players	Motivation	Satisfaction	Impact/ Interaction	Communication
Tourist	1. Reaction to: Promotion Conversations Interviews Photographs	2. Stories Diaries Conversations Letters Graffiti	3.	4. Internalization of Industry Images Photographs
Tourism Industry	5.	6. Interviews of Employees	7. Observation	8. On-site Guides Off-site Promotion (brochures, videos, advertisements, television, etc.)
Tourees	9.	10. Attitude Studies Interviews	11. Interviews Observation Newspapers Archival Research	12. Essays Drawings (of children)

Working round the left-hand side of the model, it can easily be seen how the motivation and satisfaction of tourists, service providers and locals are typically researched, underresearched or not researched as the case may be, and, if the former, the ways in which they are frequently explored (cf. section 2). The right-hand side of the model is slightly more complex since it incorporates an interactive dimension which comprises all three principal players. The third column relating to such interaction reveals that, whereas there are numerous (ethnographical) inquiries which explore the impact of tourists and tourism on the lives of destination people, and a few that examine the impact of tourism on industry personnel, apart from one or two early studies of xenophobia, stereotyping and the acquisition of cultural knowledge through interaction with hosts, there is practically nothing of a contemporary nature which investigates the effects on tourists resulting from their interaction with either industry personnel or with other members of the host society. Nor for that matter, and to the best of our knowledge, is there anything comprehensive and significant that has systematically examined the sociocultural consequences of tourists mixing with each other. Turning to the last column, it may be observed that the domain of communication through images (both pictorial and verbal) is very much the preserve of the industry as it seeks to portray both tourists and tourees (and very occasionally itself), and how this emphasis on *ego* and *alter* is reflected in the corresponding amounts of research conducted. Less work, by contrast, has been devoted to the images held by tourists of themselves, service providers and locals (although the last situation is certainly changing), and even fewer inquiries have been carried out on residents' perceptions of the visitors in their midst.

The model may therefore be considered useful to the degree that, not only does it provide a state-of-the-art appraisal of what has taken place in the last three decades of the twentieth century, but perhaps more importantly it points to gaps in incipient and cumulative knowledge, areas which may become more salient in the years ahead. It is this future outlook which constitutes the remainder of this brief presentation.

PROSPECTS OF QUALITATIVE
TOURISM RESEARCH FOR THE FUTURE

Although vacant cells in the model point to possible avenues of ulterior investigation, awareness of such gaps is not in itself a necessary or sufficient condition for their subsequent completion. There is an additional requirement for the willing acceptance of a proactive standpoint, along with the implications that such a position entails.

Elsewhere (Dann, 1999), and in greater detail, it has been argued that the future directions of tourism research reside in the adoption of one or more of three identified approaches – those of Toffler, Simmel and what has been termed 'open-ended work'. The first, epitomized in the writings of Hawkins (1993) and Ritchie (1993), typically employs variations of the Delphi technique to point to the probability and importance of events thought likely to affect tourism in the years ahead. The second emphasizes the perennial forms of tourist behaviour. By very definition, these essential qualities of strangerhood are time-transcendent and hence applicable as much to the future as to the past or present. The third approach focuses on 'areas for further research' which individuals typically highlight after reporting the results of their studies. After contextualizing their research problem (by way of a literature review of the past), they attempt to show how they have currently advanced the situation theoretically and methodologically in an original fashion. At the same time, they often acknowledge that present progress (or lack of progress) in turn leads to a further set of unanswered questions which they and others may wish to tackle in subsequent projects, projects that are literally projected from the present into the future. There are many ways of flagging their agenda and several have been identified under the headings of 'blind alleys', 'self-appropriation', 'reversing conventional wisdom', 'concept stretching', 'scope broadening', 'breaking out of the case', 'resolving paradoxes' and 'establishing new linkages' (Dann, 1999).

However, what has not been sufficiently emphasized is that, whichever of the three approaches is adopted, they are separately and collectively highly conducive to the qualitative treatment of research topics. For instance, if the Toffler approach is followed, it is clear that several of the changes identified by Ritchie (1993) and Hawkins (1993) will need qualitative investigation. Take, for example, the highly significant areas of resident responsive tourism, global lifestyles, developments in the field of health, technological innovation, socio-political arrangements, the preservation of heritage in the face of competing demand for natural resources, even the apparently simple questions of alteration in work patterns and gendered roles. All of these extremely likely occurrences will have greater or lesser impacts on tourists, destination people and the tourism industry of tomorrow. However, and more pertinent to the current argument, is the realization that every one of these topics requires qualitative treatment if it is to be satisfactorily explored, since each relates to life quality, surely a more important issue than the quantifiable standard of living.

Or again, if a Simmelian perspective is adopted, there are many areas ripe for investigation which derive from tourism as a form of strangerhood. The phenomenon of increasing urbanization, for instance, captured so tellingly in Simmel's (1950) essay on the metropolis, and a theme eminently appropriate to a study of future tourism trends, would additionally benefit from the qualitative examination of such related phenomena as attitudes to time, secrecy, friendship, authority and so on. Above all, there would be the ever-growing need to explore the corresponding reduction in freedom of generating societies as a unique condition for the expansion of tourism (Dann, 1997). Such a topic cannot be adequately tackled by asking respondents to complete the boxes of Likert scales seeking to measure degrees of authoritarianism. However, it can be dealt with more satisfactorily by using several qualitative techniques ranging from in-depth interviews to projective tests.

Finally, qualitative research is particularly appropriate to 'open-ended work'. In this regard, Lanfant (1995), for example, has argued that tourism academics should abandon such traditional and ethnocentric research props as conspicuous consumption, democratization, search for escape and, Selwyn (1996a) would add, the authenticity framework. Instead of leaning on these etic excuses for intellectual inertia, they should adopt an emic approach that allows the principal players to speak of their own situations within the context of tourism's increasingly becoming an international social fact. By taking the role of insider, and by allowing the voice of the silent Other to be heard (as Crick, 1994, has so convincingly argued), it not only suggests a qualitative approach; it demands one.

A parallel reversal of the conventional wisdom associated with 'closed work' can similarly lead to new lines of inquiry. The querying of the 'tourism as an agent of peace' rhetoric (Crick, 1989a) can lend support to those who investigate the increasingly close connection between tourism and war (Seaton, 1999; Smith, 1998), as well as to those who have relatedly identified 'dark tourism' as one of the most rapidly developing forms of tourism today and tomorrow (Dann, 1998b; Foley and Lennon, 1999; Seaton, 1996). Yet, a fascination with violent death and its emergence in a variety of tourist attractions can only be adequately tackled from a qualitative position. Seaton (forthcoming), for example, only became fully aware of the multiple ways that different types of visitors obtained diverse meanings from their patronizing battleground sites by actually joining one such tour group. In a like fashion, Hanefors (1994) only really discovered the utter dependency displayed by Swedish tourists on their courier by participating in a coach trip through Bulgaria and by listening to their conversations and interactive discussions. Had she just handed out office-generated questionnaires to her subjects as they stepped off the vehicle, she might have missed this important point altogether.

CONCLUSION

Arguing in a more general context, Berg (1989, p. 145) has suggested that:

> Qualitative methods . . . can result in either improved social scientific understanding or in meaningless gibberish.

In relation to qualitative tourism research, the preceding account endorses this appraisal. It has attempted to show that there are manifold opportunities for applying qualitative methods to the multifaceted, multimedia phenomenon of tourism. Moreover, for several of the identified topics, qualitative techniques have a unique contribution to make towards comprehending their trans-subjective nature. They cannot be adequately tackled by solely resorting to so-called objective, standardized statistical treatments imposed from outside. Nor is their importance sufficiently recognized if their various themes are simply regarded as constituting ancillary and mildly interesting issues to be explored in the preliminary stages of an inquiry rather than as research questions in their own right which should legitimately occupy an entire investigation.

However, this account, while agreeing with Berg's evaluation, has not fully examined the implications of his stark alternatives. Unlike Dann *et al.* (1988), who upset some people at the time by highlighting the weaknesses of researchers who overrelied on theory at the expense of method (the armchair types who shied away from the empirical testing of their ideas), placed too much emphasis on statistical technique to the detriment of insight (the number crunching brigade) or, worse still, those whose work was lacking in both theoretical awareness and method-ological sophistication (the collectors and disseminators of anecdotal material) – all of whom could be accused of being research deficient, if not actually producers of gibberish – this presentation has tried to focus on qualitative research that has managed to achieve a happy blend of theory and method.

Even so, and in spite of the several illustrative examples provided, a fuller evaluation of their worth has not been undertaken and still needs to be judged against the canons of the disciplines they claim to represent. Since tourism is still a field rather than a discipline, it is the application of theory and method germane to the specific social scientific discipline under which tourism is studied that must be assessed. This outstanding requirement is clearly easier to fulfil in the case of well-established disciplines within the social sciences (e.g., anthropology, psychology and sociology) than for later arrivals on the scene (e.g., business studies, marketing and management).[2]

As a corollary to this last point, and in spite of (as well as because of) an evident increase in qualitative tourism research, it is easy to predict a very real problem ahead for those who still adhere to quantitative methodologies and who wish to publish the results of their investigations. Recently, one of the leading journals in the field, *Annals of Tourism Research*, has let it be known that it will only be considering for publication articles that are social science based and do not rely on statistical techniques. While the first condition is quite in keeping with *Annals'* 'statement of purpose', the second, being an additional requirement, would seem to indicate that journal's awareness of and preference for the growing importance of qualitative methods in the social sciences. Faced with such rejection, potential authors favouring quantitative methods will thus be obliged to turn to alternative outlets for the publication of their material, a situation which could result in (if it has not already led to) a two-tier system of journals and even creeping elitism within the tourism academic community.

The full irony of such a state of affairs only becomes apparent with the realization that many contributors to tourism journals operate under a ranking system (such as the Research Assessment Exercise (RAE) in the United Kingdom) whereby, for the purpose of allocating quantities of government research funds to departments which have done measurably well, the quality of peer-reviewed journals is quantitatively assessed. However, an outlet such as *Annals of Tourism Research*, which currently receives a maximum score on the 5-point scale, would probably find such a rating procedure anathema. Instead, it would justifiably observe that, since academic papers in tourism can vary in quality even in the same issue of a quality journal, they should rather be evaluated on their innovative contribution to knowledge, i.e. their theoretical and methodological content – a criterion which is actually contained in the instructions to RAE inspectors, but one which is rarely applied (Cooper and Otley, 1998, p. 86).

We have thus surely reached a stage on entering the twenty-first century where the vicious circle given by the equation: quantitative research + quantitatively assessed publications = more funding for quantitative research, has to be seriously questioned and recast to reflect current reality. Just as tourism itself is not simply a numerical phenomenon whose success is solely measured in terms of body counts through destinational turnstiles, so too will a greater appreciation of tourism's qualitative attributes lead to parallel advances in their qualitative treatment.

NOTES

1. However, one possible survivor from this methodological meltdown is the realm of content analysis. This domain is perhaps the only one that successfully combines quantitative and qualitative approaches (Berno, 1996). It has been applied to areas as diverse as the literary theming of destinations to the different types of notices that tourists encounter. Even so, it is more than likely that its qualitative component will prevail over its quantitative dimension.
2. However, Faulkner and Ryan (1999) appear to regard tourism research and tourism management research as synonymous. Such a position is problematic, particularly since the papers which they have so admirably assembled for their special issue of *Tourism Management* devoted to methodology are clear examples of the former's calling into question the existence and viability of the latter.

REFERENCES

Albers, P. and James, W. (1988) 'Travel photography. A methodological approach'. *Annals of Tourism Research*, **15**, 134–58.

Ali, S. (1998) 'Research methodology: back to basics'. *ABAC Journal*, **18**(1), 75–98.

Babbie, E. (1995) *The Practice of Social Research* (7th edn). Belmont, Ca: Wadsworth.

Barthes, R. (1984) *Mythologies*. London: Paladin.

Berg, B. (1989) *Qualitative Research Methods for the Social Sciences*. Boston: Allyn and Bacon.

Berno, T. (1996) 'Cross-cultural research methods: content or context? A Cook Islands example'. In R. Butler and T. Hinch (eds) *Tourism and Indigenous Peoples*. London: Thomson Business Press, pp. 376–95.

Bhattacharyya, D. (1997) 'Mediating India: an analysis of a guidebook'. *Annals of Tourism Research*, **24**, 371–89.

Bruner, E. (1994) 'Abraham Lincoln as authentic reproduction: a critique of postmodernism'. *American Anthropologist*, **96**(2), 397–415.

Burns, P. and Holden, A. (1995) *Tourism. A New Perspective*. London: Prentice-Hall.

Chalfen, R. (1979) 'Photography's role in tourism: some unexplored relationships'. *Annals of Tourism Research*, **6**, 435–47.

Cohen, E. (1979) 'Rethinking the sociology of tourism'. *Annals of Tourism Research*, **6**, 18–35.

Cohen, E. (1982) 'Thai girls and farang men: the edge of ambiguity'. *Annals of Tourism Research*, **9**, 403–28.

Cohen, E. (1988) 'Traditions in the qualitative sociology of tourism'. *Annals of Tourism Research*, **15**, 29–45.

Cooper, C. and Otley, D. (1998) 'The 1996 Research Assessment Exercise for business and management'. *British Journal of Management*, **9**, 73–89.

Crick, M. (1989a) 'Representations of international tourism in the social sciences: sun, sex, sights, savings and servility'. *Annual Review of Anthropology*, **18**, 307–44.

Crick, M. (1989b) 'The hippy in Sri Lanka. A symbolic analysis of the imagery of school children in Kandy'. *Criticism, Heresy and Interpretation*, **3**, 37–54.

Crick, M. (1993) 'Obtaining information from a school-age sub-population in Sri Lanka'. In M. Crick and B. Geddes (eds) *Research Methods in the Field*. Geelong: Deakin University Press, pp. 162–85.

Crick, M. (1994) *Resplendent Sites, Discordant Voices. Sri Lankans and International Tourism*. Chur: Harwood Academic Publishers.

Dahles, H. (1996) 'The social construction of Mokum, tourism and the quest for local identity in Amsterdam'. In J. Boissevain (ed.) *Coping with Tourists. European Reactions to Mass Tourism*. Oxford: Berghahn Books, pp. 227–46.

Dann, G. (1978) 'Central America on the buses'. *The Bajan and South Caribbean*, February, 42–4.

Dann, G. (1988) 'Tourism research on the Caribbean: an evaluation'. *Leisure Sciences*, **10**, 261–80.

Dann, G. (1995) 'A socio-linguistic approach towards changing tourist imagery'. In R. Butler and D. Pearce (eds) *Change in Tourism: People, Places, Processes*. London: Routledge, pp. 114–36.

Dann, G. (1996a) *The Language of Tourism. A Sociolinguistic Perspective*. Wallingford: CAB International.

Dann, G. (1996b) 'The people of tourist brochures'. In T. Selwyn (ed.) *The Tourist Image. Myths and Myth Making in Tourism*. Chichester: Wiley, pp. 61–81.

Dann, G. (1996c) 'Images of destination people in travelogues'. In R. Butler and T. Hinch (eds) *Tourism and Indigenous Peoples*. London: International Thomson Business Press, pp. 349–75.

Dann, G. (1997) 'Tourist behaviour as controlled freedom'. In R. Bushell (ed.) *Tourism Research: Building a Better Industry. Proceedings of the Australian Tourism and Hospitality Research Conference*. Canberra: Bureau of Tourism Research, pp. 244–54.

Dann, G. (1998a) 'The pomo promo of tourism'. *Tourism, Culture and Communication*, **1**, 1–16.

Dann, G. (1998b) 'The dark side of tourism'. *Etudes et Rapports*, serie L, no. 14.

Dann, G. (1999) 'Theoretical issues for tourism's future: identifying the agenda'. In D. Pearce and R. Butler (eds) *Contemporary Issues in Tourism. Development*. London: Routledge, pp. 13–30.

Dann, G., Nash, D. and Pearce, P. (1988) 'Methodology in tourism research'. *Annals of Tourism Research*, **15**, 1–28.

Decrop, A. (1999) 'Triangulation in qualitative tourism research'. *Tourism Management*, **20**(1), 157–61.

Denzin, N. (1989) *The Research Act. A Theoretical Introduction to Sociological Methods* (3rd edn). Englewood Cliffs, NJ: Prentice-Hall.

Dooley, D. (1984) *Social Research Methods*. Englewood Cliffs: Prentice-Hall.

Echtner, C. (1999) 'The semiotic paradigm: implications for tourism research'. *Tourism Management*, **20**(1), 47–57.

Edwards, E. (1996) 'Postcards – greetings from another world'. In T. Selwyn (ed.) *The Tourist Image. Myths and Myth Making in Tourism*. Chichester: Wiley, pp. 197–221.

Faulkner, B. and Ryan, C. (1999) 'Editorial'. *Tourism Management*, **20**(2), 3–6.

Fine, E. and Speer, J. (1985) 'Tour guide performances as sight sacralization'. *Annals of Tourism Research*, **12**, 73–95.

Fjellman, S. (1992) *Vinyl Leaves. Walt Disney World and America*. Boulder: Westview Press.

Foley, M. and Lennon, J. (1999) *Dark Tourism*. London: Cassell.

Foster, G. (1986) 'South seas cruise. A case study of a short-lived society'. *Annals of Tourism Research*, **13**, 215–38.

Gamradt, J. (1995) 'Jamaican children's representations of tourism'. *Annals of Tourism Research*, **22**, 735–62.

Geertz, C. (1973) *The Interpretation of Cultures*. New York: Basic Books.

Glaser, B. and Strauss, A. (1967) *The Discovery of Grounded Theory: Strategies for Qualitative Research*. Chicago: Aldine.

Hanefors, M. (1994) 'Living the South: tourists as boundary makers and boundary markers'. Paper presented to the research committee on international tourism of the International Sociological Association, Bielefeld, 18–23 July.

Hanefors, M. and Larsson, L. (1993) 'Video strategies used by tour operators. What is really communicated?' *Tourism Management*, **14**(1), 27–33.

Hannigan, J. (1980) 'Reservations cancelled. Consumer complaints in the tourist industry'. *Annals of Tourism Research*, **7**, 366–84.

Hartmann, R. (1988) 'Combining field methods in tourism research'. *Annals of Tourism Research*, **15**, 88–105.

Hawkins, D. (1993) 'Global assessment of tourism policy: a process model'. In D. Pearce and R. Butler (eds) *Tourism Research. Critiques and Challenges*. London: Routledge, pp. 175–200.

Hollinshead, K. (1996) 'The tourism researcher as bricoleur: the new wealth and diversity of qualitative inquiry'. *Tourism Analysis*, **1**, 67–74.

Independent Television (1998) *The Tourist Trap*. ITV Channel 4.

Jackson, M., White, G. and Schmierer, C. (1996) 'Tourism experiences within an attributional framework'. *Annals of Tourism Research*, **23**, 798–810.

Jordan, F. (1997) 'An occupational hazard? Sex segregation in tourism employment'. *Tourism Management*, **18**(8), 525–34.

Karch, C. and Dann, G. (1981) 'Close encounters of the Third World'. *Human Relations*, **34**(4), 249–68.

Katriel, T. (1994) 'Performing the past: presentational styles in settlement museum interpretation', *Israel Social Science Research*, **9**(1–2), 1–26.

Keul, A. and Kuhberger, A. (1997) 'Tracking the Salzburg tourist'. *Annals of Tourism Research*, **24**, 1008–11.

Lanfant, M.-F. (1995) 'International tourism, internationalization and the challenge to identity'. In M.-F. Lanfant, J. Allcock and E. Bruner (eds) *International Tourism, Identity and Change*. London: Sage, pp. 24–43.

Laws, E. (1998) 'Conceptualizing visitor satisfaction management in heritage settings: an exploratory blueprinting analysis of Leeds Castle, Kent'. *Tourism Management*, **19**(6), 545–54.

MacCannell, D. (1989) *The Tourist. A New Theory of the Leisure Class* (2nd edn). New York: Schocken Books.

Markwell, K. (1997) 'Dimensions of photography in a nature-based tour'. *Annals of Tourism Research*, **24**, 131–55.

Maslow, A. (1954) *Motivation and Personality*. New York: Harper.

Mellinger, W. (1994) 'Toward a critical analysis of tourism representations'. *Annals of Tourism Research*, **21**, 756–79.

Mills, C. (1959) *The Sociological Imagination*. New York: Grove Press.

Moore, K. (1997) 'Tourism: escape or virtual escape?' Paper presented to the Australian Tourism and Hospitality Research Conference, Sydney, 6–9 July.

O'Barr, W. (1994) *Culture and the Ad. Exploring Otherness in the World of Advertising*. Boulder: Westview Press.

Pearce, P. (1977) 'Mental souvenirs: a study of tourists and their city maps'. *Australian Journal of Psychology*, **29**, 203–10.

Pearce, P. (1991) 'Travel stories: an analysis of self-disclosure in terms of story structure, valence and audience characteristics'. *Australian Psychologist*, **26**(3), 172–5.

Pearce, P. (1993) 'Fundamentals of tourist motivation'. In D. Pearce and R. Butler (eds) *Tourism Research. Critiques and Challenges*. London: Routledge, pp. 113–34.

Pearce, P. and Caltabiano, M. (1983) 'Inferring travel motivation from travellers' experiences'. *Journal of Travel Research*, **22**, 16–20.

Pearce, P. and Moscardo, G. (1984) 'Making sense of tourists' complaints'. *Tourism Management*, **5**(1), 20–3.

Peterson, K. (1987) 'Qualitative research methods for the travel and tourism industry'. In J. Ritchie and C. A. Goeldner (eds) *Travel, Tourism and Hospitality Research. Handbook for Managers and Researchers*. Chichester: Wiley, pp. 433–8.

Phillips, J. (1996) 'Bar girls in Bangkok. A study of open-ended prostitution'. Unpublished MPhil thesis, University of the West Indies, Barbados.

Phillips, J. (forthcoming) 'Tourist oriented prostitution in Barbados: the case of the beachboy and the white female tourist'. In K. Kempadoo (ed.) *Sun, Sex and Gold. Tourism and Sex Work in the Caribbean*. Boulder: Rowman and Littlefield.

Phillips, J. and Dann, G. (1998) 'Bar girls in central Bangkok: prostitution as entrepreneurship'. In M. Oppermann (ed.) *Sex Tourism and Prostitution. Aspects of Leisure, Recreation and Work*. New York: Cognizant Communication Corporation, pp. 60–70.

Pizam, A. (1993) 'Using unobtrusive measures in tourism research'. Paper presented to the International Academy for the Study of Tourism, Sejong Hotel, Seoul, July.

Reid, L. and Reid, S. (1993) 'Communicating tourism supplier services: building repeat visitor relationships'. *Journal of Travel and Tourism Marketing*, **2**(2/3), 3–19.

Riley, R. (1996) 'Revealing socially constructed knowledge through quasi-structured interviews and grounded theory analysis'. *Journal of Travel and Tourism Marketing*, **5**(1/2), 21–40.

Ritchie, J. (1993) 'Tourism research – policy and managerial priorities for the 1990s and beyond'. In D. Pearce and R. Butler (eds) *Tourism Research. Critiques and Challenges*. London: Routledge, pp. 201–16.

Ryan, C. (1995a) 'Learning about tourists from conversations: the over 55's in Majorca'. *Tourism Management*, **16**(3), 207–15.

Ryan, C. (1995b) *Researching Tourism Satisfaction: Issues, Concepts, Problems*. London: Routledge.

Ryan, C. (1997) 'Tourism – a mature subject discipline?' *Pacific Tourism Review*, **1**(1), 3–5.

Seaton, A. (1994) 'Tourist maps and the promotion of destination image'. *Proceedings of Research and Academic Papers*, Vol. vi. Society of Educators in Travel and Tourism of America, pp. 168–84.

Seaton, A. (1996) 'Guided by the dark: from thanatopsis to thanatourism'. *International Journal of Heritage Studies*, **2**(4), 234–44.

Seaton, A. (1999) 'War and thanatourism: Waterloo 1815–1914'. *Annals of Tourism Research*, **26**, 130–58.

Seaton, A. (forthcoming) 'Another weekend away looking for dead bodies: an interpretive study of battlefield tourism on the Somme and in Flanders'. *Tourism Recreation Research*.

Selwyn, T. (1993) 'Peter Pan in South East Asia. Views from the brochures'. In M. Hitchcock, V. King and M. Parnwell (eds) *Tourism in South East Asia*. London: Routledge, pp. 117–37.

Selwyn, T. (1996a) 'Introduction'. In T. Selwyn (ed.) *The Tourist Image. Myths and Myth Making in Tourism*. Chichester: Wiley, pp. 1–32.

Selwyn, T. 1996b) 'Atmospheric notes from the fields: reflections on myth-collecting tours'. In T. Selwyn (ed.) *The Tourist Image. Myths and Myth Making in Tourism*. Chichester: Wiley, pp. 147–61.

Simmel, G. (1950) In K. Wolff (ed.) *The Sociology of Georg Simmel*. Free Press: Glencoe.

Small, J. (1999) 'Memory work. A method for researching women's tourist experiences'. *Tourism Management*, **20**(1), 25–35.

Smith, V. (1998) 'War and tourism. An American ethnography'. *Annals of Tourism Research*, **25**, 202–27.

Thurot, J. and Thurot, G. (1983) 'The ideology of class and tourism. Confronting the discourse of advertising'. *Annals of Tourism Research*, **10**, 173–89.

Urry, J. (1990) *The Tourist Gaze. Leisure and Travel in Contemporary Societies*. London: Sage.

Uzzell, D. (1984) 'An alternative structuralist approach to the psychology of tourism marketing'. *Annals of Tourism Research*, **11**, 79–99.

van den Berghe, P. (1994) *The Quest for the Other. Ethnic Tourism in San Cristobal, Mexico*. Seattle: University of Washington Press.

van Meter, K. (1990) 'Sampling and cross-classification analysis in international social research'. In E. Oyen (ed.) *Comparative Methodology. Theory and Practice in International Social Research*. London: Sage, pp. 172–86.

Walle, A. (1996) 'Habits of thought and cultural tourism'. *Annals of Tourism Research*, **23**, 874–90.

Walle, A. (1997) 'Quantitative versus qualitative tourism research'. *Annals of Tourism Research*, **24**, 524–36.

Walmesley, D. and Jenkins, J. (1992) 'Tourism cognitive mapping of unfamiliar environments'. *Annals of Tourism Research*, **19**, 268–86.

Webb, E., Campbell, P., Schwartz, R. and Sechrest, L. (1966) *Unobtrusive Measures: Non-Reactive Research in the Social Sciences*. Chicago: Rand McNally.

Weber, M. (1968) *The Theory of Social and Economic Organization*, trans. A. Henderson and T. Parsons. New York: Free Press.

Weightman, B. (1987) 'Third World tour landscapes'. *Annals of Tourism Research*, **14**, 227–39.

CHAPTER 14

Tourist Behaviour Research – the Role of 'I' and Neural Networks

Chris Ryan

INTRODUCTION

The original brief for this chapter was to write something about future directions of tourism research. After some thought, I have to admit to being defeated! So, this chapter is an attempt to draw together two themes – one that has been recently to the fore in the considerations of tourism researchers while the second has just begun to make its presence felt. Thus this chapter falls primarily into three parts. First, it discusses the issue of subjectivity within tourism research, arguing that subjectivity is equally part of both the tourism experience and the research process, even within those studies that may be classified as positivistic. Second, the chapter will review that part of artificial intelligence research that is beginning to make its presence known in the tourism research literature, namely the use of neural networks. Finally, it will muse about whether any relationship actually exists between these disparate subjects, and whether there is value in the topic as a future research direction.

Within tourism research, as in other disciplines, a debate has occurred about the nature of the subject as a discipline, and associated with this, a discussion about pertinent research methodologies. For example, Walle briefly reviews issues about the emic and etic within anthropological approaches to tourism, and writes of how 'scholars in various disciplines have simultaneously attempted to reconcile the Achilles Heel of science with the heroic flaws of art' (Walle, 1997, p. 525). In the 1998 and 1999 Conferences of the Council of Australian Universities in Tourism and Hospitality Education, plenary sessions have debated paradigms of tourism following the terminology of Kuhn (1970). Philip Pearce is of the view that tourism is in a pre-paradigmatic state, while Bill Faulkner has sought a meta-narrative that embraces different aspects of the subject in a multi-paradigmatic approach. It is my own view that the search for a paradigm is modernistic and not entirely appropriate for a subject that exists, simultaneously, in pre-modern, modern and postmodernistic worlds. However, I think all three of us would agree that it behoves us as researchers to be well practised in the techniques we employ and to consider relationships between, and advantages and disadvantages of, each of the main approaches involved in social science research. There is an interest in research methodologies and paradigms, and this is amply illustrated by various special issues of the tourism and leisure journals which have contained articles or special issues on research methods and concepts (e.g. see D'Amore, 1997; Ryan and Faulkner, 1999). It is certainly true that the techniques used for analysing data are becoming more sophisticated, whether for example one cites Seddighi and Shearing (1997) and their use of co-integration in examining the demand for tourism in Northumbria, or in the semiotic analysis of a commentator like Hollinshead (1999) on the missing voices in the interpretation of the Alamo. It is also my suspicion that what is true of leisure studies is also true of tourism studies, namely that there is an increasing proportion of studies based upon qualitative research methods (Weissinger *et al.*, 1997).

It is in this spirit that this chapter attempts what may in fact be impossible, namely to seek an integration of qualitative and quantitative research methods, albeit from a narrow perspective. More precisely, it addresses issues of subjectivity. It begins by highlighting the role of subjectivity as the subject of research when considering tourist behaviours. It then argues that subjectivity is present on the part of the researcher through a process of reflection. Finally, it discusses how this process of reflection on part of both the researched and the researcher might be approached through conventional quantitative means and it suggests that neural modelling might present one approach. It should be noted that I do not necessarily equate qualitative research with non-positivistic research. As I have argued (Ryan, 1999a), phenomenographic research can be located within a postpositivistic ontology and epistemology in that a consensus of objectivity about the subject studied could be held to exist by the researcher who uses such an approach..

SUBJECTIVITY IN TOURISM

It will be noted that, contrary to the tradition of social science espoused by, for example, Jafar Jafari in his guidelines to contributors to *Annals of Tourism*, I have used the personal pronoun, 'I'. This is because this paper is a personal examination of the subject, and thus in terms of its integrity, the use of the personal pronoun appears justified. This usage within a culture of research, informed by work within Maoridom, will be commented upon below. Further, I must admit to, at times, agreeing with Stoller when, at the end of his study of pornography, he wrote:

With more hope that human behavior will become less malignant if we all get insight – where id was, there shall ego be? – I could enthuse that the search to understand is wonderful, and, piling on one last cliché, to agree: yes, Virginia, there is a Santa Clause.

No such luck. Logic is an idiot's delight. (Stoller, 1991, p. 226)

Given the traditional linkage between tourism and sex wherein the latter is the fourth 'S', it is surely not too fanciful to conclude that parallels exist between tourism and prostitution. Tourism is about fantasy, relaxation, the exotic if not erotic, and is often concerned, at an individual level, with id and ego if not hedonism. Whether environment and culture are prostituted for economics is a judgement that some other writers may wish to make. Hence I will argue that Stoller's observation is pertinent to tourism, and that its imperative has been recognized by other writers and commentators. 'Logic as an idiot's delight' thus has implications for the process of research as well as that which is researched. It can be objected that in business one might think that logic would be the dominant domain – but how then does one explain the nature of the British mass package holiday industry which at varying periods has taught its clientele to book late, to make judgements based on the lowest price and which has been characterized by low profit margins and varying fortunes as, on more than one occasion, the then second largest company has been bankrupted. Again, politicians seek to obtain mega-events and on occasions have left their cities with debts and excessive hotel capacity that has taken years to be removed. Hall (1992, 1994, 1997) has explained the love affair of politicians with mega-events as a search for simplicity – mega-events have a defined start and end when so much else is confusion and doubt. One might conclude that logic seems but one competing voice amongst claims of nationalism, image, feel-good factors, think big scenarios and other like factors. And, of course, one can be totally logical in argument when proceeding from a flawed initial assumption.

SUBJECTIVITY (AND VALUES) IN TOURISM RESEARCH

Does such an observation apply to tourism research? Learning about 'things', about the phenomenon that is termed tourism, is to learn not only about the multiplicity of voices belonging to the stakeholders directly involved in tourism but also other things. I can identify at least three forms of learning which are involved in tourism research. First, hopefully, something is learnt about the subject of study. Second, something is learnt about the process of learning itself, or at least about the research methodology that is being used. Finally, albeit perhaps more slowly, something is learnt about oneself. For example, in his study about tourists on a guided tour, Bruner observed that:

My double role as a tour guide serving tourists, and as an ethnographer studying them, placed me in an interstitual position between touristic and ethnographic discourse, and I must admit that I had not been aware of the ambiguities of the position in which I placed myself. As ethnographer I wanted to learn how tourists experienced the sites, but as tour guide my task was to structure that experience. . . . My talk mediated their experience and in a sense, I found myself studying myself. (Bruner, 1995, p. 230)

It would be my contention that such processes of learning of self are not restricted to ethnographic research, although it is in such research processes that I have had to grapple most intimately with the complexities of 'truths' observed, revealed and hinted at in the process of research. In 1999 a co-participant and I wrote in a paper relating to sex tourism:

The past and current involvement of the writers as friends, and as stripper and observer, mean their view is that of insider and outsider, but above all are the views of participants. The act of participation is the source of the validity of the views expressed, and acts as the boundary, which limit the meanings of those views. (Ryan and Martin, 1999, p. 200)

This view implicitly argues that the stance adopted was not that of positivism, postpositivism and nor was it that of critical theory. Rather it, at best, viewed research as an attempt to construct a text from the observed situation. Such constructions underlie, I would contend, all research efforts, including studies often categorized as empirical and positivistic. For example, a significant theme within the stream of literature relating to tourist motivations and behaviours is dependent upon various forms of psychometric testing, although subject to the caveat that rarely have the testers sought to utilize the personality tests devised by psychologists like Eynsenck or Cattell (Jackson *et al.*, 1999). Yet tourism, services marketing and leisure studies have their own equivalents, much cited and subjected to testing in order to ensure that the results of the original researchers can be replicated. Such examples would include the SERVQUAL instrument of Parasuraman, Zeithaml and Berry (1985, 1988, 1994a, 1994b), the Leisure Motivation Scale of Beard and Ragheb (1980, 1983), Plog's (1977, 1990) tests for allocentricism and psychocentrism and, arguably, Philip Pearce's Travel Career Scale (Pearce, 1988, 1991, 1993, 1996; Ryan, 1998), to mention but four. Each has given rise to a significant research output as researchers have sought to replicate the instruments, the dimensions and the findings with varying degrees of success. Yet, I long ago formed a conclusion that in many instances what the application of such scales did was simply to assess the consistency of response of the respondent. For example, if the item 'The travel agency will have up-to-date equipment and technology' correlated highly with the item 'The physical facilities at the travel agency will be visually appealing' on a SERVQUAL scale, then it should be of no surprise to learn that a factor analysis would identify a dimension, which in this case was labelled 'Tangibles' (Ryan and Cliff, 1997). I suspect that in most instances respondents would tend to provide similar scores on these items when considering a specific service situation, and in some senses the more interesting research conundrum would be if respondents did not so answer.

When it is further considered that such scales use items that are known to discriminate most powerfully between groups of respondents and patterns of response, then the underlying tendency to high correlation and the identification of a factor is emphasized even more. So, for example, if we found in a tourism situation a group of tourists who did not attach importance to tangible components and another group that did, the former would score the tangible items of the SERVQUAL scale quite lowly while the latter would score the items highly. Correlation between the different items that comprise the tangibles dimension of the SERVQUAL scale would thus be high and the factor easily ascertained using factor analysis commands on statistical software. Additionally, an application of cluster analysis commands would reveal that the total sample could be clearly divided into sub-samples that, using t-tests or ANOVA, possess differences in mean scores that are 'statistically significant'. This process would be regarded as being of use because it confirmed the SERVQUAL scale and provided marketing information as to the size of niche markets. The process would also be satisfying to the researcher for the same reasons. Equally this exercise would remain mute about the more interesting and possibly more 'real' research issues.

The 'real' replication research questions which need to be examined are those that are rarely undertaken. In the instances cited above, the original researchers undertook many hours of prior research before constructing their scales. Focus groups were held to aid the identification of key themes. Long lists of questions were formulated and tested on colleagues, used in piloted studies and then finally reduced in number to form the scales with which we are familiar. Underlying these procedures are several acts of interpretation. The respondents' interpretation of the items with which they were faced, the researchers' interpretation of and classification of comments made in focus groups and, of course, the interpretation of the statistics. Once past basic descriptive statistics, the interpretation of such data involves value judgements based upon experience. What constitutes outliers? Which number of clusters most clearly represents a summary of attitudes? Tests like Cronbach's alpha, the citing of eigenvalues and weightings – in many cases these are used to buttress the decision to select a choice from competing alternatives thought to be less optimal. In the case of mathematical modelling of attitudes through the use of techniques like linear structural equations (Lisrel), the value judgements of the researcher become even more clear in the process if not in the reporting of the findings (Reisinger and Turner, 1999). Throughout this process of modelling relationships the researcher is making value judgements about whether the results are true to the patterns of response – do they make 'sense'? I suspect there have certainly been many unreported instances where, when using atheoretical 'ad hoc' instruments such analyses do produce factors for which we use the time-honoured phrase – 'the resulting factor was difficult to interpret'.

Therefore, it can be argued, the 'real' replication of the scales being used lies not in the application of the scales to a sample and a replication of statistically defined factors, but in an attempt to replicate the emergence of dimensions through focus group work. Would replication of the processes of focus groups, repeating testing of the wording of items with colleagues – would all of these things lead to the same questions being used to construct a scale that sought to measure the same things? One suspects 'no' from such work as that of Robson and Wardle (1988) (who analysed the impact of the presence of an observer on a focus group), but equally I am not sure if in one sense it would matter overmuch.

Why this comment? Taking as an example the research undertaken by academics into the motivations of tourists, it is easy to be critical when adopting the stance of a company wishing to understand their clientele better. Unless our samples are derived from national tourist organizations, many samples, particularly by academic researchers outside of the United States, are comparatively small. Some are atheoretical. This latter criticism might be made also of the large samples used by national tourist organizations. For example, the research commissioned jointly by the New Zealand Tourism Board and the Australian Tourist Commission into the attitudes of Asian markets (e.g. New Zealand Tourism Board, 1992) towards those two countries contained long checklists of what were thought to be important. However, the study did not incorporate a structured view of measurement attitude, for example that associated with Fishbein and the importance-evaluation approach (e.g. Vaske et al., 1996). Academic researchers in this area are not immune from criticism. As noted they have not sought replication, either in terms of longitudinal studies or of specific research tools (Pearce, D., 1993). But yet! There is a commonality that, to my mind, has emerged. Tourists wish to relax, to have time with their families, to learn, to see new places, to have 'adventures' – these and similar motivations emerge time and time again. It might be said that it did not need much research to discover this. But of course the issue is the context within which these motivations arise, the importance of each motive to which groups of people under what conditions and, from the psychologist's viewpoint, how the satisfaction of these motives is incorporated into self-concepts and modes of current and future behaviour. The practical outcome is the design of better tourism products at the site or activity level. In short, I am arguing that the possible importance of any research is the context within which it is undertaken. However, these contexts are often specific to place, activity, time and people – and thus while comparisons inform, we need continually to monitor to understand better how these variables of place, activity, time and people influence the generality of results that may be found. But is the researcher part of the context?

Schechner wrote of ritualistic events that:

> A person sees the event: he sees himself seeing the event; he sees himself seeing others who are seeing the event and who, maybe, see themselves seeing the event. Thus there is the performance, the performers, the spectators; and the spectator of the spectators; and the self-seeing self that can be performer or spectator or spectator of spectators. (Schechner, 1982, p. 297)

I have often felt that is true of the researcher. It is true of quantitative research as well as more ethnographic research. In 1996 and again in 1997 a colleague, Dr Jeremy Huyton, and I, sat at various locations in the Northern Territory of Australia waiting for potential respondents to complete our questionnaires. While the results have been quantitative studies involving techniques like cluster analysis and Lisrel (Ryan and Huyton, 1998, 1999), none the less we performed a ritual role of introducing ourselves, explaining the research, leaving questionnaires with respondents, collecting questionnaires, thanking people, listening to their comments, making notes. We performed, a performance legitimized, nay, enhanced, by the use of our university status to persuade people to complete a long questionnaire. But as performers we were also spectators as we watched people complete the forms, discuss issues with their partners and perhaps look at their watches as they realized it just might take a little longer than they at first imagined.

But as performers in the research process we brought with us our past experiences, and our subjectivities. Accordingly, to speak and write of participation in the research process requires a revelation of self – as I say to my students, it is necessary to be aware of the 'bees in the bonnet' of the researcher if we are to make sense of the findings. Within the tradition of Western academic, writing a statement of self is generally not deemed appropriate, but it is of interest to note that this is changing. Again, to cite Stoller:

> It is obvious that one's observations are not the same as reality (whatever that is) but are only one's private versions of reality; that the person observing the observer – such as the reader – needs also to know about the observer in the hope that biases can be understood; that what we publicly present of our data is shaped by our personalities and by who we imagine our audience to be; that is it is less shameful to admit than ignore prejudices, for with the admission, the reader at least has a way to judge what we say. . . . Data are conditional; a fact is not a fact without being a fantasy. (Stoller, 1991, p. 4)

Thus, in the field of tourism research, Dann clearly admitted his preference when discussing theoretical constructs of tourism. He wrote:

> One's own point of view lies closest to the intermediary group, because it is based on the premise that eclecticism is the most viable approach towards theory in general, and tourism theory in particular. (Dann, 1998, p. 3)

Dann introduces in his article a number of personal observations. That, for example, postmodernity is epitomized by and perhaps coincides with the life and times of 'The King', Elvis Presley. The King lives on in simulcra, record sales and visitor numbers to Graceland (Dann, 1998, p. 2). Yet Graham is still constrained by an academic tradition where the 'I' is 'One' and the use of the passive voice is de rigueur. Other cultures do not have this problem. Living now in New Zealand I am only too aware that when Maori stand to speak, they commence with a recitation of their *whakapapa*. This term is generally translated as a statement of genealogy, but it is more than that. It is a statement of identity through the people and land with which the individual identifies, and thereby the link between the speaker and the past and generations yet to come is established.

So what is my *whakapapa* in my view of tourism research? I have come to realize that my views of tourism were shaped by a childhood spent on the beaches of the Gower Peninsular in South Wales where and when the writings of Dylan Thomas described an everyday experience to which I could easily relate. Yet, although born there, because my parents moved to Croydon to the south of London, these experiences repeated through childhood summers when I visited my grandmother meant that I was a but a visitor in a country with which I strongly identified. Now, when I visit my mother who returned many years ago to the Mumbles, I am still a stranger. During the period of my youth the motorways were built and what were deserted roads and beaches became filled with adenoidal accents of Brummies and others. I saw Dick Butler's Tourist Life Cycle Theory being re-enacted before my eyes before I had heard of either the theory or Dick. Add to this the fact of being brought up a Catholic in a land of Methodist chapels, and it can be seen that the role of *flâneur* was one that came easily to me. It is a role that also suited me initially as a researcher.

So, does this influence me when I am engaged in quantitative research that might be thought to be immune from such considerations? Let me return to my example of our laying in wait for respondents in the Northern Territory. During this time Jeremy and I observed and we became infused with the nature of the place. For several days we passed by the exhibits at Uluru-Kata Tjuta Cultural Centre and observed the interactions of tourists with Aboriginal people who gave displays. We saw, and partook to some extent, of the activities in which tourists engage. And we heard the stories of people who wished to bend our ears. Was this all without influence? It is difficult to say 'no'. It is equally difficult to say 'yes'. We don't know is the answer. But how could this influence the calculations of statistical evidence? Let us consider the processes of multivariate analysis. As anyone knows who has undertaken factor and cluster analysis, there comes a time when a decision is made as to the numbers of clusters and factors thought to exist. Is this purely an objective exercise? To cite Everitt and Dunn when they discuss principal component analysis in their book, *Applied Multivariate Data Analysis*,

> It must be emphasised that no mathematical method is, or could be, designed to give physically meaningful results. If a mathematical expression of this sort has an obvious physical meaning, it must be attributed to lucky chance, or to the fact that the data have a strongly marked structure that shows up in the analysis. Even in the latter case, quite small sampling fluctuations can upset the interpretation; for example the first two principal components may appear in reverse order, or may become confused altogether. *Reification, then, requires considerable skill and experience if it is to give a true picture of the physical meaning of the data.* (Everitt and Dunn, 1991, pp. 53–4; my italics)

Yet for Kline, reification is a potential error to be avoided. He notes that just because a latent variable is assigned a particular label, it 'does not mean that the hypothetical construct is understood or even correctly named' (Kline, 1998, p. 191). Kline continues that it must not be believed that the hypothetical construct must correspond to the real thing. However, if the latent hypothetical construct has no relationship with 'real' things, it may be asked, what is the value of the hypothesis?

The issue might arise as to whether, in our examination of the data, we unconsciously looked for clusters of visitors that matched our subjective perception of what visitors were doing. We have concluded from other work that visitors are not lay anthropologists, that many visitors who express an interest in Aboriginal culture do so within a context of their perceptions of what signifies 'The Outback' of Australia (Ryan and Huyton, 1999). It is a conclusion supported by other researchers (Murphy, 1997; Jenkins, 1998). Imagery is carried through into behavioural patterns. The perceptions that visitors possess, derived from whatever sources, are matched with their own motivations, inclinations and the role of serendipity to form actions. And we the observers may interpret these actions through our own perceptual gaze. And, as observers in the discipline of tourism, we are caught within our own discipline's categories of who tourists are. Yet, as Dann and Cohen (1996) observe, the typologies are still heuristic, and that fact alone indicates that the sociology (and by implication I might argue) the study of tourism still lacks 'powerful theoretical and analytical equipment, [and] is still very much in its infancy' (Dann and Cohen, 1996, p. 303). Urry, however, offers the perspective that among the myths of sociology is one that as a discipline it actually possesses a 'unity, coherence and common tradition' (Urry, 1995,

p. 33). Rather, argues Urry, it is parasitic and feeds off its neighbouring disciplines for its development. How much more is this true of tourism? Further, argues Urry (1995), the main characteristic of tourism is that from its origins of the social organization of travel born of modernism, it adds an aesthetic reflexity which goes beyond a cognitive and normative reflexity associated with a Habermasian tradition (1979, 1981). Urry concludes

> Travel and tourism thus transform the modern and postmodern subject. This has been shown with regard to new technologies of transportation, novel ways of socially organising travel, the growth of an aesthetic reflexity, the development of 'interpretation' in the travel industry, changes in the nature of consumption, and the 'end of tourism' *per se*. . . . Tourism is nowhere and yet everywhere. (Urry, 1995, p. 150)

Part of the reflexity can be generated by the researcher asking questions. This was brought home forcibly to me with research undertaken by Palmer (1998) in Kakadu National Park in Northern Australia. The very fact of being asked whether exposure to an Aboriginal cultural centre actually changed respondents' views on Aboriginal land claims forced them to think more about what they had seen. The process of articulation of their previously unbidden thoughts had the unexpected by-product of enhancing the satisfaction derived from their visit.

Hence, given the potential nature of tourism as an experience of reflexity, or 'reinterpretation' of what is viewed, the role of subjectivity becomes incorporated into the research process as the gaze of the researcher meets the gaze of the tourist. While I have characterized phenomenographic research as postpositivistic (Ryan, 1999a), Dann and Cohen (1996) argued that the 'I–thou' relationship of phenomenology proved useful in examining changing guest–host encounters. The same might be said of tourist–researcher relationships. The research process can hence be modelled as one where the subjectivities of tourist experience and the reinterpretation of those subjectivities in subsequent recall by tourists meet the gaze of the researcher who brings his or her own subjectivities. These latter subjectivities are born of (a) experience of being a tourist themselves, (b) being a *flâneur*, (c) past experience of research, (d) commitment to producing 'results', (e) commitment to making 'sense' of the observed and (f) general life experience.

Of course, within the wider social sciences this debate is not new. Indeed, in a review of this script Dann commented that classical social theory would recognize that much of this debate is about values and not merely subjectivity as an abstract divorced from judgement. For example, in the early years of the twentieth century Weber specifically distinguished between existential and normative knowledge and noted that the scientific treatment of value judgements may not only 'understand and empathically analyze (*nacherleben*) the desired ends and the ideals which underlie them; it can also judge them critically' (1904/1993, p. 125).

NEURAL NETWORKS – MIMIC OF THE HUMAN BRAIN

For those like myself used to generating research through quantitative techniques, the issue of subjectivity and its associated values poses a considerable challenge. Aware of subjectivity as the subject of the research, and the subjectivity of the research process, one can either treat that latter subjectivity as insidious, or as a source of illumination. On the other hand, perhaps what those based in qualitative research traditions have failed to appreciate is just how much quantitative researchers have sought to develop new modes of analysis as a development of neo-positivism (Maxim, 1999). These are many, and Russell and Faulkner (1997, 1999) and McKercher (1999), for example, have drawn our attention to at least the conceptual if not the mathematical modelling of chaos theory as an aid to better understanding some aspects of tourism. This author has sought to use neural modelling in some aspects of his own research (e.g. Ryan, 1999b). Before assessing whether this is of help, let us first outline some facets of neural modelling.

Essentially neural modelling seeks to mimic the functioning of the human brain. Unlike techniques such as non-linear regression, neural networks do not require the a priori assumption of the functional form of the model (linear, first-order polynomial, logarithmic et cetera). Unlike expert systems and fuzzy logic they do not require an elicitation of expert knowledge, which is particularly useful when a large number of variables are being considered (Petri et al., 1998). Neural networks, which may be described as a subset of the science of artificial intelligence, have been used in a range of applications. These include the outcomes of battles (Glovier, 1997), human performance under varying conditions (Hedgepeth, 1995) and investment strategies (Cheng et al., 1997). They have also been used to forecast tourist flows and behaviours (Pattie and Snyder, 1996; Law and Au, 2000).

Caudill and Butler (1990, pp. 7–8) list the characteristics of neural networks thus:

a. simple processing elements (neurodes) communicate with each other through a rich set of interconnections;
b. memories are represented by variable patterns of weighted neurodes in changing patterns of communication;
c. neural networks are not programmed – they learn;
d. operations are the functions of structures of connections, transfer functions of neurodes and learning laws;
e. neural networks act as an associative memory; they can retrieve information from partially incorrect, noisy or incomplete cues;
f. a neural network can generalize;
g. a neural network is fault tolerant; it can continue as neurodes and connections become defective. It exhibits 'graceful degradation';

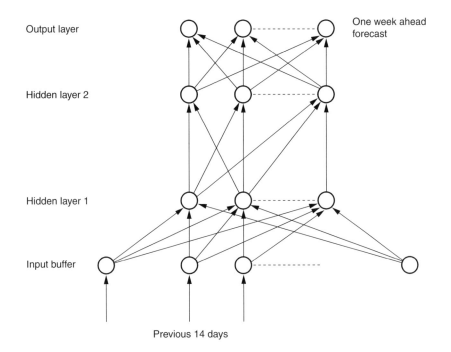

Figure 14.1 A neural network

h. a neural network acts as a processor for time-dependent spatial patterns;
i. a neural network can be self-organizing.

An example of a network is shown in Figure 14.1. This includes two 'hidden layers' which might be said to represent the interface between information being received and subsequent behaviour. It represents a learning situation where the evidence of the past fourteen days is being used to predict behaviour in the next week. In forecasting visitor behaviour to National Parks in the United States, Pattie and Snyder (1996) noted that the fundamental components of such a model include:

i the current processing element (node)
j a processing element that i is connected to
W_{ij} the weight connecting processing element j to processing element i
X_j the output of the processing element from which the connection originates
I_i the result of the summation function
t_j threshold value
F_{th} threshold function
e_j error associated with element j
LR learning rate
d_j desired output for element j

Y_j actual output of element j

M momentum factor

The output of the jth neurode in any layer is described by a summation function (U_j, the sum of inputs from the activated connecting neurodes) and an activation function (A_j, strength of communication which rests on weighting and transfer functions). For every node, j, in a layer of each of the i inputs, X_i, to that layer is multiplied by a previously established weight, W_{ij}. These are all summed together, i.e.

$$U_j = \Theta (X_i {}^* W_{ij})$$

This function is then biased by a previously established threshold value so that

$$Y_j = F_{th} (U_j + t_j)$$

Caudill and Butler (1990), Pattie and Snyder (1996) and Law and Au (2000) are among the authors who note that in back-propagation algorithms the transfer or 'squashing' function often takes the form of a logistic or sigmoid curve which modifies the weighted sum of the input values to a reasonable sum before passing the signal onto the next layer, that is the slope of the transfer function is defined as the value of Θ in the sigmoid/logistic activation function,

$$f(x) = 1/[1 = \exp(-x/\Theta]$$

If Θ is low in value the slope value is steep, and thus it is common, as described by Pattie and Snyder (1996), to experiment with ranges of values.

As a technique there is a growing number of reports which show that it is superior to alternative statistical approaches. For example Jain and Nag (1997, p. 214) report that 'neural networks consistently outperform logit models in terms of predictive accuracy'. In tourism research Pattie and Synder (1996, p. 162) reported that 'the research has found neural network models to be more accurate than five of the six traditional methods when forecasting visitor attendance.' Law and Au (2000) also concluded that a neural network outperforms multiple regression, naïve, moving average and exponential models in forecasting the demand of Japanese tourists for visiting Hong Kong. However, they also point out that drawbacks exist with neural network modelling, one being its 'looser linkage to theory' (Law and Au, 2000, p. 92); in short, it might be argued that its very replication of the human brain engenders atheoretical modelling.

THE MIMIC AND SUBJECTIVITY – A FUTURE?

Does artificial intelligence help us, as researchers, to understand better the nature of subjectivity if, as its proponents claim, it mimics the human brain? Is this a useful question to be considered? First, if it be thought that neural networks are too complex for researchers to use it must be noted that, just like statistical software, it runs on your desktop computer and examples of free software can be found on the Web, complete with demonstrations (e.g. http://www.nd.com/, the web site of NeuroDimensions Inc). Second, Stebbins (1997, p. 422) has argued that leisure studies have been characterized by 'theoretical stagnation'. Is the same true of tourism research? It is difficult to identify the key theories of the subject. Stebbins (1997, p. 422) has argued there is a lack of exploration on the part of leisure researchers. He commented that

> Leisure researchers as researchers have more in common with amateur and professional scientists than with casual leisure participants, which suggests that they should eschew accidental serendidipity in favour of trying to discover their new ideas by systematically exploring leisure groups and activities.

Similarly tourism researchers are not just tourists! However, in the postmodern world generalization may be difficult, and an experience that is tied to context and place may make the emergence of abstracted models applicable to all places and activities difficult. Our exploration may be of the particular. Hence generalities may be of limited use, and construction of theory thus difficult. It depends upon what it is we wish to theorize about. If it is about the role of tourism in our society and thus the attraction of tourism, or if it is about the identification of macroeconomic variables that determine tourist demand, then I think generalization, and thus model building, is possible. If, however, it is about the reaction of tourists to specific experiences, then generalization may be of limited use in developing management policies at site level. Yet it is often at site level that the interplay of enhancing visitor experience, improving environment, sustaining economic activity and social cohesiveness with all the management problems that are involved in seeking these ends is at its most urgent. Yet in many senses this simply describes a common social science situation – namely that there is a need for and a complementary role for both the specific and general.

Conceptual stagnation may also be associated with two contexts, the context of discovery and the context of justification. The context of discovery includes the technical modes of discovery, and thus the embracing of new methods of assessment can create new insights. Thus, if therefore neural networks can be demonstrated to possess superior predictive or interpretative capabilities than other statistical techniques, then we need to use them. If they help us to model tourist reactions to places by generating a 'black box' approach within which subjectivity is subsumed within an interplay of hidden constructs based on observed variables, then it might be said to simulate the subjective. De Ville (1996, p. 43) notes that 'Because neural predictive models are oriented to prediction, not explanation, it is usually difficult to examine the underlying dynamics.' Therein perhaps lies the nature of neural network modelling and subjectivity. As a quantitative researcher I am excited by the promise of the current generation of artificial intelligence software. As someone who spent considerable periods of time in ethnographic research, I still find the nuances of complex situations and the role of the researcher as a participant within those situations as ones characterized by the play of power. They are situations of often inconsistent context specific truths within which seeming chance is not unimportant. To encapsulate a human experience wherein, for all our cynicism, fantasies, dreams and the potential for cartharsis none the less does exist (Dann, 1996; Lodge, 1991) requires a recognition of the subjective. Research into tourist behaviour is confusing – that is why it retains its interest. Neural modelling simulates this confusion. As a simulation it does not describe but, like much theory, it creates an abstraction of processes which permit an input–output relationship to be modelled, and thus permits prediction. If site specific prediction is required by management, herein lies an important use.

It would seem that we have a tourism research conundrum. On the one hand research into tourist behaviour involves an interaction of the researcher–researched relationship with its respective subjectivities. On the other hand, there exists a tool that can mimic tourist experiences, but is bound within an empiricist 'black box'. It is to my mind an interesting conundrum and one that is not new, but yet may retain its importance as our research proceeds into a new century filled with touristic promise and developing research techniques. Finally back to my own subjectivity. It permits me to retain the role of *flâneur* – a man of the touristic crowd, but staying apart from it as I seek better to understand what tourism experiences are about within their different places.

REFERENCES

Beard, J. G. and Ragheb, M. G. (1980) 'Measuring leisure satisfaction'. *Journal of Leisure Research*, **12**(1), 20–33.

Beard, J. G. and Ragheb, M. G. (1983) 'Measuring leisure motivation'. *Journal of Leisure Research*, **15**(3), 219–28.

Bruner, E. M. (1995) 'The ethnographer/tourist in Indonesia'. In J. Allcock, E. Bruner and M.-F. Lanfant (eds) *International Tourism: Identity and Change, Anthropological and Sociological Approaches*. London: Sage, pp. 224–41.

Caudill, M. and Butler, C. (1990) *Naturally Intelligent Systems*. Boston, Mass.: Massachusetts Institute of Technology.

Cheng, W., McClain, B. W. and Kelly, C. (1997) 'Artificial neural networks make their mark as a powerful tool for investors'. *Review of Business*, **18**(4), 4–9.

D'Amore, M. (1997) 'Leisure studies in the XXIst century: toward a new legitimacy'. Special issue of *Loisir y Société*, **20**(2).

Dann, G. M. S. (1996) *The Language of Tourism: A Sociolinguistic Perspective*. Wallingford: CAB International.

Dann, G. (1999) 'The pomo promo of tourism'. *Tourism, Culture and Communication*, **1**(1), 1–16.

Dann, G. and Cohen, E. (1996) 'Towards a "new" sociology of tourism'. In Y. Apostolopoulos, S. Leivadi and A. Yiannakis (eds) *The Sociology of Tourism: Theoretical and Empirical Investigations*. London: Routledge, pp. 301–14.

De Ville, B. (1996) 'Predictive models in market research'. *Marketing Research: A Magazine of Management and Applications*, **8**(2), 43–5.

Everitt, B. S. and Dunn, G. (1991) *Applied Multivariate Data Analysis*. London, Melbourne and Auckland: Edward Arnold.

Glovier, D. A. (1997) 'Applying neural networks to predicting battle outcomes'. *Engineering Management Journal*, **9**(1), 33–40.

Habermas, J. (1979) *Communications and the Evolution of Society*. London: Heinemann.

Habermas, J. (1981) *Theorie des Kommunikativen Handels*. Frankfurt: Suhrkamp.

Hall, C. M. (1992) *Hallmark Tourist Events: Impacts, Management and Planning*. London: Belhaven Press.

Hall, C. M. (1994) *Tourism and Politics: Policy, Power and Place*. London: Belhaven Press.

Hall, C. M. (1997) 'Mega-events and their legacies'. In P. Murphy (ed.) *Quality Management in Urban Tourism*. Chichester: Wiley, pp. 75–90.

Hedgepeth, W. O. (1995) *Inference Comparison in Exploratory Neural Network and Traditional Statistical Model of Human Performance*. Norfolk, VA: Old Dominion University, Engineering Management Department.

Hollinshead, K. (1999) 'Myth and the discourse of Texas: heritage tourism and the suppression of instinctual life'. In M. Robinson and P. Boniface (eds) *Tourism and Cultural Conflicts*. Wallingford: CAB International, pp. 47–94.

Jackson, M., Schmierer, C. L. and White, G. N. (1999) 'Is there a unique tourist personality which is predictive of tourist behaviour?' In J. Molloy and J. Davies (eds) *Tourism and Hospitality: Delighting the Senses*. Proceedings of the Ninth Australian Tourism and Hospitality Research Conference, Council for Australian University Tourism and Hospitality Education (CAUTHE), Adelaide, Part 2, pp. 39–47.

Jain, B. A. and Nag, B. N. (1997) 'Performance evaluation of neural network decision models'. *Journal of Management Information Systems*, **14**(2), 201–16.

Jenkins, O. (1998) 'Visual images and stereotypes: a study of backpacker tourists to Australia'. Paper presented at the Canadian Association of Geographers' Annual Meeting.

Kline, R. B. (1998) *Principles and Practice of Structural Equation Modelling*. New York: The Guildford Press.

Kuhn, T. S. (1970) *The Structure of Scientific Revolutions*. Chicago: University of Chicago Press.

Law, R. and Au, N. (2000) 'A neural network model to forecast Japanese demand for travel to Hong Kong'. *Tourism Management*, **21**, 89–98.

Lodge, D. (1991) *Paradise News*. London: Penguin Books.

McKercher, B. (1999) 'A chaos approach to tourism'. *Tourism Management*, **20**(4), 425–34.

Maxim, P. S. (1999) *Quantitative Research Methods in the Social Sciences*. New York: Oxford University Press.

Murphy, L. (1997) 'Kangaroos, koalas and Vegemite: backpackers' images of Australia as a holiday'. Paper presented at the Australian National Tourism and Hospitality Research Conference, Griffith University, 11–14 February 1998, Jupiters Casino, Gold Coast, pp. 348–65.

New Zealand Tourism Board (1992) *Segmentation Study of the Malaysian Long Haul Holiday Market*. Wellington: New Zealand Tourism Board.

Palmer, L. (1998) 'Visitors to the Kakadu National Park and issues of Aboriginal land rights'. Paper presented in seminar series of the Centre for Indigenous Natural and Cultural Resource Management Centre, Northern Territory University, Darwin.

Parasuraman, A., Zeithaml, V. A. and Berry, L. L. (1985) 'A conceptual model of service quality and its implications for future research'. *Journal of Marketing*, **49** (Fall), 41–50.

Parasuraman, A., Zeithaml, V. A. and Berry, L. L. (1988) 'SERVQUAL: a multiple-item scale for measuring consumer perceptions of service quality research'. *Journal of Retailing*, **64** (Spring), 12–37.

Parasuraman, A., Zeithaml, V. A. and Berry, L. L. (1994a) 'Alternative scales for measuring service quality: a comparative assessment based on psychometric and diagnostic criteria'. *Journal of Retailing*, **70**(3), 201–30.

Parasuraman, A., Zeithaml, V. A. and Berry, L. L. (1994b) 'Reassessment of expectations as a comparison standard in measuring service quality: implications for further research'. *Journal of Marketing*, **58** (January), 111–24.

Pattie, D. C. and Snyder, J. (1996), 'Using a neural network to forecast visitor behaviour'. *Annals of Tourism Research*, **23**(1), 151–64.

Pearce, D. G. (1993) 'Comparative studies in tourism research'. In D. G. Pearce and R. W. Butler (eds) *Tourism Research. Critiques and Challenges*. London: Routledge, pp. 20–35.

Pearce, P. L. (1988) *The Ulysses Factor: Evaluating Visitors in Tourist Settings*. New York: Springer Verlag.

Pearce, P. L. (1991) 'Analysing tourist attractions'. *Journal of Tourism Studies*, **2**(1), 46–55.

Pearce, P. L. (1993) 'Fundamentals of tourist motivation'. In D. G. Pearce and R. W. Butler (eds) *Tourism Research. Critiques and Challenges*. London: Routledge, pp. 113–34.

Pearce, P. L. (1996) 'Recent research in tourist behaviour'. *Asia–Pacific Journal of Tourism Research*, **1**(1), 7–17

Petri, K. L., Billo, R. E. and Bidanda, B. (1998) 'A neural network process model for abrasive flow machining operations'. *Journal of Manufacturing Systems*, **17**(1), 52–64.

Plog, S. C. (1977) 'Why destinations rise and fall in popularity'. In E. M. Kelly (ed.) *Domestic and International Tourism*. Wellesley, Massachusetts: Institute of Travel Agents, pp. 26–8.

Plog, S. C. (1990) 'A carpenter's tools: an answer to Stephen L. J. Smith's review of psychocentric/allocentrism'. *Journal of Travel Research*, **28**(4), Spring, 43–4.

Reisinger, Y. and Turner, L. (1999) 'Structural equation modelling with Lisrel: application in tourism'. *Tourism Management*, **20**(1; in press).

Robson, S. and Wardle, J. (1998) 'Who's watching whom? A study of the effects of observers on group discussions'. *Journal of the Market Research Society*, **30**(3), July, 333–60.

Russell, R. and Faulkner, B. (1997) 'Chaos and complexity in tourism: in search of a new perspective'. *Pacific Tourism Review*, **1**(2), 93–102.

Russell, R. and Faulkner, B. (1999) 'Movers and shakers: chaos makers in tourism development'. *Tourism Management*, **20**(4), 411–24.

Ryan, C. (1998) 'The travel career ladder – an appraisal'. *Annals of Tourism Research*, **25**(4), 936–57.

Ryan, C. (1999a) 'Tourist experiences, phenomenographic analysis, post-positivism and neural network software'. *International Journal of Tourism Research*, **1**(in press).

Ryan, C. (1999b) 'Crocodiles as a tourist attraction'. *Journal of Sustainable Tourism* (in press).

Ryan, C. and Cliff, A. (1997) 'Do travel agencies measure up to customer expectation? An empirical investigation of travel agencies' service quality as measured by SERVQUAL'. *Journal of Travel and Tourism Marketing*, **6**(22), 1–32.

Ryan, C. and Huyton, J. (1998) 'Who is interested in Aboriginal tourism'. Paper presented at the Australian National Tourism and Hospitality Research Conference, Griffith University, 11–14 February 1998, Jupiters Casino, Gold Coast, p. 388.

Ryan, C. and Huyton, J. (1999) 'Aboriginal tourism – a linear structural relations analysis of domestic and international tourist demand'. *International Journal of Tourism Research* (in press).

Ryan, C. and Faulkner, W. (1999) 'Innovations in tourism management research and conceptualisation – editorial'. Special Issue of *Tourism Management*, **29**(1), xx.

Ryan, C. and Martin, A. (1999) 'Striptease: the silent other in sex tourism, or tourists, strippers and tales of travel'. *Delighting the Senses*, Proceedings of the Ninth Australian Tourism and

Hospitality Research Conference, Council for Australian University Tourism and Hospitality Education and Bureau of Tourism Research, Canberra, Australia, pp. 197–210.

Schechner, R. (1982) *The End of Humanism*. New York: Performing Arts Journal Publications.

Seddighi, H. R. and Shearing, D. F. (1997) 'The demand for tourism in North-East England with special reference to Northumbria: an empirical analysis'. *Tourism Management*, **18**(8), 499–512.

Stebbins, R. A. (1997) 'Exploratory research as an antidote to theoretical stagnation in leisure studies'. *Loisir y Société*, **20**(2), 421–34.

Stoller, R. J. (1991) *Porn: Myths for the Twentieth Century*. New Haven: Yale University Press.

Urry, J. (1995) *Consuming Places*. London: Routledge.

Vaske, J. J., Beaman, J., Stanley, R. and Grenier, M. (1996) 'Importance-performance and segmentation: where do we go from here'. *Journal of Travel and Tourism Marketing*, **5**(3), 225–40.

Walle, A. (1997) 'Quantitative versus qualitative tourism research'. *Annals of Tourism*, **24**(3), 524–36.

Weber, M. (1904/1993) *Die 'Objektivität' sozialwissenschaftlicher und sozialpolitischer Erkenntnis* ('Objectivity' in Social Science and Social Policy). Reproduced in J. Farganis *Readings in Social Theory – The Classic Tradition to Post-Modernism*. New York: The McGraw Hill Companies Inc., pp. 123–35.

Weissinger, E., Henderson, K. A. and Bowling, C. P. (1997) 'Toward an expanding methodological base in leisure studies: researchers' knowledge, attitudes and practices concerning qualitative research'. *Loisir y Société*, **20**(2), 434–51.

CHAPTER 15

The Resort Cycle
Two Decades On

Richard Butler

INTRODUCTION

The opportunity to revisit the resort cycle model (1980) and to comment on its continued relevance some two decades after its original publication is a task approached with some trepidation. To review one's own work is never easy, for one can all too easily perceive in it that which one wishes to see or imagines is explicit, while a reader approaching the material in a more objective fashion is more likely to see only that which is actually written. In modern-day academic literature it is extremely rare for any article to remain of interest and retain applicability for many years. Thus it is with some surprise that this writer continues to see the original article still referenced and applied in the current literature. It is not the intent in this chapter to discuss all of the applications of the model, subsequent modifications suggested for it and criticisms of the original paper. Other writers (Cooper, 1992; Prosser, 1995) have done such reviews in a comprehensive manner. Prosser, in particular, has written much of what this author would have been tempted to say, and it would be pointless to repeat or précis these earlier works. This chapter, therefore, represents a more personal discussion of the role and place of the model in tourism research, both now and in the future, rather than a full review of its use to date. The list of references includes only those works cited in the text. There are many more references not specifically cited which reflect the additional variety of ways and the frequency with which the model has been utilized over the past two decades. One element of the research literature which is conspicuously absent here is work undertaken using the model by students. Relatively little of this work makes its way into the 'official' literature in terms of journals or books, and most remains in the form of theses held in university libraries, which is unfortunate, as this body of research if it could be examined in its entirety might throw considerable light on those elements of the model still viewed as needing verification or modification.

ORIGINS

The chapter begins with an introduction that covers the origins of the model, followed by an examination of its critical elements, its current validity and future relevance. The resort cycle model as discussed here is, in fact, closer to three decades old than two. Its origins are based in the PhD work of the author and a colleague at Glasgow University in the mid-1960s, when both were examining tourism in Scotland. Pattison (1968) was studying the tourism industry in the Firth of Clyde (some 50 kilometres west of Glasgow), and this author tourism in the Scottish Highlands and Islands (Butler, 1973). At that time, in the United Kingdom as elsewhere, there was little research being undertaken on tourism at academic institutions and very little published research material. At the same time, it was becoming very apparent that the decade of the sixties was a period of considerable change in tourist destinations in a physical sense, and that these changes reflected major changes in the nature and scale of tourism itself and the tourism market.

In the context of tourism in Scotland, this period represented the end of one stage in the development of tourism in the Firth of Clyde. While one is often tempted to consider that changes taking place at the time of observation are more significant than changes that have gone before, there is no doubt that the decade of the sixties represented a very major change in tourism in this area. The old-style passenger steamers which were an integral part of the mass transport system of the area, closely integrated with the railways, were disappearing and being replaced by modern roll-on roll-off car ferries. This innovation reflected the increasing use of the car by tourists to this area and to Scotland generally. More significantly it symbolized the disappearance of the traditional form of holiday-taking in the region, namely, staying at one destination resort for one or two weeks, arriving and leaving by public transport, and thus being relatively static in location for the duration of the visit. These changes corresponded to the general breakdown of the traditional holiday pattern which had marked much of European and North American tourism during the previous century (Pattison, 1968; Stansfield, 1972). This pattern was characterized by travel by families from industrial population centres to the nearest coast for a holiday of a week or two weeks, in some cases visiting the same resort and the same hotel at the same time for many years. In some areas the husband would leave the family at the resort for the summer and commute to them at weekends. The markets were often controlled and monopolized by private rail and steam ship companies which had often integrated with hotel and infrastructure developments in the resorts they served. Changes in transportation, particularly the introduction of initially piston-driven, and then jet aircraft, far greater affluence and availability of holidays, a more peaceful world and many other factors culminated in dramatic changes in tourist travel and the development of destinations to cater for the resulting explosion in tourist numbers. The 1960s marked the end of a period of considerable stability in tourism in the older industrialized countries of Europe and North America and a period of major difficulties for the old established resort areas such as those in the Firth of Clyde which had not previously had to withstand very much competition because of transport monopolies and limited captive markets. Suddenly these resorts had to compete, not only with ones in their own country, but also with others in Europe and throughout the world. Most of them were relatively poorly equipped to do this and suffered heavily as a result. The changes in economic well-being were manifested in physical as well as economic change.

It was relatively easy to see the changes coming about, numbers of visitors at traditional resorts declining, markets changing, plant and infrastructure ageing and not being replaced, resulting in an air of gradual decay. In the Highlands of Scotland the market was changing from predominantly middle- and upper-class guests mostly staying in one centre, to a larger market of middle- to lower-middle-class tourists travelling by car and coach rather than rail, and using bed and breakfast establishments instead of hotels and private lodges and estates. Cars and coaches enabled them to move from centre to centre during the holiday. The redevelopment of places like Aviemore in Speyside and its regrettable transformation from a nineteenth-century village with one major traditional hotel and traditionally designed smaller accommodation establishments through the addition of a holiday village and many other tourist-related establishments, still widely unaccepted thirty years later, was the most dramatic example in Scotland. The trigger for these changes in the Spey Valley was the development of winter sports and with that the perception of the feasibility of a year-round tourism industry (Butler, 1973; Getz, 1983). It represented a form of rejuvenation, not so much of a place in decline, but more of a destination in change. In the Firth of Clyde, the absence of comparable rejuvenation opportunities forced the resorts there to turn to other means of survival, including roles in commuting, retirement, car ferry ports, second homes and as activity centres for yachting, golf and fishing. This pattern has been repeated in resorts in many parts of the United Kingdom and elsewhere (Cooper, 1992).

The 1960s were not a period of great conceptual development in tourism research, as noted above, primarily because there was very little tourism research being done in the academic realm. Thus, although this author, and doubtless others, was noting and recording the changes mentioned above, it was not until other examples were found in the literature that the idea of an overall model saw the light of day. In the context of the development of the resort cycle, two key tourism articles, those by Christaller (1963) and Plog (1973) provided much of the stimulus.

As well, the work of Stansfield (1972, 1978) was also of particular relevance, and it was Stansfield who coined the phrase 'the resort cycle'. The 1970s, however, perhaps as a response to the great changes which were happening in tourism itself, were a time of considerable conceptual development in tourism, albeit much of it based on 'seat of the pants' intuition and personal experience. Many of the models and concepts put forward in that decade remain and are still quoted in the literature, including the work of Cohen (1979), Doxey (1975), Plog (1973) and Smith (1977), even though relatively little of the conceptualization developed was based directly on detailed empirical research, but more on the authors' interpretation of experience and knowledge. At a time when there was little research on tourism, such a state of affairs was neither unusual nor unreasonable. It is, perhaps, a tribute to the insight of these individuals that their ideas continue to be debated and used in the current literature more than two decades later.

Of the articles noted above, two particularly appealed to this author because they provided key elements in the development of the cycle concept. In Christaller's (1963) paper, although the one argument about tourists avoiding central places is somewhat faulty, in the context of the changes in destinations there was evidence that the process being observed in Scotland had occurred in other places. As well, this paper provided a basic conceptual explanation for the changes in patterns of tourism. Plog's (1973) article was of critical importance for two reasons. First, because it suggested that the demand side of tourism was also dynamic and thus provided a basis for linking the changes in destinations (supply) with changes in visitors (demand). Second, because it was based on empirical work and statistical analysis, limited though these may appear some three decades later, which represented something of a rarity in tourism research at the time.

Other references that were of particular importance were the papers by Stansfield (1972, 1978) already noted above, which provided specific evidence of the pattern of changes in resorts in the North-Eastern USA. Although Stansfield (1978) has to be given the credit for first using the phrase 'the resort cycle' in the modern literature on tourism, in fact its use in a tourism context is much older, and evidence exists in the term being used at the end of the last century (Butler, 1989); however, this was not known when the original article (Butler, 1980) was written. Also important was the very early work of Wolfe (1952), who described both the physical and social changes in a major tourist destination in Canada, calling the changes appropriately 'The divorce from the geographic environment'. Since then, of course, there have been a large number of papers documenting other examples of change in tourist destinations, many using the resort cycle model (see, for example, Agarwal, 1994, 1997; Butler and Hinch, 1988; Cooper and Jackson, 1989; Debbage, 1990; Digence, 1997; Din, 1992; Hovinen, 1981, 1982; Ioannides, 1992; Kermath and Thomas, 1992; Meyer-Arendt, 1985; Oglethorpe, 1984; Richardson, 1986; Tooman, 1997; Weaver, 1990; Wilkinson, 1987; and Williams, 1993).

The idea of modelling the evolution of resorts came from two disparate concepts, as noted briefly in the original paper (Butler, 1980). The decision to discuss the evolution of resorts as a life cycle came from the well-known business concept of the life cycle of a product. It appeared clear to this writer, and still does, that resorts and destinations are products and should, therefore, be expected to have such a life cycle, given the inherently dynamic nature of tourism (a point well illustrated by Russell and Faulkner, 1999). They represent a product which is created, marketed, and made available in a competitive environment to the consumer (see also Gordon, 1994, on this aspect). They are subject to competition from other products and, if proved uncompetitive, are normally modified as a result of market trends and innovations. It is not unreasonable to expect that over time their appeal, as that of any product, is likely to decline, and with it, their market share. The second concept was that of the life cycle of animal species in the wild. Influential in the author's thinking was the work of the late ecologist Fraser Darling, particularly his superb study *A Herd of Red Deer* (Darling, 1936). The well-documented phenomenon of wild life populations rising and crashing as the rapidly growing population placed too great demands on resources seemed an appropriate analogy to the rise and fall of tourist visitor numbers at destinations. In an unpublished paper (Butler and Brougham, 1972) this author and a colleague quoted Darling on this phenomenon in some detail:

> Mathematicians have helped ecology enormously by their analysis of data of experimental animal populations . . . We know now the nature of the asymptotic or S curve applied to animal populations, that after a slow start of increase in a population in an ample habitat there is a sharp rise in increase or productivity until near the saturation of the habitat, whereafter the curve flattens out, making the numbers of the population more or less static. The animal manager gets ready for a catastrophic fall if he has read the signs. (Darling in Thompson and Grimble, 1968, p. 47)

These two disparate and rather unrelated concepts together provided some rationale for the challenge to what seemed the then current mode of thought with respect to tourist destinations. This was that a community, once established as a tourist destination, would always have appeal as a tourist destination, with little need to reflect and accommodate the changes taking place in the external world. Naïve though this thinking may appear at the beginning of the twenty-first century, it is necessary to remember that most developed tourist resorts in Europe and North America had been established in the middle to late nineteenth century, some, such as Brighton (Gilbert, 1939) or Atlantic City (Stansfield, 1972) even earlier than this. The market and patterns of tourism had remained relatively constant for almost a century, despite growth and the intervention of two world wars. Complacency and lack of research allowed the continued supposition that past trends would continue and the resorts would remain attractive for the foreseeable future. This point is returned to later in the chapter.

In conclusion to this rather lengthy introduction, some key points should be noted. The period before the 1980s was one of little research in tourism, although there was a growing interest in the subject by a small number of researchers. Theories and models were few, and those that were proposed were rarely based on detailed empirical research. Tourism was not thought of as a subject for serious research, and destinations, when studied, were examined as isolated case studies. At the same time there were fundamental changes occurring in the demand side of tourism which were resulting in major impacts becoming imminent on the supply side of tourism. The turbulence in the system experienced over the last two decades of the twentieth century was well established, even though its full effects had not been felt in many areas.

ELEMENTS

To comment on the model and its relevance at the beginning of the twenty-first century it is appropriate to break down the model into what this author regards as its essential elements. There has been considerable attention paid to the model over the years, much of it producing valuable comment and criticism, proposing improvements and modifications, and suggesting alternative models (see, for example, Agarwal, 1994; Bianchi, 1994; di Benedetto and Bojanic, 1993; Choy, 1992; Cooper, 1992; Debbage, 1990, 1992; Getz, 1992; Hayward, 1986, 1992; Jarviuloma, 1992; Keller, 1987; Prosser, 1995; Shaw and Williams, 1994; Smith, 1992; Strapp, 1988; Wall, 1982; and Weaver, 1988).

It can be argued, however, that in some cases the key elements, and thus the overall validity of the model, have been overlooked because of a focus on detail. At the time at which it was presented, the purpose of the model was relatively simple, to argue the case that destinations could be regarded and analysed as a product and that they would have a life cycle which would proceed through stages. Logically, it was argued, at some point this would be likely to end unless specific efforts were made to prevent this and to extend the cycle. The model attempts, perhaps ambitiously, to relate growth, change, limits and intervention in a tourism context, and to bring together the demand and supply sides of the equation. In doing this, it includes eight specific but related elements, not all of which have been addressed in the two decades since the initial appearance of the original article.

The key concept above all, is *dynamism*, or change. It may appear so obvious nowadays that change is a key component of tourism that one may wonder why this was seen as important. However, as noted above, to an industry that traditionally had not witnessed sudden change or exponential growth in the preceding century or so, it was important to stress the change and the dynamics of both sides of tourism, demand and supply. The relationship between changes in supply and changes in demand is a key aspect of resort development and may change over the life of the resort. Many early resorts were supply-led, being established to cater for a market that was only just beginning. As tourism developed and changed rapidly, many older resorts found themselves lagging behind the changes in the demand or market rather than being ahead as had been the case previously. The way they responded often determined their continued success or failure. Over the years there is little doubt that the rate of change has increased which has compounded many of their problems.

A second key element is *process*, with the model suggesting that there was a specific and common process of development of tourist destinations, which could be described and modelled. While the concept of process was not challenged directly, the argument that there is a common process was (Hayward, 1986; Wall, 1982), and one of the major areas of study with respect to the model has been the nature and commonality, or lack thereof, of the development process as proposed in the model. Many of the authors cited above have suggested and illustrated variations on the process in specific locations. However, the key argument that there is a development process through which tourist destinations pass seems generally accepted.

The third element is that of *capacity* or *limits to growth*, a concept that was strong in the resource literature in the 1960s (Hardin, 1968; Meadows *et al.*, 1972), and which this author strongly believes to be equally relevant today (Butler, 1996). The model was based in part on the belief that if demand and visitation exceeded the carrying capacity or limits of the destination, expressed in a number of ways, that the quality of the visitor experience along with the physical appearance of the destination would decline, and that this would be reflected in a subsequent decline in visitor numbers. Some support for this view is shared by Martin and Uysal (1990, p. 390) who argue that

> It is impossible to determine tourist carrying capacity outside of the context of the position of the destination areas in the life cycle. The interrelationship of the two concepts is dynamic, with the idea of change implicit in both concepts.

Fourth, although implicit rather than explicit, is the idea of *triggers*, factors which bring about change in the destination. While these were discussed to some degree in the model, they were perhaps not given the focus they might deserve. Certainly in terms of rejuvenation, and the shifting from stage to stage they are of particular relevance. They were envisaged as including innovations in areas such as transportation, and in marketing, as well as initiatives at the local and subsequently regional, national and international levels by developers. This last area was not discussed in the tourism literature and has only relatively recently been given the attention it deserves (Weaver, 1988; Russell and Faulkner, 1999).

Fifth, there is *management,* and if there is one element which has been ignored in the subsequent discussion and application of the model, it is this one. The title of the original article included 'Implications for management of resources', but perhaps because there was not a great deal of discussion of this component in the article, it has tended to be overlooked. This has resulted in criticism that the model is proposing the inevitability of decline (Hayward, 1986). In fact, this was only a part of the focus of the model, which in essence was putting forward the view that if intervention and management did not occur, then change and decline were probably inevitable. The issue of the management of tourist resorts and destinations in general, however, is something which deserves much greater attention. In reality, most tourist resorts are not managed in the strict sense that there is some agency with that responsibility. Rather, only individual elements are managed, and resort communities at best planned and promoted, with varying levels of development control. Management of tourism in the true sense rarely exists except at specific facilities.

Sixth, there is the implicit argument for a *long-term viewpoint* in the planning and management of destinations. The presumption of the model was that, if destinations are to avoid the pitfalls of overuse and subsequent decline in appeal, then looking forward from the beginning is of crucial importance. While to most private sector developers key issues are how to attract tourists in the first year of development and a decade may seem long term, in reality what is necessary is to identify how to keep tourists coming to the destination some fifty or a hundred years in the future. Such long-term planning or visioning is still very much a rarity, and reflects the unwillingness or inability of forecasters to predict beyond a decade or so with any confidence. Given the rapid rate of change in tourism which is now present, one has to sympathize with the inherent difficulties in this task.

Seventh is what may be called the *spatial* component, originally a major element in the first version of the model (Butler and Brougham, 1972), but which was much less prominent in the published version. The proposition in this respect was that, as development at a specific destination stagnated, there would be a spatial shift of development to a new destination. This could occur in the immediate vicinity, for example, in the Gold Coast region of Queensland from Coolangatta to Surfers Paradise (Russell and Faulkner, 1998), or from one region to another, for example from southern France to Spain, to Greece and then to other destinations around the Mediterranean. The change in location was assumed to reflect a number of changes in the original destination or destination area including rising costs for items such as labour and land, and decline in environmental quality.

Finally, there is the element of *universal applicability,* namely, that the model was essentially applicable to all tourist destinations. A rather presumptuous claim perhaps, but it was, after all, intended to be a general model of the tourism development process. Any model has to be applicable beyond one situation, and the limited evidence and literature available in the 1970s suggested that the process and pattern of tourist destination development was very similar across a wide variety of locations and scales.

While there are other elements and issues raised in the original paper, the above are seen as the key components and concepts introduced. It seems appropriate next to comment briefly on some of the uses and criticisms of the model in the intervening two decades.

CRITICISM, APPLICATION, AND MODIFICATION

The most quoted criticisms of the model are by Hayward (1986, 1992), who raised concerns over the identification of the stages of the model, questions of timing and scale and the suggested inevitability of the process which seemed to deny the possibilities of intervention. Wall (1982) also raised equally valid concerns over scale and whether cycles are real phenomena, while Getz (1983, 1986, 1992) discussed difficulties of using the carrying capacity concept in the context of destination planning. Most users of the model have found some points which were less applicable than others in the particular destinations which they were studying. In more recent years, Choy (1992) argued that the model had little applicability in the context of the Pacific islands because of the variety of development patterns that appeared to exist in that region, and proposed alternative cycles and processes, although one might wonder at the validity of taking the whole south Pacific as a single destination rather than the individual island states. Cohen (1979), in an article written before the model appeared, anticipated another criticism when he raised the issue of unidirectionality of such models and argued that there are probably multiple types of dynamics.

Prosser (1995) summarized the criticisms of the model as being of five types:

doubts on there being a single model of development;
limitations on the capacity issue;
conceptual limitations of the life cycle model;
lack of empirical support for the concept; and
limited practical utility of the model.

It is not the specific purpose of this chapter to refute the above and other criticisms, and particularly not those that deal with general criticisms of the product life cycle concept in broader terms (for example, Hayward, 1986 and Hart *et al.*, 1984). To do so would necessitate a far longer paper to do justice to the criticisms and to place them into appropriate contexts, and to fashion a full response where one was felt justified. Rather, some general responses will suffice.

For the most part the above criticisms are accepted to a fair degree. The original article was very short compared to many articles today, highly generalized and proposed a general principle or theory. It did not present empirical evidence to support the concept, although sufficient research has been done by many authors since to make this possible. In being so brief it left implicit items which could, and with hindsight perhaps should, have been made more explicit or expanded, and thus did leave itself open to the criticisms which have been made. Despite these quite profound criticisms, however, the model is still being used, a point that Prosser (1995, p. 9) makes,

> The extensive criticism levelled at the resort life cycle concept shows no sign of dissuading researchers from adopting the model as a framework for their research . . . the original model survives largely intact and according to some, offers the prospect of further development.

In the process of application many authors have noted how the model did not fit the specific destinations which they were studying and proposed amendments. Clearly, a model that includes all of reality is no longer a model, but some of the proposed amendments would appear to hold more general applicability than others. Again, it is not possible to note all of these here, but of particular interest to this author are those of Agarwal, Faulkner and Russell, Keller, Opperman, Strapp and Weaver. Agarwal (1994), along with others (Hovinen, 1981, 1982, for example) raises the possibility of alternative and additional stages after the stagnation stage of the original model particularly with respect to the decline stage option. Keller (1987) argued that an overlooked element, and one which could be related strongly to the stages of development, was control over development and sources of investment, an aspect also discussed by Debbage (1990, 1992).

In a similar vein, in examining the role of indigenous versus non-local investors, Weaver (1988) suggested a different process for the initial development of tourism in plantation economies, a point which deserves much more investigation, and which may have parallels in other stages and situations. Such work on developers and investors raises some of the issues discussed later in the work on entrepreneurs by Russell and Faulkner (1999). Strapp (1988) incorporated the cycle into the process of conversion of second-home destinations from conventional tourist places into retirement havens, a process which is taking place in many established tourist areas with potentially serious implications. Opperman (1998) suggested that one factor related to the cycle was decline in length of stay of visitors, and while this alone is not a major factor, it could serve as both a trigger and an explanatory factor in the stages of development. Finally, Faulkner and Russell (1997) introduce the relatively recent concept of chaos theory to tourism development and the resort cycle model. This raises some fascinating implications, not least because it deals in part with questions of agents of change or triggers in the development process, topics which have not been dealt with adequately and which should reveal much about both specific cases and general processes.

These are by no means the only modifications which have been suggested and which have potential merit for changes in the basic model, but are ones which this author finds particularly relevant to the continued application of the model.

VALIDITY AND FUTURE APPLICATION

After twenty years of review and application it is reasonable to query whether the tourism area life cycle is still a valid model for the study of tourism development and whether it can still serve as a broad conceptual framework for the study of the development process of tourism destinations. It is not surprising perhaps that this author is prepared to argue that the basic tenets of the model and the concept are as, or even more, applicable to contemporary tourism than they were to tourism development twenty years ago.

One of the predominating concepts of the 1990s has been sustainable development (Butler, 1991). In order to keep the text of this chapter longer than the list of references there will not be a discussion of that concept to any degree, nor its applicability to tourism development; other authors have done this (see, for example, Hall and Lew, 1998; Wahab and Pigram, 1997) and the *Journal of Sustainable Tourism* has almost a decade of publications on this topic. This author has argued that the original resort cycle article could legitimately be regarded an early call for the principles of sustainable development to be applied in the context of tourism destinations (Butler, 1997). The model, as noted above, contained in it what are generally accepted as the essential elements of sustainable development, namely, the need for a long-term view, the acceptance of limits to growth and development and the need for responsibility and control over development. This author believes, perhaps even more strongly than in 1980, that these principles are basic and essential if destinations are to be developed and maintained in an appropriate and sustainable manner. One of the problems with the application of the concept of sustainable development to tourism, however, is the fact that it has rarely been applied or even thought of in the context of mass tourism, and thus the application of the principles to the classic tourist resorts has been very limited (Vera and Rippin, 1996) despite arguments that these are the areas most in need of the application of such principles (Wheeller, 1993; Butler, 1997).

The number of places which are experiencing problems from overdevelopment and overuse is increasing annually. This is hardly a new problem: Wolfe commented with his usual far-sightedness on such issues almost five decades ago (Wolfe, 1952), and suggested an alternative curve of development and impacts shortly after the original model appeared (Wolfe, 1982). It appears highly likely that the rate of consumption of tourist destinations is increasing, that is, the time taken to proceed through the cycle is diminishing. Improvements in transportation, reductions in cost, savings through economies of scale, innovations in marketing and societal changes in tastes and behaviour all serve to reduce brand and place loyalty and to encourage the desire for stimulation, novelty and change for the sake of change. The 'collection', in some cases possibly instead of the enjoyment, of destinations has the potential to speed the movement of places along Plog's (1973) curve. While many tourists may like to think they are travellers rather than tourists, or allocentrics rather than psychocentrics in Plog's (1973) classification, one may argue that almost all travellers are on their way to being tourists whether they like it or realize it or not (Wheeller, 1993).

In the context of tourism development it may not be possible to prevent the process of development and subsequent decline of destinations, but it can certainly be argued that society at large does have a responsibility to avoid Hardin's 'tragedy of the commons' (1968) being repeated in most tourist destinations, an argument alluded to by this author (Butler, 1991) and discussed at more length by Healy in his article of 1994. At the heart of the resort cycle model is the principle that the development of destinations is normally evolutionary rather than revolutionary and, as a result, control and responsibility are crucial elements if development is to be appropriate and the destination survive over the long term. In the years ahead there is no reason why the model cannot continue to serve as a call for such responsibility and intervention, and as such, to have continued validity. Until there is convincing evidence that those responsible for tourism destination planning, development and management have learned the lessons from what are now regarded as past mistakes, the resort cycle model is likely to have validity in a predictive sense well into the future. Evidence (Faulkner, 1999) from some areas would suggest that there is still a reluctance in both the private and public sectors in destinations to admit that a decline may be occurring or is likely to occur in any specific destination.

CONCLUSIONS

Because it is a generalized and relatively simplistic model, it was inevitable that the resort cycle model would not fit perfectly, or necessarily even closely, all of the many specific and unique cases to which it has been applied. The question best asked, perhaps, is not whether in its original form it successfully and completely explained the process of tourist destination evolution at all locations, but rather whether it still has applicability and validity at the beginning of the twenty-first century.

The frequency of use of the model and the number of examples discussed in the literature would tend to support the view that the model still has validity in terms of being a descriptive model which has applicability in a wide variety of spatial, temporal, cultural and economic situations. It is still being used to illustrate the process of the development of tourist places in a variety of ways (Wilkinson, 1996).

Undoubtedly it provides a conceptual hook for case studies of specific locations, and given the propensity for case studies from an industry and business perspective in tourism and from the need to have specific field work examples for research, it fills a niche in tourism research methodology and conceptual development. While its ability to provide anything new after two decades has legitimately been questioned (Opperman, 1998), others continue to apply and modify the model in a variety of settings (Agarwal, forthcoming; Burns and Murphy, 1998; Goncalves and Aguas, 1997; Travel and Tourism Intelligence, 1997). Johnston (1999) has articulately expressed the ontological and epistemological attributes of the model and argues that one of its contributions is to enable analysis to go beyond simply identifying stages. He concludes that there is much more to learn about the way destinations are developed and thus a continuing role for the tourism area life cycle model. Until the destination development process is more clearly understood and short-term opportunism replaced by long-term integrated development in a controlled context, the 'tragedy of resorts' implicit in the model is likely to remain an issue of concern in the context of tourism.

REFERENCES

Agarwal, S. (1994) 'The resort cycle revisited: implications for resorts'. In C. P. Cooper and A. Lockwood (eds) *Progress in Tourism, Recreation and Hospitality Management*, Vol. 5. Chichester: John Wiley and Sons.

Agarwal, S. (forthcoming) 'The resort life-cycle, restructuring' and 'The resort: the case of contemporary British seaside tourism'. To appear in *Annals of Tourism Research*.

Bianchi, R. (1994) 'Tourism development and resort dynamics: an alternative approach'. In C. P. Cooper and A. Lockwood (eds) *Progress in Tourism, Recreation and Hospitality Management*, Vol. 5. Chichester: John Wiley and Sons.

Burns, D. and Murphy, L. (1998) 'An analysis of the promotion of marine tourism in Queensland, Australia'. In E. Laws, B. Faulkner and G. Moscardo (eds) *Embracing and Managing Change in Tourism: International Case Studies*. London: Routledge, pp. 415–30.

Butler, R. W. (1973) *The Tourism Industry of the Highlands and Islands*. PhD thesis, Glasgow: University of Glasgow.

Butler, R. W. (1980) 'The concept of a tourist area cycle of evolution and implications for management'. *The Canadian Geographer*, **24**, 5–12.

Butler, R. W. (1989) 'Tourism and tourism research'. In E. L. Jackson and T. L. Burton (eds) *Understanding Leisure and Recreation: Mapping the Past, Charting the Future*. State College, PA: Venture Publishing Inc.

Butler, R. W. (1991) 'Tourism, environment, and sustainable development'. *Environmental Conservation*, **18**(3), 201–9.

Butler, R. W. (1996) 'The concept of carrying capacity for tourism destinations: dead or merely buried?' *Progress in Tourism and Hospitality Research*, **2**(3 and 4), 283–94.

Butler, R. W. (1997) 'Modelling tourism development'. In S. Wahab and J. Pigram (eds) *Tourism and Sustainable Development*. London: Routledge, pp. 109–25.

Butler, R. W. and Brougham, J. E. (1972) 'The applicability of the asymptotic curve to the forecasting of tourism development'. Paper presented to the Research Workshop, Travel Research Association Conference, Quebec City, June 1972.

Butler R. W. and Hinch, T. (1988) 'The rejuvenation of tourism centre: Port Stanley, Ontario'. *Ontario Geography*, **32**, 29–52.

Choy, D. J. L. (1992) 'Life cycle models for Pacific island destinations'. *Journal of Travel Research*, **30**(3), 26–31.

Christaller, W. (1963) 'Some considerations of tourism location in Europe: the peripheral regions – under-developed countries – recreation areas'. *Regional Science Association Papers*, **12**, 103.

Cohen, E. (1979) 'Rethinking the sociology of tourism'. *Annals of Tourism Research*, **6**(1), 18–35.

Cooper, C. 'The life cycle concept and strategic planning for coastal resorts'. *Built Environment*, **18**(1), 57–66.

Cooper, C. and Jackson, S. (1989) 'Destination life cycle: the Isle of Man case study'. *Annals of Tourism Research*, **16**(3) 377–98.

Darling, F. F. (1936) *A Herd of Red Deer*. Oxford: Oxford University Press.

Darling, F. F. (1968) 'Ecology of land use in the Highlands and Islands'. In D. C. Thompson and I. Grimble (eds) *The Future of the Highlands and Islands*. Edinburgh: James Thin, pp. 39–65.

Debbage, K. G. (1990) 'Oligopoly and the resort cycle in the Bahamas'. *Annals of Tourism Research*, **17**, 513–27.

Debbage, K. G. (1992) 'Tourism oligopoly is at work'. *Annals of Tourism Research*, **19**(2), 355–9.

di Benedetto, C. A. and Bojanic, D. C. (1993) 'Tourism area life cycle extensions'. *Annals of Tourism Research*, **20**, 557–70.

Digence, J. (1997) 'Life cycle model'. *Annals of Tourism Research*, **24**(2), 452–4.

Din, K. H. (1992) 'The "involvement stage" in the evolution of a tourist destination'. *Tourism Recreation Research*, **17**(1), 10–20.

Doxey, G. V. (1975) 'A causation theory of visitor-resident irritants: methodology and research inferences'. *Proceedings of the Travel Research Association*, Sixth Annual Conference, San Diego, California, pp. 195–8.

Faulkner, B. (1999) 'Revisioning tourist resorts'. Presentation to CRC Review, Griffith University, Gold Coast, October.

Faulkner, B. and Russell, R. (1997) 'Chaos and complexity in tourism: in search of a new perspective'. *Pacific Tourism Review*, **1**(2), 93–102.

Getz, D. (1983) 'Capacity to absorb tourism: concepts and implications for strategic planning'. *Annals of Tourism Research*, **10**, 239–63.

Getz, D. (1986) 'Models in tourism planning: towards integration of theory and practice'. *Tourism Management*, **7**(1), 21–32.

Getz, D. (1992) 'Tourism planning and the destination life cycle'. *Annals of Tourism Research*, **19**(4), 752–70.

Gilbert, E. W. (1939) 'The growth of inland and seaside health resorts in England'. *Scottish Geographical Magazine*, **55**, 16–35.

Goncalves, V. F. da C. and Aguas, P. M. R. (1997) 'The concept of life cycle: an application to the tourist product'. *Journal of Travel Research*, **XXXVI**(2) 12–22.

Gordon, I. R. (1994) 'Crowding, competition and externalities in tourism development: a model of resort life cycles'. *Geographical Systems*, **1**, 281–308.

Hall, C. M. and Lew, A. (1998) *Sustainable Tourism: A Geographical Perspective*. Harlow: Longman.

Hardin, G. (1968) 'The tragedy of the commons'. *Science*, **162**, 1243–8.

Hart, C. W., Casserly, G. and Lawless, M. J. (1984) 'The product life cycle: how useful?' *Cornell Hotel and Restaurant Administration Quarterly*, **25**(3), 54–63.

Haywood, K. M. (1986) 'Can the tourist-area life cycle be made operational'. *Tourism Management*, **7**, 154–67.

Haywood, K. M. (1992) 'Revisiting resort cycle'. *Annals of Tourism Research*, **19**(2), 351–4.

Healy, R. G. (1994) 'The "Common Pool" problem in tourism landscapes'. *Annals of Tourism Research*, **19**(4), 596–611.

Hovinen, G. R. (1981) 'A tourist cycle in Lancaster County, Pennsylvania'. *Canadian Geographer*, **15**(3), 283–6.

Hovinen, G. R. (1982) 'Visitor cycles: outlook in tourism in Lancaster County'. *Annals of Tourism Research*, **9**, 565–83.

Ioannides, D. (1992) 'Tourism development agents: the Cypriot resort cycle'. *Annals of Tourism Research*, **19**(4), 711–21.

Jarviluoma, J. (1992) 'Alternative tourism and the evolution of tourist areas'. *Tourism Management*, **13**, 118–20.

Johnston, C. S. (1999) 'Shoring the foundations of Butler's destination area life cycle model. Part 1: ontological and epistemological considerations'. Paper presented at the Annual Meeting of the Association of American Geographers, Waikiki, Hawaii, March 1999.

Keller, C. P. (1987) 'Stages of peripheral tourism development – Canada's North West Territories'. *Tourism Management*, **8**, 20–32.

Kermath, B. M. and Thomas, R. N. (1992) 'Spatial dynamics of resorts: Sosua, Dominican Republic'. *Annals of Tourism Research*, **19**, 173–90.

King, B. (1994) 'Research on resorts: a review'. In C. P. Cooper and A. Lockwood (eds) *Progress in Tourism, Recreation and Hospitality Management*, Vol. 5. Chichester: John Wiley and Sons.

Martin, B. S. and Uysal, M. (1990) 'An examination of the relationship between carrying capacity and the tourism life cycle: management and policy implications'. *Journal of Environmental Management*, **31**, 327–33.

Meadows, D. H., Meadows, D. L, Randers, J. and Behrens, W. W. (1972) *Limits to Growth: A Report for the Club of Rome's Project on the Predicament of Mankind.* New York: Universe Books.

Meyer-Arendt, K. J. (1985) 'The Grand Isle, Louisiana resort cycle'. *Annals of Tourism Research*, **12**(3), 449–65.

Morgan, M. (1991) 'Dressing up to survive: marketing Majorca anew'. *Tourism Management*, **12**(1), 15–20.

Oglethorpe, M. (1984) 'Tourism in Malta'. *Leisure Studies*, **3**, 147–62.

Opperman, M. (1998) 'What is new with the resort cycle?' *Tourism Management*, **19**(2) 179–80.

Pattison, D. A. (1968) *Tourism in the Firth of Clyde.* Unpublished PhD thesis, Dept of Geography, University of Glasgow.

Plog, S. G. (1973) 'Why destination areas rise and fall in popularity'. *Cornell Hotel and Restaurant Administration Quarterly*, **12**(1), 13–16.

Prosser, G. M. (1995) 'Tourist destination life cycles: progress, problems and prospects'. Paper presented at National Tourism Research Conference, Melbourne, February 1995.

Richardson, S. L. (1986) 'A product life-cycle approach to urban waterfronts: the revitalization of Galveston'. *Coastal Zone Management Journal*, **14**, 21–46.

Russell, R. and Faulkner, B. (1998) 'Reliving the destination life cycle in Coolangatta: an historical perspective on the rise, decline and rejuvenation of an Australian seaside resort'. In E. Laws, B. Faulkner and G. Moscardo (eds) *Embracing and Managing Change in Tourism: International Case Studies.* London: Routledge, pp. 95–115.

Russell, R. and Faulkner, B. (1999) 'Movers and shakers: chaos makers in tourism development'. *Tourism Management*, **20**, 411–20.

Shaw, G. and Williams, A. M. (1994) *Critical Issues in Tourism: A Geographical Perspective.* Oxford: Blackwell.

Smith, R. A. (1992) 'Beach resort evolution: implications for planning'. *Annals of Tourism Research*, **19**, 304–22.

Smith, V. L. (1977) *Hosts and Guests: The Anthropology of Tourism*. Philadelphia: Pennsylvania Press.

Stansfield, C. A. (1972) 'The development of modern seaside resorts'. *Parks and Recreation*, **5**(10), 14–46.

Stansfield, C. (1978) 'Atlantic City and the resort cycle'. *Annals of Tourism Research*, **5**, 238.

Strapp, J. D. (1988) 'The resort cycle and second homes'. *Annals of Tourism Research*, **15**(4), 504–16.

Toomam, L. A. (1997) 'Applications of the life-cycle model in tourism'. *Annals of Tourism Research*, **24**(1), 214–34.

Travel and Tourism Intelligence (1997) 'Rejuvenating holiday resorts – a Spanish case study'. *Travel and Tourism Intelligence* (2), 77–93.

Vera, F. and Rippin, R. (1996) 'Decline of a Mediterranean tourist area and restructuring strategies: the Valencian Region'. In G. K. Priestley, J. A. Edwards and H. Coccossis (eds) *Sustainable Tourism? European Experiences*. Wallingford: CAB International, pp. 120–36.

Wahab, S. and Pigram, J. (eds) (1997) *Tourism and Sustainable Development*. London: Routledge.

Wall, G. (1982) 'Cycles and capacity: incipient growth or theory'. *Annals of Tourism Research*, **9**(2), 52–6.

Weaver, D. (1988) 'The evolution of a "Plantation" tourism landscape on the Caribbean island of Antigua'. *Tijdschrift voor Economische en Sociale Geografie*, **79**, 319–31.

Weaver, D. B. (1990) 'Grand Cayman Island and the resort cycle concept'. *Journal of Travel Research*, **29**(2), 9–15.

Wheeller, B. (1993) 'Sustaining the ego'. *Journal of Sustainable Tourism*, **1**(2), 121–9.

Wilkinson, P. F. (1987) 'Tourism in small island nations: a fragile independence'. *Leisure Studies*, **6**, 127–46.

Wilkinson, P. F. (1996) 'Graphical images of the Commonwealth Caribbean: the tourist area cycle of evolution'. In L. Harrison and W. Husbands (eds) *Practising Responsible Tourism*. New York: John Wiley and Sons Ltd., pp. 16–40.

Williams, M. T. (1993) 'An expansion of the tourist site cycle model: the case of Minorca (Spain)'. *Journal of Tourism Studies*, **4**(2), 24–32.

Wolfe, R. I. (1952) 'Wasaga Beach – the divorce from the geographic environment'. *The Canadian Geographer*, **2**, 57–66.

Wolfe, R. I. (1982) 'Recreational travel – the new migration revisited'. *Ontario Geography*, **19**, 103–22.

CHAPTER 16

Sustainable Tourism: Is it Sustainable?

David Weaver

INTRODUCTION

Since its introduction in the late 1980s, the concept of 'sustainable tourism' has become one of the most frequently addressed issues among tourism researchers and practitioners. While the idea of sustainability had previously been alluded to in the literature, the term itself emerged following the 1987 release of the so-called Brundtland Report, which popularized the concept of 'sustainable development' (WCED, 1987). Sustainable development, subsequently, was further publicized as the clarion call of the 1992 Rio Earth Summit and its resultant Agenda 21 manifesto. To paraphrase the definition of sustainable development proffered by the Brundtland Report, sustainable tourism can be defined as tourism that meets the needs of the current generation without compromising the ability of future generations to meet their own needs. Clearly, it is hard to disagree with the broad concept of sustainability, and this is why it is now almost universally embraced, at least in principle, as the 'great imperative' of the tourism sector and all other facets of the contemporary economy.

When first introduced during the late 1980s, sustainable tourism was widely regarded among tourism researchers as being synonymous with 'alternative tourism' (Clarke, 1997). This perception was related to the dominance at that time of the so-called 'cautionary' and 'adaptancy' platforms (Jafari, 1989), which posited that mass or large-scale tourism was inherently unsustainable. However, the 'knowledge-based' platform, which became dominant in the 1990s, de-emphasized the relationship between scale and impact. According to this view, small-scale or alternative tourism can be basically positive or negative in terms of destination impact, depending on where it is implemented and how it is managed, and the same can be said about mass tourism. Hence, the notion of sustainability was extended right across the entire spectrum of tourism activity, and not confined just to the small-scale end of that continuum (Clarke, 1997). The logic of this extension also derives from the simple observation that tourism as a whole cannot be sustainable unless mass tourism is made sustainable, since that component by definition accounts and will continue to account for the great majority of all tourism activity.

Ironically, the widespread support garnered for the principle of sustainability within the tourism sector is counterbalanced by the many fundamental disagreements that are encountered when subsequent steps are taken to implement the principle. The purpose of this chapter is to outline and discuss critically the stages that are involved in the implementation of sustainable tourism. The publication of this text in the year 2000 is appropriate in that the chapter will essentially be a critique that looks back on, and takes inventory of, a decade of sustainable tourism evolution, in order to prepare for and look forward to its further development in the new millennium.

Figure 16.1 Sample framework for implementing sustainable tourism. *Source*: Consulting and Audit Canada, 1995; Maclaren, 1996

STEPS IN THE IMPLEMENTATION OF SUSTAINABLE TOURISM

Figure 16.1 depicts a simplified and annotated sequence of stages that is commonly recommended as a procedure for implementing sustainable tourism in a destination. As such, it provides a basis for the critical analysis of this implementation process, though the stages do not necessarily always follow one another in a neat linear fashion.

DEFINING THE GOALS AND OBJECTIVES

The first basis for dissent usually occurs when the attempt is made to translate the principle of sustainable tourism into tangible goals and their associated objectives. What is to be sustained, and how is this best achieved? It is at this point that the contradictory impulses of sustainable tourism become problematic, and subject to ideological interpretation.

Sustainable or development?

There are several manifestations of this problem, one of which focuses on the component of sustainable tourism (or development) that should be stressed. For those on the more anthropocentric, pro-growth end of the ideological spectrum (i.e. the 'anthros'), the emphasis is on the 'development' portion of sustainable development – that is, sustainable tourism supports the continued growth of the tourism sector. In contrast, the more biocentric and anti-growth end of the spectrum (i.e. the 'bios') places the emphasis on the 'sustainable', that is, on the view that the continued environmental and sociocultural sustainability of the destination should take precedence over growth. Thus, the apparently universal support for sustainable development and sustainable tourism derives simply from the tendency of each side of the spectrum to focus on the element that reinforces their own ideology. Because it could therefore serve to entrench existing ideologies, Willers (1994) condemns sustainable development as 'one of the most insidious and manipulative ideas to appear in decades' (p. 131).

Intra or intergenerational equity?

A related basis for ideological conflict at the stage of goal definition is the distinction between intragenerational and intergenerational equity. The latter concept is explicit in the Brundtland definition, and is broadly supported as a pillar of sustainable development. More controversial is the intragenerational dimension, which supports the equality of outcomes at the present time. Many bios argue that intergenerational and environmental sustainability cannot be achieved without addressing current inequities between rich and poor, male and female, etc. (Frazier, 1997). Support only for intergenerational equity, they argue, may disguise support for the long-term retention of the status quo. Obviously, very different planning and management strategies are warranted depending on which of these perspectives is supported. Intragenerational sustainability, for example, requires tourism strategies that help to redress income and power differentials within a destination.

Product-led or market-led?

The market-led perspective emphasizes the sustainability of market demand, while the product-led perspective stresses the sustainability of the destination itself in terms of its environmental, social, cultural and economic integrity. Again, a definition that combines both perspectives is likely to attain widespread popularity, but risks collapse at the point when tangible goals and objectives are articulated. Advocates for the market-led approach will put the priority on measures that foster a competitive tourism industry, while, to product-led supporters, this is secondary to measures that safeguard the quality of life in the destination. Both factions will inevitably argue that the secondary objective will ultimately be attained through attention to the primary objective (i.e. their main concern). That is, a strong quality of life will result from a robust tourism industry, or, conversely, a robust tourism industry will result from maintaining the overall integrity of the destination. However, this does not reduce the potential for conflict, since the core issue is being able to put one's own agenda ahead of all others, and to have access to the resources and power that this implies.

Spatial scope of sustainability

In establishing what is to be sustained, it may be necessary to define the area to which the concern over sustainability should extend, regardless of ideology. The least complicated scenario is to consider a single operation or a single small destination, where the level of complexity is limited by the limitations of the scale, and the mandate is clearly to implement sustainability only within those narrow spatial parameters. If, on the other hand, the goal is to further the cause of global sustainability (as in the cliché 'think globally, act locally'), then very different objectives may be warranted. For example, truly to take into account global sustainability, destination managers should attempt to reduce the amount of fossil fuel consumed in transit by visiting tourists, thus possibly suggesting more of an emphasis on domestic tourists, or a reduction in long-haul visitors. Hunter (1995) refers to these two approaches, respectively, as the 'parochial' and the 'extra-parochial' approach.

Steady state and enhancive sustainability

Although not often encountered in the literature, a useful distinction with implications for goal identification can be made between steady state and enhancive sustainability.

The former is the equilibrium option that simply holds that some particular state is maintained. In material terms, this means that the rate of capital formation should equal the rate of capital depletion. In contrast, the latter is a situation where the rate of capital formation exceeds the rate of capital depletion. Such an approach is appropriate where the environmental or sociocultural conditions of a location have already deteriorated to the point where merely sustaining these same conditions is not an outcome that has any meaningful relation to sustainable development. It would be preferable in these circumstances to rebuild the integrity of the destination by, for example, encouraging the industry to improve water standards and engage in afforestation measures, or to contribute to cultural rejuvenation.

ESTABLISHING THE PLANNING AND MANAGEMENT PARAMETERS

Once the goals and objectives of sustainable development are identified, an appropriate framework for planning and management can be established. This framework will usually have to take into account the spatial, sectoral, political and temporal parameters of the implementation process.

Spatial parameters

Whether a parochial or extra-parochial approach is adopted at the goal definition stage, the reality of planning and management is that implementation will tend to occur at the parochial (e.g. municipal) level, since a jurisdiction cannot easily extend its control beyond its own boundaries. Nor can a large political unit such as a country readily assume responsibility for all functions that have to be taken into consideration in the implementation process, especially in a democratic federal system. The result is a chequerboard pattern of fragmented planning units that is haphazardly superimposed over existing tourism systems and other socio-economic and biophysical systems.

Figure 16.2 illustrates this situation. In this hypothetical scenario, a concentration of tourism activity is distributed over three municipalities, each of which formulates its own sustainable tourism strategy. The geometric boundaries of these municipalities, furthermore, have no relationship to regional biome and watershed boundaries. Hence, individual planning systems cannot possibly take into account even the regional factors that must be considered if sustainability is to be achieved, much less factors such as global warming and ozone depletion. If the goals and the planning framework of these jurisdictions are both parochial in orientation, then the potential for problems such as stress displacement is high. Stress displacement occurs when a jurisdiction addresses a problem within its own boundaries by offloading the problem to another jurisdiction. For example, a medieval walled city in Europe may ban vehicular traffic within its borders to reduce congestion and pollution, but this could lead to increased congestion

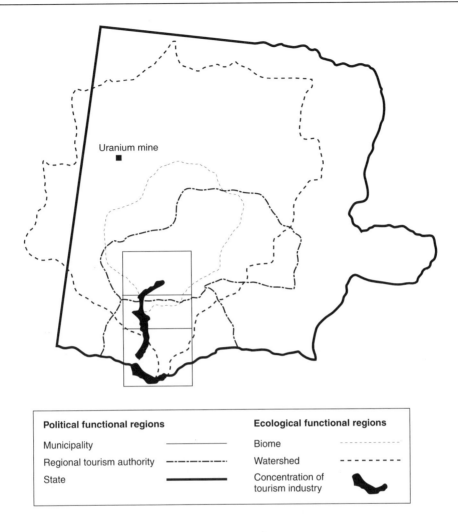

Figure 16.2 Spatial parameters for sustainable tourism: nested and overlapping functional regions

and pollution in the neighbouring municipality where everyone must now park. Another illustration is provided by the ski resort of Aspen, Colorado, where the introduction of stringent development controls led to increased development activity in down-valley communities that had previously not been impacted in any significant way by the tourism sector (Gill and Williams, 1994). Such problems could be avoided through the establishment of regional planning authorities, but these are often unpopular for a variety of reasons, including cost, the perception of redundant bureaucracy and the unwillingness of local jurisdictions to concede any power to these new super-municipal structures.

Spatial framework

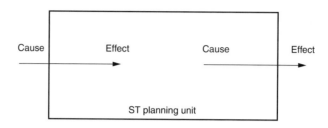

ST planning unit

Temporal framework

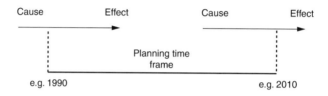

Planning time
frame

e.g. 1990   e.g. 2010

Figure 16.3 Spatial and temporal planning frameworks and discontinuities between cause and effect

Sectoral parameters

Just as a particular municipal planning jurisdiction cannot be isolated from other decisions made in adjacent or surrounding municipalities and other systems, nor can tourism be planned or managed in isolation from other economic sectors such as agriculture, mining, logging and the military – and this assumes that a coherent definition of the 'tourism industry' itself can be established (Eber, 1992). Tourism planners and academics, however, often act as if these other sectors did not exist, or were completely external to the tourism planning and management process. Yet, it is difficult to see how tourism can be made sustainable if these other stakeholders are not behaving in a sustainable way. For example, the three jurisdictions in Figure 16.2 may be managing their tourism in a sustainable way, but the integrity of the tourism sector could still be seriously affected by radioactive residues carried downstream from the uranium mine.

There is little that the tourism sector can do to influence the actions of these often incompatible sectors. Furthermore, tourism is often disadvantaged in comparison to these more traditional stakeholders in its attempt to obtain a 'fair share' of the resource base. This is because the more traditional sectors have more lobbying skill and clout with government, can demonstrate tangible economic and employment outcomes more easily than the relatively amorphous tourism sector and can claim to have had use of the resource base much earlier than tourism.

Political parameters

The parameters outlined thus far are already political to the extent that they involve issues of political jurisdiction and power. Politics actually permeate all aspects of the implementation process, constituting a filter of reality that dictates the extent to which the ideals of sustainability, the 'holistic approach', etc. can actually be achieved (Berry and Ladkin, 1997). The scope of politics includes the structure and composition of bodies that are charged with making the final decisions on all stages of the process, the lobbying processes of interest groups, the negotiation of compromises among stakeholder groups, enforcement, interacting with other jurisdictions and other sectors, etc. (Hall *et al.*, 1997). Changes in government at the local, state or national level usually induce significant readjustments in all aspects of the process. If the change involves a shift from a left-wing to a right-wing ideology, this could lead to a shift from a policy of third party regulation to an environment that favours industry self-regulation.

Temporal parameters

Intergenerational sustainability implies a long-term framework, but political exigencies usually dictate funding and implementation frameworks that are short term. Budgets, for example, seldom provide any certainty of funding beyond a one- or two-year period (Pigram, 1990). More fundamentally, the long-term trajectory of sustainable tourism is incompatible with the political necessity of obtaining the tangible short-term outcomes that will increase the likelihood of re-election. Another problem arises from the fact that causes and their subsequent effects do not always fall within the period of sustainability monitoring, a situation that mirrors the problem with spatial boundaries and makes it more difficult to understand and control the processes that influence sustainability (see above). This temporal discontinuity between cause and effect is modelled in Figure 16.3, which also depicts the same effect from a spatial perspective.

SUSTAINABILITY INDICATORS:
SELECTION, MEASUREMENT AND MONITORING

Selection

An indicator is defined by the OECD as

> a parameter, or a value derived from parameters, which provides information about a phenomenon. The indicator has significance that extends beyond the properties directly associated with the parameter value. [Environmental indicators can] reduce a large quantity of data to a

more accessible and easily understood form . . ., provide an effective early warning system for potential environmental problems [and can be used] to predict future impacts. (in Hamilton and Attwater, 1997, p. 75)

The array of indicators that should be considered in any comprehensive attempt to implement sustainable tourism is enormous, and it is beyond the financial and technical means of smaller destinations in particular to select and monitor more than a small number. Of course, the selection process is also influenced by ideology and politics – indicators of sociocultural and environmental sustainability are likely to be less of a priority for the anthros, who may instead give priority to economic variables. As well, certain indicators may not be applicable to particular destinations. The rate of agricultural land lost to tourism, for instance, is irrelevant to a destination that is already fully urbanized. But even with these qualifications, there is no consensus on any core list of indicators, both tourism and non-tourism, that all destinations should adopt as the most effective basis for measuring and monitoring sustainability. Attempts to construct such lists have been made by a number of organizations, and most notably the WTO, which includes composite indices in its core criteria (in Dymond, 1997). Composite indices attempt to combine several important variables into a single simplified measure, but these are always complicated by uncertainty as to which variables to include, and what weight to apply to each. Once the core group of indicators is selected, there then remains the problem of establishing priorities, since funding may only allow certain indicators to be subsequently measured, monitored and acted upon.

Measurement

The next step requires identification of the criteria for measuring each indicator. Obviously, indicator values must actually measure gradations of sustainability if they are to be useful as indicators, but a major problem in this regard is the lack of knowledge regarding the threshold values that indicate significant shifts. Greatly complicating this situation is the idiosyncratic nature of threshold values – what may constitute a critical value in one destination may not pertain to another similar destination. Associated with this is the need to identify benchmark values against which subsequent performance of that indicator can be gauged. The problem here is being able to position each benchmark within some spectrum of sustainability, so that it can be known whether any improvements are indicative of enhancement, or merely movement toward basic steady state sustainability.

Monitoring

The monitoring of indicators is an ongoing process that follows decisions about selection and means of measurement. Ideally, each indicator should be monitored on a spatially and temporally continuous basis. However, in reality, only a few variables are amenable to such intensive scrutiny. For example, aerial photographs and satellite imagery can provide comprehensive spatial coverage (though not on a temporally continuous basis), while temperature can be gauged continuously through time (though not on a spatially continuous basis). More typically, difficult decisions have to be made as to the best procedure for collecting sample data that will effectively represent continuous processes. The danger, however, is that interval sampling will disguise significant variations in the data. For example, concentration indicators that collect data once a month might miss the short-term but dramatic increases or decreases in traffic that are associated with special events and changes in the weather. Another important consideration is to ensure that the methods for measuring and monitoring remain consistent over the long term, so that the outcomes obtained throughout the sampling period are internally comparable, and not skewed by decisions to change the sampling criteria. Unfortunately, it is almost inevitable that these criteria will change as budget realities and technological improvements warrant adjustments to the monitoring process.

ASSESSING THE ATTAINMENT OF GOALS AND IMPLEMENTATION OF REMEDIAL ACTION

Periodically, it is necessary to assess the cumulative performance of the selected indicators, and determine what progress is being made in the direction of sustainable tourism. The task here then is to assess the relative performance of the various indicators and assess whether the original goals and objectives and, ultimately, sustainable tourism, are being achieved. Given the problems that are encountered at each stage of the process, it is questionable whether any reliable conclusions can be drawn as to the status of sustainability in the destination.

But even if such conclusions could be made, there still remains the problem of implementing remedial action where deemed necessary, and being able to ensure that sustainable practices are maintained. According to McKercher (1993), implementation ideally proceeds on the basis of perfect knowledge, a willingness of all stakeholders to compromise, the belief that solutions (in this case, to the problem of unsustainable tourism) are possible, and that undue political influences are absent. However, the reality is that the implementation stage, already the culmination of a very imperfect procedure, is hampered by inadequate and often erroneous information, the tendency of stakeholders to cling stubbornly to their own agendas and ideologies, and their further tendency to harness the political process as much as possible to further these agendas. A much higher level of resistance can also be expected at this stage, since it may entail costly attempts to change existing patterns of behaviour, and may involve the concession of power away from some stakeholders. In resisting the actual implementation of sustainable tourism measures, it is also relatively easy for the dissident forces to argue, with some merit, that such costly measures are unwarranted given the imperfect nature of the process.

CONCLUSION: WHERE TO FROM HERE?

This chapter paints a gloomy picture of the procedure involved in operationalizing sustainable tourism, and the obvious question is whether the effort is worthwhile to pursue in the first place. There are at least three reasons for arguing in the affirmative:

- If no effort at all is made, then an unsustainable outcome is virtually guaranteed. At the very least, a credible effort is likely to push the destination or product in a sustainable direction, and can produce significant outcomes in terms of knowledge and experience gained.
- Managers need to revisit the term 'indicator', which is just that in a literal sense – an indication, and not definitive evidence, of sustainability. This recognizes a reasonable amount of flexibility in the concept that is easier to cope with than a rigid standard. The emphasis, perhaps, should be placed on evidence that a destination is moving toward, or away from, a more general state of environmental, economic and sociocultural sustainability.
- Finally, it should be borne in mind that the whole debate surrounding sustainable tourism is only just over one decade old, and that great progress has been achieved during this brief period of time. This is especially evident in the extent to which evidence of sustainable practice is forthcoming from the mainstream mass tourism industry (Dymond, 1997; Goodall, 1992; Hawkes and Williams, 1993; Mowforth and Munt, 1998), notwithstanding the legitimate criticisms of this apparent trend that have been made by Wheeller (1993), Mowforth and Munt (1998) and others.

If such a degree of progress is possible in a decade (i.e. the 'foundation years'), then the prospects for the first ten years of the next century are very promising indeed, despite the problems cited in this chapter. In large part, this relates to the awareness within the industry that many facets of sustainable practice are directly and indirectly profitable, and that larger-scale operators are actually in a better position to implement sustainable practices than their smaller-scale counterparts. On the ideological front, progress will also be achieved if the moderate camps of each basic perspective are willing to work together to identify common ground. On the biocentric side, this involves the resource preservationists, while the moderate group on the anthropocentric side is the resource conservationists. Together, these two groups occupy an area or 'realm of compromise' close to the centre of the ideological spectrum.

REFERENCES

Berry, S. and Ladkin, B. (1997) 'Sustainable tourism: a regional perspective'. *Tourism Management*, **18**(7), 433–40.

Clarke, J. (1997) 'A framework of approaches to sustainable tourism'. *Journal of Sustainable Tourism*, **5**(3), 224–33.

Consulting and Auditing Canada (1995) *What Tourism Managers Need to Know: A Practical Guide to the Development and Use of Indicators of Sustainable Tourism*. Ottawa, Canada: Consulting and Auditing Canada.

Dymond, S. (1997) 'Indicators of sustainable tourism in New Zealand: a local government perspective'. *Journal of Sustainable Tourism*, **5**(4), 279–93.

Eber, S. (1992) *Beyond the Green Horizon: Principles for Sustainable Tourism*. London: World Wildlife Fund and Tourism Concern.

Frazier, J. (1997) 'Sustainable development: modern elixir or sack dress?' *Environmental Conservation*, **24**(2), 182–93.

Gill, A. and Williams, P. (1994) 'Managing growth in mountain tourism communities'. *Tourism Management*, **15**, 212–20.

Goodall, B. (1992) 'Environmental auditing for tourism'. In C. P. Cooper and A. Lockwood (eds) *Progress in Tourism, Recreation and Hospitality Management*, Volume 4. London: Belhaven Press, pp. 60–74.

Hall, C. M., Jenkins, J. and Kearsley, G. (eds) (1997) *Tourism Planning and Policy in Australia and New Zealand: Cases, Issues and Practice*. Sydney, Australia: Irwin Publishers.

Hamilton, C. and Attwater, R. (1997) 'Measuring the environment: the availability and use of environmental statistics in Australia'. *Australian Journal of Environmental Management*, **4**(2), 72–87.

Hawkes, S. and Williams, P. (eds) (1993) *The Greening of Tourism from Principles to Practice: A Casebook of Best Environmental Practice in Tourism*. Burnaby, BC, Canada: Centre for Tourism Policy and Research, Simon Fraser University.

Hunter, C. (1995) 'On the need to re-conceptualise sustainable tourism development'. *Journal of Sustainable Tourism*, **3**(3), 155–65.

Jafari, J. (1989) 'An English language literature review'. In J. Bystrzanowski (ed.) *Tourism as a Factor of Change: A Sociocultural Study*. Vienna: Centre for Research and Documentation in Social Sciences, pp. 17–60.

McKercher, B. (1993) 'The unrecognised threat to tourism: can tourism survive "sustainability"?' *Tourism Management*, **14**(2), 131–6.

Maclaren, V. (1996) 'Urban sustainability reporting'. *Journal of the American Planning Association*, **62**(2), 184–206.

Mowforth, M. and Munt, I. (1998) *Tourism and Sustainability: New Tourism in the Third World*. London: Routledge.

Pigram, J. (1990) 'Sustainable tourism: policy considerations'. *Journal of Tourism Studies*, **1**(2), 2–9.

WCED (World Commission on Environment and Development) (1987) *Our Common Future*. Oxford: Oxford University Press.

Wheeller, B. (1993) 'Sustaining the ego'. *Journal of Sustainable Tourism*, **1**(2), 129–39.

Willers, B. (1994) 'Sustainable development: a new world deception'. *Conservation Biology*, **8**, 1146–8.

CHAPTER 17

Globalization and the Economic Impacts of Tourism

Trevor Mules

INTRODUCTION

The last quarter of the twentieth century has seen increasing international movement of goods, services, people, funds and information. This erosion of national boundaries has been termed globalization, or internationalization. Tourism is in the vanguard of this trend involving the international movement of people, international payments, cross-fertilisation of culture, and international business investment in tourism infrastructure such as hotels and attractions.

Despite the gradual breakdown of national barriers, political boundaries continue to define national interest and there continues to be a demand from policy-makers for information on the economic impact of tourism on the national economy. Traditional approaches to measuring economic impact have concentrated upon multiplier effects on national economic variables such as national income (GDP), and employment.

Archer (1996), and Wagner (1997) are examples of this approach, where the multipliers have been derived from an input output model. The approach is essentially one in which tourist expenditure is classified into a number of categories such as accommodation, transport, shopping, entertainment etc. Each of these categories coincides with a sector in the input output model and each sector has its own multiplier. The tourism multiplier then becomes a weighted average of the multipliers of all the sectors that receive tourist expenditure. The weights are the proportionate amounts of expenditure by tourists in each sector.

The input-output approach is appropriate in certain circumstances. But where tourism is a large earner of foreign exchange, a significant user of the nation's land, labour, capital and natural resources, and attracts international investment, the input-output approach involves too many unrealistic assumptions to provide valid results. Skene (1993), and Adams and Parmenter (1999) advocate the computable general equilibrium (CGE) model as a way of overcoming the shortcomings of the traditional approach.

This chapter considers in some detail the merits and deficiencies of the economic models in the light of increasing globalization of tourism activity. It identifies situations when it is appropriate to use the traditional input-output multiplier approach, and indicates how increasing globalization of tourism will affect the approach taken to measuring economic impact.

GLOBALIZATION, TOURISM, AND ECONOMICS

There are two key features of globalization that affect the economic impact of tourism. Firstly, on the demand side, the rapid growth in international tourism relative to domestic tourism in many countries means that research which seeks to measure the economic impact of tourism must pay increasing attention to issues of international trade, especially currency and exchange effects. These are not so much an issue with domestic tourism.

Secondly, on the supply side the increasing globalization of business means that much of the income earned in tourism-related companies (for example, hotels, airlines) accrues to citizens (shareholders) in countries other than the tourist destination.

APPROACHES TO ECONOMIC MODELLING

It is disconcerting to non-economists that there are numerous types of economic models from which to choose when estimating the economic impact of tourism. Mules (1996) summarizes the main types of models and points out that differences between them lie in the variables which each model treats as significant or not significant. For example, traditional multipliers from input-output analysis assume that the impacts being modelled have no influence on prices, whereas CGE models explicitly model such price impacts.

The traditional multiplier approach

As indicated above, the popular approach to measuring the economic impacts of tourism is to use multipliers estimated from an input-output model of the target economy. Some of the more important implicit assumptions in this approach are that an increased number of tourists and their expenditure:

1. does not have any impact on relative prices, and so no substitution occurs,
2. has no impact on the exchange rate,

3. has no impact on resource prices such as land prices, or interest rates,
4. involves the government in reducing its deficit rather than reducing tax rates,
5. generates income which is retained in the economy where it is earned,
6. involves no economies of scale in input usage,
7. has no environmental or social costs,
8. has no feedback effects via links with other economies (both purchases and migration).

For tourism scenarios which are relatively small and localized, most of these assumptions are valid, or if they are not, the impacts can be assessed outside of the multiplier process. For example, in their study of the economic impacts of the Adelaide Grand Prix, Burns and Mules (1986) used a multiplier for tourism expenditure of 1.12 for estimating the effects on the state economy (Gross State Product), and derived estimates of the social costs outside of the input-output model.

In this situation there were relatively few international visitors, and so foreign exchange effects could be assumed away. The tourism impact was confined to a few days around the event and so there were unlikely to be any impacts of economies of scale, or any increase in resource prices due to shortages of land, labour etc. However, even in this case it could be argued that some of the profits generated in hotels, breweries, airlines, etc. accrued to entities outside the state via interstate and international ownership of the assets involved. This means that the multiplier approach has tended to overstate the true economic gain to the residents of the state in question.

Tourism multiplier effects are based on the economic structure as it existed for the target economy when the multiplier was estimated. Implicit in such estimation is a certain amount of leakage of economic activity via imports. One aspect of increased internationalization has been the increasing degree of import penetration into most sectors of the economy. This is not only an effect of fewer restrictions on international trade, but also of multinational corporations shifting their production around the world to take advantage of lower labour costs or depressed exchange rates.

Given that there is usually a lapse of time between the target year for multiplier estimation and their use in tourism impact studies, by the time multipliers are being used, they reflect an economic structure that has been made obsolete by the globalization processes. Again, the approach is likely to overestimate the economic impacts of tourism expenditure because it does not allow for the greater leakage to imports that is occurring relative to that which was occurring at the time of estimation of the multipliers.

The multiplier approach is likely to be appropriate for modelling the economic impacts of small special events, or events with limited international visitor attraction, or for tourism generally to small regions. However, in the latter case it is important to be wary of price effects which are not explicitly accounted for in the traditional approach.

For example, the city of Cairns in northern Australia developed historically around sugar cane, fishing and other primary commodities. In the 1980s and 1990s Cairns experienced a rapid growth in inbound international tourism, and the infrastructure investment associated with mass tourism. The investment and growth in tourism pushed up land prices, and wage rates, which reduced the profitability of sugar cane farming.

The input-output based multiplier approach would not explicitly take account of this negative effect on other industries. This is not to say that a competent researcher would not be able to incorporate such effects into the research into tourism's economic impacts, but it would be a separate calculation to the impacts of the expenditure of tourists on accommodation, shopping etc.

The point here is that the term 'economic impact' needs to be interpreted more widely than has traditionally been the case. The usual approach, such as Archer (1977) and Bicak and Altinary (1996), is restricted to the *positive* effects of expenditure by tourists on the hospitality, transport and other affected sectors. To be comprehensive, the studies should include an allowance for any negative effects, such as the impacts on costs in other industries.

Effects which the traditional approach excludes are not always negative. For example, special events such as the Olympic Games, or Formula One Grand Prix, may have positive promotional effects for both business and tourism. Local businesses may be able to use the event as a way of hosting clients and customers. The inaugural 1985 Australian Grand Prix in Adelaide reportedly resulted in deals being done in the corporate hospitality tents (Bentick, 1986).

While the traditional multiplier approach does not explicitly include many effects as listed above, researchers have tended to rely on the method, and to graft other effects on to the results. This approach to other effects has two problems which may or may not be significant, depending upon the circumstances:

i.   the decision of what to evaluate and what not to include becomes arbitrary. Ideally the economic model should be comprehensive, but all models face the same choice of what to make endogenous, and what to leave out;

ii. there may be complicated feedback effects which are not taken into account. For example, a study of the economic impacts of international tourism in Cairns may well measure the impact on land prices as an 'add-on' to the usual impact of tourism expenditure. But such land price increases may deter tourism infrastructure development which may in turn reduce the growth in visitor numbers that has been projected.

The very widespread nature of the multiplier approach makes it generally accessible and many researchers and consultants find it relatively easy to use. It is widely understood by, and easily explained to, policy-makers. And it is relatively cheap compared with the alternative, such as a CGE approach. Adams and Parmenter (1999, p. 119) comment that 'in small regional economies . . . the range of mechanisms encompassed by a general equilibrium model, over and above those included in an input-output model, may not be of much practical importance'.

Globalization and the multiplier approach

Tourism multipliers which are derived from input output models depend for their values in part on the 'open-ness' of the host economy to international trade. The more open the host economy (i.e. the lower are trade barriers such as tariffs) the greater the leakage effect to imports of an input-output multiplier and therefore the lower the multiplier value.

Paradoxically, in Australia the tourism multiplier actually rose from 0.80 in 1973–74 (Bureau of Industry Economics, 1979, p. 74) to 0.863 in 1995–96 (O'Dea, 1997, p.A3). This is despite the share of imports in GDP rising from 14 per cent to 20 per cent due to the globalization of trade. It appears that the sectors of the economy which most attract tourism expenditure have moved against the trend of increased reliance on imports.

The general equilibrium approach

Whereas the input-output multiplier approach to modelling tourism's economic impacts is very much driven by tourists' expenditures, and how they generate economic activity in supplying industries such as accommodation, transport, retailing and so on, the general equilibrium approach makes explicit many more economic impacts. For example, the general equilibrium model is able to include as endogenous effects the impacts on prices and wages, the response of government to changes in government revenue, the effects in financial markets on such variables as interest rates and exchange rates.

Because general equilibrium models are more comprehensive, they are able to take account of global/international effects such as exchange rates and imports. However, the process of opening up to many more influences also requires more information and/or more assumptions. For example, if an increase in tourism causes a rise in room rates at hotels, is it across the board, or only for five star? If the latter, does it only affect international visitors, and if so, how do they respond? Do they reduce the length of their stay, do they substitute in favour of cheaper accommodation or do they maintain their accommodation and give up something else, such as souvenir shopping?

Skene (1993) showed how significant such questions could be when analysing changes in numbers of international visitors to Australia. He used a CGE model for Australia, and estimated a multiplier for tourist expenditure of either 1.8 or 11.4, depending upon what was assumed about the behaviour of government. In the 11.4 case it was assumed that tax revenue rose as a result of tourism, and that the government spent the extra revenue, thereby increasing GDP. In the 1.8 case it was assumed that the extra revenue was used to reduce the government deficit, and so no extra government expenditure occurred.

The general point to emerge from this example is that the meaning of 'economic impact' depends upon the economic setting in which the phenomenon of interest (an increase in tourism) occurs. The impact on typical economic variables such as GDP, employment etc. depends upon whether GDP is growing or declining under other influences such as world commodity prices and volumes, tariff and exchange rate scenarios, international interest rate regimes and so on.

Given the tendency at the time of writing for the world's financial markets to regard the USA Treasury interest rate as some kind of benchmark, the impact of tourism on a country such as Australia depends upon what the researcher assumes to be the stance of US monetary policy.

These points illustrate some of the problems in using general equilibrium models. In general, despite such problems, the approach is widely used in non-tourism studies. Bhattacharyya (1996) reviews CGE modelling of energy and environmental issues, while Partridge and Rickman (1998) review CGE approaches to regional economic modelling and analysis. The approach is also widely used in trade and tax modelling. For example, Bernheim, Scholz and Shoven (1991) modelled consumption tax issues, while Gazel, Hewings and Sonis (1995) modelled impacts of the USA–Canada free trade agreement.

Skene (1993) and Adams and Parmenter (1995) are examples of CGE modelling of international tourism in Australia. In both studies the emphasis is on the impacts of tourism expenditure, and both studies show the importance of the impact of tourism's foreign exchange earnings. In particular, Adams and Parmenter allowed the extra earning of foreign exchange to raise the value of the A$ in foreign exchange markets, thereby reducing the A$ earnings of traditional export industries such as mining and agriculture. In the Australian case this result had significant and somewhat perverse regional implications.

The negative impacts on mining and agriculture were particularly significant for the state of Queensland, which is also the State where much of the growth in Australia's inbound tourism has occurred. Table 17.1 below is reproduced from Adams and Parmenter (1999) in which they make the point that 'the expansionary effects of tourism in Queensland depend primarily on the extent to which tourism to Queensland increases, the contractionary effects are driven by the whole of the national increase in tourism, all of which contributes to the strengthening of the real exchange rate'.

Table 17.1 compares the impacts of a 10 per cent increase in the growth in international tourism to Australia on the Gross State Product (GSP) of two states, Victoria and Queensland. The economy of Victoria is less dependent upon inbound tourism, mining or agriculture, and is more dependent upon manufacturing and service industries.

The table shows that the direct or first-round effect is bigger on Queensland's rate of growth of GSP than on Victoria's, a reflection of Queensland's greater share of inbound tourism (22 per cent compared with 17 per cent; Bureau of Tourism Research, International Visitor Survey, 1996). However, the impact on the air transport industry is greater in Victoria, since major service companies in air transport are located in Victoria.

The negative impact on traditional export industries is six times greater for Queensland than for Victoria, a result which causes the overall impact of growth in tourism to be negative for Queensland, whereas the positive effects on its air transport industry makes Victoria's overall impact positive.

This result appears to be at odds with conventional wisdom and with facts. The Australian Bureau of Statistics' review of the Queensland economy (ABS, 1990, Catalogue No. 1315.3, 'Queensland During the 1980s') stated that tourism, mining and in-migration were the three driving forces of economic growth in the Queensland economy during the 1980s. State accounts data for Australia shows Queensland's average annual rate of growth of GSP over the period 1990–91 to 1997–98 to be 6.1 per cent, while over the same period Victoria's was only 3.3 per cent.

The reasons for the apparent contradiction is that the CGE modelling results of Adams and Parmenter are comparative, and are in a static economic setting. That is to say the model compares two situations, one with higher tourism growth than the other. The results are negative for Queensland because higher tourism growth results in lower growth for traditional export industries because of the exchange rate effects. This is not saying that Queensland is growing less fast than Victoria, only that it is growing less fast than it would otherwise do.

The static nature of the modelling also contributes to the perverse results. Queensland has experienced substantial in-migration from other states over the past 15–20 years. From 1976 to 1996, Queensland's average annual rate of population increase was 2.1 per cent, compared with a national average of 1.3 per cent. Some of this population flow has been driven by employment opportunities which in turn derive from the stimulus to local tourism industries from the growth in tourism. Adams and Parmenter's CGE modelling did not take this dynamic effect into account.

A further point to note is that, while Queensland may appear to lose GSP growth in traditional export industries such as mining and agriculture, this is something of an illusion, because while the GSP in these industries may be *generated* in Queensland, a good percentage of it accrues to the foreign owners of mining companies and pastoral holdings, rather than to Queenslanders. The losses to Queensland are thus overstated by the Adams and Parmenter modelling.

The work of Skene (1993) and Adams and Parmenter (1995, 1999) pertains to modelling the economic impacts of tourism in Australia using CGE models. There is almost no research of this type on tourism outside Australia, with the exception being Zhou *et al.* (1997) in which a CGE model for Hawaii was used to measure the

Table 17.1 Effects of a 10 percentage point increase in the national rate of growth of international tourism on Gross State Product in Victoria and Queensland. *Source:* Adams and Parmenter (1999)

	Victoria	Queensland
	Percentage	
Contributions of:		
first-round effect on local tourism industries	0.007	0.017
air transport (including aircraft maintenance)	0.032	0.022
traditional exports	−0.014	−0.080
other industries	0.039	−0.050
Average annual rate of growth of GSP	0.064	−0.091

Table 17.2 Impacts on Hawaiian industry output of a 10 per cent decline in visitor expenditure. *Source:* Zhou *et al.* (1997)

Industry	CGE Model Result %	Input-Output Result %
Manufacturing	−4.54	−10.43
Construction	−0.77	−1.75
Transportation	−7.25	−10.41
Communication	−5.32	−8.15
Trade	−6.37	−6.95
Restaurants and Bars	−8.25	−9.40
Hotels	−9.65	−11.22
Services	−4.28	−4.52

economic impacts of a 10 per cent decline in tourism expenditure. Presumably their interest in a *decline* in expenditure was motivated by the effects of the Asian financial crisis and the poor economic performance of the Japanese economy.

They point out that tourism 'accounts for nearly 35 per cent of the Hawaii Gross State Product' (Zhou *et al.*, 1997, p. 77) and they compare output effects estimated from the CGE model with those estimated using the traditional input-output model. They find that the input-output approach gives consistently larger declines in output in every industry (see Table 17.2). The reason is that the CGE model allows prices to moderate in the face of declining demand, the input output model does not. This price effect tends to moderate the reduction in demand in the CGE model.

Interestingly, they do not allow for any exchange rate effect, or for any other financial effect. This is because Hawaii is part of the larger US financial system, and although tourism is a large part of the Hawaii economy, Hawaiian tourism is not a large part of the US economy. Thus they elect to run their CGE model with the exchange rate and other exports both fixed. This contrasts with the Adams and Parmenter work in Australia.

TOURISM AND INTERNATIONAL TRADE

Estimates by Australia's Bureau of Tourism Research (1998) show tourist expenditure in Australia by Australian residents to be 3.4 times as great as tourist expenditure by foreign visitors. This means that the economic impacts of Australians as tourists in their own country far outweigh the impacts of foreign tourists in Australia. However, the growth in tourist numbers and expenditure over the last two decades has been much higher in the international arena than for domestic tourism.

International tourism to Australia has grown by an annual average of 12.3 per cent over the period 1992 to 1997 (Office of National Tourism, 1998). Over the same period, domestic visitor nights grew at an average annual rate of 3.1 per cent (Bureau of Tourism Research, 1998). This has placed inbound tourism in the forefront as an export industry and as an earner of foreign exchange. According to the Office of National Tourism (1998), tourism accounted for 12.6 per cent of Australia's export earnings, compared with 9.6 per cent for coal exports, and 7.3 per cent for gold exports.

The balance of payments effects of tourism

International tourism is an export of services in the balance of payments of the host country. It also increases the need for imports in the host country, both as a component of visitor expenditure, and as a component of the expenditure by industries which cater for tourists. This induced import effect has been modelled by CGE modellers in Australia, but with ambiguous results which depend upon the assumptions made.

Adams and Parmenter (1991) experimented with various assumptions about the 'economic environment' within which tourism growth occurred. These included a constraint on capacity of tourism supplying industries, a constraint on the government's borrowing and a constraint on national expenditure. In every case they found that the induced increase in imports exceeded the boost to export receipts from tourism, such that the international balance of trade effect was negative.

Skene (1993) assumed a fixed exchange rate, the result being a much smaller increase in imports, and a net improvement in the balance of trade. This assumption is not very realistic, and so the actual impact on imports is likely to be greater than Skene's range of 0.4 per cent to 1.9 per cent (Skene, 1993, p. 17).

It might be thought that only international tourism and not domestic tourism has significant implications for a country's international balance of payments.

Indeed, international tourism is a rapidly growing segment of international trade in services, and services in turn are replacing goods as the prime movers of international trade. However, it must be remembered that, while foreign inbound tourism earns export receipts for a country, domestic tourism has international balance of payments effects via the demand for imports that domestic tourism generates. Domestic tourists use travel and accommodation services which in turn require imports of aircraft, fuel, hotel equipment, restaurant equipment and so on. In most countries, even relatively self-sufficient ones like the USA, a proportion of such items is imported, either by choice or by necessity.

This is not the only negative impact that domestic tourists have on their international balance of payments. As has been indicated above, domestic travel within Australia has been growing at 3 per cent per year, yet domestic *outbound* travel is growing at over 5 per cent per year (Office of National Tourism, 1998). This development is a function of greater affluence, the falling cost of international travel relative to domestic travel, and the proportion of the population with family links in other countries.

Domestic outbound travel has the same effect on the international balance of payments of a country as buying an imported motor car. It is an import and adds to the import debits in the international accounts. It is an economic impact of tourism which rarely gets modelled by economic modellers, unless in terms of the expenditure impacts in the host country. For example, Gamage and Vu (1996) used traditional input-output modelling to estimate the economic impacts on Vietnam of Australian visitors. However, no attention was paid to the impact on the Australian economy.

It is clear that tourism, whether domestic or international, has profound impacts on the host country's international balance of payments which have either been overlooked by economic modellers, or not modelled in a realistic fashion. With deregulated financial markets, this effect also has implications for the host's exchange rate.

The exchange rate effect of tourism

Where tourism is a major earner of foreign currency, it adds a supply to the foreign exchange market which would not be there if tourism were not so large. This reduces the cost of foreign currency below what it would otherwise be, or put another way, increases the value of the domestic currency beyond what it would otherwise be.

Figure 17.1 below depicts this scenario where the domestic currency is the A$, and the foreign currency is the yen. The growth in international tourism (from Japan) into Australia has pushed the supply of yen out from S_1 to S_2, lowering the price of yen from A$1 per Y100 to A0.75 per Y100. Put the other way, one Australian dollar is now worth Y133, up from Y100, ie a 1/3 appreciation in the exchange rate.

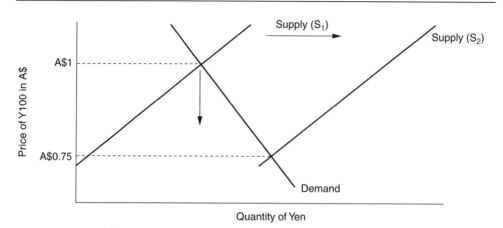

Figure 17.1 Demand and supply of yen in Australia

The supply of foreign currency into Australia due to tourism earnings grew by 10.5 per cent per year over the period 1992–93 to 1997–98, and foreign exchange credits from tourism accounted for 12 per cent of total export credits (Office of National Tourism, 1998). If all else was constant, this would mean a 1.26 per cent annual growth in total export credits due to the growth in tourism receipts from inbound visitors.

To estimate the effect that this would have on the exchange rate, information is needed on the elasticity of demand for foreign currency as depicted in Figure 17.1. If a demand elasticity of minus 1 is assumed, the increased supply of foreign currency caused by tourism would raise the exchange rate by 1.26 per cent per year.

The demand elasticity is actually likely to be less than 1 because the demand for foreign currency reflects the demand for imports. The high proportion of industrial supplies in Australian imports suggests that this demand is likely to be inelastic because of the lack of readily available substitutes, meaning that the exchange rate appreciation caused by the growth in international tourism is likely to exceed 1.26 per cent per year. This analysis is modified by the effect of investment in tourism infrastructure and the consequent increase in imports of such items as aircraft, hotel equipment, coaches etc. These extra demands for foreign currency will tend to eat up the extra supply coming from tourists. However, Skene (1993) suggests that for Australia, under most assumptions, the net effect on the balance of trade is still strongly positive.

On the face of it, this seems to be a good thing. A higher value of a nation's currency is often taken as a symbol of economic success, making imports cheaper and indicating a high desire by foreigners to purchase domestic goods and services. However, where other industries besides tourism are earning foreign exchange through exporting, a higher exchange rate damages their prospects. For example, coal exports (8.4 per cent of Australian export receipts) are paid for in terms which are contractually specified in foreign currency (either $US or yen). Since an appreciation of the exchange rate makes foreign currency translate into less domestic currency, the growth in international inbound tourism indirectly harms the local coal industry.

The above phenomenon is known in the international economics literature as the 'Dutch disease', following the tendency for manufacturing in The Netherlands to slump in the wake of expansion of oil exports from the North Sea (Lindert and Pugel, 1996, p. 81). It has been specifically modelled in relation to tourism in Australia by Adams and Parmenter (1995), and by the Centre for International Economics (1988). In the latter, the squeeze on non-tourism exports is explained by tourism bidding up prices for land and labour rather than through the exchange rate. The irony in the notion of tourism growth harming mining exports is that in the 1970s, mining was the villain, with writers such as Gregory (1976) warning that the growth in mineral exports from Australia would be damaging to what were then traditional agricultural exports.

The exchange rate effect has been highlighted by economic modellers such as Adams and Parmenter (1995) when modelling the economic impacts of growth in foreign tourism in Australia. Strangely it has received no mention in non-Australian studies. For example, Archer (1995) modelled the economic impacts of tourism in Bermuda without any allowance for exchange rate effects, although he did note that, since 80 per cent of tourist expenditure in Bermuda is by US citizens, the value of the US dollar was an important determinant of the economic impact of tourism in Bermuda.

Similarly, Archer and Fletcher (1996) used a traditional input-output approach to measuring the economic impact of tourism in the Seychelles. The 'Dutch disease' effect is perhaps not particularly relevant to an economy such as Bermuda's, where there are really no other export industries to be squeezed by an exchange rate appreciation. For the Seychelles, agriculture and fishing are relatively significant export industries where a negative economic impact from the exchange rate appreciation would be expected.

The story is very different for Korea, where Lee and Kwon (1997) carried out a study on the economic impacts of casino tourism. They found that casino tourists accounted for some 93.7 per cent of casino revenue in Korea (Lee and Kwon, 1997, p. 57), making the casino tourism industry more export oriented than the motor vehicle or electronics industries. Despite this, and despite Korea exporting almost 80 per cent of motor vehicle production, and 60 per cent of television set production, they make no allowance for the growth in casino tourism receipts squeezing Korea's traditional manufacturing exports via the exchange rate effect. Their analysis is a traditional input-output one, with no reference to any effects in international trade and finance.

To conclude this section on the exchange rate effects of tourism, it is necessary to consider the general issue of what determines the exchange rate. Following financial deregulation throughout much of the Western world during the 1970s and 1980s, currencies have been determined by market forces of supply and demand as depicted in Figure 17.1. Or have they? There is a strand of economics that attempts to explain exchange rate movements in terms of relative interest rate differentials (Blundell-Wignall and Browne, 1991). That is, if Australian interest rates are above, say, US interest rates, then foreign funds flow into Australia pushing up the value of the A$.

In the long run, if the model depicted in Figure 17.1 is applicable, the value of a currency is determined by the ratio of its export prices to its import prices, i.e. its terms of trade. A rise in the price of coal on world markets would shift the supply curve in Figure 17.1 to the right in coal exporting countries, thereby raising the value of their currencies (reducing the cost of foreign currency).

Gruen and Wilkinson (1994) found that a 1 per cent rise in the terms of trade 'leads to an appreciation of the Australian real exchange rate of about 0.3 to 0.5 per cent' (Gruen and Wilkinson, 1994, p. 214). However, they also found that a 1 percentage point interest differential leads to a 2 to 3.5 per cent appreciation. This raises the question of interest rates, and how growth in tourism receipts impacts on a country's interest rates.

Globalization of tourism supply

One aspect of globalization is the increasing foreign ownership of tourism businesses. High-profile cases such as the dominance of Japanese ownership of hotels in Waikiki and Australia's Gold Coast give the impression that substantial ownership of tourism assets are in foreign hands. Further evidence to support this notion is the 25 per cent of Qantas owned by British Airways, and the 50 per cent of Ansett Australia owned by Air New Zealand.

The implication of foreign ownership for economic impact measurement lies with the variable GDP which is the conventional variable used for the exercise. GDP is a measure of all income (and indirect taxes) at the point of generation. Thus the wages paid and profits earned in a hotel are included in the GDP. But profits do not necessarily accrue to residents of the host economy. Foreign ownership means that the profits accrue to the owners who are residents of a country other than the host. Whether the profits are actually taken out of the country or re-invested in the host economy does not matter. The point is that they represent part of GDP which is not at the disposal of residents. In their national accounts, most countries treat income accruing to non residents as part of the difference between GDP and Gross Disposable Income. In Australia, despite perceptions of increasing foreign ownership of business generally, this gap has stood at between 3 per cent and 4 per cent for all of the 1990s.

But what of foreign ownership in tourism? Is the GDP being generated in tourism accruing in large amount to non residents? Using Australian data for

1995–96, O'Dea (1997) estimated total GDP in tourism to be $26.88 billion. In the same year the Australian Bureau of Statistics estimated that for all industries, income accruing to non residents was $19.874 billion. Dwyer *et al.* (1990) estimated foreign investment in tourism to be 8.4 per cent of all foreign investment in Australia. If we assume that 8.4 per cent of all foreign income earned in Australia was in the tourism sector, then this would make the foreign income earned in tourism $1.669 billion, or 6.2 per cent of the total GDP in tourism for the year.

Thus it would seem that while GDP may overestimate the amount of income which tourism makes available to residents of the host country, the margin is not great. Of course the margin may be increasing. This is an area where further research is warranted.

STRATEGIC CONSIDERATIONS

Whatever economic model is used to measure the economic impact of tourism, the results of the exercise must be kept in proper perspective. Tourism is an internationally traded service, and economic models cannot predict the future course of world trade and finance. A recent illustration of the inability of models to predict the future was the collapse in Asian exchange rates and financial markets over 1997–98. The importance of this point is that when governments are making decisions about tourism development, they are making strategic economic decisions that will impact on their economies for several years into the future. These decisions need to take account of future trends in international trade, not just the pattern of past trade.

When Gregory (1976) was warning that growth in Australia's mineral exports would harm traditional agricultural exports, farm products accounted for 34 per cent of Australia's total export receipts (ABARE, 1996). By 1996 this figure had fallen to 20 per cent. Over the same period mineral exports rose from 27 per cent to 35 per cent. Does this mean that the government should have halted mining development in order to preserve rural exports? To do so would have been ill-considered strategy, as rural exports are in long-term decline as a share in Australia's total exports, having stood at 71 per cent in 1956–57, and 49 per cent in 1966–67. This is a reflection of trends in consumer choices worldwide which gave greater prominence to manufactured goods and less prominence to primary products.

In recent decades this shifting of consumer preferences has tended to favour services. Hence travel credits have risen from 6 per cent of total exports in the mid-1980s to 10 per cent in the mid 1990s. Over the same period mineral exports fell from 42 per cent to 35 per cent of total exports. To attempt to halt the decline in the prominence of mineral exports by limiting tourism development would damage the country's future prospects in international trade.

In a world where growth in traded consumer services exceeds growth in demand for goods, nations which have a comparative advantage in tourism should accept that acting strategically in favour of tourism may have some negative impacts on other industries. However, this is a far better outcome for the nation than would occur under the alternative scenario.

REFERENCES

ABARE (1996) *Australian Commodity Statistics*. Canberra: Australian Bureau of Agricultural and Resource Economics, December.

ABS (1990) 'Queensland During the 1980's'. Brisbane: Australian Bureau of Statistics Catalogue No. 1315.3.

Adams, P.D. and B.R. Parmenter (1991) *The Medium Term Significance of International Tourism for the Australian Economy*, Canberra: Bureau of Tourism Research.

Adams, P. D. and Parmenter, B. R. (1995) 'An Applied General Equilibrium Analysis of the Effects of Tourism in a Quite Small, Quite Open Economy', *Applied Economics*, **27**, 985–994.

Adams, P. D. and Parmenter, B. R. (1999) 'General Equilibrium Models', Chapter 10 in *Valuing Tourism: Methods and Techniques*, Canberra: Occasional Paper No. 28, Bureau of Tourism Research.

Archer, B. H. (1977) *Tourism Multipliers: The State of the Art*, Bangor Occasional Papers in Economics, No. 11. Bangor: University of Wales Press.

Archer, B. H. (1995) 'Importance of Tourism for the Economy of Bermuda' *Annals of Tourism Research*, **22**,4, 918–30.

Archer, B. H. (1996) 'Economic impact analysis'. *Annals of Tourism Research*, **23**(4), 704–7.

Archer, Brian and Fletcher, John (1996) 'The economic impact of tourism in the Seychelles'. *Annals of Tourism Research*, **23**(1), 32–47.

Bentick, B. L. (1986) 'The role of the Grand Prix in promoting South Australian entrepreneurship'. In J. P. A. Burns, J. H. Hatch and T. J. Mules (eds) *The Adelaide Grand Prix: The Impact of a Special Event*, Ch. 9. Adelaide: Centre for South Australian Economic Studies.

Bernheim, B. D., Scholz, K. J. and Shoven, J. B. (1991) 'Consumption taxation in general equilibrium models: how reliable are simulation results?' In B. D. Bernheim and J. B. Shoven (eds) *National Savings and Economic Performance*. Chicago: University of Chicago Press.

Bhattacharyya, S. C. (1996) 'Applied general equilibrium models for energy studies: a survey'. *Energy Economics*, **18**, 145–64.

Bicak, H. A. and Altinary, M. (1996) 'Economic impact of Israeli tourists on North Cypress'. *Annals of Tourism Research*, **23**, 928–31.

Blundell-Wignall, A. and Browne, F. (1991) *Increasing Financial Market Integration, Real Exchange Rates and Macroeconomic Adjustment*. OECD Economics and Statistics Department Working Paper, cited in David W. R. Gruen and Jenny Wilkinson (1994) 'Australia's real exchange rate – is it explained by the terms of trade or by real interest differentials?' *Economic Record*, **70**(209), 204–19. Melbourne: Economic Society of Australia.

Bureau of Tourism Research (1996) *International Visitor Survey*. Canberra: BTR.

Bureau of Tourism Research (1998) *Australian Tourism 1998 Data Card*. Canberra: BTR.

Burns, J. P. A. and Mules, T. J. (1986) 'A framework for the analysis of major special events'. In J. P. A. Burns, J. H. Hatch and T. J. Mules (eds) *The Adelaide Grand Prix: The Impact of a Special Event*. Adelaide: Centre for South Australian Economic Studies.

Centre for International Economics (1988) *Economic Effects of International Tourism*. Canberra: Centre for International Economics.

Dwyer, L., Findlay, O. and Forsyth, P. (1990) *Foreign Investment in Australian Tourism*. Bureau of Tourism Research. Occasional Paper No. 6.

Gamage, Ari and Vu, Minh Duc (1996) 'Measuring the economic impact of tourist arrivals: a comparison of expatriate and non-expatriate travellers from Australia to Vietnam'. Paper presented to the National Tourism and Hospitality Conference, Coffs Harbor.

Gazel, R., Hewings, G. J. D. and Sonis, M. (1995) 'Trade, sensitivity and feedbacks: interregional impacts of the US–Canada Free Trade Agreement'. In J. C. J. M. van den Bergh, P. Nijkamp and P. Rietveld (eds) *Recent Advances in Spatial Equilibrium Modelling*. New York: Springer.

Gregory, R. G. (1976) 'Some implications of the growth of the mining sector'. *Australian Journal of Agricultural Economics*, **20**, 97–104.

Gruen, David W. R. and Wilkinson, Jenny (1994) 'Australia's real exchange rate – is it explained by the terms of trade or by real interest differentials?' *Economic Record*, **70**(209), 204–19.

KPMG Management Consulting (1996) *Business, Economic and Social Review of the IndyCar Event*. Brisbane: KPMG Management Consulting.

Lee, Choong-Ki and Kwon, Kyung-Sang (1997) 'The economic impact of the casino industry in South Korea'. *Journal of Travel Research*, summer, 52–8.

Lindert, Peter H. and Pugel, Thomas A. (1996) *International Economics* (10th edition). Chicago: Irwin.

Mules, Trevor (1996) 'Kate Fischer or Liz Hurley – which model shall I use?' Paper presented to Australian National Tourism Research Conference, Coffs Harbor.

O'Dea, Daniel (1997) *Tourism's Indirect Economic Effects 1995–6*. Bureau of Tourism Research. Research Paper No. 4.

Office of National Tourism (1998) *Tourism Industry Trends*, Issue Number 5. Canberra: Department of Industry, Science and Tourism.

Partridge, Mark D. and Rickman, Dan S. (1998) 'Regional computable general equilibrium modeling: a survey and critical appraisal'. *International Regional Science Review*, **21**(3), 205–50.

Price Waterhouse (1989) *Economic Impact Assessment of the 1988 Australian Formula One Grand Prix*. Adelaide: Australian Formula One Grand Prix Board.

Skene, John (1993) *The Economic Impact of Growth in Visitor Expenditure – A Quantitative Assessment*. Working Paper No. 92. Canberra: Bureau of Industry Economics.

Wagner, John E. (1997) 'Estimating the economic impacts of tourism'. *Annals of Tourism Research*, **24**(3), 592–608.

Zhou, Deying, Yanagida, John F., Chakravorty, Ujjayant and Leung, PingSun (1997) 'Estimating economic impacts from tourism'. *Annals of Tourism Research*, **24**(1), 76–89.

CHAPTER 18

Turbulence, Chaos and Complexity in Tourism Systems: A Research Direction for the New Millennium

Bill Faulkner and Roslyn Russell

INTRODUCTION

As a domain of human activity at the global level, tourism is a relatively recent, twentieth-century, phenomenon and it has only become the subject of a coherent field of research in the second half of this century. This history partly explains the emergence of tourism as a multidisciplinary field of study, rather than a discipline in its own right (Graburn and Jafari, 1991; Gunn, 1994), as the prior existence of many established social science disciplines provided the conceptual and methodological foundations for research and education. On the one hand, it can be reasonably claimed that this genesis of the tourism field has been an important strength because it has brought diverse perspectives to bear on what has been increasingly recognized as a multifaceted phenomenon. On the other hand, it also means that a large part of tourism research has inherited the Newtonian or Cartesian research tradition, which has dominated many of the social science disciplines that have influenced the evolution of the field (Faulkner and Russell, 1997). This is especially so since, as observed by Graham Dann and Joan Phillips in Chapter 13, positivistically inclined business and management-oriented disciplines have become more prominent, at the expense of traditional disciplines (anthropology, sociology, psychology). Although a Newtonian paradigm has arguably been instrumental in advancing our knowledge in tourism, it is equally true that it has resulted in certain aspects of tourism being poorly understood. In particular, conventional approaches to tourism research are more attuned to the analysis of relatively stable systems, resulting in large gaps in the understanding of turbulent phases in tourism development and the underlying dynamics of change (Hall, 1995; Laws *et al.*, 1998).

As we face the dawn of the new millennium, it is perhaps timely for us to assess the adequacy of the conceptual and methodological tools currently used by tourism researchers. If, as suggested above, the dominant paradigm is deficient as a basis for understanding change, then we clearly need to modify our approach. This is particularly so if, as argued later in this chapter, the world of the late twentieth century and the new millennium has become, and is becoming, increasingly turbulent. In this chapter, we elaborate on the case for adopting chaos theory, and the allied complexity perspective, as a more useful conceptual foundation for understanding change in, and the dynamics of, tourism systems (Faulkner and Russell, 1997; Russell and Faulkner, 1999). In doing so, we begin with an outline of the chaos perspective and its distinctiveness from the Newtonian paradigm. The nexus between three types of events that are often associated with increased turbulence and change in the tourism industry (disasters, crises and entrepreneurial activity) is then described in terms of the chaos framework. Finally, the question of turbulence as a global trend is addressed to demonstrate the potential relevance of the chaos perspective to tourism research in the new millennium.

CHAOS AND COMPLEXITY

Like most of their counterparts in other social sciences, tourism researchers have traditionally focused on aspects of tourist behaviour and tourism development patterns that exhibit order, linearity and equilibrium, while eschewing situations where disorder, non-linearity and disequilibrium are more apparent. This is because the parent disciplines from which tourism studies have been derived have generally adhered to the Cartesian or Newtonian paradigm of scientific inquiry. The Newtonian tradition in the social sciences has essentially endeavoured to emulate nineteenth-century physics by precisely measuring social behaviour and relationships in positivistic, quantitative terms. It is founded on a reductionist position, which sees small changes in the initial conditions of a system being invariably reflected in small changes in the final state. By elaborating on the fundamental limitations of this paradigm at this stage, we can bring a sharper focus to bear on the distinctiveness of the alternative, chaos theory based, approach.

As a derivative of classical physics, the Newtonian/Cartesian paradigm propagated a reductionist world-view, whereby objects and events are understood in terms of their constituent parts and these are assumed to fit together like cogs in a clockwork machine. Every event is therefore determined by initial conditions that are, at least in principle, predictable with some degree of precision owing to the predominance of linear or quasi-linear relationships. Small changes at the outset yield correspondingly small shifts in the final state of the system (Capra, 1982). As Prigogine and Stengers (1985) have emphasized, this approach has tended to concentrate on those aspects of systems where stability, order, uniformity and equilibrium are accentuated. Meanwhile, situations where instability, disorder, non-linearity and disequilibrium are more prevalent tend to be construed as aberrations and are therefore ignored, and variations from the 'norm' that offend the elegance of conventional explanatory frameworks are often assumed away as being attributable to 'noise' or 'exogenous factors' (Toohey, 1994). The fact that such variations have the potential to signal an underlying turbulence, which may precipitate fundamental shifts in the system, means that our understanding of the dynamics of change is limited. Thus, in the tourism field, key events (and individuals) that are ultimately responsible for triggering major shifts in the configuration of tourist behaviour and development have often been filtered out of the research process.

Chaos theory provides an alternative perspective, which enables us to gain a deeper understanding of the change process. In contrast to the traditional paradigm described above, chaos theory sees systems as being inherently complex and unstable. Small changes, individual differences and random externalities are therefore recognized as having the potential to precipitate major realignments in systems through disequilibriating positive feedback processes. Non-linear relationships therefore prevail in such systems, which are driven by self-organizing, adaptive tendencies to produce new complex ('emergent') configurations. This perspective offers a more meaningful framework for examining and understanding change by virtue of its appreciation of turbulence as a feature of most systems. While many systems may normally exhibit the steady state characteristics epitomized by the Newtonian model, they are nevertheless periodically disturbed by changes in their environment, or internal structural changes, which precipitate a phase of turbulence until a new steady state configuration is established. In this context, chaos should not be seen as simply a lack of order or a condition reflecting the degeneration of a system, but rather as a creative phase leading to a new, more complex order (Peat, 1991). There is therefore a linkage between chaos and the notion of complexity.

Key propositions of the chaos/complexity perspective that distinguish it from the Newtonian/Cartesian view are outlined in Table 18.1. A central distinction draws on the living systems metaphor (Gleick, 1987; Peat, 1991; Prigogine and Stengers, 1985; Capra, 1996), which in turn highlights the complexity factor. The reductionist approach of the Newtonian paradigm dissects systems into their component parts and interprets the behaviour of the system additively in terms of the static relationships between these parts. Individual parts are examined in isolation, with mechanistic, clock-like relationships being assumed. We therefore lose sight of the potential for situations to arise where synergies result in 'the whole being greater

Table 18.1 The Cartesian–Newtonian versus chaos–complexity models.
Source: Faulkner and Russell, 1997

Cartesian–Newtonian Model	Chaos–Complexity Model
Based on nineteenth-century Newtonian physics (deterministic, reductionist clockwork model).	Based on biological model of living systems (structure, patterns, self-organization).
Systems seen as structurally simple, with a tendency towards linear or quasi-linear relationships between variables.	Systems viewed as inherently complex, with a tendency towards non-linear relationships being more prevalent.
Systems tend towards equilibrium and are driven by negative feedback.	Systems are inherently unstable and positive feedback driven processes are more common.
Individual differences, externalities and exogenous influences that create deviations from the norm are exceptional, noise-generating factors.	Individual differences and random externalities provide the driving force for variety, adaptation and complexity.

than the sum of its parts' and where the system exhibits a dynamic, lifelike emergent complexity (Capra, 1982). The chaos perspective captures the lifelike, self-organizing characteristics of systems, and in this sense it appreciates that systems are inherently complex and unstable, and focuses attention on the prevalence of non-linear relationships. Of particular relevance to this chapter's interest in the roles of entrepreneurs, disasters and crises in the turbulence of tourism systems is the proposition that individual differences and random externalities provide the driving force for variety, adaptation and complexity.

There are several concepts associated with the chaos/complexity perspective that have particular relevance to our interpretation of the role of disasters, crises and entrepreneurial activity in the turbulence of tourism systems.

- *The 'butterfly effect'*: reference to the butterfly effect was inspired by the work of the atmospheric physicist, Edward Lorenz, whose computer simulations of global weather patterns demonstrated that it was feasible for a butterfly flapping its wings in Beijing to initiate a series of effects resulting in a cyclone in Florida (Gleick, 1987, pp. 20–3; Lorenz, 1993). In more general terms, this effect reflects the inherent non-linearity of many systems and refers to situations where a small and apparently insignificant change or perturbation can precipitate a chain reaction that culminates in a fundamental shift in the structure of the system or a dramatic large-scale event. In the steady state systems assumed by the Newtonian paradigm, such small changes in the initial state are associated with equally small shifts overall, as any disturbances are ameliorated by a negative feedback process that restores equilibrium within the system. On the other hand, in lifelike systems, where positive feedback and non-linear relationships are more prevalent, the effects of even minor random disturbances are accentuated and magnified by mutually reinforcing positive feedback loops. In the tourism context, therefore, it is feasible for an initiative of a single entrepreneur or a single event (crisis or disaster) to precipitate a major shift in the evolution of a tourist destination. The changes introduced by these events can reverberate throughout the destination in question as other enterprises within the system adjust and find new niches, resulting in a new configuration of linkages.

- *Lock-in effect*: Paradoxically, while the positive feedback driven, self-organizing tendencies described above implies a system in a constant state of flux, these tendencies can also be responsible for creating inertia within the system. Thus, it is possible that an accident of history, or an initiative of an entrepreneur, can be responsible for the establishment of such a strong network of mutually reinforcing relationships that these endure long after the initiating conditions have been superseded. Through this 'lock-in effect' (Waldrop, 1992), it is possible for an innovation introduced by an entrepreneur in the past to have a lasting effect, despite changes in the conditions that would otherwise make the original response redundant. At a tourist destination, the lock-in effect might be evident in the continuing concentration of tourist accommodation capacity and attractions around a location, which was originally advantaged by access to rail transport. With the passage of time, rail transport might have become less relevant as a means of access for tourists, but the original location might retain its dominance owing to agglomeration effects.

- *'Edge of Chaos' and 'Phase Shift'*: Edge of chaos is a situation where a system is in a state of tenuous equilibrium, on the verge of collapsing into a rapidly changing state, with new dynamics for a future evolution (Waldrop, 1992). The interlocking relationships between the components of a system means that, in accord with the butterfly effect, if just one agent experiences a shock or mutation large enough to knock it out of equilibrium, this may be enough to create the necessity of other agents to change and adjust. In turn, this may induce an avalanche of changes until a new equilibrium is reached. Crucially, no such equilibrium is permanent. The equilibrium of the system is punctuated, with long periods of relative stasis (phases) interrupted by bursts of evolutionary change (phase shifts). Each phase shift may be associated with changes that precipitate the extinction of unsustainable or 'unfit' enterprises, while creating new opportunities for those enterprises capable of adapting. Entrepreneurs or significant events (crises and disasters) are at the forefront of phase shifts in individual destinations as they respond creatively to new opportunities or threats arising from changes in the external environment. In the process, they generate changes that, in turn, demand adaptive responses on the part of other enterprises within (and beyond) the destination. Phases in a destination's evolution are periods when a relatively stable profile of tourism activities exists and this is reflected in a corresponding stability in the profile of visitors. A phase shift might be induced by factors such as: changes in the socio-economic environment that affect market demand patterns; gradual or sudden changes in the natural environment that impinge on the sustainability of tourism development; technological innovations that create new opportunities in the market place; and initiatives elsewhere that affect the competitiveness of the destination. As emphasized in the next section, these changes are often associated with significant events such as crises and disasters.

CRISES AND DISASTERS

In the tradition of the Newtonian paradigm, early management theory generally emphasized the relative stability of both internal and external environments of organizations and, as a consequence, issues associated with how they cope with change and crises were not addressed (Booth, 1993). If the implications of change were considered at all, this was viewed in terms of the challenge of coping with gradual (relatively predictable) change, rather than sudden changes which might test the organization's ability to adjust. Such situations might be described as crises or disasters, depending on the distinctions referred to below.

A definition of crises, which reflects the general usage of the term, is provided by Selbst (1978), who refers to a crisis as '[any] action or failure to act that interferes with an [organization's] on-going functions, the acceptable attainment of its objectives, its viability or survival, or that has a detrimental personal effect as perceived by the majority of its employees, clients or constituents'. By referring to 'any action or failure to act', it is implied that the event in question is in some way attributable to the organization itself. This definition of crises therefore seems to exclude situations where the survival of an organization or community is placed in jeopardy because of events over which those involved have little or no control. For example, tornadoes, floods and earthquakes can hardly be regarded as self-induced, although communities in vulnerable areas can take steps to minimize the impacts of such events. Thus, for the purposes of this analysis, it is proposed that 'crisis' be used to describe a situation where the root cause of an event is, to some extent, self-inflicted through such problems as inept managers, inappropriate management structures and practices or a failure to adapt to change. On the other hand, 'disaster' will be used to refer to situations where an enterprise (or collection of enterprises in the case of a tourist destination) is confronted with sudden unpredictable catastrophic changes over which it has little control.

We can therefore envisage a spectrum of events such as that depicted in Figure 18.1, with crises located at one extreme and disasters at the other. However, it is not always clear where we locate specific events along this continuum because, even in the case of natural disasters, the damage experienced is often partially attributable to human action. Good management can avoid crises to some degree, but must equally incorporate strategies for coping with the unexpected event over which the organization has little control. Frequently, the recognition of a critical problem that might eventually precipitate a crisis becomes a matter of too little too late largely because, as Booth (1993, p. 106) observes, 'standard procedures tend to block out or try to redefine the abnormal as normal'. This problem is probably more relevant to the genesis of crisis, where organizations fail to adapt to gradual change. However, it might also apply to disaster situations, to the extent that the tendency to ignore warnings of an impending disaster often leave communities unprepared when it actually happens.

We have distinguished between crises and disasters in terms of the degree to which the event in question is self-inflicted. Thus, the former represent situations where the causes of the problem are associated with ongoing change and the failure of organizations to adapt to this, while the latter is triggered by sudden events over which the organization has relatively little control. Notwithstanding this distinction, crises and disasters have the common feature of impacting on organizations or communities 'with such severity that the affected community has to respond by taking exceptional measures' (Carter, 1991, p. xxiii). Booth places a similar emphasis on the necessity of 'exceptional measures' in the community's response by referring to the necessity of non-routine responses, but he adds that stress is created by the suddenness of the change and the pressure it places on adaptive capabilities. Thus, a crisis is described as 'a situation faced by an individual, group or organization which they are unable to cope with by the use of normal routine procedures and in which stress is created by sudden change' (Booth, 1993, p. 86).

Several other authors have attempted to distil the essential characteristics of disaster or crisis situations (Fink, 1986, p. 20; Keon-McMullan, 1997, p. 9; Weiner and Kahn, 1972, p. 21). A synthesis of these contributions produces the following key ingredients:

- a triggering event, which is so significant that it challenges the existing structure, routine operations or survival of the organization;

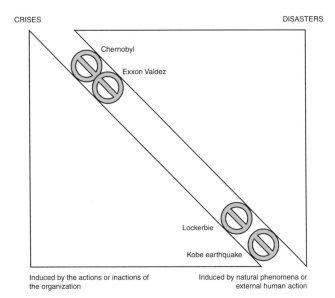

CRISES

DISASTERS

Chernobyl

Exxon Valdez

Lockerbie

Kobe earthquake

Induced by the actions or inactions of
the organization

Induced by natural phenomena or
external human action

Figure 18.1 Crises and disasters

- high threat, short decision time and an element of surprise and urgency;
- a perception of an inability to cope among those directly affected;
- a turning point, when decisive change, which may have both positive and negative connotations, is imminent. As Keon-McMullan (1997, p. 9) emphasizes, 'even if the crisis is successfully managed, the organization will have undergone significant change';
- characterized by 'fluid, unstable, dynamic' situations (Fink, 1986, p. 20).

Crises and disasters epitomize chaos phenomena in terms of all three dimensions mentioned in the previous section. First, the ossification of obsolete structures implied by lock-in tendencies contributes to the eventual exposure of the organization or destination to crises. Equally, the features of crises/disaster situations highlighted above point to the presence of the butterfly effect, especially when the role of 'triggering events' and the 'fluid, unstable, dynamic' nature of disaster situations are considered. The butterfly effect is most obvious in natural disasters such as cyclones, avalanches and volcanic activity, which have been recognized as an increasingly prevalent hazard for tourism activities because of the attractiveness of exotic tropical destinations that are particularly exposed to these types of disasters (Murphy and Bayley, 1989). However, this effect might be equally relevant in situations where a crisis has been precipitated by a single, seemingly insignificant event. An example of the latter, in the tourism context, might be a case where a single act of violence towards a tourist at a particular destination attracts media attention which is out of proportion with the severity of the event and, as a consequence, causes significant damage to the image and attractiveness of the destination.

The association between disasters and crises with 'turning points' highlights how even apparently stable systems are frequently 'at the edge of chaos'. Here a seemingly insignificant event may be enough to precipitate instability and change on such a scale that the integrity and coherence of the system appear to be threatened. Fink emphasizes the ubiquity of the 'edge of chaos' condition in business when he suggested that businesses generally are a crisis waiting to happen – i.e. 'any time you (i.e. managers) are not in crisis, you are instead in a pre-crisis, or prodromal mode' (Fink, 1986, p. 7). In his view, the essence of crisis management thus becomes 'the art of removing much of the risk and uncertainty to allow you to achieve more control over your destiny' (Fink, 1986, p. 15).

Both in the common usage of the terms and in many of the definitions referred to above, crises and disasters are associated with negative and threatening impacts of the event. This is particularly so in Selbst's (1978) definition introduced at the beginning of this section. However, as Fink (1986) emphasizes, the Webster dictionary definition of a crisis refers to such events as being 'a turning point for better or worse'. Crises and disasters therefore have transformational connotations, with each such event having potential positive (e.g. stimulus to innovation, recognition of new markets, etc.), as well as negative outcomes. There are many instances of natural disasters that have positive as well as negative outcomes. For example, while seasonal floods in riverine areas of Peninsula Malaysia bring disruption to communities within the area, they also replenish the productive capacity of riverine alluvial soils upon which the region's agricultural industry is so dependent (Chan, 1995). Similarly, a crisis might provide a valuable catalyst for the modernization of an organization's management procedures and thus enhance its survival in the longer term.

Again, this is consistent with elements of chaos theory, that see chaos as essentially creative, rather than a purely destructive, process. Once a system is pushed past some point of criticality by some crisis or disaster, it may well be destroyed as an entity, it might be restored to a configuration resembling its pre-crisis/disaster state, or a totally new and more effective configuration might emerge. The potential for both destructive and positively creative forces being unleashed by the chaos associated with crises and disasters is illustrated in Berman and Roel's (1993, p. 82) description of reactions to the 1985 Mexico City earthquake:

> Crises bring about marked regressions as well as opportunities for creativity and new options. They are turning points in which regressive tendencies uncover discrimination (and) resentment about ethnic and socioeconomic differences . . .: yet they also trigger progressive potentials and solidarity.

ENTREPRENEURIAL ACTIVITY

Entrepreneurs are generally regarded as 'someone who perceives an opportunity and creates an organization to pursue it' (Bygrave, 1993). This description is, perhaps, an understatement of the proactive inclinations of entrepreneurs, to the extent that it could be construed as implying they passively wait for opportunities to emerge. Clearly, many entrepreneurs go beyond this by actually creating their opportunities and, in terms of the chaos perspective, they disturb the equilibrium of business systems with a 'perennial gale of creative destruction' (Schumpeter, 1949). It follows that the evolution of a tourism destination can be construed as an ongoing tension between entrepreneurs, who are the agents of change, and planners, whose role is to moderate or at least control change within certain parameters (Lewis and Green, 1998). The modus operandi of these two sets of actors respectively, therefore, parallels the opposing perspectives of the chaos and Newtonian paradigms. This point is partially conceded by a number of authors who have observed that the traditional models used in the management field are inadequate for dealing with the complexities of entrepreneurial behaviour (Stevenson and Harmeling, 1990; Bygrave, 1993; Smilor and Feeser, 1991).

The linkage between crises and disasters, as defined in the previous section, and entrepreneurial behaviour can be described in terms of a twofold relationship involving opportunities and changes induced at three levels. First, crises and disasters may create opportunities that might be exploited by entrepreneurs either because the event causes the demise of a competitor, and thus creates a new market niche, or it may produce a new set of market conditions that suit the particular strengths of the entrepreneurial organization. Second, a more proactive and progressive organization (or destination) may be instrumental in inducing a crisis in a less progressive organization if its actions result in changes that render the latter less competitive, and eventually non-viable. Third, entrepreneurial entities are themselves agents of change, and some of the intended and unintended changes they produce have the potential to cause disasters or crises for others. There are numerous examples of environmental disasters that are directly attributable to the excesses of entrepreneurial activity. In such cases, a combination of greed, ignorance and poor management practices with regard to exposure to hazards and environmental carrying capacities, and an insufficient appreciation of environmental conservation considerations, have produced unsustainable outcomes that ultimately produce the disaster. In this setting, what might be described as a crisis for the organization responsible for the event, is a disaster for the many other parties affected.

Entrepreneurs are therefore linked with crises and disasters by virtue of their sensitivity to new opportunities created by crises/disasters and their role as agents of change. This linkage, however, has not been explored in the considerable amount of research on entrepreneurial behaviour generally over the last decade (e.g. Stevenson and Harmeling, 1990; Bygrave, 1993; Smilor and Feeser, 1991; Stacey, 1992; Storey, 1994). The same observation applies to the somewhat more limited attention that has been given to aspects of entrepreneurial activity in the tourism context (Barr, 1990; Echtner, 1995; Kaspar, 1989; Koh, 1996; Lewis and Green, 1998; Snepenger *et al.*, 1995). Similarly, very few authors in either the general field or in the tourism setting specifically, have drawn attention to the relevance of the chaos perspective to understanding the dynamics of entrepreneurial behaviour. Lewis and Green (1998) and Russell and Faulkner (1999) are the exceptions in this regard, and the following elaboration is based on the interpretation contained in the latter paper.

Stacey (1992) implicitly recognized the potential utility of the chaos perspective in the context of management research generally by proposing that the whole world of business needs to be approached with a new perspective, one which recognizes instability, turbulence and complexity not as unavoidable environmental factors to be endured, but as integral and vital ingredients for the creativity and innovation which are so essential for adaptation and long-term survival of economic systems. Similarly, the relevance of the chaos perspective to the analysis of entrepreneurial events is alluded to by Bygrave (1993, p. 257), who highlights as fundamental ingredients such features as a change of state, outcome sensitivity to initial conditions, discontinuities, holistic and dynamic processes and uniqueness. Through its preoccupation with stability and linear change, the conventional approach is oblivious of the entrepreneur-induced discontinuities and dramatic shifts that are illuminated by the chaos perspective. Change processes are therefore poorly understood, and the most interesting and dynamic aspects of socio-economic phenomena are relegated to the fringe of the research agenda.

The entrepreneurial process involves a change of state from being without to having the venture, and this involves a discontinuity in the sense that the new situation is not necessarily a natural progression from what existed in the past. Entrepreneurial episodes are holistic in that they cannot be understood using reductionist approaches, where the components are disassembled and examined in isolation from each other. As emphasized earlier in this chapter, there are synergies between the components, which means that the whole is greater than the sum of the parts. The description of the process as being extremely sensitive to initial condition suggests that, in accord with the butterfly effect, small changes in some variables can have a disproportionate impact on the outcomes. As suggested by Bygrave (1993, p. 258), therefore, the entrepreneurial process is incredibly sensitive to a multiplicity of antecedent variables, with tiny changes in any one of a myriad of input variables being capable of producing huge changes in the outcome. Prediction of outcomes with the mathematical precision of the Newtonian approach is therefore impossible.

Finally, the reference to the uniqueness of entrepreneurial events highlights the tendency of traditional approaches to focus on larger numbers of cases and averages and, as a consequence, ignores outliers. Yet, as Stevenson and Harmeling (1990, p. 8) emphasize, the study of entrepreneurship is concerned with 'the few who have made a difference or who desire to'. They add that 'those who succeed in accomplishing that which normal analysis deems to be impossible do so by exploiting small advantages, recognizing the importance of timing, recruiting allies, and exercising creativity that goes well beyond the norm' (p. 8). The 'butterfly effect', and the related notion of sensitivity to initial conditions, are partially explained in terms of the leverage entrepreneurs achieve from small advantages through their ability to identify opportunities and create the organizations and alliances required to maximize the benefits derived from these opportunities. Wherever there is a fundamental interest in change process and turning points in socio-economic phenomena, therefore, it is the outliers who make the difference and warrant attention, rather than the averages.

The above interpretation of entrepreneurial behaviour provides a useful backdrop for elaborating on the contrasting modus operandi of entrepreneurs and planners referred to earlier in this section. The existence of a spectrum of decision-makers, ranging from 'promoters' or entrepreneurs at one extreme to 'trustees' or administrators at the other, has been identified by Stevenson, Roberts and Grusebeck (1985). The latter can be equated with planners and regulators in terms of their mindset and mode of behaviour. As Stevenson *et al.* observe, firms may themselves become dominated by administrators (regulators) and, as a consequence, entrepreneurial behaviour may be stifled internally. Where this happens, the vitality and adaptability of the firm will eventually be compromised by its own inertia. One style of decision-making (entrepreneurs) focuses on creating and exploiting new opportunities, while the other is more concerned with fulfilling their responsibilities within the constraints of the parameters of past practices and the resources under their control. Karl Weick's discussion of self-designing systems highlights how aspects of entrepreneurial behaviour can be built into organizations in order to increase their adaptability. In the process, elements of the contrast between entrepreneurial and regulator behaviour are illuminated when he refers to moribund organizations (incapable of self-design) as:

- valuing 'forecasts rather than improvization';
- dwelling 'on constraints rather than opportunities';
- borrowing solutions rather than inventing new ones;
- removing doubt rather than encouraging it;
- being content with final solutions rather than continuously experimenting;
- discouraging contradictions rather than seeking them. (Weick, 1977, p. 37)

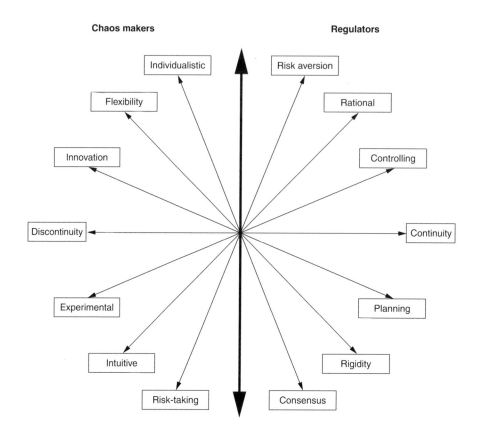

Figure 18.2 Contrasting modi operandi of entrepreneurs/chaos-makers and regulators. *Source*: Russell and Faulkner, 1999

The contrasting styles of entrepreneurs (chaos-makers) and planners (regulators) are summarized in Figure 18.2. Here, the risk-taking inclinations of the entrepreneur are contrasted with the tendency of planners to avoid risks and establish greater certainty and predictability within their domain of responsibility. Similarly, the intuitive, experimental and innovative characteristics of the entrepreneur are diametrically opposed to the more calculated approach of the planner, who is more intent upon providing conventional solutions that have been thoroughly tested elsewhere. The planners' brief is to provide rigid parameters for development in order to produce a degree of continuity that is consistent with some consensus within the community regarding preferred outcomes. On the other hand, entrepreneurs seek the flexibility that is required for them to respond to new threats and opportunities within their environment, while their innovative and individualistic pursuit of their own ends means that they produce discontinuities in the direction of development. The effect of the planners/regulators, therefore, is to establish a 'Newtonian' regime of equilibrium and linear change, whereas the entrepreneurs/chaos-makers are associated with the disequilibrium, non-linearity and spontaneity described by the chaos/complexity model. Through their actions, the chaos-makers are responsible for the 'lifelike' characteristics tourism system, whereby new coherent configurations of supply and demand are constantly emerging in response to changing conditions.

TURBULENCE IN TOURISM SYSTEMS

From the above discussion, we can arrive at the synthesis depicted in Figure 18.3, which sees a combination of crises, disasters and entrepreneurial events underpinning the turbulence of tourism systems. Crises and disasters are interrelated in the sense that the distinction between the two is somewhat blurred and, to some extent, dependent upon the perspective which is adopted. On the basis of the distinction made earlier in this chapter, it is possible for the same event to become simultaneously a crisis for one organization, to the extent that it might be self-induced, and a disaster for another if there is substantial collateral damage. Furthermore, there is an interrelationship between entrepreneurial behaviour, on the one hand, and crises and disasters, on the other, to the degree that the former produces change and the latter produces opportunities for entrepreneurs to exploit. Meanwhile, in addition to entrepreneurial activity, crises and disasters can be triggered by natural events such as cyclones, floods and earthquakes. There is a third source of change, which, for the purposes of the present exercise, has been coupled with natural phenomena within the schema. These are events induced by malevolent human action associated with political and sociopathic phenomena, such as acts of war, terrorism or sabotage. Such events are obviously not natural and, if anything, can be aligned with entrepreneurial activity to the extent that the latter involves elements of self-interested predatory behaviour which is, to some degree, immoral. Furthermore, acts of war or terrorism can be construed as a form of entrepreneurism in the sense that, in Bygrave's (1993) terms, they involve the perception of an opportunity and the creation of an organization to pursue it. However, equating violent extremism with entrepreneurism has the potential to distort the analysis of the role of conventional entrepreneurism within the tourism system. Therefore, in the context of the present exercise, it is convenient to regard acts of violence as being external triggers resembling natural disasters.

As we enter into the second millennium, there is a general perception that the world has become more disaster and crisis-prone, and that turbulence is therefore an increasingly common part of modern life. Crises may have indeed become more frequent if, as Toffler (1970) has suggested, the pace of change in our social, political and economic systems has accelerated under the impetus of technological innovation to such an extent that the ability of organizations and individuals within

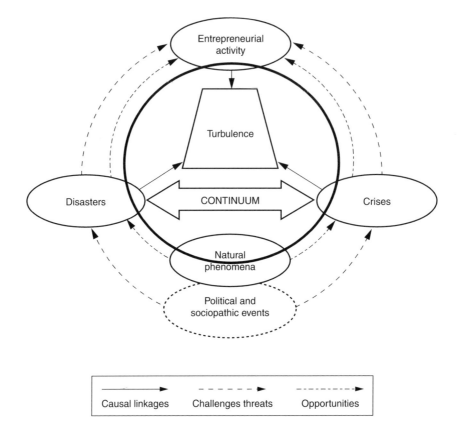

Figure 18.3 Turbulence in tourism systems

them to adapt has been greatly tested. These processes are essentially driven by entrepreneurial activity. Lags in the adaptive process might therefore be expected to be more prevalent, as are the crises these produce. Disasters, on the other hand, have been linked with natural and other events, which are more random than the seemingly constant change in social, political and economic processes. The underlying rationale for any increase in the incidence of this type of event is therefore less obvious. Could it be, for instance, that the apparent increase in the frequency of natural disasters is a consequence of the fact that the global scale of modern mass communication systems has resulted in fewer natural disasters now going unnoticed? This issue is examined specifically below for the purposes of both elaborating on some of the interactions described earlier, and highlighting the importance of building on the foundations provided by chaos theory to improve our capacity to analyse turbulence and change phenomena in the future.

Blaikie, Cannon, Davis and Wisner (1994) draw on a range of data sets relating to natural disasters to show that, while the number of natural hazard events (earthquakes, eruptions, floods or cyclones) has not increased in recent decades, the number of disasters (defined in terms of declarations of disaster areas, economic value of losses and the number of victims) has. Meanwhile, Horlick-Jones *et al.* (1991) question the proposition that disasters are becoming more frequent on statistical grounds, although they suggest that disasters themselves may be changing in the form of their expression in such a way that the definition of disasters has become too fluid for statistical time series purposes. This is, in a sense, conceding the point already made in relation to the distinction between crisis and disaster. That is, crises and disasters are the extremes in a continuum of events and, for many events along this spectrum, the process of attributing the causes to the actions (or lack of action) of the community (or organization) concerned, or to natural events outside its control, is seldom a straightforward process. As the following discussion will reveal, even the incidence of natural disasters, such as floods and landslides, has been linked to changes brought about by human activities.

Various authors have commented on the apparent increasing frequency of disasters (Blaikie *et al.*, 1994; Burton *et al.*, 1978) and, among the factors cited as reasons for this, the following are the most common:

- global population growth;
- urbanization;
- global economic pressures;
- war as a global pressure; and
- impacts of technology.

Many of these factors overlap with, and reinforce, each other, as the following elaboration illustrates.

Population growth

Population growth has been seen as a contributing factor. However, as emphasized by Blaikie *et al.* (1994), this is not for the simplistic reason that, with the larger population, more people become the victims of disaster because there are more of them in dangerous places. The linkage is not explained in terms of increasing numbers per se, but in terms of inequities in political and economic structures that force disadvantaged groups into marginal land use systems in vulnerable areas (Brammer, 1990; Hartmann and Standing, 1989). In their elaboration of this point, Blaikie *et al.* (1994, pp. 3–4, 5) provide an insight, which again highlights the blurring of the distinction between crises and disasters:

> The crucial point in understanding why disasters occur is that it is not only natural events that cause them. They are also the product of the social, political and economic environment (as distinct from the natural environment) because of the way it structures the lives of different groups

343

of people. There is a danger in treating disasters as something peculiar, as events, which deserve their own special focus. By being separated from the social frameworks that influence how hazards affect people, too much emphasis on doing something about disasters is put on natural hazards themselves, and not nearly enough on the social environments and its processes. . . The 'natural and 'human' are so inextricably bound together in almost all disaster situations, especially when viewed in enlarged time and space framework, that disasters cannot be understood to be 'natural` in any straightforward way.

Urbanization

Rapid urban growth in developing and developed countries alike has brought with it lapses in urban planning, which have resulted in extensions of urban (or tourism) development into increasingly hazardous areas. Furthermore, the impacts of urban development on catchment areas have made them more hazardous. An example of these effects is the many instances where flood plains and swamp areas are converted into housing estates or tourism resorts. This results in the compounding effects of increased run-off from urbanization of the catchment and a reduced capacity of waterways to accommodate this run-off owing to the filling in of the flood plains. This phenomenon has resulted in the 'growth management' approach to urban planning being advocated, the general idea of which is 'to prevent development in hazardous areas . . . or to ensure that structures are designed to withstand hazards and that public facilities that are crucial to responding to disaster . . . are available' (Berke, 1998, p. 77).

Global economic pressures

Blaikie *et al.* (1994) have argued that declining commodity prices, along with external pressures for Third World countries to reduce foreign debt, have resulted in an overexploitation of natural resources in order to increase exports, and a decline in public sector investment in infrastructure and essential services. Environmental effects such as deforestation have therefore made some areas more susceptible to floods and landslides, while the infrastructure necessary to ameliorate and respond to the impacts of extreme natural events has been downgraded. A study by Ford (1987, cited in Blaikie *et al.* 1994, p. 40) provides an example of the latter effect in Jamaica, where external monetary pressures necessitated structural adjustment involving major increases in interest and home mortgage rates, which resulted in low maintenance in homes and buildings. These conditions resulted in the hurricanes of 1988 and 1989 having a more devastating effect.

War as a global pressure

The increasingly destructive capabilities of the technology of modern warfare make this most unfortunate aspect of human activity a disaster-producing hazard in its own right. However, warfare can add to many of the problems referred to above by virtue of its tendency to trigger large-scale migrations of displaced people, who then put pressure on the carrying capacity of receiving areas and thus intensify the risk of crises or disasters. Conversely, warfare can render affected areas inaccessible for productive purposes and thus increase pressure on other areas.

The impact of technology

In observing that our environment appears to have become increasingly 'turbulent and crisis prone', Richardson has suggested this might be because we have not only become a more crowded world, but also we have a more powerful technology that has the capacity to generate disasters. As the spectre of the Millennium Bug illustrates, for instance, computer failures can bring to a standstill major computer-driven systems. The complexity of technology-based systems means that they are more prone to the 'butterfly effect' described earlier. Small changes or failures in the system can precipitate major displacement through mutually reinforcing positive feedback processes. Mitroff (1988) has alluded to this in his reference to the role of the interaction between information technology and economic systems in creating wild swings in the financial system. Meanwhile, the role of technology in exposing humankind to 'natural' disasters is succinctly described in the following remarks by Burton *et al.* (1978, pp. 1–2):

> In a time of extraordinary human effort to control the natural world, the global toll from extreme events of nature is increasing . . . It may well be that the ways in which mankind deploys its resources and technology in attempts to cope with extreme events of nature are inducing greater rather than less damage and that the process of rapid social change work in their own way to place more people at risk and make them more vulnerable. . . . To sum up, the global toll of natural disaster rises at least as fast as the increase in population and material wealth, and probably faster.

Whether the incidence of natural disasters is increasing, or it is simply a matter of each disaster having more devastating effects, as the above summary suggests, it is apparent we live in an increasingly complex world and this has contributed to making us more crisis/disaster prone. Complexity, in this context, refers to an intricacy and coherence of natural and human systems, which complicates the process of isolating cause and effect relationships in the manner so often assumed as being possible in traditional research. This complexity is explicit in Richardson's (1994, pp. 66–7) itemization of the features of complex systems that make them so vulnerable. These features include:

- diversity – numerous factors govern the behaviour of the system, making it difficult to isolate cause and effect definitively;
- interactivity – these numerous factors are interrelated in a complex way, making it difficult to influence one in isolation from the others;
- invisibility – the factors with the potential to trigger crisis or disasters are often apparently distant and therefore not within the scope of the management's normal range of considerations;
- ambiguity – cause-effect relationships are problematic, sometimes apparently contradictory and therefore often open to debate (e.g. carbon emissions/global warming linkage);
- incremental change –the major impacts of the threatening situation are often only felt with the occurrence of some triggering event and after the onset of the crisis has occurred in an insidious way (boiled frog syndrome); and
- new phenomena – insufficient time has elapsed for the phenomenon to be observed and understood.

CONCLUSION

As in the case of most of the mainstream social science disciplines that have provided the foundations for its development, the conventional approach to research in the tourism field reflects the dominance of the traditional Newtonian paradigm. Thus, a reductionist approach that implicitly assumes the clockwork model of the universe has been emphasized, simple linear or quasi-linear relationships have been assumed to prevail and individual differences, externalities and exogenous influences that create deviations from the norm are dismissed as exceptional noise-generating factors. While this approach has served us well in underpinning our understanding of tourism systems, it has only done so to the extent that these systems are stable. In reality, we live in an environment which has always been turbulent to some degree and is, arguably, becoming more so. Disasters, crises and change induced by entrepreneurial activity (including technological innovation) are becoming more prevalent and tourism systems are, more often than not, in a constant state of change and flux as a consequence. We therefore need the conceptual and methodological tools to analyse turbulence and change more effectively.

This chapter has argued that chaos theory and the allied complexity perspective provide the basis for an alternative conceptual, which has the potential to help tourism researchers to develop an understanding of the dynamics of change more effectively. Within this approach, the 'noise-generating factors' and 'outliers' that so often provide the triggers for instability and change will become the focus

of attention. So too will the apparently small changes that are magnified by positive feedback processes to become the drivers of major phase shifts in the structure of the system. Furthermore, by regarding tourism systems (at the enterprise, destination or network of destinations levels) as being generally in a state of tenuous equilibrium (edge of chaos), rather than intrinsically stable, we might be in a better position to anticipate and manage change. Ultimately, an emerging sub-field of 'change' research in tourism, based on the chaos paradigm, will need to come to grips with less spectacular and subtle events that influence the dynamics of change. However, an examination of more dramatic instances of disasters, crises and entrepreneurial activity would appear to offer the best prospects for providing an initial impetus for this line of research.

REFERENCES

Barr, T. (1990) 'From quirky islanders to entrepreneurial magnates: the transition of the Whitsundays'. *Journal of Tourism Studies*, **1**(2), 26–32.

Berke, P. R. (1998) 'Reducing natural hazard risks through state growth management'. *Journal of the American Planning Association*, **64**(1), 76–87.

Berman, R. and Roel, G. (1993) 'Encounter with death and destruction: the 1985 Mexico City earthquake'. *Group Analysis*, **26**, 91–89.

Blaikie, P., Cannon, T., Davis, I. and Wisner, B. (1994) *At Risk: Natural Hazards, People's Vulnerability and Disasters*. London: Routledge.

Booth, S. (1993) *Crisis Management Strategy: Competition and Change in Modern Enterprises*. New York: Routledge.

Brammer, H. (1990) 'Floods in Bangladesh: a geographic background to the 1987 and 1988 floods'. *Geographical Journal*, **156**(1), 12–22.

Burton, I., Kates, R. W. and White, G. F. (1978) *The Environment as Hazard*. New York: Oxford University Press.

Bygrave, W. D. (1993) 'Theory building in the entrepreneurship paradigm'. *Journal of Business Venturing*, **8**, 255–80.

Capra. F. (1982) *The Turning Point*. London: Flamingo.

Capra, F. (1996) *The Web of Life*. London: Harper Collins Publishers.

Carter, W. H. (1991) *Disaster Management. A Disaster Manager's Handbook*. Manila: Asian Development Bank.

Chan, N. W. (1995) 'Flood disaster management in Malaysia; an evaluation of the effectiveness of government resettlement schemes'. *Disaster Prevention and Management*, **4**(4), 22–9.

Echtner, C. M. (1995) 'Entrepreneurial training in developing countries'. *Annals of Tourism Research*, **22**(1), 119–34.

Faulkner, B. (1998) 'Introduction'. In E. Laws, B. Faulkner and G. Moscardo (eds) *Embracing and Managing Change in Tourism: International Case Studies*. London: Routledge, pp. 1–10.

Faulkner, B. and Russell, R. (1997) 'Chaos and complexity in tourism: in search of a new perspective'. *Pacific Tourism Review*, **1**(2), 93–102.

Fink, S. (1986) *Crisis Management*. New York: American Association of Management.

Ford, K. (1987) 'Private correspondence with Ian Davis'. In P. Blaikie, T. Cannon, I. Davis and B. Wisner (1994) *At Risk: Natural Hazards, People's Vulnerability and Disasters*. London: Routledge.

Gleick, J. (1987) *Chaos: Making a New Science*. London: Heinemann.

Graburn, N. H. H. and Jafari, J. (1991) 'Tourism social research'. *Special Issue: Annals of Tourism Research*, **18**(1).

Gunn, C. (1994) 'A perspective on the purpose and nature of tourism research methods'. In J. R. B. Ritchie and C. R. Goeldner (eds) *Travel, Tourism and Hospitality Research: A Handbook for Managers and Researchers* (2nd edn). New York: John Wiley, pp. 3–11.

Hall, C. M. (1995) 'In search of common ground: reflections on sustainability, complexity and process in the tourism system' – a discussion between C. Michael Hall and Richard W. Butler. *Journal of Sustainable Tourism*, **3**(2), 99–105.

Hartmann, B. and Standing, H. (1989) *The Poverty of Population Control: Family Planning and Health Policy in Bangladesh*. London: Bangladesh International Action Group.

Horlick-Jones, T., Fortune, J. and Peters, G. (1991) 'Measuring disaster trends part two: statistics and underlying processes'. *Disaster Management*, **4**(1), 41–4.

Kaspar, C. (1989) 'The significance of enterprise culture for tourism enterprises'. *The Tourist Review*, **44**(3), 2–4.

Keon-McMullan, C. (1997) 'Crisis: when does a molehill become a mountain?' *Disaster Prevention and Management*, **6**(1), 4–10.

Koh, K. Y. (1996) 'The tourism entrepreneurial process: a conceptualisation and implications for research and development'. *The Tourist Review*, **51**(4), 24–41.

Laws, E., Faulkner, B. and Moscardo, G. (eds) (1998) *Embracing and Managing Change in Tourism: International Case Studies*. London: Routledge.

Lewis, R. and Green, S. (1998) 'Planning for stability and managing chaos: the case of Alpine ski resorts'. In E. Laws, B. Faulkner and G. Moscardo (eds) *Embracing and Managing Change in Tourism: International Case Studies*. London: Routledge, pp. 138–60.

Lorenz, E. (1993) *The Essence of Chaos*. Washington: University of Washington Press.

Mitroff, I. I. (1988) *Break-away Thinking*. New York: John Wiley.

Murphy, P. E. and Bayley, R. (1989) 'Tourism and disaster planning'. *Geographical Review*, **79**(1), 36–46.

Peat, F. D. (1991) *The Philosopher's Stone: Chaos, Synchronicity and the Hidden Order of the World*. New York: Bantam.

Prigogine, I. and Stengers, I. (1985) *Order Out of Chaos*. London: Flamingo.

Richardson, B. (1994) 'Crisis management and the management strategy: time to "loop the loop"'. *Disaster Prevention and Management*, **3**(3), 59–80.

Russell, R. and Faulkner, B. (1998) 'Reliving the destination life cycle in Coolangatta: an historical perspective on the rise, decline and rejuvenation of an Australian seaside resort'. In E. Laws, B. Faulkner and G. Moscardo (eds) *Embracing and Managing Change in Tourism: International Case Studies*. London: Routledge, pp. 95–115.

Russell, R. and Faulkner, B. (1999) 'Movers and shakers: chaos makers in tourism development'. *Tourism Management*, **20**(4), 411–23.

Schumpeter, J. A. (1949) *The Theory of Economic Development*. Cambridge, MA: Harvard University Press.

Selbst, P. (1978) 'The containment and control of organizational crises'. In J. Sutherland (ed.) *Management Handbook for Public Administrators*. New York: Van Nostrand.

Smilor, R. W. and Feeser, H. R. (1991) 'Chaos and the entrepreneurial process: patterns and policy implications for technology entrepreneurship'. *Journal of Business Venturing*, **6**, 165–72.

Snepenger, D. J., Johnson, J. D. and Rasker, R. (1995) 'Travel-stimulated entrepreneurial migration'. *Journal of Travel Research*, **34**(1), 40–4.

Stacey, R. D. (1992) *Managing Chaos: Dynamic Business Strategies in an Unpredictable World*. London: Kogan Page.

Stevenson, H. and Harmeling, S. (1990) 'Entrepreneurial management's need for a more "chaotic" theory'. *Journal of Business Venturing*, **5**, 1–14.

Stevenson, H., Roberts, M. J. and Grousbeck, H. I. (1985) *New Business Ventures and the Entrepreneur* (2nd edn). Illinois: Irwin.

Storey, D. J. (1994) *Understanding the Small Business Sector*. London: Routledge.

Toffler, A. (1970) *Future Shock*. London: Bodley Head.

Toohey, B. (1994) *Tumbling Dice*. Melbourne: Heinemann.

Waldrop, M. (1992) *Complexity: The Emerging Science and the Edge of Order and Chaos*. London: Simon and Schuster / Penguin.

Weick, K. E. (1977) 'Organisation design: organisations as self-designing systems'. *Organizational Dynamics*, Autumn, 31–46.

Weiner, A. J. and Kahn, H. (1972) 'Crisis and arms control'. In C. F. Hermann (ed.) *International Crises: Insights from Behaviour Research*. New York: The Free Press, p. 21.

Index